Glory
for
Sale

FANS, DOLLARS AND THE NEW NFL

by Jon Morgan

bancroft
press

Baltimore MD

Published by Bancroft Press
P.O. Box 65360, Baltimore, MD 21209. (410) 358-0658.

ISBN 0-9631246-5-X
Library of Congress Catalog Card Number 97-73064
Printed in the United States of America

First edition

Designed by Melinda Russell, Bancroft Press
Distributed to the trade by National Book Network, Lanham, MD

For Carol Frigo, my wife and best friend.
And our daughters, Hannah, Allison and Rachel.
It's OK to come back into the basement now, girls.

ACKNOWLEDGMENTS

I owe thanks to more people than I can name, but here are a few:
My structural editor, Ann Sjoerdsma, who skillfully, patiently, and even
cheerfully crafted a book out of 130,000 stray words. And my publisher/
editor, Bruce Bortz, who not only conceived the idea of this book but took
a gamble on me. Also, my bosses at The Sun, *Jack Gibbons and Molly*
Dunham Glassman, for giving me the best job in journalism.

Among those generous with their time, recollections or encouragement
were Herb Belgrad, James Biggar, Ordell Braase, James Considine, Bruce
Gaines, Tony Grossi, Timothy Heider, Arthur Hirsch, Mike Klingaman,
Stephen Koff, Robert Leffler, Nancy Lesic, Laura Lippman, Laura Martinez
Massie, Creighton Miller, Mike Preston, Michael D. Roberts, Jeff Schudel,
Matthew Tanner, Jack Torry, Tom Waldron and John Ziemann.

Of course, the work is my own and I take responsibility for any errors
or omissions.

The
American
Dream

Those of us who played in the NFL can always recall at least one moment when we looked up from the grass, glazed in sweat, head pounding in the heat, to see the visage of our team's owner contentedly looking on. At that moment, we wondered what it would be like to own a team. Most knew that a drive for money burned in our core and that owners had more of it than any of us.

Oh, I know, some players like to reminisce about the old days when athletes played for the love of the game. But that's like pining for your old girlfriend: you always remember her better than she really was. I don't know if any NFL players ever really played just for the love of the game, but I do know this: No sane person would ever do the things you have to do to yourself, physically, mentally, and emotionally, in order to play in today's NFL if someone wasn't dangling a big bag of cash in front of them. No, money is at the bottom of it all. Players know the score; it's a multibillion dollar business. And they want their cut.

One thing I never did as a player was think about owners in the human sense. To me, they were insulated, pampered people — the idle rich, who were sponging off of our bone-jarring efforts. Of course, like most of the rest of us, they are still human beings who live out their lives, part tragedy, part comedy. Granted, some of them are silver-spooners, and their teams are playthings. Others are entrepreneurs who made fortunes in oil or computers or shoes, men who've crammed their office walls with endless power photos, honors and awards and are now proud possessors of the biggest, best, most testosterone-induced trophy of them all: an NFL team. But even these men eat and sleep and breathe. They know, like us, the sting of failure and the charge of success. A few, especially the NFL old-timers, have more in common with the rest of us than we ever suspected.

In *Glory for Sale*, we begin to understand fully why Art Modell, one of those old-timers, moved his venerated NFL franchise out of Cleveland. For the first time, in a public forum, we see Modell as a human being. We learn that his very presence in the league was the result of an outrageous speculation, an all-or-nothing gamble decades ago that just happened to pay off. We also learn that NFL franchises, back in the days before football was king, were not unlike today's professional lacrosse teams. Which of us would risk everything we had on one of those franchises? That is what Modell did. There were few others like him who were willing to gamble, but those who played won big. NFL franchises are now not only worth close to $300 million apiece, but they give their owners a power and a prestige worth twice that. Football has become our national religion, and NFL owners are the druids. Men of business, men of state, men of war: All are inexorably drawn toward the people who own and control these teams.

Yet, those owners are no more immune to greed and incompetence and chicanery and worry than the rest of us. What happened to Art Modell has happened to each of us at some time or other. The move from Cleveland, I contend, happened to him more than it happened to even the most stalwart of Browns fans. Haven't we all trusted someone only to discover later that we were deceived, and what's worse, that the deceiver is pointing the finger of blame at us? Haven't most of us entered into an agreement with a contractor or a car salesman only to later find that they not only failed to live up to their end of the bargain, but never intended to do so in the first place?

Make no mistake, this book does not exonerate Art Modell. It takes pointed note of his hypocrisy. What *Glory for Sale* does is humanize Modell. It leaves us with the realization that, were we in this man's shoes, we'd have done the very same thing. It's all well and good for any of us (especially our slippery politicians) to stand back and cry foul at Modell's apostasy. It's certainly possible to see him as an elitist owner and power monger, and it's just as possible to give him no pity because his "type," which "has everything," is held to a higher standard than everyone else. Yet no man felt more ache in his craw during this debacle than Modell himself. The fans lost their team, but only for a short time.

Modell lost a part of his life. He built that team. He paid its prodigious bills. He leveraged everything he had to hang onto it. Fans may have paid their $25 for a ticket and worn the team colors, but I dare say they got their money's worth in entertainment and then some. From my experience as an opposing player, I know what the energy was like in Cleveland's Municipal Stadium. I felt those "Dawg Pound" biscuits raining down on my helmet. I heard those gut-rending cheers when the Browns scored and when they won. That is what fans paid for; that is what they got. They never paid to have Art Modell watch the team he gambled on so many years ago whisked out the window to creditors in a bankruptcy court. They never paid him to flush down the drain the legacy he created for his children and grandchildren. Those were rights they didn't earn. The name and colors and records of their Browns, yes, those things belong to Cleveland and its fans. But no more.

When you read this book, you too will realize that Art Modell did exactly what you would have done. He saved himself and his family, while leaving the thing which was most important (the team name and colors) to the community he loved, the community that vilified him nonetheless. This was not a man who betrayed a train-load of children to the Nazi's. The only thing Modell did was create a temporary hiatus for Browns football in Cleveland. Though my life has orbited this game, I believe that such a development is disconcerting at best, and certainly not criminal. Cleveland Browns football will live on, as it should. People must realize that they were whipped into a frenzy by the very politicians who made it impossible for Modell to stay.

You are about to learn what happened in those back rooms of power over the years, the events that made Modell's move from Cleveland inevitable. For the first time, you will be privy to all the political shenanigans, false promises and shady deals you always suspected were occurring. Jon Morgan adeptly takes you into the engine of the NFL. What you'll find there are the same machinations that turn the wheels of our politics, our corporations, our world of entertainment and our very lives. What you'll see are people just like you. We all want to get ahead, to make it big. When you subscribe to the American dream, there's no sense blaming Art Modell for doing the same.

In
Charm
City

Art Modell didn't look like a man who had just added $75 million to his fortune.

Slumped in a chair, his arms tightly across his bulging middle, the white-haired owner of the Cleveland Browns looked tired and old, every bit of his 70 years. His face was worn and puffy from many sleepless nights.

Age had long ago rounded Modell's features and broadened his once sturdy, athletic build. But it had left him with an expression of perpetual bemusement — the cocked grin of a kindly uncle who always seems on the verge of cracking a joke.

Not today. Not on Nov. 6, 1995.

For most of the spectators waiting to hear Modell speak in a downtown Baltimore parking lot, the moment was one of celebration; Modell was bringing the National Football League back to the city. His fabled Browns were headed for the Colts' Memorial Stadium where they'd play until the opening of their own new, state-of-the-art stadium in the fall of 1998.

For Baltimoreans, it had been 12 painful years since their beloved Colts had slipped out of town. The team had loaded its gear into green and yellow Mayflower vans bound for Indianapolis on a snowy March 1984 night. Not even the mayor, who had worked so hard to keep the gloried franchise, was notified of the move.

But that was ancient history now. For today, in a sun-drenched, noon photo opportunity, Art Modell was announcing the Browns' arrival. Ten television stations — four from Baltimore and six from Cleveland — were there to record the event. Sports network ESPN was beaming it live to cable watchers nationwide. Once again, there would be NFL football in "Charm City," the popular nickname for Maryland's largest city.

Though news reports had predicted the announcement days before, Maryland officials and Modell had withheld public confirmation until today, until they could hold this celebration on the spot where the new stadium would be built. Maryland Governor Parris Glendening and Baltimore Mayor Kurt L. Schmoke had already called their Ohio counterparts to tell them the news. At 4 a.m., local newsrooms had received faxes announcing "Football is coming back to Baltimore!" but not mentioning the team they had all reported already.

About 100 invited guests were seated in folding chairs in front of a makeshift stage, built a few feet above a parking lot serving baseball's Oriole Park at Camden Yards. Potted plants lined the gray and dark brown dais. Gray upholstered chairs with sturdy, dark wooden legs were neatly arranged. The dais, the furniture, the dark suits on the speakers — all lent the scene the look of an outdoor, corporate board meeting.

In fact, this was the ultimate board meeting: a jarring collision of sport and business. One of the most avidly supported franchises in sports was jilting its fans in favor of the profit potential of a new stadium and the corporate dollars it would attract.

Baltimore, long the prototypical "victim" of the NFL, was now a plunderer. But among the city's celebrants, there was little sign of irony or remorse. The gubernatorial seal of Maryland, with its heraldic crest, was hung on the podium, and the yellow and black flags of Baltimore and Maryland flapped to the rear of the stage.

Some of the veterans of the city's long football wars assembled: There were officials of the Maryland Stadium Authority, the agency formed in the wake of the Colts' departure to procure another NFL team and to make sure that the baseball Orioles didn't leave in the meantime. The authority's executive director, Bruce Hoffman, an engineer who had overseen the construction of Oriole Park, sat in the front row. He would now be called upon to supervise the new football stadium. Maryland state Senators John Pica and Tommy Bromwell, who had helped to draft the eminent-domain legislation that spooked Colts' owner Robert Irsay into leaving in 1984, were there, too. The two Baltimore-area lawmakers had fought for years to maintain funding for the stadium, beating back opponents' arguments that there were better uses for the public money. That fight was about to get even uglier.

Another 100 or so "uninvited" guests positioned themselves to the side of the stage and pushed against yellow police barricades. They erupted in a boisterous chant of "Art, Art, Art," when Modell's dark limousine arrived in a five-car motorcade, escorted by motorcycle cops.

Many fans waved handmade signs. "If you build it they will come," read one. Another, parodying a popular Budweiser TV commercial, said: "Art Modell, We Love You Man." Still other signs expressed Baltimoreans' resentment over NFL Commissioner Paul Tagliabue's role in denying the city an expansion team: "Tagliabue Can't Stop Us Now."

Many Baltimore fans were jubilant. That morning, some had scoured local stores for Browns hats, sweaters and other gear. They crossed out "Cleveland" with magic markers or masking tape and replaced it with "Baltimore." Bootleg Baltimore Browns T-shirts were already for sale.

The sky was a cloudless blue — Colts blue — and the temperature a crisp 55 degrees. It was sweatshirt and football weather in Baltimore, a city which had nurtured the NFL through its shaky adolescence and had never quite adjusted to autumn without the game.

Modell, seated between Glendening and Schmoke, remained stone-faced. This was the sort of occasion that he generally craved, one that thrust him to the center of attention and cast him as a hero. But Modell had been in public life long enough to know what this day actually meant. He had seen the vilification of owners who had moved their teams. He himself had been among the most critical when the Colts left Baltimore and Al Davis stunned Oakland by moving his Raiders.

He knew what was coming.

As he waited for his turn to speak, Modell scanned the crowd warily through his silver-rimmed bifocals. Sharing the dais with him, cheerfully talking, were some of the most important people in his life, including his son, David, who ran the Browns' marketing operation and was widely assumed to be the owner in waiting, and his good friend Alfred Lerner, a billionaire Cleveland financier. Lerner, who began amassing his fortune as a $75-a-week furniture salesman in Baltimore, was a part-owner of the Browns. He had made the introductions that resulted in the team's move to Baltimore.

Spotting a familiar face, Modell briefly smiled, got up and reached down to shake the outstretched hand of William Donald Schaefer, who had been mayor of Baltimore when the Colts left. During his two terms as Maryland's governor, Schaefer had made the return of the NFL a personal crusade. But he had been banished this day to a seat in the audience, so as not to upstage his successor. Though both men were Democrats, Glendening's slim election victory a year earlier had come with no help from Schaefer.

Cameras clicked and whirred as Schaefer and Modell shook hands. The two men went way back together. Modell had flirted with Baltimore for years, first hinting a decade ago that he might be interested in bringing a team to town. He and Schaefer held a number of secret meetings a year after the Colts left. They discussed a new stadium, possibly to be shared with the Orioles, and how Modell would sell the Browns, move to Baltimore and become its "owner in waiting" as he pursued an expansion franchise. The talks went on for several years, raising the hopes of city officials, but nothing ever came of them. Later, when the NFL added expansion franchises, Modell expressed support for the city's application — except when it counted. During deliberations inside the NFL owners meetings, Modell helped to sink Baltimore's application.

The crowd, recognizing the role the former governor had played in securing stadium funding and fighting the good fight, applauded warmly. Schaefer smiled and waved.

Maryland Stadium Authority chairman John Moag, Jr., who sold the Browns on Baltimore, stepped to the podium to begin the ceremony. Only the second chairman in the Authority's nine-year existence, Moag had held the volunteer post for 11 months. He was off to a very good start.

Moag asked the crowd for a moment of silence for Yitzhak Rabin. The assassinated Israeli prime minister was being buried that day in Jerusalem.

Then Moag, a Baltimore-based Congressional lobbyist, turned to the happier business at hand. He introduced the people lined up behind him and acknowledged the many dignitaries in the audience. Clearly out of his element, Moag shifted from foot to foot and leaned awkwardly down to the microphone. A relative newcomer on the Maryland political stage, Moag had been a behind-the-scenes player for years and a hustler all of his life. From making a few bucks parking cars on his family's lawn before Colts games, to greasing the skids of a client's legislation as a Washington lobbyist, Moag had long known how to exploit an advantage. But most of his work was done, sometimes with a wink and a nudge, in Capitol Hill hallways and offices. He wasn't used to the intense scrutiny and criticism that the Browns deal would draw.

He urged the crowd to show compassion for Cleveland fans who, he noted, were going through a wrenching process all too familiar to Baltimoreans.

"Our elation is accompanied by pain that we know so well," Moag said.

He suggested that this should be a moment of "pensive reflection" for Baltimoreans. Then he introduced his boss, Governor Parris Glendening, who betrayed not a trace of pensiveness or reflection.

An ordinary and earnest speaker on his best days, Glendening delivered a graceless performance that would haunt him for months.

"This is a great day for Baltimore. This is a great day for the state of Maryland. And, personally, this is a great day to be governor," he said to rousing cheers.

Glendening spoke of the great tradition of the Browns, seeming to miss the point that the team's great tradition and its civic association made its theft all the more hurtful for Clevelanders and NFL fans. The move was, as Cleveland-born comic Martin Mull would quip later that day, like finding out the Eiffel Tower had been moved to Nebraska.

But Maryland's newly elected governor was eager for a success during a year filled with missteps. He waved a Browns beer mug in the air and playfully taunted reporters. "You just never asked the right question," Glendening teased.

"I said I would never comment until we had a signed lease with an NFL team. You never asked me if we had a signed lease," he said, holding aloft the Browns' memorandum of understanding with Maryland. "The Browns are coming to Baltimore!"

Moag and Glendening had convinced Modell that he needed to act quickly. If he delayed, they told him, he would lose out on the state's generous offer of a publicly financed stadium leased on exceedingly favorable terms. The agreement had been secretly signed early on the morning of Oct. 27, aboard Lerner's private plane at Baltimore-Washington International Airport. It was not supposed to be announced until after the 1995 football season, to avoid a plunge in Browns ticket sales and the spectacle of a lame-duck team playing before a hostile home crowd. But word leaked, and the announcement was pushed up a month.

Glendening pridefully compared the negotiations to "Kissinger-style shuttle diplomacy" — a comment that seemed all the more inappropriate in light of the Rabin funeral that day. But the governor clearly reveled in his deal making, in the hushed meetings and the "secret knock" on the airplane door.

"I'm sure all of us involved will never forget the early morning calls, the late evening calls and the weekend visits. It was fun, no question about it,'" he gushed.

Even Modell cringed. A Baltimore *Sun* columnist later dubbed Glendening "Governor Gloat-dening." Opponents of the move would replay a tape of his speech on TV sports talk shows, and in homes across the country as Baltimore, overnight, was transformed from sympathetic victim to greedy thief.

The reaction stunned Glendening. "Where do these people think franchises come from?" he would later ask, exasperated. A former political science professor at the University of Maryland, Glendening was a shrewd calculator of action and reaction. But he had miscalculated this one.

He thought he had pulled off the sort of political coup that a governor could only pray for. He had brought the National Football League back to Baltimore, filling a painful void. He had achieved in 11 months what Schaefer, a vastly more popular and passionate governor, had spent 11 fruitless years trying to accomplish. This should have been Glendening's day to step out from Schaefer's long shadow.

Here he was, just a few hundred feet away from two of Schaefer's most enduring monuments: Oriole Park at Camden Yards and Baltimore's Inner Harbor. The universally acclaimed "retro" ball park was partly responsible for a stadium building boom then underway across the nation. The Orioles had gone from a backwater franchise to one of the richest teams in professional sports, thus demonstrating to team owners the mesmerizing wealth that could be theirs with a new stadium. Even Modell had fallen under the spell.

And the success of the Inner Harbor, an upscale retail complex off to the east, had convinced countless other cities, including Cleveland, to reclaim their waterfronts and rejuvenate their downtowns. The Inner Harbor's shops and restaurants had brought tourists and residents flocking to a once-shunned industrial district and revived the city's self-image.

By putting the baseball and football parks in Camden Yards, Schaefer had managed to extend the reach of the Inner Harbor a few blocks west, connecting the waterfront with a working-class neighborhood. And, he hoped, that would keep up the momentum of the city's development.

But in the coming weeks, the former governor would join the chorus of critics of the Browns deal, suggesting that he wouldn't have done such a dastardly deed, that he wouldn't have given away so much. Schaefer was just being opportunistic. During his time, he had offered similar, or better deals, to other NFL team owners. Today, however, Schaefer said he was pleased to see his dream realized — although he understood how Clevelanders felt. He, too, had experienced that awful "kick in the stomach."

"I feel sorry for the mayor of Cleveland," he said when the cameras converged on him, as they would several times during the one-hour ceremony.

A fan shouted to Schaefer, "You were the quarterback....They came in the fourth quarter."

Indeed, Schaefer *had* muscled the funding for the stadium through the Maryland General Assembly, but he had been unable, despite personal intervention with NFL owners, to close the deal.

Glendening paid only passing homage to Schaefer, crediting him with "laying the groundwork" for the day.

"Don, we appreciate it," he said perfunctorily from the podium.

The new governor needed all of the credit he could get, and he hoped the day's celebration would help put behind him the nagging questions of his election. His margin of victory had been a humiliating 5,993 votes despite the 2-to-1 registration advantage Democrats enjoy in Maryland over Republicans. He had carried only three of Maryland's 24 jurisdictions. But they were the three biggest. One was Baltimore City.

As Glendening was soon to learn, times had changed since 1987 when Schaefer, running a state that foolishly considered itself "recession proof," had converted his 82-percent election victory in '86 into legislative approval for two stadiums at Camden Yards. It was a half-billion-dollar chunk of pork that Schaefer had hoped would win back the affections of the NFL and keep the Orioles from leaving town.

But by 1995, a fiercely conservative Congress was slashing federal agencies — many of them staffed by Marylanders earning fat paychecks. This, and a continuing erosion of Maryland's industrial base, had pushed the state into a malaise that lingered after the national economy had recovered. While negotiating a costly deal with the Browns, Glendening was reducing aid for the state's disabled citizens and eliminating education programs for prisoners — causes dear to both Glendening and his lieutenant governor, Kathleen Kennedy Townsend, a member of America's first family of liberalism.

Several people in the audience raised the point with heckles and signs.

After Glendening introduced him, Modell moved slowly to the podium. Months of negotiations and soul-searching were now complete, and he was transplanting his treasured Browns, one of the most respected franchises in the NFL, to a new city and a new stadium. It had been an agonizing decision.

For years, Modell had watched lesser team owners such as the Raiders' renegade Al Davis and the Colts' boozy Bob Irsay boost their personal fortunes with team moves. In the past year alone, three team owners had announced or completed lucrative moves to new addresses: the Los Angeles Rams' Georgia Frontiere, the Houston Oilers' Bud Adams, and, again, Davis, who was returning to the city he had once fought the league for the right to abandon. Even Malcolm Glazer, owner of the Tampa Bay Buccaneers for less than a year, was shopping around for a new home. And Ken Behring of the Seattle Seahawks was looking to move his team to Los Angeles.

Modell had opposed all of these moves, and had forcefully warned his fellow owners that such instability squandered the fan loyalty that he and the other "old guard" league men had spent years building.

But now he was joining the gold rush. And he was getting one of the best claims of all: A stadium whose every square foot was designed to make him money. Maryland would spend $200 million building a luxury stadium with skyboxes, club seats, high-tech scoreboards and anything else anyone could think of. All Modell had to pay was the cost of running the facility. He would even be allowed to book concerts and other events there and split the proceeds with the state.

The deal would lift Modell out from under crushing debt. Years of questionable business deals and free-agent signings had cost him dearly and failed to deliver what he most wanted: a Super Bowl trophy. Meanwhile, the league's economics were fast shifting against owners such as him who were confined to old stadiums. Merely filling the seats — something the league mastered years before — was no longer enough to ensure success for a team. Now the owners were boosting profits by systematically driving up the value of ticket sales by driving up the price. The best way to do that: sell them to corporations that were willing to pay hundreds of thousands of dollars a season for climate-controlled suites in which they could romance clients and strike deals. Of course, old wrecks such as Cleveland's Municipal Stadium, as historic as they were, would never do for the cellular phone set.

Modell was slow to recognize this change and even slower to act. He had mastered his sport in the era when season tickets were sold one by one through personal appearances over rubbery chicken at Rotary Club luncheons. No one did it better than Modell. He was funny. He was charming. And he was hard to refuse when he came around with a pocketful of tickets and promises for a winning season. But now teams like the Carolina Panthers and Jacksonville Jaguars, new franchises playing in new or like-new stadiums, were generating more cash from each of their skyboxes than Modell could wring from 1,000 season tickets. And they were a threat on the field. Suddenly Modell's shtick was obsolete.

Also outdated was his approach to local politics. At one time, Modell moved easily along the corridors of power. He had bankrolled candidates, especially Republican ones. He was generous with charities. He served on the right boards and political committees, staying in touch with the powerful men who got things done. He could pick up the phone and quickly reach a mayor, governor or even the President. For decades this gave him and his franchise everything they needed. When he decided he ought to run the city-owned stadium himself, he worked adroitly to get it accomplished.

But the characters and rules had all changed over the past 10 years. Unfamiliar faces were in charge back at Cleveland's City Hall. Modell was no longer a master of his own fate. He had tried to play by the old rules to get a new stadium, and he had failed miserably. He backed a loser for mayor. He worked clumsily behind the scenes, confusing even his supporters about what he needed or wanted. He wanted the community to repay him for his years of service, but he didn't want to beg. He took it as a point of pride that he never threatened to move the team. But threatening to move was how Stadium Wars were being fought and won in the 1990s.

Modell, relying on the winks and good will that had served him well in previous decades, had let civic leaders push him to the end of a line he should have headed. They were more worried about losing the Indians. The hapless Tribe had, after all, threatened to change cities almost as many times as it had changed managers. And the franchise's new owner, Dick Jacobs, was precisely the sort of hard-nosed millionaire who could move a team. He had even brought in baseball's commissioner to underscore the threat: build a new stadium or lose the team. Though a Cleveland resident, Jacobs was largely a mystery to most of the city, rarely involving himself in the usual civic functions and boards.

Not Modell. He was a stalwart community man and notoriously soft touch. He could never break the heart of his adopted home town. He was, after all, from Brooklyn and vividly recalled the pain of the Dodgers move west — the first truly shocking franchise relocation of the modern era. When Modell promised, as he often did, never to move the Browns, city leaders believed him. He even kept his demands low, insisting a renovation — rather than a new building — would suffice. The Browns leave Cleveland? That would be like the Bears jilting Chicago or the Giants deserting New York.

Or the Colts leaving Baltimore.

For Jacobs, who had no reservations about threatening to move his team, Cleveland had constructed a Camden Yards-class facility. Same for the NBA Cavaliers. In fact, the city was on a veritable spending spree, putting up a multimillion dollar hall of fame for rock 'n' roll musicians, a new science center and associated public works projects. And, as Modell learned the hard way, the money was fast running out.

More than anything else, the new stadiums in Cleveland demonstrated to Modell what could be done in a new venue. The Indians, a perennial doormat of the American League, and were Modell's rent-paying subtenants at Municipal Stadium,.took in so much at their highly acclaimed Jacobs Field that they could afford to shop aggressively in the free agent market. The team made it that season to their first World Series in 41 years. They, not the Browns, were now the talk of Cleveland. Long-time corporate customers were cancelling their skyboxes at Municipal Stadium and signing up at "the Jake."

And Modell, as he liked to say, was still "trying to get indoor plumbing."

He was exaggerating, of course. Municipal was old and decrepit, but it had primitive skyboxes and some amenities many other teams lacked. By some accounts, he was earning more in revenue from his stadium than most other NFL teams. But it was both falling down and falling behind the times. Upkeep was gobbling up his profits. Modell had borrowed all he could the year before to sign free agents and still fell a game shy of going to the Super Bowl. In 1995, the team was off to a lackluster start. His health was poor. The banks were wary of letting him pile on more debt. He needed to act fast if he was going to get to the big show.

Even Cleveland officials acknowledged that their stadium renovation plan was worth a fraction of what Baltimore was offering. Cleveland had cobbled together a complicated, $170 million package of loans, up front payments from businesses, and taxes on cigarettes, booze and parking to rebuild 64-year-old Municipal Stadium from the ground up. A voters' referendum on one part of the funding was scheduled for the next day, Nov. 7. But Modell, who was routinely being savaged in the Cleveland press for everything from bad player trades to bad punts, didn't think it would pass and wasn't convinced it would be enough if it did.

Meanwhile, Maryland had been ready for eight years with legislation that permitted it to build a stadium financed by the proceeds from a special sports-theme instant lottery. This same sort of mechanism had built Oriole Park. The land for the football palace had been bought and cleared. All that was needed was a signature on a lease — which Modell had provided — and the bonds would be sold and the bulldozers rolled out. Or so Maryland officials said.

Stadiums had become a key factor of NFL economics. Moving to a new stadium would catapult Modell's franchise overnight to among the most valuable in sports, easily adding $75 million to $100 million to its worth. It was a windfall unimaginable to Modell, a high school dropout who had borrowed everything he could 34 years earlier to buy the Browns for $3.9 million.

The Maryland deal even included a provision that allowed Modell to raise $80 million through "permanent seat licenses," a pernicious trend then sweeping sports. A PSL was a one-time fee that gave a fan the right and obligation to purchase a season ticket each year. It typically ranged from a few hundred dollars to a few thousand.

Modell thought Cleveland, with its thousands of longtime season ticket holders, would never go for PSLs, at least not in an old stadium. But the Maryland deal allowed Modell to immediately go out and obtain a $50 million loan backed by the expected proceeds of the license sales. It was a much-needed infusion of cash.

So it was more than professional courtesy that prompted Modell to introduce his new banker, Frank Bramble, to the Baltimore audience. Bramble, then in charge of Maryland National Bank, was a Lerner protogé who had worked with him to rescue and then sell the state's largest bank. Bramble arranged Modell's $50 million line of credit and was happy to stand and take a bow when introduced.

Modell knew that deserting Cleveland would cost him. He would lose much of what he held dear, especially his stature in Cleveland, where he had once been so popular his name had been mentioned as a candidate for high office.

Decades of friendships and familiar routines would now be broken. His cherished mansion in the Cleveland suburbs, where he and his wife, the former actress Patricia Breslin, had entertained the stars of Hollywood and Republican politics, and where Pat's two children, David, and John, had grown up as Art's adopted sons, would have to be sold.

His revered position within the NFL, a fraternity of vast wealth and celebrity, would also be shaken. His place in the Pro Football Hall of Fame — he had been nominated for the class of 1996 — was in jeopardy. And he would no longer be able to go out in public without a bodyguard for fear that a zealous Browns fan would carry out one of the death threats already pouring in by fax, phone and letter.

"This has been a very tough road for my family and me," Modell sadly told the Baltimore crowd.

"I leave my home of 35 years and a good part of my heart there. I can never forget the kindness of the people of Cleveland."

Modell managed a few one-liners, but for the most part his remarks were forced and defensive. He looked down often, speaking softly.

"I know what you went through 11 years ago because that is exactly what is happening in Cleveland right now," Modell said.

"I am deeply, deeply sorry from the bottom of my heart."

Looking over the heads of the Cleveland sportswriters whose favor he had courted over the years, Modell spoke flatly of his pleasure at being in Baltimore. He recalled the great Browns-Colts games of the 1950s and 1960s, when the two teams were perennial contenders for championships and strong-armed quarterbacks like Otto Graham and Johnny Unitas were at the helm.

The Colts and Browns were founded just a year apart, in a short-lived league born in the post-World War II sports boom. In their prime, they were among the most respected franchises, winning hearts and championships in an age when the grass was real and face masks were a novelty. The earth shook when the two teams met at riotous Memorial Stadium or cavernous Municipal

Stadium. Titles were often on the line, and the outcomes were never assured.

Football may have made its millions in the glamorous media capitals of New York and Los Angeles, but it first connected with fans in working-class cities like Cleveland and Baltimore. It was in industrial centers, among the smokestacks and the steamships, that the National Football League built its following, game by game, often played in stadiums built for baseball.

It hardly seemed likely that storied, old-guard franchises like the Browns or the Colts would ever forsake their longtime fans, whose adoration knew no bounds.

If there were any doubt about how the public would react to the Browns' move, an unidentified messenger in the parking lot that afternoon settled it. Standing silently behind the police barricades, among the revelers, the man held a one-word sign above his head: "$hame."

During a brief question-and-answer period, reporters shot accusatory questions at Modell, and the beleaguered Browns owner mounted a rambling defense.

"The fans have supported the Browns for years, but frankly, it came down to a simple proposition. I had no choice," he said.

He said he had been losing millions of dollars in Cleveland — a point that would later be disputed by the NFL — and had been unable to negotiate a suitable stadium deal. The Baltimore agreement, he said, was "far beyond the capacity" of Cleveland to match.

"I was not going to put myself in the position of demanding something and then being accused time and time again of being an extortionist, a shakedown artist and what-have-you," he said.

Such characterizations sliced Modell. Although his antics had worn on many of the Cleveland fans, he had always been a national spokesman for the NFL's better instincts, for putting the fans before dollars and tradition ahead of quick profits. He wasn't an oilman turned part-time sports magnate like the Dallas Cowboys' Jerry Jones; he was a football man. This was his only business.

But now he had become the symbol of the cash obsession of modern sports. *Sports Illustrated*, which had teed off on Colts owner Irsay after his move, would depict Modell on its cover as a pudgy cartoon caricature slugging a Browns fan in the gut. The headline: "Modell Sucker-punches Cleveland."

At rallies in downtown Cleveland — the downtown he had helped to revive — Modell would be hanged in effigy. The message boards at the airport, which usually displayed bright snippets of civic boosterism, would be reset to blink "Stop Art Modell!" non-stop. No explanation was necessary; even out-of-town visitors knew what was meant.

The team's nationwide network of Browns Backers also energized to the crusade. Faxes from Backers in every state would be sent to every NFL team owner. Thousands of signatures would be collected on petitions. The Internet would crackle with derisive commentary on Modell; one World Wide Web home page would offer visitors the chance to download color photos showing the mock executions of Modell, his son David, and Browns coach Bill Belichick.

The man who had spent so many years building the NFL was suddenly its darkest villain. The message was painfully obvious to fans across the country: If Modell, one of the supposed good guys of sports, could do this to fans as faithful as the Browns' fans, what team was safe?

This was not how Modell had seen it ending. When he begged and borrowed the money to buy the Browns in 1961, Modell was a glib, 35-year-old Madison Avenue ad man of modest means and grand ambition. He could never have foreseen the spectacular success of the NFL or his eventual role as a symbol of its troubles.

The league had fought off all comers and now stood alone atop the world's richest sports market, arrogantly picking and choosing from among obsequious cities trying to join the club.

Baltimore had been one of the most persistent losers. Many in the city had come to embrace conspiracy theories to explain why team after team kept ending up elsewhere. Most involved commissioner Paul Tagliabue and Washington Redskins owner Jack Kent Cooke collaborating to mold Baltimore and Washington into a common market for the Redskins. In fact, Cooke and other Redskins owners going back 50 years had viewed Baltimore as a part of their territory and had fought to keep competitors out. But no Redskins squad ever captured the hearts of Baltimore fans.

In the heady years of the '60s and '70s, when the NFL took what was essentially a college sport, nurtured it with TV dollars, and watched as it grew into an awesome marketing giant, Modell had been the ultimate insider and team player. As one of former commissioner Pete Rozelle's most trusted allies, he had spent 31 years at the head of the NFL television committee, negotiating one blockbuster deal after another. Modell helped to cultivate the all-important "league-think" that enabled the sport to prosper while its bickering rivals in baseball, hockey and basketball lurched from crisis to crisis.

He also chaired the NFL's labor committee when negotiations resulted in the first collective bargaining agreement with players. He served on committees overseeing everything from the NFL's merger with the AFL to expansion; in the late 1960s, he was even, briefly, the only elected president the NFL ever had.

But success had its price. The collegial NFL that Modell joined and helped to develop was barely recognizable now. Selfish upstarts like Jerry Jones, who deposed Modell from the television committee and went on to earn even more money for owners, brought harsher sensibilities to the business side of the league.

The television networks were now paying the NFL $1 billion annually to broadcast its games. Each year, the Browns were earning from TV rights about 10 times what Modell paid for his franchise. Moving to Baltimore would give Modell all the advantages of the new NFL he had resisted — the NFL that had all of the fans it needed and was courting corporate clients with $2,970 season tickets, $3,000 seat licenses, and $200,000 a year skyboxes.

Mayor Schmoke expressed most eloquently the misgivings even football-hungry Baltimoreans were feeling that day. Cleveland and Baltimore — both waterfront cities living in the twilight of their industrial heydays — had long been culturally and economically linked. Now they were soulmates, forever joined by betrayals they had suffered at the hands of an NFL franchise, he said.

As happy as he was to see football back, Schmoke said there was a difference between "joy and unrestrained joy."

"I know that the people of Baltimore are not unmindful of the hurt felt by the people of Cleveland," Schmoke told the crowd. "We share that legacy, and hope Cleveland gets a team."

As it would turn out, Maryland's plunder of Cleveland soon would take on national implications. Baltimore and its Colts had achieved a relationship unique in sports — the crooked smile and gritty play of quarterback superstar Johnny Unitas still resonated along the city's working piers and sweaty steel mills. But Colts mania had all but flickered out by the time the Mayflower vans rolled in 1984. Irsay had bought the team and systematically broken the bonds. When the team crept out of town, the average game attendance had dwindled to an embarrassing 41,000.

Not so in Cleveland. The city that had roared for Jim Brown, Frank Ryan and Lou Groza in the 1960s was at least polite enough to keep showing up in the disappointing 1990s. An average of 70,000 boisterous, dog-biscuit throwing fans continued to pack crumbling Municipal Stadium to watch the underachieving likes of Bernie Kosar and Vinny Testaverde. On Nov. 6, 1995, the team's record was 4-5. But its TV ratings and attendance were among the best in the league.

Schmoke, a friend of Cleveland Mayor Michael White, shared breakfast with him that morning at a downtown Baltimore hotel, after which White rushed to hold a competing press conference and to begin his long fight to save the Browns. Although their styles could not be more different — White was a man of passionate oratory, while Schmoke was studious and wonkish — the two shared a generational and racial bond. They were among the best and brightest of the black political leaders who tried to translate the victories of the Civil Rights Movement into the nuts and bolts of municipal management. Both men followed into office popular white mayors who had gone on to state governorships, Schaefer in Baltimore and George V. Voinovich in Cleveland, and both were thought to be on similar paths. Schmoke and White were struggling to establish their own legacies in a time of crushing indifference to their old-line industrial cities.

But unlike White, Schmoke was a true sports fan and athlete. He had quarterbacked his team in the City-Poly game, an annual athletic showcase of Baltimore's best college-prep high schools, City College and Polytechnic Institute. The game was played each year before a screaming crowd at Memorial Stadium, the kingdom once ruled by the Colts' Unitas, Art Donovan and Ray Berry. Schmoke had lived through the glory years of the Colts and had fought to bring the NFL back to his city.

White, on the other hand, rarely attended Browns games and

viewed sports teams from the perspective of an urban planner, not a fan. When the Indians' Jacobs Field was being planned, he realized that the complex would bring more people and dollars downtown if it were connected to an arena that could host 41 NBA games and hundreds of concerts, revivals and other events. He talked the owners of the Cavaliers into abandoning their profitable, 15-year-old suburban arena for a new one to be built adjacent to Jacobs Field.

Of course, this meant holding the Browns' demands off for a while. But at the time, the delay didn't seem too risky. Modell said he would never move. And there was no hint of Cleveland's impending investment crisis and other financial calamities that would make building a football stadium even tougher.

Although neither White nor Schmoke had known it, their cities had been on a collision course for more than a decade. A host of economic and legal upheavals within the league had changed forever the relationship between cities and fans. Stadiums were now king, and Cleveland was learning the lessons of Baltimore.

White and Schmoke were on opposite sides of an ugly, national debate about sports and money. Over breakfast, Schmoke advised White to heed the orderly Baltimore plan of 1984 and begin preparing for a return of the NFL down the road. White said thanks, but made it clear he was going to fight like hell to stop the Browns' move in its tracks.

The Cleveland mayor then picked up the tab.

Later, at his own press conference at a hotel a few blocks away, White accused Modell of duplicity and dishonesty. He said the team owner had used Cleveland as "a doormat to cut a better deal."

"We have not been dealt with fairly. We have not been dealt with honestly. And we are not going to go away," White said.

The city's lawyers, in court early that morning, had won a temporary court order blocking the Browns from leaving until a hearing could be held to determine if the team was in violation of its lease.

"We have been wronged. I did not come here to go through the motions. We are going to do what it takes. The principle of how we've been treated is worth fighting for," White said.

Back at Camden Yards, Schmoke, Glendening, Modell and

other officials retired to a catered reception for some of the city's corporate and political elite. Modell began the process of carving out his place in a new city, starting all over again, just as he had done 30 years before in Cleveland.

Modell then boarded a plane for his winter home in Florida. The Battle for the Browns had begun.

CHAPTER ONE

The
Upstart
League

T he National Football League traces its roots to a 1920 meeting of starry-eyed sportsmen in a car dealer's showroom in Canton, Ohio. But it wasn't really established as a national force until television discovered it in the 1960s.

In the early decades, franchises such as the Akron Pros, Pottsville Maroons and Staten Island Stapletons paid their players by the game and formed and collapsed as fast as a line of scrimmage. Baseball was the undisputed national pastime. Boxing and horse racing also were big fan favorites. But football remained primarily a popular college game that defied repeated attempts at professional league organization.

By 1946, the NFL was still worrying about franchises going broke when a competitor, the All-American Football Conference, suddenly took the field. The new league was organized by *Chicago Tribune* sports editor Arch Ward and several investors. The NFL had spurned their efforts to gain an expansion franchise, which they hoped to move to Los Angeles. The bid was defeated by the Cardinals and Bears, teams then slugging it out in Chicago, and now planning to end the cross-town competition by winning approval for the Cardinals to move to L.A. The Chicago teams instead got a third competitor: The AAFC Chicago Rockets, later to be called the Hornets.

The AAFC was stocked with former college football stars returning from the war. It consisted of eight franchises, many taking advantage of the nation's coliseum-building frenzy in the 1920s and 1930s: The Rockets played at Soldier Field; the Miami Seahawks at the Orange Bowl; the Cleveland Browns at Cleveland Municipal Stadium; the San Francisco 49ers at Kezar Stadium; the New York Yankees at Yankee Stadium; the Brooklyn Dodgers at Ebbets Field; the Buffalo Bills at Civic Stadium and the Los Angeles Dons at the Los Angeles Coliseum.

The upstart league had an innovative form of revenue sharing that years later would be adopted by the NFL. The visiting AAFC franchise would receive the greater of $15,000 or 40 percent of the gross gate receipts. United Airlines was signed up to fly teams among the cities. NFL players took the train.

Using a tried and true strategy, the National Football League ignored the new rival. The first American Football League had expired without much fuss in 1926 after a single season. A decade later, AFL II came along and lasted just two seasons, losing money and disbanding after the NFL lured away its coveted Cleveland Rams franchise. A third AFL played in 1940 and 1941, but in smaller markets not contested by the NFL, and quickly died.

In light of this history, NFL Commissioner Elmer Layden had plenty of reason in 1946 to brush off a pair of AAFC-appointed emissaries, Cleveland Browns coach Paul Brown and Chicago investor John Keeshin, who wanted to meet to talk about mutual interests.

"Let them get a ball first," Layden sneered when asked if the AAFC would ever play the NFL.

But the AAFC proved a surprising success with fans. In its second, third and fourth years, it actually out-drew the NFL in average game attendance, provoking the first true "football war" for fans and ticket sales. The inevitable bidding for players left teams in both leagues claiming they were losing money almost from the start.

Not all AAFC franchises were successful, though. Some struggled. The hapless Miami Seahawks drew an average of 7,164 fans to the Orange Bowl in the first season — the worst attendance in football and barely a third of the league's average. The team's AAFC-worst 3-11 record landed it in the basement of the Eastern

Division despite a mid-season turnover of almost the entire roster. Financially, the team was awash in red ink, and its rivals had to contribute cash to keep it afloat. The league even filed charges against the franchise for violating indebtedness rules.

Days after the last game of the inaugural season, AAFC team owners met and decided they'd had enough of Miami. They expelled the franchise.

But the slot didn't stay open long. The league turned immediately to a city that had come close to getting a team the first time around: Baltimore. Baltimore had been considered for one of the charter franchises in 1944 when the league held its first organizational meeting. Investor and former heavyweight boxing champion Gene Tunney and league founder Ward had even gone to Baltimore and applied for use of its Municipal Stadium.

But Tunney pulled out two months later, saying he was worried that World War II would last longer than expected and the league's debut would be delayed. Other investors expressed interest, but none was able to complete the deal, and the franchise destined for Maryland was given instead to Miami.

A week after their demise, the resurrected Seahawks headed for Baltimore. The city had its first professional football team.

In its 1947 manual, the AAFC expressed high hopes for Baltimore and disdain for Miami: "Baltimore shows every indication of being one of professional football's greatest strongholds. So, in this instance, the worst has been replaced by the best."

Washingtonian Robert Ridgway Rodenberg, a 38-year-old Harvard-educated journalist turned short-movie producer turned Army spy turned sports team owner and bon vivant, took over the franchise. "Seahawks" not being a suitable name for the Maryland city, Rodenberg wanted to call the Baltimore team the Whirlaways, after the horse that had won the 1941 Kentucky Derby. But someone suggested the name was too long. A name-the-team contest was held, and the "Colts" won. Winner Charles Evans of Middle River, Md., said he thought it reflected well on the state's thoroughbred racing history, which dated back to before the American Revolution.

Still wearing Miami's silver and green, the Colts played their first game in Baltimore on Sept. 7, 1947, against the AAFC Brooklyn Dodgers, who wore bright yellow jerseys.

The game was played at Baltimore's Municipal Stadium, a structure that pre-dated Memorial Stadium on 33rd Street in the city's Waverly neighborhood. A wooden, 50,000-seat, single-deck oval, Municipal had been built in 1922 with the hope of landing the annual Army-Navy game. (It was played there only twice, and the stadium became known as "lonely acres.")

Municipal's splintery benches were built directly on sloped earthen banks using a primitive construction technique that was fast and easy but not very pretty. With no major-league team in town, however, nobody gave much thought to stadiums, pretty or otherwise. Reserved seats that season sold for $1.50 to $3.50 a game.

On hand for the franchise's debut was the AAFC's new commissioner, former Navy fullback Jonas H. Ingram, a retired four-star admiral who had been commander-in-chief of the Atlantic fleet. His acceptance of the AAFC job lent the fledgling league some badly needed credibility.

Optimism was not strong for a Colts win. The team had lost its first two exhibition games. The 27,418 fans who turned out for the regular-season debut were treated to periods of drizzle and drenching rain in the first half, and sun and mud in the second. But, it turned out to be a much better game than anyone expected.

Baltimore got lucky on the opening play. Brooklyn's Elmore Harris fielded the kickoff on his own 5-yard line and advanced to the 25, where he was hit hard and fumbled. An alert but disoriented Brooklyn Dodger guard named Harry Buffington scooped up the ball and ran, but got turned around by some tacklers and ended up darting into his own end zone. He tried to pass the ball, but it was batted down. Colts fullback Jim Castiglia jumped on it, scoring Baltimore's first touchdown — on the first play of the first game. Castiglia, out of Georgetown, became the city's first bona fide football star.

Brooklyn rebounded, however, and held a 7-6 lead when the teams retired for halftime. On the opening kick of the second half, Billy Hillenbrand, a 6-foot, 188-pound Colts halfback out of the University of Indiana via the Chicago Rockets, fixed that. He caught the ball on the 5-yard line and ran it back 95 yards for a touchdown. A 57-yard punt return by Hillenbrand cemented the Colts' 16-7 victory.

After the game, Rodenberg said, "I knew Baltimore would go

for pro football in a big way. We are not promising a pennant winner ... but we'll guarantee interesting football. This is a great day
for me despite miserable weather."

The next morning's newspapers showed the Colts atop the
conference's Eastern division — for the first and last time.

The next week, the team lost to San Francisco, 14-7, then
braced for a game in Cleveland against the mighty Browns, who
had won the AAFC's first championship.

Ouch.

The Browns, led by quarterback Otto Graham and fullback
Marion Motley, scored three touchdowns in the game's first 10 minutes. The final score of 28-0 put the Colts into third place in their
four-team division. They then went on to lose to the Yankees, to tie
the 49ers and to drop consecutive losses to Buffalo and Los Angeles.

The Colts' strong quarterback, Bud Schwenk, a Browns alum-
nus who would set several records that season, couldn't save them
from some embarrassing disasters. On Oct. 26, they lost to Los
Angeles, 56-0, the most lopsided score in the league's short history.

"The Dons, scoring in every period, toyed with the ineffective
Colts throughout the second half," *The Sun* glumly reported.

The season limped to a conclusion on Dec. 7 with another
debacle against Cleveland. A crowd of 20,574 turned out in
Baltimore's Municipal Stadium on a cold and rainy day to see
Graham throw two touchdowns in the first 11 minutes — off his
earlier pace but impressive nonetheless. Two minutes into the second half, he connected for another TD pass. Graham left the game
early to save his energy for a tougher opponent. The Browns went
on to post a 42-0 shutout win.

The Colts won only two of 14 games that first season and
ended up last in their division, matching the previous season
record of the defunct Miami Seahawks. Only the Chicago Rockets'
1-13 record was worse. The Colts were outscored 377 to 167 and
outrun 2,665 yards to 1,161 yards. The only bright spot was quarterback Schwenk, who managed a respectable 2,337 yards passing.

But he didn't return the next season.

At the box office, the Colts weren't much better. They drew an
average crowd of 14,261, which was not big enough to earn a profit. It was also third-worst in the eight-team league. Worry over the
future of football in Baltimore — something that was destined to

become a municipal obsession — led Mayor Tommy D'Alesandro to convene a "Save the Colts" summit. A group of 16 civic leaders was recruited to buy the team from Rodenberg, whose post-game parties were eating into receipts.

Among those who contributed $10,000 were radio executive R.C. "Jake" Embry and McCormick Spice Co. chief Charles McCormick. A public stock offering in the spring of 1948 also raised $200,000.

The group talked the league into a "help the weak" aid plan for endangered franchises such as the Colts. In that effort, Cleveland gave Baltimore a quarterback, Y. A. Tittle. He went on the next season to post record rookie numbers, completing 55.7 percent of his passes for 2,522 yards. During one stretch, he threw 115 straight passes with no interceptions and 68 completions, for a 59-percent completion rate.

Tittle helped the team go 7-7 in 1948, winning a playoff berth. But the Colts lost in the post-season to the Buffalo Bills. Average game attendance that year hit 29,244, exceeding by a few hundred the average of both the AAFC and the rival NFL (28,691). Still, the team lost money, and there was pressure in the league to drop the franchise, which seemed to be an obstacle to merger negotiations then under way with the National Football League.

The NFL's Washington Redskins, just 40 miles to the south, were not interested in a merger that would bring a competitor so close to them. Prior to the AAFC's debut, the Redskins had played some exhibition games in Baltimore, and owner George Preston Marshall was keen on developing a following in the city.

Colts president Walter S. Driskill alluded to these troubles in the team's 1949 publicity book, commenting: "Despite the talk of Baltimore losing its franchise, despite the unfounded rumors that the All-America Football Conference could not operate in opposition to another league, and despite long weeks of doubt about our stadium, the football faithful of this city and its environs have shown that they want, and will support, the local club."

The Colts' average-game attendance fell that next season to 21,768, but was still on par with the NFL and ranked fourth-best in the AAFC. Doubts remained about the franchise's future, however, so D'Alesandro planned a "Save the Colts" exhibition game for the following August. All tickets would be sold for a princely $5, the cost of a box seat at the time. The mayor challenged Baltimore to buy 50,000 tickets to the game, and he personally vowed to move 10,000 of them.

The effort was falling well short of its goal when peace finally came between the AAFC and the NFL.

The larger league, which had resisted recognizing the AAFC for four years, finally admitted in 1950 that the rivalry was driving up player costs and driving down profits. Terms were struck to bring three AAFC teams into the NFL: the Cleveland Browns, the San Francisco 49ers and, though just barely, the Baltimore Colts.

Without question, Cleveland was the strongest AAFC franchise. The Browns had won all four league championships and gone undefeated in 1948. Their success on the field was so overwhelming that it actually hastened the demise of the league: Fans came to see the AAFC as the Browns vs. Everyone Else.

The AAFC Yankees were purchased by the NFL New York Bulldogs, and the latter franchise was canceled. (The Yankees went belly-up two seasons later, leaving the city's football fans to the Giants.)

None of the AAFC franchises invited into the NFL competed in an existing NFL market, so the merger restored the NFL's monopoly. The Colts agreed to pay Redskins owner Marshall $150,000 for "invading" his territory. He publicly predicted the Colts would not survive.

He was right. Baltimore's NFL initiation was painful from the start. Their first game was a grudge match against the Redskins, led by future Hall of Fame quarterback Sammy Baugh. The Skins won 38-14. Attendance for the game, played in Baltimore, was a respectable 26,267. That anyone showed up at all was a marvel: The Colts hadn't won a home game since 1948 and had just lost seven straight pre-season exhibitions.

Next up was Cleveland and another drubbing inflicted by Otto Graham, 31-0. Then it was the Rams' turn. They demolished the Colts, 70-27, posting the highest regular-season winning score ever recorded in the National Football League. The game's 14 touchdowns tied a record, and its 10 extra points set one. Between them, the two teams gained an astounding 989 yards, most of them by the Rams.

Predictably, the fans were turned off.

Only 12,971 fans turned out for Baltimore's next home game, against the Green Bay Packers. The Colts actually won, 41-21, recording their first, and nearly last, NFL victory. The delirious fans carried Tittle from the field. But they sobered up by the final home game: Only 12,059 watched the Detroit Lions club the Colts, 45-21.

Baltimore finished its first season in the NFL with a league-worst record of 1-11. The team was outscored by a margin of better than 2 to 1. Home game attendance averaged a scant 15,837, well shy of the 25,000 the team said it needed to break even.

But Baltimore *Sun* sports editor Jesse A. Linthicum, a virtual Colts cheerleader, found a bright side to even this: "The attendance was not sufficient to give the club an even break but, all things considered, the total was deemed satisfactory."

Not quite.

By this time, the Colts had been repeatedly shored up by the community. Rodenberg gave up control after the first season, admitting that the venture was broke. Civic leaders passed around management of the franchise like a United Way chairmanship until, in 1950, local businessman Abe Watner agreed to guarantee the team's operations for a year. Any profit was to go to charity.

Under Watner, things went from bad to worse. The team lost every game, and Watner cut expenses sharply. Finally, on Jan. 18, 1951, Watner asked the other NFL team owners, then meeting in Chicago, for help. It was a desperate act, but Watner was hoping the NFL owners would come through for the Colts like the AAFC owners had. He was wrong.

NFL owners, warned by Marshall that such a request might be made, heeded Marshall's urgings and turned Watner down.

Watner now threw in the towel. The other owners voted to pay him $50,000 for his players, who were put into a draft. The Packers bought the Colts' helmets. And the team's landlord auctioned off equipment to pay back-rent.

Marshall then announced that he was going to make Redskin fans of Baltimoreans. The city seethed at the duplicity, and the Baltimore City Council came close to passing an ordinance to bar the Washington team from Municipal Stadium. Watner, now Baltimore's Public Enemy No. 1, left for a Florida vacation.

But the game wasn't quite over.

The Colts board of directors, which wasn't notified of

Watner's plans until after the fact, filed suit against him and the National Football League. Spurred into action by the litigation, the NFL started negotiations. Commissioner Bert Bell admitted that the league was wrong in allowing Watner to abandon the franchise and offered to revive the team if its debt could be cleared.

Baltimore's attorney, an aggressive litigator named William D. MacMillan, of Semmes, Bowen and Semmes, didn't think this was enough. The team would still be weak, he argued. He went ahead with the lawsuit, alleging restraint of trade, antitrust violations and anything else he could think of.

The lawsuit was the first of several that Baltimore would file to win sports teams. It was also an early whiff of smoke from a fierce battle that still rages in the NFL — the fight over antitrust.

Designed to ensure competition among large corporations, antitrust laws were not easy to apply to oddball organizations such as sports leagues. Were they single companies with dozens of branch offices? Or were they a consortium of competing companies?

The distinction is not trivial. If a league is a single company, then it is free to determine where to put its operations just as McDonalds can open and close restaurants. But if leagues are viewed as a collection of competing businesses, then they should be barred from fixing prices, driving competitors out of their markets and otherwise colluding to the disadvantage of consumers.

The notion of "antitrust" developed in the late 1800s, when the end of the Civil War brought a new industrialization to the nation's economy. It didn't take long for major manufacturers to figure out that they could make more money if they stopped competing with each other.

At first, industrial barons were content to meet in smoke-filled rooms and agree among themselves on how much kerosene, whiskey or sugar they would make and how much they would charge.

As the economy grew, so did the need for more complicated agreements. In 1881, Cleveland industrialist John D. Rockefeller, who co-owned the Standard Oil Co. of Ohio, revolutionized the trust concept. He convinced stockholders of dozens of other firms in related businesses — mostly refineries — to turn over control of their companies to a "trust," with its own board of trustees, that he would preside over.

The Standard Oil Trust quickly gained a stranglehold over competitors, who often were forced to join the trust or get out of the business. The trust demanded, and received, cut-rate prices from suppliers. It told retailers from whom to buy and what to charge. If retailers bought from the trust's competitors, their supply would be cut off. At its peak, the Standard Oil Trust controlled 95 percent of the nation's oil business.

Consumers and populist politicians soon took aim at Standard Oil and the trusts then in tight control of railroading, steel making, and other vital industries. In 1890, the U.S. Congress passed the Sherman Antitrust Act, sponsored by Ohio Senator John Sherman, to outlaw monopolies or attempts to form monopolies. Because it was a federal law, however, the Sherman Act only applied to businesses engaged in interstate commerce. It wasn't until 1911, after some contradictory court decisions, that "trust-busting" federal lawyers succeeded in getting the U.S. Supreme Court to break up Standard Oil.

Not long after, the trustbusters caught up with professional sports. At first glance, sports leagues appeared to be monopolies: The teams share profits, set prices, decide who does and doesn't get into the business and collectively drive down the price of labor.

One of the first test cases was brought by Ned Hanlon, owner of the defunct Baltimore Terrapins: He sued baseball's National League for purposely driving the Terrapins' Federal League out of business in 1915 after only two seasons. Dissatisfied with the terms of an agreement reached in an earlier lawsuit against the Federal League, he pursued his case all the way to the Supreme Court.

There, in an eloquent 1922 decision that still reverberates, the legendary Justice Oliver Wendell Holmes ruled that baseball is exempt from antitrust law. Putting on a baseball game for money isn't "commerce" in the strict sense of the word, he wrote. And even though the teams cross state lines to play each other, the transportation is incidental, not essential, to the business, so they really aren't engaged in interstate trade. The Sherman Antitrust Act, he decided, did not apply.

Subsequent courts have been openly skeptical of that ruling and have narrowed its scope greatly, but, because the decision still stands, it affords baseball a unique protection few other industries enjoy. The Supreme Court has since suggested that Congress settle the issue legislatively, but it has so far demurred.

For years, the NFL assumed Justice Holmes' exemption applied to it as well. It found out otherwise in 1957 when the Court decided *Radovich v. National Football League.*

A guard with the Detroit Lions, George Radovich left the team in 1946 to care for his sick father in Los Angeles, where he played for the Los Angeles Dons of the All-American Football Conference. After his playing career had ended, Radovich applied to be a coach with the San Francisco Clippers of the Pacific Coast League, an NFL affiliate. It was then he learned that the NFL had blacklisted him. Radovich sued, and his case made it to the U.S. Supreme Court, which ruled that the National Football League, and every sport except baseball, had to conform to the antitrust laws.

Though that landmark decision was still a few years off when MacMillan filed the Baltimore Colts' lawsuit in 1951, the NFL had to be nervous about the unsettled nature of antitrust law and sports. The matter was heard in Baltimore, and the judge turned out to be a devout Colts fan. A number of his preliminary rulings went Baltimore's way. Had it lost, the NFL could have been forced to pay hefty damages.

Then, on Dec. 3, 1952, before the final court ruling, Commissioner Bell said that the city could have another franchise if it sold 15,000 season tickets in six weeks. That goal was reached in less than five weeks, and Baltimore was back in the NFL.

This time, though, it was assigned a franchise even weaker than the Seahawks: The Dallas Texans. The team was not only broke, but quite likely cursed. A year earlier, the Texans had been the New York Yankees. They failed in New York and almost moved to Baltimore in 1951, but chose Dallas instead. The experiment in Texas was disastrous: The Texans drew so poorly that they abandoned their hometown after just four home games and became a permanent road team based in Hershey, PA.

After the season, the franchise reverted back to the NFL, which awarded it to Baltimore. The team came to town with a big defensive end named Art Donovan and some blue and white uniforms.

Unhappy about the Colts' turn of fortune, the Redskins' Marshall took steps to see that it would never happen again. In

1953, he had this clause inserted into the NFL bylaws: "In the event the Baltimore franchise is forfeited or surrendered, or is transferred to a City other than Baltimore, all rights to the Baltimore Territory shall invest in the Washington Redskins, and the area included in the Baltimore Territory shall be reconstituted and become part of the Home Territory of the Washington Redskins."

• • •

Meanwhile, Baltimore realized that if it wanted to play in the big leagues, it would need a big-league stadium. Its initial stadium drive took on the overtones of a full-fledged civic crusade. Community leaders saw a new sports venue as a way to anchor some of the new wealth that had come into the city during World War II. Steel factories and shipyards were still sprawling, but their size was dissipating with post-war demobilization.

Baltimore was then the nation's ninth largest city. It hit its population zenith in 1950 with 949,708. In 1945, a 78-citizen mayoral committee reported to Mayor Theodore McKeldin that "Baltimore stands today at a civic crossroad. There is no avoiding the unpleasant truth that until recently Baltimore was being outrun by a number of younger cities in the race for national and international prominence."

War, the report said, had changed that, but only temporarily. "It is for the leaders of Baltimore and Maryland to see that the reversal is permanent," it concluded.

The committee suggested a rather bold solution, one that reflected the hotbed of high-tech engineering that Baltimore had become: A 100,000-seat, circular stadium with a thin, metal roof to be supported not by vision-obscuring columns, but by air pressure. No one had ever built such a "domed" stadium. Though the basic design had been patented by a couple of New York men, committee member Glenn L. Martin, an eccentric but brilliant aviation pioneer, championed the cause in Baltimore. His company, which would later evolve into the aerospace giant Lockheed Martin, ran a factory complex to the east of the city where bombers were built, the best known being the Marauder.

Martin argued that the new stadium would draw attention and prestige to the city, and help retain its bright young people, who were then seeking success elsewhere. More pragmatic minds prevailed, however, and the air-supported dome debuted much later in more innovative cities. Instead of building a trend-setting monument, Baltimore put together a bargain-basement stadium that was obsolete almost from its first game.

Construction occurred in phases, as various funding levies were passed. The first allowed for a $3.5 million, single-deck, 20,000-seat concrete structure. Work began on that in 1949 and was completed a year later, amid optimism that the new park would not only keep the Colts happy but attract a Major League Baseball team. Baltimore was home to the International League Orioles, and there was rampant speculation that some major-league teams were looking for new homes.

The new structure went up on 33rd Street at the site of the old Municipal Stadium, which had been called "Babe Ruth Stadium" in its final years. Planners thought this location had two advantages: It was in a crowded residential neighborhood, which meant that fans could walk to the games, and it would cost less to rebuild on the same site than to build on a new one.

"Memorial Stadium was built where it was because we only had $3.5 million to spend," Robert C. "Jake" Embry, a community leader involved in the effort, recalled in 1991. "The old wooden sta-dium, with utilities, was already there, and the cost of bringing in new utilities to any of the other sites ... would have been $1 million."

It was obvious that the new stadium needed a second deck, but the matter was controversial. The voters soundly rejected a bonding referendum for an upper deck of the "Babe Ruth Stadium." Then someone got the bright idea to connect the project with the nation's bountiful, post-war patriotism. The stadium was renamed "Memorial Stadium," and voters were told it would be dedicated to the war dead. That did the trick. A second vote in 1953 approved $3 million for "Memorial Stadium."

Double-decked and shaped like a horseshoe, it contained almost no wood — a relief to a city that had lived through the fiery destruction of the first Oriole Park 10 years before. The new struc-ture's exterior was a handsome mix of red brick and sandy-colored concrete. Fans walked to the upper decks on broad ramps that switched back and forth like a mountain trail. The structure easily accommodated baseball, with home plate situated in the bottom of the "U." But football was a little trickier: The dugouts had to be covered with plywood, and the stadium's open, north end needed to be filled in with temporary bleachers. Temporary seats could also be added along the sidelines.

To emphasize the patriotism of the project, an urn with dirt from overseas military cemeteries was put on display inside. And stainless steel, art-deco lettering graced the giant facade at the stadium's southern end, reading: "Time will not dim the glory of their deeds."

Despite these touches, it was obvious that some corners had been cut in the design. The upper deck, for example, was held aloft by giant, concrete pillars instead of by the "cantilever" system used in other parks. The pillars cost less, but they pushed the upper deck back from the field, thus limiting the prices that could be charged for those seats. They also left thousands of lower-deck seats with obstructed views. In addition, many of the original seats were wooden bleachers, and the stadium lacked a roof. No double-decked stadium had ever been built without a cover for the upstairs fans.

These shortcomings notwithstanding, the structure did what was hoped: It attracted the attention of Major League Baseball. The first flicker of interest came before the second deck was even added, from an investor who wanted to buy the Boston Braves and move them to Baltimore. That deal fell through. But the next one was more successful.

The St. Louis Browns, despite the best promotional efforts of their young and free-wheeling owner Bill Veeck, were a disaster on the field and at the gate. In their last year in St. Louis, they lost nearly two-thirds of their games and couldn't have blasted fans away from the National League Cardinals if they'd had explosives. The Browns' attendance averaged 3,860 a game, barely a third of what the Cards were drawing.

In 1953, when millionaire brewer August Busch, of Anheuser Busch fame, bought the Cardinals, Veeck figured he'd better get out fast. He looked first to Los Angeles, but found no suitable stadium. He then considered Milwaukee, but the Braves beat him there. That left Baltimore.

The city promised to add the second deck to Memorial Stadium and offered the Browns liberal lease terms. Veeck agreed, and on March 11, 1953, he asked his fellow owners for permission to make the move east. The other owners, disenchanted with Veeck's maverick ways, turned him down on March 16 and again on Sept. 27. Baltimore community leaders saw what was happening and rounded up some investors to buy out Veeck. They also threatened legal and political challenges to baseball's cherished antitrust status.

The threat of litigation again turned the tide. The owners approved the move, and it was announced Sept. 29, effective the next season. Thus, the first Browns team — the St. Louis Browns — arranged to move to Baltimore. They became the Orioles.

Vice President Richard M. Nixon threw out the first pitch at Memorial Stadium in 1954.

For Charm City, it was sweet redemption: The last time major league baseball had allowed a team to move was 52 years earlier, when the first Baltimore Orioles' American League franchise went north to New York and was renamed the Yankees.

The Orioles' arrival was also indicative of an unprecedented sports expansion going on in Baltimore. In the span of a few years, the city, which previously contented itself with horse racing, minor league baseball, and duckpin bowling, acquired three major league teams. Besides the Colts and Orioles, there was also the Baltimore Bullets. This 1947 expansion team of the Basketball Association of America joined the National Basketball Association when the leagues merged in 1948. Baltimore, it seemed, was on its way.

CHAPTER TWO

That Old Colt Fever

Memorial Stadium was still under construction when the Colts, wearing their Texas blue-and-white uniforms, started play there.

New owner Carroll Rosenbloom, a Baltimore native, knew some football, having played the sport at the University of Pennsylvania under then coach and later NFL Commissioner Bert Bell. As a young man, Rosenbloom took over his father's textile business, landing lucrative military contracts for uniforms and parachutes. Fabulously wealthy, he was growing bored with business when Bell approached him about taking over the Colts.

The commissioner wanted an owner who had both deep pockets and a competitive spirit. Rosenbloom lived primarily in New York, but had an estate in Baltimore and fit the bill. After some initial hemming and hawing, Rosenbloom agreed to make the purchase. Some local investors helped to raise the money to pay off the Redskins' territorial fee.

The team began the 1953 season with a blockbuster trade. The Colts swapped five Baltimore players for 10 Cleveland Browns. Among the players who came over were future coach Don Shula, Bert Rechichar, Carl Taseff, and Art Spinney.

The new players got the team off on the right track: The Colts upset the Chicago Bears, 13-9, in their first game, when Rechichar kicked a then-NFL record 56-yard field goal. But they soon lapsed into the ways of the old Colts and finished the season 3-9, dropping their last seven games.

The next season, the team hired a new coach, Weeb Ewbank, a longtime assistant coach in Paul Brown's Cleveland football machine. Ewbank promised Rosenbloom a contender in five years. Even before he formally took over the job, Ewbank made some crucial contributions.

After Ewbank signed with the Colts, Brown went to Bell to insist that Ewbank, who had supervised Cleveland's planning for the upcoming player draft, remain with Cleveland until *after* the draft. Bell agreed. So, on draft day, Ewbank was still working for the Browns — theoretically.

It wasn't a trivial request. When it came to spotting great new talent, Paul Brown had no equal. To the draft, he brought a disciplined research methodology never before seen in the game. So he was understandably seething on draft day in 1954 when the Baltimore Colts seemed to be reading his mind, picking players he had identified as top potentials. Some of them were obscure men whose talents Brown thought could be developed.

In the 20th round, for example, the Colts made the unlikely pick of a nearsighted, pigeon-toed receiver from Southern Methodist University named Raymond Berry. Paul Brown had had his eye on the upperclassman and intended to take him.

In the next round, the Colts snagged another Brown pick, Robert Lade, an unheralded lineman from Nebraska State Teachers College. The Cleveland coach was so angry now that his face turned bright red, and he suspiciously eyed his assistant, Ewbank, seated next to him. Brown didn't know how, but he was sure there was a leak in his organization.

He was right. Ewbank had been passing notes to the Colts through John Steadman, a sportswriter for *The Baltimore News-Post*. And the Colts had not hesitated to take advantage of this inside information.

Still, in Ewbank's first season, the Colts posted another disappointing record. They went 3-9, the same as the year before. Then gradually they began to improve. For the 1955 season, Ewbank and General Manager Don Kellett engineered some key drafts, picking up quarterback George Shaw, running back Alan "The Horse" Ameche and center/linebacker Dick Szymanski. The team won its first three games, finishing with a franchise-best 5-6-1 record and Shaw getting named rookie of the year. But, sadly, his career was about to be cut short by injury.

Luckily, Ewbank and Kellett had arranged for a backup. In 1956, they gambled on a young untried quarterback cut by the Pittsburgh Steelers. John Constantine Unitas turned out to be more than the average understudy.

An all-star at his Pittsburgh high school, Unitas had a hard time talking his way onto a college team. Coaches just couldn't imagine the 6-foot, 138-pound kid striking fear in the hearts of his opponents. Notre Dame and Indiana both told him to get lost. Pittsburgh, his hometown university, offered him a scholarship, but he flunked the admissions test.

Finally, the University of Louisville signed him. He failed the exam there, too, but appealed to the admissions board and was admitted on probation with a football scholarship. Unitas put on some weight, won some games, and finished with a solid but unspectacular record.

The Steelers drafted him in the ninth round. But Pittsburgh already had three other quarterbacks and wasn't very impressed with Unitas in training camp, where he spent most of his time on the sidelines playing catch with owner Art Rooney's son. Unitas was cut without even appearing in an exhibition game. He hitch-hiked home.

But Unitas didn't quit easily. He learned perseverance by shoveling coal at 75 cents a ton for his mother. She had taken over the family business after Unitas' father died. The young player sent a telegram to Cleveland coach Paul Brown alerting him of his unex-pected availability. Brown, who had an especially good sense of quarterback talent, was interested, but had just talked his star QB, Otto Graham, out of retiring.

Brown called Unitas and told him Cleveland was set for the season with Graham and backup George Ratterman. But he would like to see Unitas at the Browns' training camp the next summer, if he was still available.

In the meantime, Unitas took up semi-pro football, playing on a trash-strewn, grassless junior high school field in Pittsburgh's

Bloomington section. He was the starting quarterback for the Bloomington Rams of the Greater Pittsburgh League and was paid $6 a game. During the week, he worked construction for $125 a week to help provide for his wife and new baby.

How Unitas came to the Colts' attention is in dispute. Some accounts have an anonymous fan writing Ewbank a letter. Another has GM Don Kellett poring over waiver lists, recognizing Unitas' name, and tracking him down through his Bloomington Rams coach, who was touting another long-forgotten player. In any case, Kellett made what later would be remembered as one of the most fateful, 80-cent phone calls in football history. He invited Unitas to a tryout, and the eager young athlete accepted. Having checked out the Colts roster, Unitas knew that the only other backup QB was a rookie and concluded that his chances of playing were better in Baltimore than in Cleveland.

He also had an advantage with Ewbank. Some members of Ewbank's coaching staff were familiar with Unitas from Pittsburgh and his college days. Ewbank himself knew the coach at Louisville and called him for his assessment. The Colts ended up signing Unitas as a backup to Shaw for $7,000.

The new Colts quarterback was astounded by Baltimore and its football devotion. During the 1956 training camp, the team held a scrimmage at Memorial Stadium, an annual event whose proceeds went to police boys' clubs. (Tickets cost $1.)

"So I walk out on the field, and there's 48,000 people there to see a scrimmage!" he recalled much later. "I've never seen that many people in all my life. I said, 'What the f— is going on?' And these crazy people are hollering and screaming 'Colts! Colts!'"

Unitas warmed the bench for a couple of weeks. Then, on Oct. 21, 1956, he got his shot. The Colts were playing Chicago at Wrigley Field, then home to both the Bears and the baseball Cubs, and Shaw went down with a torn knee ligament, ending his career and launching Unitas'.

It wasn't a pretty debut to say the least.

Unitas' first pass was intercepted and returned for a touchdown. On the Colts' next play from scrimmage, Unitas fumbled a handoff to Ameche. The Bears recovered and scored again. In another possession, Unitas fumbled yet another handoff, and the Bears scored yet again. The 20-14 lead he had inherited from Shaw dissolved into a 58-27 Chicago win.

But he got better. A lot better.

Although the Colts poked around for a new passer, Unitas started the next game and led the team to a 28-21 defeat of the Packers. A week later, he cemented his role with the team by pulling off an upset win over the Cleveland Browns, 21-7. Coach Paul Brown got his first glimpse of the star QB who slipped away.

That year, Unitas set an NFL record completion rate for a rookie, hitting his receivers more than 55 percent of the time. The next year, he was named league Most Valuable Player, and the Colts broke .500 with a 7-5 record. Then in 1958, the Colts won their first six games and all of their home games, and made it to the championship game.

His Colt teammates were awed by the command Unitas took in the huddle. He didn't ask for input, nor did he tolerate dissent. Unitas jealously guarded his right to call plays, basing his decisions on field reports that his receivers and linesmen brought back. He often ignored suggestions sent in by the coach. Fortunately, Ewbank — in contrast to Paul Brown's domineering ways — encouraged his team leaders to think for themselves.

Having learned the game in the age of two-way football, Unitas could read a defense as well as anyone. Loping up to the line of scrimmage with his stooped shoulders and gangly arms, he would calmly glance right, then glance left, and casually discard the play called in the huddle, going with something radically different. His teammates learned to pay close attention.

Opponents, too, were often caught off guard by Unitas' gambling instincts and uncanny diversions: He would regularly look one way and throw another, or double-pump the ball at decoy receivers, to draw the defense to the wrong side of the field.

Though he weighed less than 200 pounds and was not particularly fast, Unitas had enormous hands. He threw with a unique overhand style that sent short passes spiraling like bullets and long bombs downfield with pinpoint accuracy, often landing safely in a receiver's hands, mere inches out of a defender's reach.

He would go for the long bomb when a first down was only a short run away. "Why go for six yards when you can go for six *points*?" he used to say. And he'd sometimes throw a pass and run downfield to block for the receiver. Other times, he could be seen tossing a game-winning pass and then confidently walking off the field, head down and certain that the pass would find its mark.

The man had nerves of steel. He figured that, after taking the snap from center, he could count on exactly 2.5 seconds before releasing his passes, so he designed his plays accordingly. He would wait until the last possible moment to fire off a pass, lining up receivers just where he wanted them. When he ran, he always scrambled for the extra yard, disdaining the now-common practice of stepping out of bounds or sliding into tacklers.

Unitas also suffered a lot of punishment. Rushers had standing orders to shut down Unitas and the Colts' pass-heavy offense. But he almost always got back up for more.

In a 1958 game against Green Bay, Unitas was carted off the field with three broken ribs and a punctured lung. He came back four games later, helping to complete a franchise-best 9-3 season.

Before he retired in 1973, Unitas would be named league MVP two more times. He would play in 10 Pro Bowls and set 22 NFL records, gaining 40,239 yards and 290 touchdowns on 2,830 completions. During one remarkable stretch, he threw at least one touchdown pass in 47 straight games — a feat comparable to Joe DiMaggio's 56-game hitting streak in baseball.

• • •

It was the 1958 championship game, however, that first brought the 25-year-old Unitas to national attention. Played before 64,185 fans at Yankee Stadium, the game proved to be a thriller of historic proportions and helped to firmly establish the National Football League.

The timing couldn't have been better for the NFL: The popularity of New York's "big blue team of destiny," the Giants, had network television executives hoping for better results from their nationwide broadcast of the championship game. The first two contests had hardly been cliffhangers: New York routed Chicago, 47-7, and Detroit pummeled Cleveland, 50-14.

Among the players on the field Dec. 29, 1958, were some of the best in the game, many of them destined for the Pro Football Hall of Fame. For the Colts: Unitas, Ameche, Berry, Donovan, Lenny Moore, and Gino Marchetti. For the Giants: Frank Gifford,

Pat Summerall, Sam Huff, Rosey Grier, and Charley Conerly.

New York had beaten Baltimore, 24-21, in the regular season and was the heavy favorite.

Offensive end and kicker Summerall, who would become even better known as an NFL sportscaster, put the Giants ahead 3-0 in the first quarter. But a pair of fumbles by another future sportscaster, New York halfback Frank Gifford, were quickly converted into Colt touchdowns, the second one scored after a dramatic 88-yard drive led by Unitas.

In the second quarter, emotions were already running high when the Giants' famous linebacker Sam Huff pushed Berry out of bounds and, according to Ewbank, kneed the receiver in the groin for good measure. The enraged coach exchanged a few words with Huff and punched him squarely on the chin. Player intensity promptly escalated.

The Colts went into the second half with a 14-3 lead. Unitas led the team down to the Giants' 3-yard line, where New York's vaunted defense finally came to life. The front line stopped two straight quarterback sneaks. Then, on third down and goal to go, several Colts players missed the call. Unitas was to pitch back to Ameche, who then was supposed to pass to tight end Jim Mutscheller. But "The Horse" thought he was supposed to run with the ball, and paid no attention to Mutscheller, who was open in the end zone. The Colts lost yardage on the play.

The momentum suddenly switched to New York, and journeyman quarterback "Chuckin' Charlie" Conerly went to work. Conerly, the NFL's rookie of the year in 1948, had led the Giants to the championship in 1956. Now, he started a drive culminating in a touchdown rush by fullback Mel Triplett.

In engineering the Giants' comeback, Conerly had some unusual help. A Polaroid snapshot taken by Giants owner Wellington Mara in the first half showed the Colts' secondary over-shifting to the strong side. Conerly thus could anticipate, and exploit, the alignment of the Colts defense.

After another series of passes, hand-offs and fakes, Conerly had his team up 17-14, 53 seconds into the fourth quarter. A pair of Baltimore drives went nowhere, and Conerly soon found himself on his own 40-yard line needing four yards for a first down.

Attempting to stop a second down Giants run, the Colts' great defensive end Gino Marchetti broke his leg, and Gifford, the ball carrier, later would claim that the official mismarked his forward progress, denying the team a first down. A third-down sweep by Gifford for the final yard was stopped short of scrimmage by the Colts' Donovan and Ordell Braase — inches away from a first down, continued possession of the ball, and, with only minutes on the clock, what seemed a sure win.

N.Y. Coach Jim Lee Howell, figuring his league-best defense could protect the Giants lead, called for a punt. It turned out to be a fateful error. Unitas was back in the driver's seat for what later would become his trademark two-minute drill, a no-huddle offensive explosion that the team practiced each week. Unitas quickly rediscovered his first half footing and adroitly moved the ball downfield with precision passes to future Hall of Famer Raymond Berry.

With just 30 seconds remaining, Colts kicker Steve Myhra tied the game with a field goal, which led to the NFL's first overtime. (The rules then provided for ties in the regular season and overtimes in the post-season, but no teams had yet needed one.) The Giants won the coin toss and opted to receive, but, on their first offensive possession, came up one yard shy of a first down.

Unitas — just three years from the sandlots of Pittsburgh — was suddenly cast in the starring role of a nationally televised drama. He took over on his own 20-yard line and kept the Giants off balance through 80 yards of brilliant play-calling.

First, he handed off to halfback L.G. Dupre for 10 yard and three yard gains, then hit Ameche for another first down. Dupre ran again but was taken down well short of the first down. On the next play, Unitas was sacked. Now on third and long, the spindly quarterback took the snap and looked downfield for Lenny Moore, but found him covered. Berry was open, but he was short of the first-down marker. As his offensive line strained to protect him against the oncoming Giants, Unitas calmly waved Berry deeper and hit him with a rocket pass for the first down.

A 21-yard run by Ameche and a 12-yard pass to Berry got Baltimore to the Giant 8-yard line, where the Colts called a timeout. The crowd expected a field goal, followed by a riotous celebration in the streets of Baltimore. But Ewbank had little confidence in Myhra, an erratic kicker on his best days, and told Unitas to keep it on the ground with a handoff to Ameche. Unitas quickly discarded his coach's advice and in the huddle called for a sideline pass to Mutscheller, who was to take the pass over his outside shoulder so the ball would go out of bounds if he was covered. The tight end caught the ball at the 1-yard line and slid out of bounds on the frozen turf.

Eight minutes and 15 seconds into the overtime, Unitas slapped the ball into Ameche's gut and watched as a picture-perfect block by Moore opened a gaping hole on the Giants' left side. The Horse's head-first gallop across the goal line, captured in a black-and-white photo, is still one of the most recognizable moments in football and can be found framed and hanging in taverns and homes all across the Baltimore area.

Later, Ewbank would joke that he had missed his self-imposed deadline of delivering a championship to Rosenbloom in five years. It took him five years, eight minutes, he would say.

The victory set off fireworks in Charm City but cast a pall over Yankee Stadium. Among the dejected fans headed home was a young ad man named Art Modell, who had watched the game from an upper-deck seat.

"It had all the drama you would want," Modell recalled years later. "It confirmed my belief that the game [NFL] was here to stay."

Associated Press sportswriter Jack Hand wrote, "If they play pro football for 100 years, they never can top Baltimore's first championship snatched dramatically in a sudden-death playoff, 23-17, after New York refused to gamble."

Between them, the two teams established 12 NFL championship records. Berry caught 12 passes for 178 yards, bettering reception and yardage records set, respectively, by the Browns' Dante Lavelli (11 catches) in 1950 and by the Redskins' Wayne Millner (160 yards) in 1937. With 349 yards passing, Unitas surpassed Redskin Sammy Baugh's previous mark of 335 yards, set against the Bears in 1937. Both the Giants' six fumbles and the Colts' four recoveries were also records.

"Never had there been a game like this one," wrote Tex Maule in *Sports Illustrated*. "When there are so many high points, it is not easy to pick the highest. But for the 60,000 and more fans who packed Yankee Stadium for the third week in a row, the moment they will never forget — the moment with which they will eternally bore their grandchildren — came when, with less than 10 seconds to play and the clock remorselessly moving, the Baltimore Colts kicked a field goal which put the professional football championship in a 17-17 tie and necessitated a historic sudden-death overtime period. Although it was far from apparent at the time, this was the end of the line for the fabulous New York Giants, eastern titleholders by virtue of three stunning victories over a great Cleveland team."

Television executives couldn't have been happier. They now had a game that everyone was talking about. Unitas even turned down an invitation to appear on Ed Sullivan's variety show.

The 1958 telecast was not without its mishaps, though. The broadcast abruptly halted in the middle of its exciting finish when someone tripped over an electrical cord on the field. Play was stopped. One account has a quick-thinking network exec delaying the game, and thus giving technicians time to fix the problem, by imitating a drunk on the field.

Two years later, the NFL had its first network contract, permanently plugged into the money-machine life support of TV.

• • •

The 1958 game also kindled a remarkable romance between Baltimore and its Colts. A sweaty city of steel mills and stevedores, Baltimore was viewed by much of the nation as a smokestack among the glistening skyscrapers of the Eastern seaboard.

The post-World War II boom had brought new wealth and sophistication to New York, Philadelphia, and Washington. But Baltimore, bulked up by wartime shipyards and aircraft factories, was still strictly a blue-collar town best known for its crab houses and sleazy red-light district.

Still, in 1958, the Baltimore Colts were the undisputed champions of the world. And they had gotten there with an unlikely collection of regular-Joe superstars with ethnic names and strong work ethics.

Unitas, with his crooked teeth and understated manner, wasn't exactly a media darling. Yet fans thrilled to the sight of him — his spindly legs and black high-top shoes, fading back in the pocket.

Ray Berry, his favorite receiver, was an obsessive athlete who ran and re-ran plays with Unitas after hours during training camp.

Tall, eccentric and bright, Berry wasn't very fast. He became one of the greatest receivers in football by sheer dint of his determination. Berry figured there were 18 basic catches in football, 12 on short passes and 6 on long ones. He practiced these with relentless repetition, often setting up a net so he could have passes fired at him and not have to waste time running down the missed balls.

Berry played in shoes with soles of differing thickness because one of his legs was shorter than the other. The imbalance made his high-stepping gait look wild and out of control to pursuing tacklers. He also wore a corset for a back injury and contact lenses for nearsightedness. To make sure that he played at precisely the 182 pounds he favored, he took a scale with him on the road.

Part acrobat and part computer, Berry could run an elaborate pass route and turn at the last moment to receive a ball just as it floated down. He could catch a ball with his fingertips while leaning far over a sideline, his toes stretched safely in bounds.

Drafted by the Colts in 1954, Berry played with the team until 1967. When his career ended, he had caught 631 passes for 9,275 yards — an NFL record that would stand for years. He was inducted into the Hall of Fame in 1973.

If Berry was the team's graceful jungle cat, Art Donovan was its rhinoceros. He stood 6-foot-3 and weighed 265 pounds. A beer-swilling, foul-mouthed defensive tackle, Donovan became the first Colt in the Hall of Fame when inducted in 1968. He titled his irreverent football autobiography, "Fatso."

Known as much for his locker-room pranks as for his effectiveness in stopping both the pass and the run, Donovan literally anchored the team's defense during its early years. He had a clause in his contract that required him to pay a fine if his weight ever exceeded 270 pounds. Every Sunday, he delighted in upsetting Berry's routine by borrowing his hairbrush without asking. Donovan later went on to fame as a voice of early-era, tough-guy football with appearances on David Letterman's late-night TV talk show.

Colt Gino Marchetti, who at age 18 fought Nazis at the Battle of the Bulge, was almost unstoppable as a defensive end. He retired in 1963 but came back the next year, only to retire again. Three years later, with the Colts' defensive line ravaged by injuries and Marchetti now 40 years-old, he again put on the uniform and again menaced NFL offenses. He, too, was voted a Hall of Fame berth. Known as "Gino the Giant," he would pace the locker room before games like a caged lion and developed a reputation for "playing mad." Quarterbacks learned to fear his brutal sacks. A 1969 poll of sportswriters voted Marchetti the best defensive lineman of the NFL's first half-century.

The career of fleet-footed running back Lenny Moore appeared near an end in 1964, but then he went on to score a record 20 touchdowns and helped take the team to the title game that year. Known as "Spats" because of the heavy taping he put on his ankles before games, Moore redefined the role of a back, proving equally dangerous when running and when receiving.

Then there was Gene "Big Daddy" Lipscomb, a 6-foot-6, nearly 300-pound tackle who would knock the senses out of an opponent and then help him back to his feet. He refined the role of a defensive lineman by reading the other team's play and stalking the ball carrier instead of just plugging up the middle.

Operating in the era before free agency and mega-salaries, these Colts wove themselves into the fabric of the Baltimore community. They would show up at the local punt, pass ,and kick competitions and tour the local schools, talking to students. Personal appearances and hospital visits were considered part of the job, one that didn't pay all that well.

Unitas earned his highest salary, $250,000, in 1974 during his last season. By then, he had been traded to the San Diego Chargers. The money was about 10 times what he got from the Colts after winning the '58 championship. During his early days, Unitas worked in the off-season as an ironworker; later, he supplemented his gridiron pay as a salesman.

Running back Tom Matte said he and Unitas and other players would often lug their bruised bodies down to the team's offices on Mondays to autograph pictures for fans who wrote to request them. The Colts policy was to give out snapshots to anyone who asked, and plenty did.

Many Colts retained ties to Baltimore well past their playing years. Ameche and Marchetti opened hamburger joints, called Ameche's and Gino's respectively. The Horse touted a special "35 sauce," named for the jersey number he wore. Both restaurant chains are now out of business.

Tackle Jim Parker opened a liquor store, Jim Parker's Pub Inc., which is still operating. And Art Donovan bought the Valley Country Club in Towson, Md., outside Baltimore, in 1955, and still owns it.

• • •

The Colts repeated as champions in 1959, again beating the Giants, 31-16, this time in Baltimore. The Giants led 9-7 after three quarters, thanks to three field goals by Pat Summerall. The Colts defense came alive in the fourth quarter, though, intercepting the Giants three times for scores.

It seemed the start of something great.

But the next few seasons, the team struggled, going 6-6 in 1960, 8-6 in '61 and 7-7 in '62. Not until the Colts made another withdrawal from the Cleveland Browns' savings account did they turn around: In 1963, Paul Brown protogé Don Shula became Baltimore's head coach.

Drafted out of college in 1951 by Coach Brown, Shula played as a Cleveland defensive back for two years. He then donned a Colts uniform for four years and that of the Redskins for a year, before starting his coaching career.

In Shula's first year, the Colts finished in third place, with an 8-6 record. But the next season they came back strong, posting a 12-2 record and winning the NFL Western Conference. In their first championship game since 1959, they faced the Browns. Shula's familiarity with his opponent proved of little value, however: The Colts lost 27-0.

The next season the Colts went 10-3-1 and tied for the conference lead. Apparently headed for a rematch with the Browns, they first had to knock off the 10-3-1 Packers in a divisional playoff without the services of Unitas, who tore a knee ligament in Week 12 when two Chicago Bears tackles sandwiched him. His backup, Gary Cuozzo, separated a shoulder in the next game, which the Colts lost to the Packers, 42-27.

Shula picked up another back-up quarterback, 36-year-old veteran Ed Brown, but he had a spotty record, and Shula didn't have much confidence in him. Instead, the coach decided to gamble on a nonquarterback to lead the team into the final game, and, he hoped, the post-season.

Colt halfback Tom Matte had quarterbacked at Ohio State University, where coach Woody Hayes had his QBs running and handing off more than passing. Matte had only three days to practice for his new role when he led the Colts against the Rams in the regular-season finale. To help him in the huddle, he wrote a crib sheet on his wristband, listing all of the Colts offensive plays and assignments.

Matte turned in a gutsy performance, running more than he threw. When a pass was essential, Shula sent Ed Brown in. Both passes Matte threw that day fell incomplete, but he gained 99 yards on the ground, and the Colts won 20-17. They had earned the right to face Vince Lombardi's Packers in an unusual tie-breaker game for the divisional crown.

Against the Packers, Matte would be completely on his own. Brown had joined the roster too late to be eligible for post-season play. The game was played at Lambeau Field in Green Bay on the day after Christmas. It was a relatively balmy 28 degrees.

Baltimore got a lucky break on the opening drive. Green Bay quarterback Bart Starr hit Bill Anderson for a short gain, but the ball was knocked loose. Colts linebacker Don Shinnick scooped it up and headed for the end zone. Starr was the only man in position to stop Shinnick, but Colts safety Jim Welch took him out with a shoulder. Shinnick scored, and Starr left the game with bruised ribs.

The Colts, capitalizing on Matte's able footwork, led 10-0 at the half. But the Packers came roaring back. They stopped the Colts' opening drive, then got a break of their own. Baltimore punter Tom Gilburg fielded a high snap, and the Packers knocked him down, taking over the ball at the Colts' 35. A few plays later, halfback Paul Hornung went in for a Packers' TD.

With 1:58 left in the game, Green Bay found itself at Baltimore's 15, behind 10-7. Field-goal kicker Don Chandler trotted out, but his attempt was high and slicing. Or so it appeared. Chandler twisted his face at what he thought was a miss, but the official shocked everyone by signaling a good kick. The score was tied, and the game went into overtime.

The Colts protested vigorously. A Baltimore newspaper printed a series of photographs, taken from the game film, that showed the kick was no good. Years later, Chandler admitted that he, too, thought the ball sailed wide. Nonetheless, he connected for real in OT to win the game for the Packers, 13-10.

The next season, the NFL began putting a pair of officials under the goal posts during field-goal attempts. It also added 10 feet to the uprights, bringing them to 20 feet; the added height became known as "Baltimore extensions." Matte's cheat-sheet wristbands, but not Matte, ended up in the Hall of Fame.

The Packers went on to beat the Browns, 23-12, in the championship. And the Colts headed to the "playoff bowl," a short-lived annual match of second-place finishers that the players dubbed the "toilet bowl." Baltimore beat the Dallas Cowboys in Miami 35-3.

In 1966, the Colts again ended up in the toilet bowl, posting a 9-5 record, second in the Western Conference. They beat the Philadelphia Eagles 20-14.

The 1967 season was an even bigger heartbreaker. Unbeaten in 13 games, with an 11-0-2 record, the Colts dropped their last game, 34-10, to the Rams and lost a chance at the post-season. But Baltimore came roaring back in 1968, despite losing Unitas to an elbow injury in the last pre-season game.

Backup QB Earl Morrall proved more than up to the task. The Colts won their first five games, lost one to the Cleveland Browns, then finished the season with eight straight victories. Their 13-1 record put them atop of what was then called the Coastal Division. They knocked out the Minnesota Vikings 24-14 for the conference championship, then thrashed the Browns 34-0 for the 1968 NFL championship.

The NFL, then in the early stages of a merger with the rival American Football League, still kept a separate regular season schedule but was pitting its champions against the AFL's in a grand finale. The Super Bowl, won by the NFL's Packers the first two years, had become an emotional outlet for the bitterness the two leagues had built up during their six years of "football wars."

Thanks to the Packers' wins in Super Bowl I and II, the older NFL had a smug sense of superiority. The Colts were heavily favored to extend the league's winning streak in Super Bowl III, set for Jan. 12, 1969, in Miami's Orange Bowl. Few fans or analysts took seriously the 13 of 23 interleague preseason games that the AFL had won. "Just a quirk," NFL stalwarts reassured themselves.

Heading into the Super Bowl, the AFL's New York Jets were

18-point underdogs. Colts owner Carroll Rosenbloom had already planned the victory party: He had a 10-piece band and several cases of champagne waiting at his Florida home. Party invitations had been sent.

But three days before the game, at a dinner hosted by the Miami Touchdown Club at the Miami Springs Villa, the Jets' brash, young quarterback Joe Namath made a stunning prediction. At the close of remarks made during an award acceptance, Namath said, "And we're going to win Sunday, I'll guarantee you."

No question, Namath was good. In fact, the bidding for his services between the AFL and NFL had pushed his salary to nearly $400,000 and helped to convince the leagues to negotiate the merger. But was he good enough to guarantee a victory over the 15-1 Colts, a team some considered one of the best in NFL history?

Sadly, for Colts fans, Namath and the Jets were more than just talk. On the Colts' first possession, they moved the ball easily to the Jets' 19. But Morrall went three downs and out, and the Colts' place-kicker missed an easy 27-yard field-goal attempt. It was a bad omen for Baltimore.

Morrall was intercepted three times in the first half. By the time he was replaced by Unitas in the fourth quarter, he had completed only 6 of 17 passes for 71 yards. And by then, the Jets had scored two field goals, bringing the score to 13-0. Unitas, his arm still sore, managed to lead the Colts to a touchdown in the game's final minutes, but the effort only prevented a shutout. The game ended with Namath and the Jets on top, 16-7.

And the victorious coach? None other than Paul Brown's protégé and the Colts' one-time head coach Weeb Ewbank, who had taken over the Jets in 1963.

The Colts' loss was a crushing blow for the National Football League.

"We were absolutely thunderstruck," recalled Art Modell, who was then overseeing merger talks as the NFL's president.

Guests at Rosenbloom's post-game party barely spoke above a whisper. A man not easily given to humility, Rosenbloom was humbled.

"It was like a mortuary," Modell said.

Baltimore fans were despondent for weeks. But they eventually got their due: The Colts came back two years later with an 11-

2-1 record, and beat the Cincinnati Bengals for the divisional title and the Oakland Raiders for the conference championship, before facing the Dallas Cowboys in Super Bowl IV. This time, the Colts were the AFL team. They won, 16-13, on a 32-yard field goal by Jim O'Brien in the last five seconds of the game.

(Don Shula, it should be noted, had left Baltimore by this time, taking the head coaching job at the Miami Dolphins, where he soon would make NFL history. With quarterback Bob Griese at the helm, the 1972-73 Dolphins became the only modern-day undefeated team; they capped off the feat with a victory over the Washington Redskins, 14-7, in Super Bowl VII. They then returned to beat the Minnesota Vikings, 24-7, in Super Bowl VIII. The winningest coach in NFL history, Shula was inducted into the Football Hall of Fame in 1997, during his first year of eligibility.)

· · ·

For a city that had spent decades rooting for minor-league baseball teams, Baltimore had a joyful awakening to football's big leagues. In fact, even after the Orioles moved to town and became champions, the city's heart stayed on the gridiron. In 1966, the Colts sold out every home game on their way to a relatively lackluster 9-5 season, while the Orioles averaged less than 18,000 per game on their way to their first World Series victory. The Orioles even failed to fill Memorial Stadium for the decisive game of the Series, when a home run by slugger Frank Robinson beat the much-favored Los Angeles Dodgers. The Orioles swept in four games.

Beginning with a 1964 contest against the Chicago Bears, the Colts played before sold-out home crowds for 51 straight games — setting an NFL record. The crowds were so boisterous that Memorial Stadium was called by one sportswriter "the world's largest outdoor insane asylum."

The stadium even attracted its own free-lance cheerleaders. Leonard Burrier was a mild-mannered, beer-drinking owner of a Baltimore tire shop in 1975 when he decided to liven things up at Memorial Stadium. While watching the Colts play the Browns, he stood up, did a little twist, and contorted his body into the letters "C," "O," "L," "T," "S." Before he knew it, all of Section 32 was shouting out the letters in unison, and Burrier was "The Big

Wheel," destined to become a part of Colts lore.

The Big Wheel could be seen most Sundays running around the stadium and performing his human spelling bee on the tops of the baseball dugouts. Sometimes, an accomplice would hold up a sign over his head reading "APPLAUSE," but it was rarely needed.

Between plays, a white horse named "Dixie" would gallop around the field as the Baltimore Colts Marching Band, a venerable holdover from AAFC days, brought the crowd to its feet, and sometimes to tears, with the Colts' fight song.

Season tickets became so hard to get that they were passed down in wills, and their ownership was contested in divorces. The fight song was played on jukeboxes in waterfront bars and at weddings in fashionable suburbs. Colts Corral fan clubs were formed, and many of their members would meet the team at the airport when it returned from road games.

One of the most zealous fans was Hurst "Loudy" Loudenslager, a round-faced supply sergeant with the Maryland National Guard whose affection for the team became a local legend. He founded Colts Corral No. 2 along with fellow National Guardsmen who met monthly at Baltimore's castle-like Fifth Regiment Armory to plan trips to Colts away games. In the 1960s, Loudy began the tradition of seeing the players off and welcoming them back at the airport. He missed only one trip, and only because he was suffering from heart problems.

When the Vietnam War threatened to take some promising Colts, Loudy helped them enlist in the National Guard to avoid the draft.

Loudenslager's wife Flo baked black-walnut cakes for players and coaches on their birthdays and estimated making 900 cakes over the course of 30 years. Their family club-room basement became a shrine of blue-and-white jerseys, game balls, used cleats, and personal notes of thanks from Baltimore Hall of Famers.

When Loudy died in 1989, he was laid out in a white Colts T-shirt with blue shorts. His coffin was decorated with floral footballs and horseshoes. Among his pallbearers were some appreciative former Colts, including Johnny Unitas and Art Donovan.

Some of Baltimore's other fans went on to their own distinctive brands of fame. A young Tom Clancy, destined to become a best-selling author, watched games from upper deck seats with his mailman father.

Future film maker Barry Levinson was also there, enjoying the hysteria that he would later dramatize in "Diner," an autobio-graphical movie account of growing up in Baltimore during the height of Colts madness.

Then there was Baltimore poet Ogden Nash, the Colts' unof-ficial poet laureate, who wrote glowingly of "that old Colt fever."

In 1972, though, the fever broke.

CHAPTER THREE

The Legend of
Paul, Jim,
and Art

Thirty-six-year-old Paul Brown was already a football phenomenon in 1944 when he got a call inviting him to coach a
Cleveland team in the new All-American Football Conference.

Brown had created champions out of several high school and
college football teams. During the war, he took a leave of absence
from his job as coach of the Ohio State Buckeyes to be coach and
athletic officer at the Great Lakes Naval Training Station north of
Chicago. He was in the process of leading the Navy team to a
record 9-2-1 and thinking about life after the military, when Arthur
"Mickey" McBride called.

A wealthy Cleveland taxicab magnate with investments in
real estate, horse racing, and printing, McBride had been spurned
in an offer to buy his hometown Cleveland Rams of the National
Football League. So, in the summer of '44, he joined five other
investors, including The *Chicago Tribune*'s Arch Ward and his
friend, actor Don Ameche, in St. Louis to map out strategy for a
new league to start up after the war — when the Army would stop
drafting all of the players.

When the group announced formation of the AAFC on Sept.
3, few people paid it much attention, especially officials of the
National Football League. They had other problems to worry

about. The war, for example, was siphoning off all the players. The Rams were so depleted of players that they took a season off. Several teams —Pittsburgh and Philadelphia one year and Pittsburgh and the Chicago Cardinals the next — merged temporarily. Two other leagues that were planned for war's end — the TransAmerica League and the United States Football League — faded when the AAFC moved forward.

Designated owner of the new Cleveland team, McBride started to round up a staff. He knew he needed a coach of stature to give the fledgling operation credibility. A few calls to sportswriter friends brought an immediate and enthusiastic nomination: Ohio State's Paul Brown.

Born Sept. 7, 1908, Brown was a native of Norwalk, Ohio, and played football at Ohio's Massilon High School, a nationally recognized powerhouse. Brown weighed only 100 pounds when he reported for team duty but grew into a 130-pound quarterback by his junior year.

"When he was my quarterback, his voice rang with inspiration as he called the plays. The kids believed in him, and he ran them like a Napoleon," Dave Stewart, Brown's coach at Massilon, recalled years later.

Brown enrolled at Ohio State but discovered that, at 135 pounds, he wasn't big enough for Big Ten football. He transferred to Miami University at Oxford, Ohio and became a notable runner and passer.

After graduation, Brown coached Maryland's Severn Prep, a Naval Academy preparatory school outside Annapolis. Over two years, his teams amassed a record of 16 wins, one loss, and a tie.

In his spare time, Brown attended law school and considered a legal career. But in 1932, he landed the coveted job of head coach at his alma mater, Massilon, and he never looked back.

Brown rebuilt the school's football program, then in the doldrums, with an organized, disciplined style that was to become his hallmark. The team posted a 6-3 record his first year, then went 8-2 and 9-1 in the next two. His success was such that Massilon expanded its stadium seating from 5,000 to 21,000. In 1940, the high school team drew more fans than any college team in the state except the Ohio State Buckeyes.

When the top coaching position opened at Ohio State in 1941, the state's governor received letters from fans supporting Brown for the job. He got it, and in three years racked up 18 wins, 8 losses, and 1 tie. During his second season, the Buckeyes won the national crown.

When he took over the Cleveland team, Brown received terms as lucrative as any coach had ever seen: a $1,000-a-month retainer until the end of the war, then $20,000 and 15 percent of the team's profits per season. Brown's appointment rated bigger headlines in Cleveland than the start of the All-American Football Conference itself.

The coach's reputation alone was enough to run the Cleveland Rams — the NFL's reigning champions — out of town in 1945. The Rams had started in Cleveland in 1936 as part of a six-team league called the American Football League. It was the second league to adopt the AFL name, and its history was short and troubled. Its first title game was canceled because unpaid players for the Boston franchise refused to participate.

In the second season, the Rams applied for, and received, membership in the National Football League.

The NFL Rams finished no better than third in their first six seasons. In 1943, the team suspended play while its owners served in the military. The 1944 season proved a disappointment, but the team rebounded in 1945, finishing 9-1 behind quarterback Bob Waterfield. The Rams even beat QB Sammy Baugh and his Washington Redskins, 15-14, for the NFL title that year.

Despite this success, the Rams suffered from anemic attendance. The franchise played its home games at a number of stadiums — primarily tiny League Park — and owner Dan Reeves complained of losing money. His season-ticket base was only about 200.

Understandably, Reeves wanted no part of competing against a Paul Brown team. Compounding Reeves' worries, McBride had signed a long-term lease at the larger Municipal Stadium, thus shutting the Rams out. So on Jan. 11, 1946, Reeves asked for, and received, NFL permission to move to Los Angeles. He agreed to subsidize his opponents' travel expenses to California in exchange for getting first crack at the lucrative and fast-growing L.A. market, which had been pumped up by wartime industry. Cleveland was left to the new All-American Football Conference.

With Brown signed up, McBride was ready to go. He had several co-investors, including Robert H. Gries, a wealthy Clevelander whose family had founded the retail giant May Co. and who had been a charter investor in the Rams.

A contest was held to name the team, and John J. Harnett of Lawrence, Mass., won a $1,000 war bond with his entry of the Panthers. His name was drawn from a pool of 36 people who had suggested the same name. McBride soon discovered, however, that a defunct semi-pro team called the Panthers had played in town. So he picked another name popular with the fans: The Browns, for the team's already famous coach.

• • •

Unlike the Rams, the Browns picked one home base: Municipal Stadium.

The 15-year-old stadium was then a marvel to behold and a vivid reflection of its time. Conceived in the 1920s as part of a grand downtown development that produced a city hall, a county courthouse, a public library, and other landmarks, the stadium earned the voters' approval — a 3-to-2 margin on a bond referendum — the same day in 1928 that Herbert Hoover was elected president.

Cleveland was then the nation's sixth largest city and a muscular, industrial giant. Visionary civic leaders had taken care to ensure that a transportation infrastructure existed to keep the city connected commercially to the world, first with the Erie Canal and later with a pioneering downtown airport. Cleveland's steel making, started during the Civil War, flourished during the go-go 1920s.

The new stadium reflected the city's optimism and sturdy personality. It was immense — as tall as an 11-story building and 800 feet long — and could seat 78,189. Among stadiums that provided fans with seat backs, it was the largest in the world. With temporary seating brought in, the capacity could be pushed to 110,000. A walk around its perimeter was a half-mile excursion, and lights allowed for the playing of night games.

The huge stadium was built on a lakefront landfill, stabilized by enormous wooden pilings driven deep into the soil, a system that mimicked Europe's great cathedral buildings. Viewed from above, its double-decked seating concourses formed the shape of a flat tire — not quite round and not quite oblong.

The stadium's squat, sturdy base was built with 3.3 million yellow clay bricks. About halfway up the stadium, a recessed aluminum superstructure began that blended into an overhang to protect upper-deck fans. The idea was that the aluminum would provide a visual transition between the bricks and the sky, reducing the heft of what was an enormous structure.

The job ran over budget, to slightly more than $3 million, and never seemed to live up to its boosters' expectations. Talk of hosting the 1932 Olympics there proved empty; the games went instead to Los Angeles' mammoth Memorial Coliseum. Cleveland stadium was christened on July 2, 1931, to a disappointing crowd of about 8,000 — 75,000 had been expected. Said Cleveland Mayor John Marshall, "The ancient world never saw a structure like this."

The next day, at the stadium's first athletic event, the crowd was again below expectations: Only 36,936 turned out to see Max Schmeling defend his heavyweight boxing title against Young Stribling. Schmeling won by a TKO in the 15th round.

The sprawling, three-and-one-half-acre field was oversized for most sports. At first, Cleveland's Indians, who played much of their 1932 and all of their 1933 seasons at Municipal, found it too large. They returned to their old, cozier haunts at League Park on Lexington and East 66th streets for all but weekend and holiday games. It wasn't until 1946 that the Indians relocated permanently to Municipal Stadium.

(No ballplayer ever hit a home run into Municipal's centerfield bleachers, although Mickey Mantle came close. The Indians eventually had to install a false outfield wall to return the long ball to the game.)

Football debuted at the stadium on Sept. 9, 1931, when a short-lived NFL team, also called the Cleveland Indians — many early football teams adopted the names of the more established teams in town — played an exhibition game against a semi-pro team. The Rams played there intermittently until they left for the West Coast.

In its first game, McBride's new team, the Browns, set a pro-football attendance record. A crowd of 60,135 turned out on Sept. 6, 1946, to watch the Browns rout, 44-0, the lowly Miami Seahawks, soon to disband and to resurface as the Baltimore Colts. Both the turnout and the score were due in no small measure to Paul Brown, a strategist extraordinaire.

Blending an accountant's bookish organization with the discipline of a Marine, Brown introduced stopwatches and X's and O's to the game. His players spent hours in classrooms learning plays, and sat for Sunday exams during training camp. Brown gave IQ tests, studied game films, and mentored some of the best players and coaches in the game.

He even invented the face mask. During a 1953 game against the San Francisco 49ers, Browns quarterback Otto Graham took several punches to the face, and doctors needed 15 stitches to sew up the gash in his mouth. Brown instructed an assistant to attach an inch-thick piece of clear plastic to Graham's helmet.

Stalking the sidelines in his usual white T-shirt, black baseball cap, and brown slacks, the intense coach added finesse and intellect to a game then dominated by a "three-yards-and-a-cloud-of-dust" style of offense. He hired full-time assistant coaches, scouted college players, and generally reinvented football.

Under Brown, Cleveland became the artful Athens to the black-and-blue Sparta symbolized by the Chicago Bears. The coach brought precision passing into a game dominated for decades by hand-to-hand ground combat.

"Everyone knew their parts. Paul Brown scripted tightly. He wanted it done his way, and you did it," recalled Dante Lavelli, a charter member of the Browns.

Lavelli backed up offensive end John Yonaker, but in the opening game against the Seahawks, Yonaker dropped a pass, and Brown yanked him. Lavelli got the call.

Yonaker, whom Brown derisively called "glue hands" after the drop, went on to play defense. Lavelli ended up with 386 receptions and 62 touchdowns over a 10-year career that peaked with induction into the Hall of Fame.

Unquestionably, Brown managed with fear, and no player dared to challenge his authority. He insisted that players wear business suits while on the road and told his men to consider themselves the New York Yankees of football.

"We won so much that the people got stale," said Lavelli. "But Paul Brown used to say he didn't care if there were only seven people in the stands, he still wanted to win."

Brown was also one of the first professional football coaches to use black players. He never talked about what was then contro-versial integration; he just did it.

Browns fullback Marion Motley and linebacker Bill Willis were the only black players in the AAFC in 1946, the year before Jackie Robinson broke the color barrier in baseball. The Rams had a pair of black players that season, too, the first in the NFL since 1933. But the National Football League would still have an all-white team as late as 1961 — the Washington Redskins, then the southernmost team.

• • •

Paul Brown had a jeweler's eye for talent. One of his first picks as Browns head coach was Otto Graham, a three-sport, eight-letter athlete from Northwestern University whom Brown had dis-covered the hard way. Brown's Buckeyes lost to Northwestern's Wildcats. Graham handed his future coach the only loss of his first season in Columbus.

Never mind that Graham had been drafted by the NFL's Detroit Lions and was to report there as soon as his military duty was over. Brown caught up with the quarterback at Glenview Naval Air Station in Glenview, Ill. He convinced the $75-a-month cadet to join the still nameless and playerless Cleveland team in exchange for a signing bonus, a two-year contract, and $250 a month in earnest money until the end of the war.

Brown's investment paid off handsomely. By the time he retired in 1955, Graham had led his team to a stunning 94-15-3 record, and the Browns had played in a league or conference championship game each of his 10 years. Graham's touch became legendary. Whether he threw a high-arching pass downfield or a quick sideline pass, he elevated passing to an art form. Sending a receiver down the sidelines, Graham would often hit him the split-second before he stepped out of bounds.

Graham had a career 55.7 percent pass-completion rate — sec-ond only to Baugh on the all-time record list at the time of his retire-ment. A third of the Browns' points during his tenure were scored off of Graham's passes. The Cleveland QB's average gain per com-pletion, 8.6 yards, is still the best ever. Sid Luckman, at 8.42 yards with the Chicago Bears, and Steve Young, at 8.18 yards with the

Tampa Bay Buccaneers, are his closest rivals.

From 1953 to 1955, Graham led the NFL in yardage and in completion percentage; in 1952, he threw the most TD passes. In 1951 and again from 1953 through 1955, Graham was voted all-pro honors. In 1953 and 1955, he was selected as league player of the year.

And this was in the era of two-way football, when players played both offense and defense.

"The test of a quarterback is where his team finishes. By that standard, Otto Graham was the best of all time," Brown would later say.

Graham and his coach led Cleveland on a romp that will likely never be matched by another team in a professional sports league. In the AAFC's four years, the Browns not only won every title, but 47 of 54 games, losing just four times and fighting to a draw three times.

Only two teams beat them, each one twice: San Francisco and Los Angeles.

The Browns so dominated their league that fans in other cities grew bored of the repetition and lost interest. When the AAFC and NFL merged in 1950, the Browns went on to puncture the older league's obvious sense of superiority.

Cleveland went 10-2 in its first NFL season, outscoring its opponents 310 to 144. In their first game in the new league, the Browns defeated the NFL champion Philadelphia Eagles, 35-10. At the end of the season, they beat the New York Giants in a playoff and then faced the Los Angeles Rams (previously the Cleveland Rams) for the 1950 championship.

The game, played on frozen turf in Cleveland's Municipal Stadium the day before Christmas, was a high scoring grudge match played in leather helmets without face masks. It is still remembered as one of the best football games ever played.

Eight participants would later be elected to the Hall of Fame: the Browns' Graham, Lavelli, Motley and Groza; and the Rams' Bob Waterfield, Norm Van Brocklin, Tom Fears, and Elroy Hirsch.

Surprisingly, the Rams were the favorite, largely because of residual skepticism about the Browns' AAFC background, but also because the Rams had scored an average of nearly 40 points per game during the 12-game season.

A fast-throwing team, the Rams had two quarterbacks, Waterfield and Van Brocklin, who combined during the regular season for more than 300 yards a game. But Van Brocklin would sit out the Cleveland game with a broken rib.

The Browns, meantime, came into the game with the NFL's best defense, having held their regular-season opponents to an average of 12 points a game. Though the strong-armed Graham had an average year for him — 1,943 yards and 14 TDS — Motley led the NFL in rushing with 810 yards. And Lou "The Toe" Groza had kicked a field goal in 10 consecutive games.

Groza, in fact, was a virtual scoring machine: The Browns scored a league-leading 14 field goals that year, for a 66.5 percent attempt/completion rate. The ageless placekicker, who doubled as a defensive tackle, would rack up 1,608 points over a 21-season career.

The matchup proved an offensive explosion from the start. On the first call from scrimmage, the Rams ran a crafty play in which three of their most dangerous scorers — Hirsch, Fears, and Verda Smith — were deployed as decoys. On the snap, the trio ran to the right, drawing the Browns defense with them. Running back Glenn Davis, hesitating a moment as if to block, zipped to the left, catching Waterfield's pass and streaking past the secondary for an 82-yard touchdown.

After 27 seconds, the Rams led 7-0.

Though a little less flashy, the Browns wasted little time in responding, taking six plays to cover 72 yards — 21 on the ground by Graham and another 31 on a TD pass. Groza tied the score with the point-after conversion.

The Rams came back with a pair of Waterfield passes to Fears and moved swiftly downfield. Six plays later, Los Angeles scored, taking a seven point lead.

The first three series had consumed only 15 plays but resulted in 3 touchdowns and 21 points.

The teams then settled down and traded the lead throughout the cold afternoon.

With three minutes to go, it appeared that the Rams would eke out a one-point victory, 28-27. But no one bothered to tell Cleveland that.

Otto Graham bulldozed the ball down to the Rams' 30-yard

line and on fourth down, instead of electing to go for a field goal, tried to run for a first down. He fumbled, and the Rams recovered

Heartbroken fans headed for the exits, but didn't get far; four plays later, Cleveland's defense stopped the Rams cold. A 51-yard punt and return left the Browns 68 daunting yards from the goal line with a minute, 50 seconds remaining.

Graham came out roaring, running the ball himself for 14 yards and moving his offense to the Browns' 46. He then threw left for 15 yards and right for 16. Another completed pass brought the ball to the Los Angeles 11, where Brown called for a quarterback sneak, to squeeze out a few extra yards and enhance Groza's chances. Lou "The Toe" would be kicking the potential game-winning field goal into a brisk wind.

The move worked.

With 28 seconds on the clock, and the stadium crowd on its feet, the ball soared 16 yards through the uprights. Final score: 30-28, Cleveland.

The Browns won the next three division titles, but lost each championship match — to Los Angeles, Detroit, and Detroit again. Then the team rallied to win back-to-back championships, beating Detroit and Los Angeles.

The community's support of the team was abundant from the start. Players returning from road games were mobbed at the train station by boisterous crowds. To congratulate players, enthusiastic supporters rushed onto the train as it arrived. Often, they were serenaded by Frankie Yankovich and his then-famous, Cleveland-based polka band.

"Fans in Chicago and New York didn't wait up for their vanquished players to return home. They were too cosmopolitan for that. It was fun then," Dante Lavelli recalled years later.

In 1953, amid the winning, McBride sold the team's controlling interest for $600,000 to an investment group headed by Cleveland industrialist David R. Jones. Jones, the city's first boxing commissioner, had been a stockholder in the Indians during Bill Veeck's regime. Bob Gries and his family remained major stockholders, but a new investor, Nationwide Insurance Co., now owned a piece of the team, too.

One of the first things the new owners did was take out a large life insurance policy on Paul Brown in recognition of his value to the organization.

The team's $600,000 sale price was then a record for a football franchise and signaled that the NFL, and Cleveland football, had grown more solid by the season.

In 1956, though, Browns fans suffered through a startling first: a losing season. Otto Graham had retired the season before, and the magic seemed gone. The team's 5-7 finish was both a disappointment and a reminder that team members were human.

Ironically, their poor finish gave the Browns a good enough position in the draft to pick up a player who would not only revive the franchise but give football itself a strong boost. Even more than Otto Graham, he would come to symbolize Cleveland's football glory — a player who seemed a football dynasty unto himself.

• • •

Broad-shouldered, 6-foot-2, and 230 pounds, running back Jim Brown had excelled at every sport he tried at Syracuse University. He averaged 13 points a game in basketball, scored 187 points in football, became one of the greatest lacrosse players in the school's history, and mastered the high jump for the track team.

Over his nine NFL seasons, Brown would run, catch, and even throw the ball. He would establish himself as one of the greatest ball carriers the game had ever known or will ever know. He gained 12,312 yards rushing and led the NFL in total yardage per season eight times and in touchdowns five times. He ran for more than 100 yards in 58 games.

Until O.J. Simpson's 2,003-yard season in 1973 — over an expanded 16-game schedule — Brown held the single-season rushing record, too. In 1963, he rushed for an extraordinary 1,863 yards, averaging 6.4 yards per carry.

Brown was born Feb. 17, 1936, in Simons, Ga., and later moved to a wealthy Long Island neighborhood with his mother, who worked as a domestic. There, two community leaders, recognizing his athletic talent, informally adopted Brown and contributed greatly to his career. They were Ed Walsh, his high school football coach, and Kenneth Malloy, a local sports booster and attorney who raised money to get Brown into Syracuse. (Malloy went on to become chief justice of the New York Supreme Court.)

Jim Brown and Paul Brown had a respectful, but not friendly, relationship. The running back bristled under the coach's tight control. He flourished later under the looser hand of the coach's successor, Blanton Collier, a former high school algebra teacher.

"Paul didn't hold me down. I only had one complaint with him and that is when he became too conservative. I loved his discipline, I loved his administrative talent. He was very blunt. He liked the running game so it suited me," Jim Brown said in a 1996 interview.

But the retired running back left no doubt about his preference in style. "Under Blanton, we just played and had fun. It wasn't uptight. Paul had everyone scared to death," he said.

Despite his reputation as a brooding loner, Jim Brown developed a taste for Hollywood. He left football and a league-high $65,000 salary at the top of his game when only 29. He went on to appear in more than 30 movies, including the top-grossing "The Dirty Dozen" with Lee Marvin.

At the same time, Brown involved himself in black self-help organizations, assisting minority entrepreneurs in getting started. Later, he became active in a prison counseling program that stressed self-esteem as a way to restart young, damaged lives.

Brown was the NFL's rookie of the year in 1957, when he helped his team win the divisional title. The next season, Cleveland made it to the playoffs, but lost to the Giants. Soon, attendance at Browns' home games hit 500,000 a season.

Brown was overwhelmed by the response of the fans.

"It was a love affair. Whatever was going on, the fans were great. The kids went to the games with their fathers and mothers and those kids would grow up. They shared a life with me. We shared every one of those victories and some of those runs. We were like family. When I would go out into the little towns and hamlets and met someone for the first time, we all shared something," Jim Brown said.

The team then slid into its longest post-season drought in history. Though still posting winning records, the Browns couldn't nudge themselves into the playoffs. Players, including Jim Brown, began to think the unthinkable. Publicly, they suggested that Paul Brown was the root of the team's problems, that he needed to change for the Browns to win.

In 1960, the team was sold again. Nationwide Insurance, which had acquired a 30-percent interest, decided to take its profits and get out. The new owner, a New York advertising executive, was not as willing to cede team operations to Paul Brown. Art Modell and the coach began butting heads early.

Although their fan following remained large, the Browns seemed to be running out of steam. In 1962, they hadn't won a title in five years, and they'd missed the playoffs the past four. They had just posted their worst record — 7-6-1 — since 1956.

While players complained openly about Brown's dictatorial ways, Modell grew weary. Though the making of key player decisions was the coach's express prerogative under the existing contract, the rookie owner was more than a little irritated at Brown's failure to involve him in any way. In the middle of a Cleveland newspaper strike , Modell decided to fire his famous coach.

Though timed to reduce bad press, Paul Brown's forced departure was acrimonious: Modell had Brown's desk emptied into a cardboard box and the contents left on the porch of his home. The team continued to pay Brown the $82,500 stipulated in his contract for the next six years. But the legendary coach became a consultant-on-call who was never called.

Mutual acquaintances believe the break was inevitable. Both men had big egos, and both wanted credit for the team's popularity. There was also a vast difference in their styles. The prickly Brown thought winning games was the best way to keep the franchise healthy. Modell believed in marketing and public relations.

In his 1979 autobiography, Paul Brown devoted an entire chapter to his falling out with Modell. He claimed the new team owner plotted to get rid of him from the start, and intentionally sowed discontent among the coaches and players.

"During the first two years between his coming to the Browns and my dismissal, I lived through a period of almost constant 'intrigue,'" Brown wrote. "Player was set against player; the loyalty of my coaching staff was questioned, and attempts made to find out which ones were 'Paul Brown men'; public criticism of my coaching was encouraged among the players and steadfastly carried on by management through the media..."

A major disagreement between the owner and the coach occurred over the use of Ernie Davis, a running back who had broken many of Jim Brown's records at Syracuse. Paul Brown liked Davis so much he struck a deal with the Redskins, whereby they'd draft Davis in 1961 and then trade him to the Browns. But shortly after he arrived in Cleveland, Davis was diagnosed with terminal leukemia. A doctor neighbor of Brown advised against playing Davis because his ability to heal from injuries was weakened.

According to Brown, Modell wanted to play Davis to gain some public relations benefit from his investment.

"Finally, Modell came to me one day and said, 'Put him in a game and let him play. We have a big investment in him, and I'd like a chance to get some of it back. It doesn't matter how long he plays; just let him run back a kick, let him do anything, just so we can get a story in the paper saying he's going to play, and the fans will come to see him. If he has to go, why not let him have a little fun?'" Brown wrote.

Brown said he then contacted NFL Commissioner Pete Rozelle, who instructed him not to play Davis and promised to overrule any decision to do otherwise. Davis died on May 18, 1963 without ever playing in a pro game.

The incident put his relationship with Modell in "the deep freeze," Brown recalled. In early 1963, Brown was called into Modell's office and fired.

Brown said Modell told him during their last meeting: "This team can never fully be mine as long as you are here because whenever anyone thinks of the Cleveland Browns, they think of you. Every time I come to the stadium, I feel that I am invading your domain, and from now on there can be only one dominant image."

When Brown's autobiography came out, Modell denied the Davis story and filed a grievance with his friend, Rozelle. The commissioner fined Brown $10,000 for violating a league rule against criticizing another team's official. Brown, then owner of the Cincinnati Bengals, paid the fine, but said he stood by his account.
Vic Ippolito, the Browns' doctor at the time of the Davis incident, claimed the player's disease was in remission and that he could safely play. Ippolito supported Modell's version of the event, saying that the Browns owner only wanted to give Davis a chance to play before he died.

Years after the fact, Modell offered a more benign justification for firing Brown. He related a conversation with the coach early in Modell's ownership:

"I grew up in New York City, and we played football in the streets. We used sewer plates as guides for our passes," he explained.

"Well, one day Brown came into my office, and I said, 'Paul, I have a sure-fire touchdown play. Have your end run down to the first sewer plate and then cut around the second to the third and have the quarterback hit him with a pass. It's a touchdown every time.'

"He didn't even smile, and I knew then I would have to fire him. I couldn't have a coach without a bit of humor in him."

In 1967, the very year he went into the Pro Football Hall of Fame, and just four years after leaving Cleveland, Paul Brown founded the Bengals, an AFL expansion team brought into the NFL through its merger with the AFL. He and other investors scraped together the $7.5 million expansion fee, and his reputation put them over the top. The owners borrowed the name Bengals from a defunct Cincinnati team of the 1930s.

Then 60 years old, Brown began assembling a team from scratch. In 1970, his Bengals moved into shiny, new Riverfront Stadium on Cincinnati's Ohio River. Brown himself coached the team through 1975 but had lost his touch. The team went 55-56-1 during his tenure, including 5-7 against the Browns.

"Every time we played the Browns, the coaches talked about how PB wanted this game," said former Bengals guard Joe Walter. "If there was any game of the year he wanted, this was it."

The Bengals gradually improved, however, and, in 1982, under coach Forrest Gregg, a Hall-of-Fame Green Bay Packers tackle, they made it into Super Bowl XVI. Young Joe Montana's controlled passing and Ray Wersching's dependable field-goal kicking gave the San Francisco 49ers what appeared to be an insurmountable 20-0 halftime lead. But the Bengals, under QB Kenny Anderson, came back. The 49ers held on to win, 26-21, the first of Montana's four Super Bowl triumphs.

Unfortunately for the Bengals, in their only other NFL championship trip, they met Montana and his favorite receiver, Jerry Rice. In January 1989, they lost Super Bowl XXIII to the 49ers, 20-16.

Paul Brown died on Aug. 5, 1991, leaving the Cincinnati team to his son, Michael Brown. It would be up to the younger Brown to rediscover winning and to solve the problem of Riverfront Stadium's premature obsolescence. It was a problem that many NFL cities were facing in the uncertain '90s.

CHAPTER FOUR

Modell's
Dynasty

T hough it was to be played on Cleveland's home turf two days after Christmas, the 1964 NFL championship game was expected to be a romp for the visiting Baltimore Colts. The championship trophy, most of the experts predicted, was a gift waiting to be unwrapped by quarterback Johnny Unitas and Baltimore's other superstars.

Weeks before the game, *Sports Illustrated* proclaimed: "This year it is yawningly conceded that the Eastern champion — probably Cleveland — will be playing merely for the dubious pleasure of being thrashed by Baltimore on Dec. 27."

New owner Art Modell wasn't so sure. The team's glory days had run out, but his Browns did enjoy a successful 10-3-1 season that year and the former powerhouse did appear to be on the rebound.

To the 12-2 Colts, who were thriving under the direction of the NFL's youngest coach, Don Shula, championship years appeared dead ahead. The Colts' fearsome roster had eight players headed for the Pro Bowl that postseason. Johnny U. was still in his prime, calling the plays like a field marshal. The league's Most Valuable Player that season, Unitas had been picked off only 6 times in 305 pass attempts. And his favorite target, Raymond Berry, had averaged better than 15 yards a reception.

The Colts had the game's best offense, ranking first in touchdowns and compiling the third highest point total in NFL history. On defense, they were No. 1 in sacks. Defensive end Gino Marchetti, who had retired the year before but been cajoled back into service, was again stalking opponents like a hungry bear.

Lenny Moore, who had been trade bait in the off-season, came bursting back to life and turned in a career year with an NFL-record 20 touchdowns. And perennial Pro Bowler Jim Parker was still dominating at offensive tackle.

The Browns, by contrast, had a leaky defense that had allowed more than 20 points a game, the worst in the league. They were especially susceptible to the blitz, a Colts specialty. Cleveland had some solid performers, but they seemed overmatched by Baltimore, even playing before 79,000 mostly hometown fans.

Overall, the Browns' chances of winning seemed as bleak as the weather. It was so cold that gas-fueled heaters had been set up a few days before the game to defrost the turf.

The Browns quarterback, the prematurely gray Frank Ryan, was a certified genius with a doctorate in mathematics. Though he had led the NFL that year with 25 touchdown passes, he was no Unitas, and tended to run hot and cold.

But Ryan did have Paul Warfield to throw to — a rookie wide receiver from Ohio State who ran up more than 1,000 yards that season, scored a dozen touchdowns, and eventually entered the Hall of Fame with more than 5,000 yards and an average of 19 yards-plus per catch.

And the Browns still had their sensational fullback Jim Brown, who led the NFL in rushing that season with 1,446 yards in 280 carries. In a single game against Dallas, Old Number 32 carried the ball 26 times for a dominating 188 yards.

Still, Cleveland's greatest asset was probably on the sideline. Second-year head coach Blanton Collier had learned his trade under Paul Brown and was a master at spotting and exploiting an opponent's weakness. He had also coached Baltimore coach Don Shula, then a defensive back with the Browns, and employed him as an assistant coach at the University of Kentucky.

Reviewing game films before the big day, Collier found a sizable chink in the Colts' armor: The nimble-footed Unitas tended to fade back and shuffle in the direction of his intended receiver.

With the extra half-second warning afforded by Unitas' footwork, the Browns defenders could cover his primary target before he could get the ball off. This would force the quarterback to focus on his second choice of receivers and give the Browns rushers additional time to swarm.

Armed with this knowledge, and aided by a 20-mile-an-hour wind that favored the Browns' ground attack over the Colts' aerial fireworks, Collier's players shut down the great Unitas. All day, he tried desperately to find an open receiver, scrambling from the pocket and adjusting his line of fire. But nothing worked. He threw two interceptions and no touchdowns.

The Browns won, 27-0.

It was a sweet moment for Art Modell. Only four years in the league and he had a world champion.

The other NFL owners, many of them league founders like the Steelers' Art Rooney and the Bears' George Halas, had viewed the newcomer with suspicion. Now they would have to accord Modell the respect of a winner and grudgingly admit him into the inner circle of the fraternity.

The victory also vindicated Modell's astounding and controversial decision to fire Paul Brown.

Like his predecessor, Collier was a skillful tactician. But the bespectacled and soft-spoken Collier had a warmer personality. He seemed more of a father figure to the players than Brown, the stern taskmaster.

Collier also let his quarterback change plays at the line of scrimmage. And he gave Jim Brown the flexibility to adjust to the defense on the field, things that the iron-fisted Paul Brown strictly forbade.

The players responded gratefully.

In 1963, Brown posted his single-season record 1,863 yards — more than a mile. He also led the league in scoring, with 90 points. The same year, Ryan passed for a respectable 2,026 yards. It wasn't quite good enough. Though the Browns posted a 10-4 record, they failed to make the playoffs.

The next year, the Browns of old seemed to be back. They dispatched opponents with ease, culminating with the defeat of the mighty Colts in the NFL's 1964 championship game.

• • •

Though poised for greatness, the National Football League was still a fledgling — not unlike Art Modell, who was long on dreams and short on capital.

Modell grew up in Brooklyn's Borough Park, an orthodox Jewish neighborhood where store keepers would close up for the Saturday Sabbath. Modell's father, George, pioneered electronics retailing, selling radios when they were still bulky crystal sets. One by one he assembled a chain of 11 stores in the New York area. For the very young Art and his two older sisters, this meant a childhood of relative luxury — including chauffeurs and vacations on the New Jersey shore.

Then, with the suddenness of an early frost, the family's lifestyle crashed. George Modell lost everything in the stock market collapse of 1929, declared bankruptcy, and became a traveling wine salesman barely able to scrape together a living.

The Modell family struggled, like much of America in the Depression and some of it after World War II. Art passed the time playing stickball, pinball, and pool with his pals, one of whom was future comedian Buddy Hackett.

At age 8, Modell developed a passion for football, rooting for the Brooklyn Dodgers, an early NFL franchise that in 1946 would jump to the AAFC. Attending the Thanksgiving Day game between the Giants and Dodgers became an annual ritual for him. He and a cousin would walk to Ebbets Field and pay 25 cents for seats behind the Dodgers' bench.

Modell was enthralled by the exploits of the Dodgers' Roy "Father" Lumpkin, who played with reckless abandon and without a helmet. Modell and his pals would field their own teams in the streets and synchronize pass plays using manhole covers and sewer grates as markers.

Like their baseball namesake, the Dodgers brought distinction and pride to Modell's working-class borough. Walking down neighborhood streets on game days, Modell would hear the voices of radio broadcasters Red Barber and Vin Scully coming from each row-house stoop.

Years later, when the baseball Dodgers moved to Los Angeles, Modell was among the anguished fans left behind wondering how their world had been turned so desperately upside down.

Modell played catcher for his high school baseball team and even thought of making a career out of the game. But then in 1939, when he was just 14, disaster struck again. His father died.

The circumstances of George Modell's death were scandalous, although Art Modell would not find that out until 1983, when *The Akron Beacon Journal* dredged up the story.

George Modell was found alone and unconscious early one day in a tourist cabin in Austin, Texas. The night before, he had registered with a woman. Hours later, explaining that he had had a drink against doctor's orders and passed out, the woman asked cabin employees to help her pick Modell up and put him on the bed. When he was found the next day, the woman had vanished. Modell was taken to a hospital, where doctors said he had a trace of pneumonia, but probably not a fatal case. He died at 6 p.m. that evening.

The death certificate blamed "toxemia ... probably related to alcoholism."

Modell, who had been devoted to his father, said later he was not convinced of these details, but he made a point of never setting foot in Austin to find out.

One thing was sure: To get through the lean times, the elder Modell had cashed in and spent all of his life insurance, leaving his family utterly penniless. Suddenly, Art was the man of the house. "His death left me obsessed with becoming a success," the Browns owner recalled. "I wanted to make something of myself. I had no inheritance, nothing to fall back on."

To earn money for his family, Modell dropped out of high school the next year. He lied about his age to get a job as an electrician's helper and cleaned ships at Bethlehem Steel's New York shipyard for 45 cents an hour. At night, he took courses at New York University and earned his high school diploma.

In 1943, World War II was raging, and the 18-year-old Modell was dead-set on joining the Marines. His mother, concerned for his safety, talked him out of it, but he nonetheless signed up for the Army Air Force. After basic training, he worked a ground-maintenance assignment at Lowry Air Force Base outside Denver. There, he signed up for the base's baseball team, and his defensive prowess — he was just an average hitter — caught the attention of commanders.

Modell was soon assigned to the physical education wing. He spent the rest of his duty moving from base to base in California, New Mexico, Mississippi, and Nebraska, leading the physical training, or "P.T.," required of each G.I.

Under the Army's dependent program, he was able to send his mother some money, which the military matched. He also got night jobs when he could, often working as an oiler for railroads.

"I would lay in my bunk in the barracks and dream of the day when I would get out and make a success of myself," he said.

After the war, Modell returned to New York and, intrigued with the nascent television industry, attended the American Theater Wing on the G.I. Bill. Once a week, his class would visit the studios of WZXJT in Jamaica, N.Y., to practice TV basics: camera work, play acting, and directing.

"There were only 5,000 TV sets in New York, and I thought if I could get an education in TV, that I could build on it because I thought TV would be a big thing one day," Modell said. "It was new and exciting."

A natural performer in social settings, Modell was attracted to show business, especially movies. He was convinced that the new TV technology could extend the reach of motion pictures. The few television shows then being produced were barely successful, and the industry's future was in some doubt. But Modell had vision.

"I just felt television was going to take off because I thought it was a great way to reach people, to entertain them," he said.

He and another student, Charlie Harbruck, formed Modell and Harbruck Television Productions. They printed up glossy business cards listing the address and phone number of a $5-a-month answering service. They then set out to find shows to produce.

A dashing figure, Art Modell stood only 5-foot-8, but he had a beefy, athletic build, dark, wavy hair, and a jovial, salesman's disposition. He was often at the center of attention, which was precisely where he liked to be.

One day, Modell had an idea: If he and Harbruck could get grocers to mount televisions in their stores, their company could provide advertisers with a captive market of shoppers. Modell stopped by the offices of WPIX, a New York TV station owned by *The New York Daily News*, and said he wanted to buy six hours of programming time each day. The receptionist took his card and name.

When the general manager came in and saw that someone wanted to buy such a big block of air time, he ran up the street to the address listed on Modell's card — the answering service. There, Modell assumes, he was greeted by a roomful of harried women with telephone headsets on their heads and cigarettes dangling from their lips.

It was the last Modell heard from WPIX.

But he then talked ABC into giving the idea a try and, in November 1948, Modell and Harbruck started producing the city's first daytime TV show, "Market Melodies." The program provided a critically unacclaimed series of cooking tips, music, and dramatic presentations — anything to fill the time. It aired from 2 p.m. to 4 p.m. Monday through Friday, and from 10 a.m. to noon on Saturday — the peak grocery-shopping hours.

New York's Grand Union grocery stores soon agreed to try out the TV experiment. Modell borrowed $10,000 from an uncle, leased 100 sets, and mounted them at Grand Union stores. Then with some ABC people, he lined up sponsors. He was finally up and running. Sort of.

The finicky television sets proved too much bother for the grocers. Every time a train rumbled by, the sets had to be retuned, and Grand Union eventually demanded their removal from the stores. But by then the show had built up an at-home audience, and television set ownership was rapidly growing. ABC kept the show on the air another six years, until 1954.

"This guy was a wonder," recalled former Grand Union executive William Brady.

"He always got along. He always had an angle. He was determined to know the right people and, at the time, I was one of the right people."

Brady helped the persistent Modell land a job as Grand Union's account executive with the L.H. Hartman Co. ad agency, thus giving him the opportunity to bring his chutzpa and list of TV sponsors to a place where they would be immediately appreciated: high-flying, post-war Madison Avenue.

The firm's focus was on liquor ads, which were prohibited on TV. But the agency also wanted to open a television department. So it hired Modell, who worked his way up to partnership. On the side, he invested in an upstate New York champagne maker.

In 1960, the Hartman agency dissolved, and Modell took his accounts to a new firm, Kastor, Hilton, Chesley, Clifford & Atherton, where he served as a senior vice president. He had an office with a terrace in the penthouse (it was the Associated Press building), and was there less than a year when a call came from his friend Vincent Andrews.

Andrews, a New York agent, represented some of the biggest names in the fledgling television industry, including Dennis James, host of the "Original Amateur Hour" from 1948 to 1960 and emcee of the short-lived 1956 quiz show, "High Finance."

Andrews had heard the Browns were for sale from Frederick "Curly" Morrison, a Browns running back (1954-56) then working as a CBS salesman. Morrison immediately thought of his boss, CBS president and television pioneer, William S. Paley, as a potential buyer. CBS, at the time, was negotiating for the first contractual rights to broadcast NFL games.

"I was one of about three people who knew," recalled Morrison, who figured the TV money alone would recoup any investment in the team.

Paley instructed Morrison to put together a deal to buy the Browns. They negotiated a price of $3.92 million and were preparing to fly to Cleveland to make a $500,000 deposit when, days before settlement, the CBS president backed out, apparently nervous over a possible conflict of interest. The NFL was about to become a major commercial client of his network. It wasn't clear that there would be anything illegal about Paley's football team ownership, but CBS was considering innovations that would require a good relationship with federal regulators, and Paley didn't want to compromise the network in any way, Morrison said.

That's when Morrison called Andrews to ask him to pull together a group of high-profile clients who might want to buy the Browns. But this plan, too, had collapsed, by the time Andrews phoned Modell.

Modell, an established football fanatic, not only rooted for the NFL Giants, but was one of the team's earliest season ticket holders at the Polo Grounds. When Morrison told him in a meeting about the impending CBS-NFL television deal, Modell didn't need a lot of convincing.

"He was a dynamic guy with a lot of marketing ideas,"

Morrison said. "He understood advertising and television — he understood the medium as well as anyone."

The young ad man could barely contain himself. Morrison and some of the Browns' representatives initially refused to tell him which team they were selling. Modell thought — and dreamed — it might be the Giants and was momentarily disappointed to learn it was the Browns.

But he had watched enough Browns games to know that owning the franchise was the chance of a lifetime.

He rushed to Cleveland — a city he had never visited before — and accepted the asking price, $3.925 million. It was a record for an NFL franchise. Later, he found out that the only other bidder had offered just $2.8 million.

Modell celebrated with a game at Municipal Stadium, sitting near the 50-yard line of the cavernous stadium's upper deck and watching the Browns beat the Chicago Bears, 42-0, in a blinding blizzard.

His next task was raising the money. Andrews, slated to be a co-investor, dropped out at the last moment. Modell scrambled and signed on brewery baron Rudolph Schaeffer, who put up $250,000 in the hope of expanding his beer sales to Cleveland.

With about $25,000 to his name, Modell borrowed all of his $250,000 share from a bank, and the two men made a nonrefundable $500,000 deposit on Jan. 25, 1961. The sellers gave them 90 days to raise the remainder.

Modell issued Browns stock, keeping 25 percent for himself and giving another 25 percent to Schaeffer — but in a trust controlled by Modell. The rest was parceled out to other investors. Among them: the team's coach, Paul Brown; its president and attorney; a banking friend of Modell; and a few of Modell's New York advertising associates.

Then Modell made a decision he would later regret. Hungry for cash, he let some of the team's previous minority partners buy into the new ownership. The biggest chunk — 28 percent — was sold to Robert H. Gries and some of his relatives.

The Grieses, an old Cleveland family (they settled in the city in 1830), had been part of the city's football history from the beginning — as charter investors in the Rams in 1936 and with the AAFC Browns in 1946.

Gries could have bought the team outright. But he didn't want the bother or the public glare of running a team.

He instead helped Modell by putting up $425,000 for his 28 percent share, and he called his friend, the chairman of Cleveland's Union Commerce Bank, to smooth the way for a $2.5 million loan to Modell. Modell disputes Gries' role in arranging the loan, saying it was Modell's New York banker — and brother of his future wife — who made the key introduction. But in either case, it was a nice piece of financial wizardry. For only a fraction of the sale price, Modell took control of one of the premier franchises in a sport about to burst onto the national scene.

For Modell, who would never be accused of having a great financial mind, the purchase would prove the most astute of his life.

● ● ●

Though not quite ready for prime time, the National Football League in 1961 was attracting fans at an impressive clip. On average, games drew slightly more than 40,000 fans, a respectable number in any sport. And attendance was growing fast.

It had taken the NFL 13 years to go from 1 million tickets sold in a season to 2 million. Another six years were needed to pass the 3 million mark. Only four more were required to hit 4 million in 1962, Modell's first full year as an owner.

The growth was not just in the major cities, such as New York and Los Angeles, where teams were packing in more than 350,000 fans per season. It also came in a handful of acknowledged football "hotbeds," such as Baltimore and Cleveland, which in 1960 had the NFL's third and fourth best attendance, respectively.

The NFL posted growth so dramatic that it attracted the sincerest form of flattery: imitation. The American Football League, actually the fourth entity to use that name, took the field in 1960.

Founded by rejected NFL applicant Lamar Hunt, the new league put teams in Dallas, Boston, Buffalo, Denver, Houston, New York, Los Angeles and Oakland, Calif.

The upstart league also added a few new rules to jazz things up, including a team option, after a touchdown, of trying for a one-point kick or a two-point run/pass conversion. It also put players' names on their jerseys.

At first, as it had with the previous AFLs and the AAFC, the NFL tried to ignore the new league. In 1965, talk of a cooperative college draft, for example, was dismissed by at least one NFL team owner — Art Modell.

"I don't believe in a common draft. This is my opinion, not that of the rest of the owners," Modell told reporters at the annual owners' meeting in Palm Desert, Calif. "But I do not feel we of the NFL have to deal with the AFL. We have the best game, the best organization, tradition, and everything else. Why should we be bothered by the other league?"

Indeed, AFL game attendance in the early years barely registered. The Los Angeles Chargers drew so badly — only 9,928 fans watched the team clinch the divisional title — that they moved to San Diego after only one season.

But the NFL was keenly aware that its future markets were being raided. So it quickly added teams in Dallas and Minnesota and moved the Cardinals from Chicago to St. Louis. (This last move pleased the networks, which disliked blacking out games in the nation's second largest market — something made necessary because the Cardinals weren't selling out.)

Football was clearly booming. The country had gone almost overnight from 12 teams in one league to 22 in two. By 1963, *U.S. News and World Report* would declare that "one of the strongest American business booms now underway is that in pro football."

• • •

When Modell bought the Browns, Alvin Ray "Pete" Rozelle had been on the job as NFL commissioner for about a year. A compromise candidate among the owners, he succeeded Bert Bell, who had died of a heart attack on the sidelines of a Philadelphia Eagles game. When he became the "Boy Czar" of football, Rozelle was serving as general manager of the Los Angeles Rams.

It had taken the owners 23 ballots over nine days to elect him, with the final vote going 7-4. Little did they know that the baby-faced Rozelle would change the face of American sports.

A public relations expert, Rozelle recognized early the credibility that media coverage could lend to a sport. He also saw the potential of television, a medium that baseball owners had been leery of: They feared it would reduce attendance, but Rozelle saw it as a potent complement.

"He was the ultimate commissioner. He understood his business and the sport and the role of the networks," recalled Robert Wussler, who, as president of CBS Sports, negotiated some blockbuster football deals with Rozelle.

Within a year of taking office, Rozelle moved the league's headquarters from Bala Cynwyd, a suburb outside of Philadelphia that Bell had favored, to New York, the nation's media capital. Soon he was pushing team owners to jointly market the league's television rights. He wanted a single league-wide package.

It would be a major departure. At the time, each team sold its own rights, creating a hodgepodge of broadcasts and fees ranging from $120,000 in Green Bay, Wis., to $370,000 in New York. This created considerable instability among franchises. Some NFL teams were going out of business and jumping to rival leagues as late as the 1950s. For small-town teams, it was hard to survive bad seasons or even a stretch of bad Sunday weather.

The AFL, on the other hand, had adopted the single-contract idea from the start. It signed a $2-million deal with ABC that gave each team about $250,000 a year and almost certainly spared it the fate of the three previous AFLs. In signing the ABC deal, the AFL was taking a legal gamble. The NFL had lost a 1953 court case involving its policy of blacking out some games. Later, the NFL asked the same judge if his decision meant that the league couldn't sign up a single network to televise its games. The judge said that was exactly what it meant.

But Rozelle was determined. He thought he could negotiate more money for a league-wide broadcasting package than the individual teams could on their own. And, he figured, if those revenues were shared equally, weaker franchises would not go out of business or become perennial losers. First, though, he had to convince his employers, the NFL team owners.

The big-market teams growing rich on their contracts weren't too keen on the idea. But Rozelle, in one of the first demonstrations of his legendary ability to persuade the notoriously independent-minded team owners, talked them into it in 1960. His next obstacle was the U.S. Congress, which would have to approve a special provision granting the league a broadcast exemption from antitrust laws.

In 1961, Congress passed, and President John F. Kennedy signed, the Sports Antitrust Broadcast Act. The new law permitted the National Football League, or any other sports league, to market its broadcast rights as a package and thus prevent the networks from striking the best deals they could with only the individual teams whose games they wanted. It was a ground-breaking measure, and it vastly increased the power of the league offices.

It also set the altar for the coming marriage of television and sports. With a steady, predictable flow of cash from TV, professional sports teams would no longer survive or die exclusively on their game attendance revenues.

Rozelle and his NFL were now off and running. CBS agreed to add the teams that it wasn't then carrying for an annual rights package worth $4.65 million, or $330,000 per team. When the package expired in 1964, the network anted up even more — a total of $14.1 million, or $1 million per team.

Rozelle assembled a crack team of whiz kids to help him negotiate with the networks. They shrewdly analyzed advertising rates, ratings, and demographics and used them to drive up the fees the networks would pay. In the process, former TV executive and ad man Art Modell became a critical inside player, the point man between the commissioner's office and the NFL owners. He took over the chairmanship of the NFL's television committee in 1962 and held the job for 31 years.

Modell's go-along temperament also made him a natural apostle for Rozelle's philosophy of "league think," the one-for-all, all-for-one attitude that dominated football in these formative years. He soon became one of Rozelle's top allies and confidants. Only a few team owners, including Wellington Mara of the New York Giants and Art Rooney of the Pittsburgh Steelers, were involved in every element of the sport.

Modell "was in Rozelle's inner sanctum," said Wussler, the former CBS executive.

During TV negotiations, Modell would often break the ice with a well-timed quip. He served as the eyes and ears of the team owners.

As an accommodation to television, which would now be paying heavily for NFL games, the league agreed to special time-outs for commercials and created two new "two-minute warnings," during which advertisers would have access to viewers when they were unlikely to switch the channel. When the league added the Atlanta Falcons in 1965, growing TV money was a major reason the expansion fee was set at a robust $8.5 million.

Modell's investment was now beginning to look very shrewd. The Browns' value had already more than doubled in five years. In 1965, he had further enhanced his holdings by having the team borrow money and buy out Schaeffer's share for $1.5 million.

The champion Browns were also packing them in at the gate. Game attendance at Cleveland's Municipal Stadium averaged more than 79,000 in 1965 — the highest in the NFL. The team was winning and making money, and no one missed Paul Brown.

Art Modell had arrived.

The man who had quit high school after his father's death now lived in a five-room, 24th-floor, lakefront apartment. He always had a new car, often a Cadillac or Buick, which was outfitted with a high-quality stereo tuned to classical music.

He was also one of the city's most desirable bachelors. He held court at downtown nightclubs and consorted with some of the city's most colorful denizens, including future Yankees owner George Steinbrenner, then a Cleveland-based industrialist.

Every day after work, Modell and his cronies gathered at a Cleveland nightspot. Among the most famous was the Pewter Mug. They met at Table 14, a Formica-topped table equipped with a telephone so the men could be reached by their offices. The tussles between Modell and Steinbrenner for the check at Table 14 became famous. So did the frivolity and spirited give-and-take among developers, journalists, judges, cops, lawyers, and ne'er-do-wells.

"At its zenith, Table 14 was more informative than the City Club, more interesting than the six o'clock news, and more relevant than either," wrote one participant, journalist Michael D. Roberts. "Out-of-town reporters would visit and write about the table. For a time, it was, other than the orchestra, the only bright spot in town."

Initially apprehensive about the smooth-talking New Yorker, native Clevelanders were starting to warm to Modell. He was being invited to big city events and onto the boards of important civic organizations.

"He went out of his way to accommodate people and be part of the community," recalled Creighton Miller, a Cleveland attorney and Table 14 regular who helped found the Browns and the NFL Players Association.

• • •

Even more good news was headed Modell's way. In 1966, the American Football League and the National Football League announced a phased-in merger, to begin that year.

Unlike its predecessors, the new AFL really was beginning to amount to something. Not only did it have its own television contract, but it was luring fans away from the NFL and driving up player costs.

The bidding for athletes had become competitive.

One early competition pitted the AFL's New York Jets against the NFL's St. Louis Cardinals for the services of Joe Namath, a much-acclaimed quarterback in Bear Bryant's University of Alabama football machine. (Namath originally had wanted to go to the University of Maryland, but his test scores weren't high enough.)

Upon his graduation in 1965, the flamboyant athlete hired a lawyer to sort out the offers. The Jets won with what was then a record: a $387,000 annual salary and a new Lincoln convertible.

That same year, the Green Bay Packers spent $1 million signing running backs Donny Anderson of Texas Tech and Jim Grabowski of Illinois. Altogether, the two leagues spent $7 million on draft choices for the 1966 season.

To Modell and many other team owners, the salary spiral loomed as a potential disaster. The Namath deal could do "irreparable harm" to the game, Modell complained to reporters.

"Think of the problems that arise when a $12,000-a-season center snaps the ball to a $400,000-a-year quarterback. There has to be some resentment," Modell said.

In April 1966, it looked like the football wars were going to get even bloodier. Appointed the AFL's commissioner, Oakland Raiders executive Al Davis drew up an aggressive battle plan that called for enhancing league status through the acquisition of top players, chiefly quarterbacks. The Raiders claimed to have landed the Rams' star QB, Roman Gabriel, although the Rams denied it.

There were also rumors that Packers halfback Paul Hornung and Bears tight end Mike Ditka were headed to AFL teams.

Even before Davis' appointment, the NFL's leaders were getting nervous about the AFL. Rozelle, Modell and a handful of influential NFL owners gave Dallas Cowboys president and general manager Tex Schramm the go-ahead to meet with his fellow Texan, AFL co-founder Lamar Hunt, to see if he had any interest in a merger. Hunt owned the AFL's Kansas City Chiefs, which had started out in Dallas in 1959 as the second-team Texans (the first being the eventual Baltimore Colts). The Texans moved to K.C. in 1963, but Hunt kept his personal residence in Dallas.

At Love Field in Dallas on April 4, days before Davis became AFL commissioner, Schramm and Hunt met secretly under a statue of a Texas Ranger. Walking to Schramm's car, both said they saw the virtue of a merger. But both had to sell it to their respective partners, and there would be a lot of resentment and resistance on both sides. For six years, the NFL had denigrated the AFL, hoping it would fold. The AFL had reveled in the competition and proved worthy of the challenge.

Talks took place quietly over the next few months and, in June, Rozelle announced the deal. As with the AAFC merger 15 years before, the AFL-NFL union included terms favoring the older league. The nine AFL teams agreed to pay the 15 NFL clubs $18 million in principal and interest over 20 years. The Giants and 49ers, now facing same-league competition in their markets, received $8 million and $6 million, respectively.

Rozelle would reign supreme over the merged structure, and each league would add an expansion franchise in 1967, with two more teams to be added later. Beginning the next season, they would hold a common draft which almost immediately ended the short-lived spiral of player salaries. The merger on the field would occur gradually, with AFL and NFL teams set to play each other only in pre-season exhibitions and in a season-ending championship.

The first inter-league showdown, played on Jan. 15, 1967 at Los Angeles Memorial Coliseum, pitted the NFL Green Bay Packers against the AFL Kansas City Chiefs. It was no mere football game. Each league viewed it as the first and last chance to prove superiority before the merged draft began watering down differences.

"The rivalry was intense and the hatred was deep.... It was like Michigan and Ohio State," recalled Modell.

In a planning session, Hunt referred to the game as a veritable "super bowl" of football, according to Modell. The name stuck, informally, at first. The rest is history.

In planning for that first championship, the leagues proved loyal to their respective TV networks, which had brought them financial stability. They settled on a novel compromise. Both NBC and CBS would air the game, sharing camera equipment. But each would sell its own advertising, bring in its own affiliates, and do its own pre-game show.

This was the last time the matter would be handled this way. Future Super Bowl rights would alternate between the networks.

On game day, Modell sat in the Coliseum next to Maria Lombardi, the wife of Packers coach Vince Lombardi. The tension was excruciating, he recalled. "There was enormous pressure imposed on Vince by the league. We had to establish league superiority," Modell noted.

Lombardi was so nervous before the game that his body trembled noticeably. But he came through for the NFL. The Packers won, 35–10.

The next day, NFL team owners held a regularly scheduled organizational meeting. When Lombardi walked in, he received a standing ovation.

The leagues' merger (and resulting monopoly) still required congressional approval, but Rozelle secured it in 1966 with typical aplomb. He recruited two of Washington's most powerful forces as allies: Senator Russell Long and Representative Hale Boggs, both Louisiana Democrats.

The lawmakers were much moved by Rozelle's appeal to sportsmanship — and by his promise to put an NFL franchise in New Orleans, LA. The Senate passed the bill by voice vote, and the House of Representatives approved it as a rider to an anti-inflation tax credit bill. This kept it out of the Judiciary Committee and away from a chairman who was opposed. Less than two weeks later, New Orleans received the Saints' NFL franchise.

The newly reconstituted NFL had immense profit potential. The networks would no longer have a pair of leagues to bid off one another. And the team owners could set limits, formally or otherwise, on player pay. The "Rozelle rule," for example, effectively eliminated free-agent movement by authorizing the commissioner to order a team acquiring a free agent to compensate — through such items as cash or draft picks — the team giving up the player. Eventually, though, the rule was struck down in court.

The new league went through a restructuring period, guided by two presidents elected by the AFL and the NFL. AFL owners picked Milt Woodard, a paid staff member (Al Davis returned to Oakland). In 1967, NFL owners unanimously elected Modell as their unpaid president and re-elected him annually for the next three years. He also chaired the labor committee in the touchy negotiations that led to the first collective bargaining agreement with players in 1968.

"He was a young guy ... with a lot of ideas. He saw the potential for pro football," remembered Ordell Braase, the Colts defensive end (1957 to 1968) who served as the players' union president during its formative years.

The AFL-NFL merger required a realignment of divisions to balance out what would become two conferences, the American and the National. Owners were generally reluctant to jump divisions because it meant severing long-standing and profitable rivalries. The issue actually threatened to scuttle the merger.

Then in 1969, the Browns' Art Modell, the Colts' Carroll Rosenbloom, and the Steelers' Art Rooney agreed to switch into the AFC at the start of the 1970 season. The other NFL owners paid the three teams $2.5 million each in compensation. The agreement broke a 36-hour logjam at an owners' meeting and made the AFL merger final. It also evened out the rights package for NBC, which was then broadcasting AFL games and had insisted on bigger markets to keep its ad rates up.

The omnipresent Modell was in on the ground floor of another crucial NFL innovation: In 1970, as chairman of the broadcast committee, he helped to negotiate the league's Monday night football package.

Initially, the idea was to have a prime-time game on Friday nights. Modell and Rozelle flew to Detroit together to secure a sponsorship from Ford Motor Co. The automaker, then headed by maverick CEO Lee Iaccoca, readily agreed.

Congress, however, balked. Lawmakers were opposed to

anything that could hurt college games then being aired in a number of districts on Friday and Saturday nights. The NFL switched to Monday nights, but its signature network, CBS, wasn't interested. That was the time slot for its top-rated "Caroll Burnett Show" and the "Andy Griffith Show" (later "Mayberry RFD"). NBC was doing pretty well on Mondays with "Rowan & Martin's Laugh-in" and the NBC "Monday Night Movie."

ABC took the bait. It soon established such strong ratings that it took over ownership of Monday nights during football season and hasn't let go since.

Some team owners had been skeptical about getting fans to come out to games played on a week night, but not so Modell. He volunteered his Browns and their enormous stadium for the first "Monday Night" game, played in 1970. Some 85,000 fans turned out to watch the Browns beat the Jets, 31-21.

"Monday Night Football" soon became a gold mine. ABC signed a three-year deal to pay the NFL $8.5 million a season for the rights to broadcast 13 prime-time games. That brought the combined TV network payout to the league to almost $50 million a season, or $1.9 million a team.

Four years later, the league renewed the Monday night package for $13 million, bringing the NFL's TV take to $57.6 million. The trajectory only got steeper in ensuing years.

Although they complained at renewal time, the network executives knew exactly why they were agreeing to ever-larger sums. Football games not only drew large audiences, but they attracted hordes of free-spending young men. Because they increasingly were not reading newspapers or watching the evening news, advertisers were finding it very hard to reach them. Football brought them all to their TV sets at once and put them in a good mood — hence the enthusiasm for football among the nation's beer brewers.

These TV deals brought important changes to the National Football League. First and foremost, teams and team owners were now much richer and did not have to worry about going out of business.

But television also changed the role of the ticket-buying fan. Although still an important source of money, ticket receipts declined as a percentage of team profits. Screaming, face-painted fans evolved into props for TV broadcasts. To TV viewers, the message was implicit: If 65,000 fans were crowded into the stadium, it must be an important sporting event. With their boisterous crowds, cities like Baltimore and Cleveland became TV favorites.

The TV packages also made it harder for a new professional football league to form and compete for players. This proved to be the case in 1974, when the World Football League took the field with 12 teams, 6 of them in NFL cities.

The WFL scheduled its season to start earlier than the NFL's; it also added a few new rules to increase the action. For example, receptions were ruled fair even if only one of the receiver's feet was in bounds, as in college football.

The new league even managed to sign a $1.6 million contract with a cable network — each team's share was worth $130,000 a year — and pried a couple of big-name players, such as the Miami Dolphins' Larry Csonka, away from the NFL.

But the WFL just couldn't match the salaries of the NFL, enriched from television to the tune of $2.2 million a team, or 17 times as much. And because the big-city WFL teams failed to catch fire, the league lost most of its TV money in its second season. This turned the WFL, with its rosters of NFL-shunned players, into a minor league of sorts. Football fans noticed the difference. WFL teams failed, moved, and generally danced around until the middle of the second season, when the whole league died.

The TV bonanza brought other repercussions: NFL players began pushing for a bigger share of football's revenue and won some concessions after brief pre-season strikes in 1974 and 1975. But the owners still held the upper hand.

• • •

In 1978, a poll showed 70 percent of the nation's sports fans followed football, compared with 54 percent pursuing baseball. The message was clear: The country had a new pastime.

Modell, who estimated his net worth at $14 million that year, was clearly enjoying the ride. According to a newspaper survey taken in the early 1980s, he was the second most powerful person in the NFL, with only Rozelle ahead of him. He was, in effect, one of the most powerful men in all of professional sports.

As he befriended politicians and corporate titans alike, his role and clout in Cleveland were also growing.

And at his side now was a wife, Pat Breslin, an Irish-Catholic and fellow New Yorker who had grown up in Bronxville, Westchester County, where her father was a prosecutor.

Breslin earned a degree in psychology, with a minor in speech and drama, from New York's College of New Rochelle. She performed in a few Broadway plays, then went to Hollywood, where she picked up a few movie and TV parts, appearing on "General Hospital," "Peyton Place," and "The Twilight Zone."

Though her brother, Eddie, was one of his New York bankers, Modell was actually introduced to Breslin by Dan Reeves, then the owner of the Los Angeles Rams, in a Santa Monica, Calif., restaurant. They married four months later, in 1969, in Las Vegas, and Modell adopted her two sons, John and David.

The family moved to a five-bedroom, Tudor mansion built on 29 wooded acres in Waite Hill, a tony Cleveland suburb. There, Modell installed in his basement a reminder of his Brooklyn past — a 100-year-old pool table. He also had a swimming pool, private tennis courts, and access to an exclusive golf course.

Modell's visits to the Pewter Mug dwindled as his new wife, who had high society aspirations, began scheduling him for black-tie events. The new couple, rebuffed by Cleveland's old-money East side, soon found a thriving community in the city's changing managerial class. Executives of Cleveland commerce, increasingly being run by out-of-town firms, soon supplanted the old guard. And the Modells were at the heart of the conversion.

Their home became a fixture in Cleveland's society. They hosted celebrities such as Lucille Ball and gave $1,000-a-plate fund-raisers for Republican heavyweights. Senator Bob Dole and presidents Gerald Ford and George Bush all came calling.

NFL team owners are always sought out by community leaders, if for no other reason than to get choice stadium seats. But the gregarious Modell ingratiated himself with the chieftains of the city's commerce and culture.

He became a patron of the arts, a benefactor of charities, and a general fix-it man often called in to solve intractable community problems. Once, he saved a football league for poor children. On another occasion, he served as foreman of the county grand jury.

As a court-appointed receiver for the bankrupt Sheraton

Hotel, Modell convinced investors to put up $18 million and revive it as the Stouffer Renaissance Cleveland Hotel. He also preserved a crucial downtown block at a time when money and residents were flowing out of the city. The block would serve as the hub of a downtown revival.

"He really took the lead in that effort, and those were dark days for downtown Cleveland," said Richard W. Pogue, former managing partner of Jones, Day, a Cleveland law firm intimately involved in city affairs.

"Art did a lot of things in the background also that he never got credit for."

Modell's most ambitious, and important, community project was the resurrection of Municipal Stadium — an effort that would make him a hero and, he felt certain, a richer man.

He was wrong. Municipal would ultimately haunt him as his greatest blunder.

In 1972, the stadium was costing the city $500,000 a year beyond what it was taking in in revenue. And major repairs were needed: The electrical system was rotting, plumbing was leaking, and the cement was crumbling.

In lease negotiations with the city that year, Modell vociferously complained about the stadium, suggesting that a major renovation or replacement was necessary. A blue-ribbon panel, headed by Modell's chum Steinbrenner, confirmed Modell's opinions in a December 1972 report to the mayor.

"We feel that the chances of long-term success would be greatly enhanced if the operation of Cleveland Stadium could be removed from political considerations and placed in the hands of business-oriented management ... to take over the existing stadium on a long-term lease," the report concluded.

In case the city wasn't listening, Modell not-so-quietly bought nearly 200 acres of land in a suburb called Strongsville, just off the Ohio Turnpike, about 18 miles from downtown Cleveland. He even had a model of a new stadium built and put on display in Browns headquarters.

According to Browns partner Robert Gries, studies had shown that a stadium on the Strongsville site would be so expensive, and local opposition would be so fierce, that the project was almost infeasible.

"At best, it would have been a fight all the way," Gries said.

Modell's actions, along with his refusal to sign a lease with the city, did indeed shake up City Hall. The mayor pleaded with Modell not to move, saying the loss of the team would damage efforts to save Cleveland's downtown.

Modell relented. Instead, he made an offer based on the Steinbrenner report: He would fix up the stadium if its operations were turned over to him. And he would sign a 25-year lease and invest $10 million into the stadium over the next 10 years. Political leaders were relieved when the details were hammered out.

Modell also seemed relieved. He had been quietly urging the NFL to consider letting owners like himself sell stock to the public. In one letter to his fellow owners, he noted a "liquidity problem."

The deal with the city soon opened new sources of borrowing, the life-blood of Modell's business style and something that would prove disastrous again and again in his career.

Modell formed the Cleveland Stadium Corp. with a few other investors — including Steinbrenner — and became his own landlord. After some vigorous negotiations, he signed the Indians as subtenants, ending for a time the baseball team's wanderlust. (The franchise threatened to move to New Orleans in 1971.)

At last, it seemed, the city's sports fans could relax. In 1980, Cleveland Mayor George Voinovich told the Cleveland *Plain Dealer*, "If the city had held on to the stadium, it probably would be closed today."

• • •

For his community involvement, Modell racked up a den full of civic awards and commendations. Cleveland's John Carroll University gave him an honorary law degree. The Cleveland Sales and Marketing Club named him its 1983 Executive of the Year. The city's Variety Club declared him "Super Citizen." The Ohio Sports Media Association awarded him the "Pride of Cleveland Award."

"I could call Art any time for a donation for any cause, regardless of the beneficiaries' race, color, or creed, and the check would be in the mail the next day," said Sam Miller, a community leader and friend.

Modell joined the boards of the city's biggest banks and its telephone company, as well as Cleveland State University and the renowned medical center, Cleveland Clinic. He eventually became president of Cleveland Clinic's board of directors, the most prestigious voluntary post in the city.

A friend got him a seat on 20th Century Fox's board of directors, where he served alongside Henry Kissinger and Gerald Ford.

Twice, Republican leaders tried to get Modell to run for governor or lieutenant governor of Ohio. He declined both overtures.

On Nov. 11, 1981, when 1,100 people turned out for a $150-a-plate appreciation dinner honoring the team owner, Modell's legacy seemed assured. The National Conference of Christians and Jews gave him the Human Relations Award. United Nations Ambassador Jeanne Kirkpatrick was the keynote speaker.

The night was filled with toasts and plaudits for Modell who, in 20 years, had won over the skeptical Ohio city and was now viewed as one of its most important assets.

Engraved on the silver medal awarded him that night were these words: "Champion of Brotherhood."

CHAPTER FIVE

The
Irsay
Watch

William Donald Schaefer was lying in the bed of his West Baltimore row house shortly before midnight on March 28, 1984, listening to the radio, when he first heard the news. The Colts, Baltimore's beloved NFL team, were loading their gear into a caravan of green and yellow Mayflower moving vans for a one-way trip to Indianapolis.

The city, and its mayor, would never be the same.

Schaefer was not much of an athlete or sports fan. His attendance at a game was more ceremonial than passionate, like the Queen attending a cricket match. But he had built his political reputation on accomplishing the impossible for his city and appeasing a millionaire team owner like Robert Irsay Jr., intent on breaking fans' hearts, had seemed like another task entirely within the realm of the possible.

He had been wrong.

"Do it now" wasn't just the anthem of Schaefer's administration. It was his personal mantra. If, on one of his frequent Sunday drives through the city, he spotted a rain-soaked mattress or other bit of untidiness in an alley, he would fire off a tersely worded "action memo" to a hapless department head first thing Monday. City workers who valued their careers and hearing knew to have the trucks dispatched by lunchtime.

Schaefer squeezed money out of Washington long after the federal bureaucrats said they were out. He turned litter control into a game called "trashball" by having the city's sidewalk trash cans made up to look like basketball hoops, complete with exhortations to "dunk one for Baltimore." He sold broken-down homes for $1 each to anybody promising to fix one up. He even sold potholes as Valentine's Day gifts. For a $35 check to the city, someone could have a hole patched and pink hearts painted on a favored piece of fresh asphalt. A cheerful notice and a "Pothole Patch Doll" would then be mailed to the object of the buyer's affection.

A brooding man of 5 feet, 9 inches, Schaefer exuded an authority that made him seem taller. He had steely blue eyes and spoke in the distinctive accent of his city. In his lexicon, Baltimore was "Bawlmer" and inactivity in office a felony.

Born in 1921 in West Baltimore and trained as a lawyer, he lived much of his life — even after his political ascension — in the same row house with his widowed mother, Tululu. Schaefer lost his first two races for City Hall but prevailed in 1955. Once in office, he developed a reputation as something of an oddball, working long hours and laboring over his votes even when outnumbered on the City Council 19 to 1.

He was elected city council president in 1967, and four years later ran for mayor with the backing of some of the city's powerful political bosses. In a three-way Democratic primary, he won with 56 percent of the vote, and, because Baltimore was a heavily Democratic city, easily went on to win the general election against token Republican opposition. Election Day, Nov. 2, 1971, was his 50th birthday.

A confirmed bachelor, Schaefer was married to his job. His "rule by tantrum" created a near makeover of Baltimore. He oversaw the transformation of rat-infested fruit-cargo piers into the Inner Harbor, a waterfront attraction of shops and restaurants that opened in 1980 and became a symbol of the city's resurgence. Similarly, he found the money to have highways, hotels, and a subway built, despite a rising conservative political tide against public spending and cities.

Each time a new public works project opened, he was sure to be there to cut the ribbon with oversized scissors. And he was sure to leave behind some surface painted with the slogan, "From the Citizens of Baltimore and Mayor William Donald Schaefer."

Occasionally, his publicity efforts touched on the bizarre, such as when he jumped into the seal pool at Baltimore's new National Aquarium wearing a one-piece Gay Nineties bathing suit and holding a rubber duck. He had pledged to take the swim if the aquarium didn't open on time. It didn't, but Schaefer and the city gained tons of positive national attention when he stylishly fulfilled his promise.

Schaefer was little interested in studies or theory, and in reality, the city continued to deteriorate along with the rest of urban America during his tenure. Baltimore lost population and wealth and added crime and despair at frightening rates. It remained one of the nation's poorest cities, ranking at the top of almost every measurement of urban ill, from unwed pregnancy to infants born HIV-positive.

But what Schaefer could control — the brick and mortar of governing — he did as well as anyone, winning applause from such disparate observers as conservative columnist George Will, the National League of Cities, and management guru Tom Peters.

In 1984, Richard Ben Cramer, in *Esquire* magazine, dubbed him the "Best Mayor in America," writing: "The mayor never read Aristotle, Lewis Mumford or Jane Jacobs on the city; he won't talk theory for five minutes, has no articulate opinion on civil rights, or gay rights, or women in the workplace; he never could TV-sermonize on The Challenge of Urban America like San Antonio's handsome Henry Cisneros, neither could nor would blow his horn like New York's Edward Koch; he'll never make a *New Republic* mayor, or even a *60 Minutes* mayor. But great mayors never travel well."

Baltimore voters rewarded Schaefer handsomely. He was elected mayor four times, often by astounding margins and carrying nearly every city precinct, even after black residents became the majority — a demographic shift that frequently spells political doom for white incumbents like Schaefer.

When he decided to run for governor in 1986, his reputation as a "can do," if quirky, chief executive easily overcame the state's natural suspicion of Baltimore's political clout. He captured 82 percent of the vote, setting a new state record. He was handily reelected four years later.

As governor, he pushed through the Maryland General Assembly major overhauls of education, economic development, and other state functions while winning funding for a slew of Baltimore public works projects, from a trolley line to the two new sports stadiums. He would lash out at cabinet members, dress down government workers, skirt open-bidding rules, and otherwise work through, around, or over opposition to get it done.

So it was more than the disappointment of losing the Colts that kept him up that March night in 1984. It was the anger of being snubbed, and the helplessness it symbolized. Schaefer had spent years negotiating with Irsay, the mercurial Colts owner, and had wrung from him what he thought was at least one inviolate commitment: Call before you move the team.

But there was no call that night. The next morning, Schaefer's only greeting came from a gaggle of reporters, who would later debate whether the mayor was crying when he came out to meet them.

"He didn't call his old friend, Don," Schaefer told the media, sardonically recalling the public promise Irsay had repeated a few months earlier to "call my old friend Don Schaefer."

"In a way, this gets very personal to me, when I thought someone would at least pick up the phone and say to me, 'I'm going,'" he said. "I'm trying to retain what little dignity I have left in this matter. If the Colts had to sneak out of town at night, it degrades a great city."

• • •

The late-night theatrics of the Colts' move may have been shocking, but the actual move wasn't. The crisis had been building for years.

Team owner Carroll Rosenbloom had long groused publicly and privately about Memorial Stadium. The fans were flocking to Colts games, but the place barely handled 60,000. And it suited baseball much better than it did football. The upper deck did not circle the stadium; instead, it ended at the 50-yard line, so half of the best seats were missing. Plans to expand capacity usually involved adding more end-zone, not upper-deck, seating.

And the stadium's location was awful. Traffic would tie up

the streets for hours; and on game days, neighborhood residents would become prisoners of their own homes. A provision of the city charter prohibited spectator sporting events from starting on a Sunday before 2 p.m. This blue law, which dated back at least to the stadium's opening, meant the Colts were the only NFL team in the nation that didn't observe the traditional 1 p.m. starting time. Rosenbloom complained, but area religious leaders vigorously defended the law as a way to allow parishioners to get in and out of church before the onslaught of fans.

Moreover, the Colts owner had to share his team's home with a cotenant. At one time, NFL team owners gladly accepted second-class citizenship in facilities, but those days were fast ending, and Rosenbloom knew it. Whenever he asked for something for the stadium, the Orioles asked for something different. Scheduling games, changing the seating plan, adding vendors — all became a contest that Schaefer was called upon to referee. Sometimes, the two team owners would sit in his office and refuse to speak to each other, relaying messages through the mayor like bickering children.

"You needed an interpreter standing between them when they'd meet," Schaefer recalled later.

Rosenbloom was selling every ticket he could print, and it irked him that his capacity was limited by the baseball team. When the Orioles' season ended, the city added 5,000 temporary stadium seats. But this addition was delayed if the Orioles went into post-season play, leaving some Colts season-ticket holders with no seats at all for early-season games.

The city's leases with the two teams also favored the Orioles, reflecting the greater priority put on acquiring a major league baseball team in 1954 than a football team in a fledgling league. The Orioles had control over stadium concessions and parking — even during football games.

Rosenbloom had all the money he wanted and little use for the hassle. Memorial Stadium just wouldn't do. So he started dealing.

In 1965, he announced he would build his own stadium, possibly in partnership with the Orioles. He asked only that the city tear down Memorial Stadium so that it wouldn't attract a competing American Football League team. He thought the downtown area would be the best place for a new stadium.

Mayor Theodore McKeldin received the idea warmly: "I'm

for anything that is big, new, and progressive," he told reporters.

But Rosenbloom was soon complaining about a lack of city support for the project and a lack of suitable real estate. His relationship with Orioles owner — local beer magnate Jerold Hoffberger — grew icy as the two disagreed on the parameters of the project and how it would be financed.

By 1972, Rosenbloom wasn't talking to Hoffberger, and he declared that he wouldn't talk to the city either. He announced that the team wouldn't return to Memorial Stadium after its lease ran out that season.

"We aren't interested in negotiating with the city any more …. I'm tired of being the bad guy no matter what happens in Baltimore," Rosenbloom said in late 1971.

"When we offered to put up money for stadium improvements, Rosenbloom and the Colts were ogres, forcing their will on people. If the city offers to build a practice field, or do something that would benefit the Colts, we are squandering the taxpayers' money. If we want to build our own stadium, we're bad. No matter what, we're wrong."

Rosenbloom flirted with a new and eager suitor: Tampa, FL. Rosenbloom himself was living most of the time in Florida, flying in on game days and leaving his son, Steve, in charge of the team in Baltimore. Under fire from the media for charging season-ticket holders for pre-season games — a now common practice just getting under way then — he moved his team training camp to Tampa.

In 1972, he scheduled three exhibition games in Tampa, but none in Baltimore. Tampa fans gobbled up the tickets, and community leaders offered to enlarge the city's stadium and build a practice facility next door if the team would move there. Word leaked out, and Baltimore fans responded by wearing T-shirts that warned, "Don't Tampa with our Colts."

Rosenbloom remained intrigued with Tampa, so much so that he asked Rozelle about permanently moving the Colts there. Rozelle said no. And that was that. No one ever thought of moving a team in defiance of the commissioner.

"Carroll called me and said he had just spoken with the commissioner, and the commissioner said, 'no way,'" recalled Leonard Levy, a Tampa businessman and sports-minded civic booster, in 1997.

But, Levy added, Rosenbloom also told him: "Leonard, I give you my word that no one will get a franchise before Tampa."

Rosenbloom kept his word: Tampa won a franchise in the league's next expansion, 1974.

Rosenbloom had other ideas for getting out of Baltimore. In 1971, his friend — Los Angeles Rams owner Dan Reeves, the man who moved the Rams from Cleveland to L.A. in 1946 — died of cancer. Rosenbloom thought first of buying the Rams and giving the Colts to his son. But Rozelle nixed this idea, too; he thought it would be a conflict of interest to have two franchises owned by such close relatives.

So Rosenbloom hatched another scheme, one that would get him out of Memorial Stadium and in with a new team in a warm-weather climate. He figured if he could line up someone to buy the Rams, he could convince that "buyer" to "swap" the franchise for the Colts and some cash.

Brokering the deal was Joe Thomas, recently fired as director of player personnel for the Miami Dolphins and trying to get back into the game. Thomas put Rosenbloom in touch with Willard "Bud" Keland, a Racine, Wis., real estate developer and former partner in the Dolphins. Keland agreed to the swap and to cut in Bob Irsay, a buddy from his Florida country club, for 1 percent.

When the parties gathered in NFL Commissioner Pete Rozelle's New York office to consummate the deal, however, Keland came up short of cash. He tried to get Irsay to put up the bulk of the money, but insisted on operating the team himself. Irsay didn't want any part of that arrangement and quickly began to see little need for Keland.

"As it turned out, at 3 o'clock in the afternoon, I had to come up with all the money. So, instead of owning 1 percent, I ended up owning 100 percent," Irsay recalled years later.

Under an arrangement worked out in advance, Irsay bought the Rams for $19 million and simultaneously traded them for Rosenbloom's Colts and about $3 million in cash. When all the transactions were settled, Irsay figured he had paid $13 million.

This gave Rosenbloom a team in a vastly more valuable — not to mention prestigious — market and spared him millions of dollars in capital-gains taxes he would have faced had he sold the Colts outright and bought the Rams.

And so, on July 13, 1972, Irsay, a 48-year-old industrial heating and air conditioning contractor from Chicago, became the owner of the Baltimore Colts.

In interviews with the Baltimore *Sun* soon afterward, Irsay sought to calm fears in the community about the team falling into out-of-town ownership. He said he hadn't wanted to keep the Rams.

"I didn't particularly like the idea of traveling for hours to Los Angeles," he explained, "and the situation there needs a lot more work than the present situation with the Colts, who have such fine personnel, a lot of team spirit, and an outstanding organization. I have no plans to make any changes, because things are going so well."

He also said he liked his coach, Don McCafferty, and would honor Johnny Unitas' personal services contract with Rosenbloom, which called for 10 years of employment after his quarterbacking days were over.

"I won't be an interfering owner," he pledged.

"I bought the Colts to play in Baltimore. I have no thought of taking them elsewhere. We have a great team in a great sports town where there have been sellouts. Why move?"

It was just what Baltimore wanted to hear.

• • •

But Irsay didn't waste any time remaking the organization in his own image. He appointed Thomas vice president and general manager; and five games into the new season, the two men fired McCafferty, despite his Super Bowl victory at the end of the 1970 season. Irsay then benched Unitas for a game against the Jets, even though he had bombed the team a month earlier for 396 yards. The next year, he not only traded the Baltimore great to San Diego, but called in $600,000 in loans he said Rosenbloom had made to Colt players.

Irsay soon developed a reputation for meddlesome management, calling in plays from the owner's box and berating coaches and players from the sidelines. In 1974, he walked down to the field in the second half of a game against the Eagles and strongly suggested to coach Howard Schnellenberger that he replace struggling quarterback Marty Domres with Bert Jones. Schnellenberger told Irsay to leave the team's bench, and the Colts went on to lose 30-10.

After the game, Irsay appeared again — this time in the team's locker room — where he fired Schnellenberger, then in his second season, and surprised his GM, Thomas, by naming *him* coach.

In 1979, Irsay gave place kicker Toni Linhart a $10,000 raise after missing three field goals in a 13-10 loss to the Browns. Four days later, the Colts owner cut him from the team.

In the second half of a 1981 game against the Eagles, Irsay manned the headphones in the coaches' booth and called in plays to Mike McCormack, his sixth head coach.

In 12 seasons in Baltimore, Irsay went through eight head coaches. The franchise's once proud reputation grew so ragged that first-round college draftee John Elway refused to sign with the Colts in 1983. After an embarrassing standoff, Irsay traded the promising QB to the Denver Broncos — to the surprise of both Ernie Accorsi, the Colts general manager and chief negotiator, and Colts head coach Frank Kush.

Meanwhile, Irsay did little to endear himself to the Baltimore community. He lived in the Chicago area and, on most game days, flew in and out of Baltimore on his private plane. He dabbled in Baltimore philanthropy, but never became deeply involved in the society of the city.

He also began cutting expenses on even the smallest items. Ended under Irsay's regime was the Colts' popular and long-standing practice of handing out free player photographs to any fan who requested them.

"Rosenbloom wanted us to get out in the community. Irsay didn't give a shit. People got tired of the way he managed the team," remembered former running back and sometime-quarterback Tom Matte.

In the Irsay era, the Colts payroll was cut, and the team's performance slumped. The World Champions sank to a 39-percent winning percentage, with a regular-season game record of 68-104-1.

But the Baltimore Colts did enjoy a bit of a resurgence with coach Ted Marchibroda, a former NFL quarterback and offensive assistant under George Allen at both the L.A. Rams and the Redskins.

Marchibroda engineered the first NFL single-season team turnaround from last place to first, when he led the Colts to a 10-4 record in 1975. The previous season, under Schnellenberger and Thomas, the team had won only two of 14 games. Under Marchibroda, they won the AFC Eastern Division title in three consecutive seasons — 1975, 1976 (11-3) and 1977 (10-4) — but they lost in the playoffs, falling victim to Pittsburgh twice and once to Oakland.

After two 5-11 seasons in 1978 and 1979, the Colts' second winningest coach — behind Don Shula — was fired. But Marchibroda would return to the organization in Indianapolis, where he would build another champion.

The fans responded predictably: Between 1972 and 1983, Baltimore attendance plummeted from an average of 60,000 a game, 10 percent above the NFL average, to just 41,000 — 9 percent below it. The crowd of 27,934 that showed up on Dec. 18, 1983, for what turned out to be the Colts' last game, was only 516 fans larger than the one that turned out for the first Colts game in 1947.

Despite the slumping attendance, the Colts remained one of the most profitable teams in the NFL. These were the days when the key to making money was keeping expenses low and soaking up the growing network television revenues. In their last season in Baltimore, the Colts had the lowest NFL player payroll and the third highest operating profit, $5.1 million. Even with one of the highest debt loads — Irsay was paying $1.4 million a year in interest, the second highest in the NFL — the team generated a total profit of $4 million that year.

"A man who could screw up professional football in Baltimore would foul the water at Lourdes or flatten the beer at Munich," wrote sportswriter and native Baltimorean Frank Deford in *Sports Illustrated* in April 1984.

The other NFL owners and league officials had a similar opinion of Irsay, who became known for rambling diatribes and incoherent outbursts at meetings.

"I don't think Bob's ever had a lot of stature among the other owners. He's never really contributed anything substantial," one team executive said in 1996.

"He will get up and make some off-the-wall speech and people will look around and ask, 'What did he say?'"

During a debate among the owners about allowing quarter-backs to communicate with their coaches via helmet radios, Irsay spoke against the idea, citing Soviet bugs found in the U.S. embassy in Moscow. If the Communists could bug our embassy, he asked, how secure could a coach's communications with his players be?

"I don't like to use the word buffoon, but that's how the other owners view him," the executive said.

As his reputation in Baltimore soured, reporters began probing into Irsay's past and discovered that much of what he said about it was fiction.

Repeatedly in interviews and in team publications, Irsay claimed to have been a poor Catholic kid who survived the tough streets of Chicago and worked his way through the University of Illinois, washing dishes for a fraternity and playing football on the side. He humbly allowed how his leg had been injured by a hand grenade while he was serving as a Marine during World War II in New Guinea. He claimed to have risen to the rank of first lieutenant.

None of it was true.

His younger brother, Ronald, and his mother, Elaine, said he was raised Jewish. The family name, in fact, was Israel before it was changed during Irsay's youth. Although the family background wasn't rich, it wasn't poor either, relatives recalled.

The owner's unique view of his own background, and his insistence on publicly identifying his biological father as a "stepfather," clearly did not sit well with the family. In 1986, Elaine Irsay described son Bob this way to *Sports Illustrated*: "He's a devil on earth, that one. He stole all our money and said good-bye... He was a bad boy."

She and other family members accused Bob of driving his father out of business after the elder Irsay suffered a heart attack.

Charles Irsay ran Acord Ventilating Co., a sheet metal contracting company in Chicago. Bob worked for his father until they had a falling out, and they reached a settlement in which the son received a big account he had brought into the company, along with some tools and vehicles. He then started his own competing company, and Charles' business went into decline. Ronald quit college to try to rescue Acord, but it failed two and a half years later.

"I don't know how else to say this, but my brother tried to run my father out of business," said Ronald Irsay, 55, in 1996. "Bob actually worked to try to destroy his own father. Oh, he's a real sweetheart, all right."

The University of Illinois reported that Irsay attended classes there from 1940 to 1942 but never graduated and never played football on the school's team. The Marines said he was discharged as a sergeant in 1943 after a run-in with military authorities involving the theft of a jeep. According to the Pentagon, he never served overseas.

Most galling to Baltimoreans was Irsay's early and obvious wanderlust. Beginning in 1976, just four years after buying the Colts, he shopped the team to any city that seemed interested. The courtship was often public. He investigated moving the team to Phoenix, Memphis, Los Angeles, New York, Indianapolis, and Jacksonville, Fla.

He complained about sharing an outdated stadium with a baseball team, and about the city's reluctance to invest in new facilities. He accused the city's "fair-weather" fans of refusing to support a team of less than championship caliber.

• • •

Schaefer became Baltimore's mayor at a time of extraordinary enthusiasm and success for the city's sports teams. Urban ills were fast closing in on his city, but on the playing field at least, Baltimore was a champion.

The Orioles had just come off a season that landed them in the World Series for the second year in a row. The Colts had won Super Bowl V in January 1971 and had come within a game of playing in the championship the next year. The Baltimore Bullets won the National Basketball Association Eastern Division title in 1971, only to lose the championship to Lew Alcindor (later known as Kareem Abdul-Jabbar) and the Milwaukee Bucks. The sports pages nationwide were full of stories about Unitas; the Orioles' Robinsons, Frank and Brooks, and pitcher Jim Palmer; and Bullet stars Wes Unseld and Earl Monroe.

For a compulsive booster like Schaefer, it was hard not to see the benefits of playing in the big leagues, no matter what the costs.

He got his first hint of the costs, however, in 1972 when

Bullets owner Abe Pollin, complaining about the difficulty of draw-ing fans to the downtown Baltimore Civic Center, announced he was moving his franchise to a new facility to be built in Landover, Md., outside Washington. Pollin even changed the team name to the Washington Bullets. Thus, Baltimore's first major-league team in the modern era became the first to flee.

Worries ran rampant that the other two teams would soon fol-low the Bullets' lead. The Colts' and Orioles' owners contributed to the jitters with frank assessments of Memorial Stadium.

On Feb. 15, 1972, Schaefer and Maryland Governor Marvin Mandel named an ad hoc commission to examine the city's stadi-um needs. The report, completed a month later, was not kind to the 33rd Street edifice. Among the flaws cited: 10,000 of its seats had "less than desirable" views; 20,000 were bench seats with no backs; and 7,000 were temporary bleachers installed for football games. Space wasn't adequate for the front offices of either the baseball or football teams, and the teams had to share locker rooms. The field rated poorly, and bathrooms were in short supply.

"Many of the problems relate to the limited, $6 million bud-get at initial construction which necessarily precluded many design and comfort amenities. Considering that the city has obtained near-ly 20 years' use from the small investment, the stadium has served a satisfactory economic life," the report said.

Mandel, a former semi-pro baseball player and Baltimore politico, announced that the state would help the city build a new stadium. He then submitted and guided through the 1972 General Assembly legislation to create the Maryland Sports Complex Authority. Its purpose was to "provide for a sports complex and related facilities in the greater Baltimore region."

Mandel thus began the process that would eventually create a new stadium. But the action was, in Rosenbloom's eyes, too little, too late. He went ahead with his swap of the Colts and rebuked the fledgling Authority for "not doing a thing."

Elsewhere in the country, a virtual boom in stadium building was underway. Pre-World War II-era stadiums were crumbling, sports attendance was soaring, and the leagues were expanding. An increasingly suburban fan base and a new reluctance to use mass transit overwhelmed the limited parking available in most older parks.

The NFL, meantime, was emerging as an economic and political powerhouse. For a brief period, this worked to the advantage of football and major league baseball. New, multipurpose stadiums were winning approval in cities that might have been reluctant to build parks for one major-league tenant.

The first domed stadium, the $43 million Astrodome, opened in Houston in 1965 and was a marvel. Dubbed "the eighth wonder of the world," it had heat, air conditioning, large scoreboards, wide seats, easy parking, luxury boxes, and artificial turf. And both baseball and football could be played in it. The sports world took notice of the innovations, and the Astrodome became one of the most influential stadiums of the century.

In 1966, the St. Louis Cardinals baseball and football teams moved into the privately developed Busch Stadium. The place looked like a flying saucer perched on the banks of the Mississippi River, but it was an engineer's dream. After a baseball game, a switch could be thrown and whole sections of seats, mounted on tracks, would automatically retract; high-pressure hoses would clean off the foul lines; and a hydraulic lift would lower the pitcher's mound into the ground. New sideline seating would also emerge and pieces of artificial turf would be rolled out to fill in the gaps on the field. Nine hours later, presto! A football stadium.

But none of the seats was especially good, and the ambiance was as sterile as a strip mall. Still, it was cheap — $25 million — and easy.

Over the next several years, the design — perhaps the last-gasp of multisport stadiums — was duplicated in Cincinnati, Philadelphia, Atlanta, and Pittsburgh. Sharing a stadium meant compromising on architecture and splitting the revenue from any advertising and luxury seats, but no one thought anything of it. The teams even signed leases guaranteeing their cities a return on the investment.

The New England Patriots, Kansas City's Chiefs and Royals, and the Dallas Cowboys also got new stadiums during this period. Work was underway on stadiums in New Jersey and Buffalo. New Orleans and Detroit would soon have domes. A similar, domed stadium was suggested for Baltimore, with the support of Schaefer and others.

Planners of Baltimore's project consulted with some of the

architects who had designed the New Orleans Superdome, and from those conversations the original estimates emerged: At a cost as low as $78 million, the Baltimore facility could accommodate 70,000 fans for football, 55,000 for baseball, and 20,000 as an arena. Two potential sites were eyed: the land under Memorial Stadium and an industrial area west of the city's Inner Harbor. The latter, a 27-acre site owned by the Chesapeake & Ohio Railroad, was known for its most prominent feature. The Camden Station was the birthplace of the nation's railroad industry, a spot where the once-mighty Port of Baltimore fed cargo to rail cars for the steam-powered trip into the American heartland. During its heyday, the station was the grandest in the country. It took its name from the adjacent Camden Street, which, in turn, was named for English nobleman Charles Pratt, the Earl of Camden. He was an outspoken supporter of the colonies in the British House of Commons prior to the Revolutionary War. Completed in 1856, it served as the gateway to the nation's capital for the entire Northeast. It was also a stop for escaping slaves on the Underground Railroad. In 1861, the first blood of the Civil War was spilled in front of the station when Confederate sympathizers attacked a Massachusetts infantry unit on its way to a Washington-bound train.

Abraham Lincoln passed through the station several times. On the first, when he was en route to his 1861 presidential inaugural, his railcar was secretly moved through town in the middle of the night to thwart a rumored assassination attempt. Lincoln visited again on his way to and from the Gettysburg battlefield, where he delivered his most famous address. And his funeral train stopped in Camden Station on its way to his burial site in Springfield, Ill.

The station's neighborhood also boasted some illustrious baseball history. Babe Ruth's father ran a tavern nearby, and the young George Herman lived upstairs for a while. Years later, in 1954, the Orioles made their grand entrance in Baltimore at the station, disembarking after a two-game, season-opening series in Detroit.

By 1972, however, the rail yard was gasping its last. The national highway system and the airline industry had stolen most of its passengers, and cargo was being loaded directly on the piers, circumventing the need for the long Camden warehouse. Mayor

Schaefer thought it the perfect place for a stadium.

"Let me make it perfectly clear that I have supported the downtown stadium compatible with the Inner Harbor project. As far as I'm concerned, there's one area, the downtown area," he told reporters at a 1972 press conference.

The "Baltodome" idea attracted some support, but not enough, despite backers' assertion that the public contribution would be limited to city and state loans.

That same year, Maryland Sports Complex Authority chairman Edmond Rovner issued an important reminder to opponents and supporters alike: "A major consideration in Mr. Irsay's trading of franchises was the city's firm commitment to proceed with these plans."

Not surprisingly, in May 1973, the Authority issued a report saying that neither the Colts nor the Orioles would sign a long-term lease at the old ball park.

"It is the authority's conclusion that under these circumstances, no assurance can be given that the teams would remain in Baltimore at Memorial Stadium except on a short-term basis," the report said.

The authority proposed a new facility, to be built at Camden Yards and to be shared by both teams. A multipurpose plan was drawn up for a $114 million stadium, convention center, and parking garage complex.

But the timing was awful for raising public money for sports in Baltimore. The city was suffering a dizzying loss of residents and tax dollars. Corporations were fleeing to the Sun Belt and citizens were heading to the suburbs. Baltimore lost 12 percent of its population in the 1970s, dropping from 905,000 to less than 800,000. It also suffered badly in the race riots of the late 1960s. Most of the state's attention was focused on the more urgent matters of civil rights and Vietnam.

On Feb. 27, 1974, Governor Mandel pulled the plug on the idea. Too much else was going on, including a teachers' strike in Baltimore and election campaigns waged across the state. Besides, he said, the Orioles and Colts had failed to commit to long-term leases at the proposed complex. As governor, he would not support state-backed financing of the proposal, which opponents feared would force taxpayers to make up any revenue shortfalls.

A spokesman explained that the Governor had decided not to back the legislation because of "other problems, other priorities, and other needs that have to be met."

The Orioles' Hoffberger told *The Sun* he was disappointed with the governor's decision. If attendance fails to pick up and no new complex is built, he said, "I will bow to the will of the people. I think the people of Baltimore will have told us what they want to tell us. First, they don't want a new park and, second, they don't want a club."

Irsay, though, took Mandel at his word that the project was delayed, not dumped.

"It's not a matter of saying there will be no stadium. It's a matter of getting the facts together so everybody is happy when they build the stadium," Irsay told the newspaper.

"I'm a patient man. I think the people of Baltimore are going to see those new stadiums [in New Orleans and Seattle] opening in a year or two around the country and they are going to realize they need a stadium ... for conventions and other things besides football."

The stadium delay sparked an immediate increase in rumors that one or both of Baltimore's teams were moving. Asked about the Colts, Commissioner Rozelle said, "I don't think [they] will move. It will be a burden on Irsay financially, but the team will stay in Baltimore."

Led by Hyman A. Pressman, Baltimore's penny-pinching comptroller who favored rehabbing Memorial Stadium, opponents tried to make sure the ambitious stadium project was indeed dead. They collected signatures and placed on the fall ballot a cleverly worded amendment to the city's charter.

Question "P" called for proclaiming "the 33rd Street stadium as a memorial to war veterans and prohibiting use of city funds for construction of any other stadium."

Fueled by the same patriotism that helped build the stadium, the measure passed 56 percent to 44 percent.

• • •

Schaefer, who had opposed Question P, now was even more fearful about the instability of the city's sports teams, and about retaining Baltimore's major-league status. Developments over the ensuing years only heightened his concern. In 1976, Irsay acknowledged publicly that he had received an "attractive offer" to move the club to Phoenix. A few months later, before the 1977 Super Bowl in Los Angeles, he told reporters: "I can get the [NFL team owners'] votes. We can move if we want to."

"I like Baltimore and I want to stay there, but when are we going to find out something about our stadium?" he asked. "I'm getting offers from towns like Indianapolis to build me a new stadium and give me other inducements to move there. I don't want to, but I'd like to see some action in Baltimore."

Meantime, the Orioles franchise fell into the hands of out-of-town owners. In 1979, Jerry Hoffberger sold 80 percent of the Orioles to Washington-based attorney Edward Bennett Williams for $10.5 million. Soon, Williams was complaining about the team's accommodations. In an August 1979 interview with *The Washington Post*, he lamented the team's poor attendance numbers and declared the coming season a "trial year" for the fans of Baltimore.

He tossed in a few digs at Memorial Stadium, too, saying that, because of stadium traffic, it had taken him hours to get home after a recent game.

"Memorial Stadium has inadequate parking and inadequate access and egress. Frankly, I don't know if those problems will ever be solvable at that location," Williams suggested.

Irsay's actions were no more comforting. On Aug. 15, Jacksonville officials flew him by helicopter onto the field of the Gator Bowl for a garish "love-in." Irsay smiled broadly and flashed thumbs-up while being entertained by cheerleaders, skydivers and 50,000 fans, all trying to demonstrate the city's desire for the Colts.

Irsay said Jacksonville's offer was compelling, as were the inducements being offered by Memphis and Los Angeles. Though he later denied it, reports out of Jacksonville quoted the team owner as telling officials, "It's not a matter of if I'm leaving [Baltimore], but where I'm going."

That fall, Irsay put his team's possible relocation onto the agenda for the NFL owners' meeting. But, before the meeting was to occur, offers of new stadium renovations in Maryland convinced him to remove it.

On Dec. 11, 1979, he issued a statement: "We want to stay here ... and bring Baltimore and Maryland a championship like we have in the past. That is all we are committed to."

• • •

Meanwhile, a storm was brewing out west that would soon be felt in nearly every sports town in the country, especially Baltimore.

Rosenbloom, never satisfied with the Los Angeles Memorial Coliseum, announced on July 25, 1979 that he was moving the Rams to Anaheim, an L.A. suburb best known as the home of Disneyland. Various leagues had eyed the city for some time. The rival American Football League, under then-commissioner Al Davis, had once considered it for an expansion franchise.

A few months later, Rosenbloom drowned in a swimming accident. His widow, Georgia, and son Steve went ahead with the planned move to Anaheim and began play in 1980. That freed the L.A. Coliseum, and the huge Los Angeles market, for another team.

As part of its efforts to refill the stadium, the Los Angeles Memorial Coliseum Commission asked the NFL if expansion was on the horizon. It wasn't. The city then began talking to teams that might be interested in moving, including the Colts. But the commission came across a significant impediment — the league's bylaws. The rules required unanimous consent before a team could move into another's territory, defined as a 75-mile radius around its home field. This effectively gave the Rams a veto over anyone else moving to L.A.

The Coliseum Commission sued the NFL, charging that the rule contradicted the nation's antitrust laws, which were designed to ensure competition among businesses. But a judge soon dismissed the case, reasoning that the city didn't have a team committed to moving there and, therefore, didn't have standing to bring a suit.

Davis, now the owner of the Oakland Raiders and a friend of Rosenbloom, quickly solved the commission's "standing" problem while creating a new one for the league. On March 1, 1980 he signed a memorandum of understanding to move his Raiders to Los Angeles.

The move shocked the sporting world. The Raiders had enjoyed 12 years of sellouts in Oakland despite some of the highest ticket prices in the league. Fan support seemed exceptional. And there was little financial distress. The Raiders were among the top five NFL franchises in revenue, having earned profits of $2 million in 1978 and $1.5 million in 1979.

But Davis, always a maverick, cited grievances that were ahead of his time and provided a glimpse of stadium battles to come. He complained that his facility had no skyboxes and that he got none of the revenue from parking and concessions. Because he had to share the facility with a baseball team, he said, the Raiders were always forced to play their first three games of the season away from home.

In what were acrimonious negotiations, Davis demanded more stadium renovations than Oakland city fathers were willing to pay for. In addition, he said he asked for, but did not receive, support from Rozelle to move to L.A. The commissioner said he'd allow the Minnesota Vikings to move to Los Angeles; the team promptly received a new stadium in Minnesota.

"We had the best record in professional football. The [Oakland] coliseum was selling out. But the Raiders did not have certain of the things that I thought were necessary to be competitive in the 1980s, the things that other stadiums were getting that were being built," Davis explained to a Senate committee a few years later.

At a special meeting of team owners in early 1980, he acknowledged his intention to move to Los Angeles without asking for their approval.

Rozelle was not pleased at the prospect of teams roaming the country and was even less happy about the anarchy that would result if team owners defied the governing structure he had assembled.

"I, for one, regret that any club in the NFL should sacrifice so much in the way of good will, moral commitment, and fan loyalty for nothing more than an increase in its profit potential," Rozelle said later.

He appointed a committee of team owners to investigate, and he put his trusted ally, Art Modell, on it.

Modell was already on record as strongly opposing the Raiders' move. He had been quoted as saying that casual team relocations would hurt the NFL's image and that the league had a moral obligation to stand by the loyal fans of Oakland.

Davis and Modell were philosophical opposites, and each detested the other. To Davis, Modell was a spineless pack runner. To Modell, Davis was a selfish and dangerous man bent on destroying the league's success.

In a 1980 deposition in the matter, Modell spoke for the old-guard traditionalists then running the league, saying that the NFL valued its "image of stability, of loyalty for our people. We don't move around for the buck ... it would be bad for the league's image if teams hopscotched around the country.

"I have never been involved in any veteran franchise transfer since I've been in football, and that's 20 years now. It's just not good for the Browns to announce tomorrow that we are moving into Yankee Stadium in New York because I got a better offer from the landlord. I'm sorry. I feel that very deeply." With Davis and several other owners abstaining, the league voted 22-0 to disallow the Raiders' move to L.A.

"I have no idea what the future will bring, except the ownership is steadfast in the belief that the constitution and bylaws, which have gotten the league where it is, must be preserved," Modell told a Cleveland reporter after the meeting. "I wish Al [Davis] had not done what he did, and I hope he accepts the decision we have reached."

Never one to let collegiality get in the way of what he wanted, Davis largely ignored the committee's vote. The league then filed a breach of contract suit against him, and won a restraining order forbidding the Raiders from moving.

Meanwhile, Los Angeles officials revived their lawsuit, and Davis joined it. By this time, to remove the appearance that it was deliberately shielding its franchises from competition, the NFL, on advice of counsel, had softened its rules on relocation. It removed the old Redskins' clause that prevented a team from moving to Baltimore without compensating the Washington team. And it revised downward the number of owners needed to approve a relocation to a city already with a team— from 100 percent to 75 percent.

The Raiders insisted that, despite the recent rule changes, the NFL remained a cartel made up of competing franchises. These franchises couldn't conspire to keep out competitors any more than Exxon, Mobil, and Texaco could jointly set gas prices, they argued. Keeping them out of Los Angeles amounted to an illegal conspiracy to protect the Rams' turf.

The NFL claimed in its filing that it was really a single business and that the individual clubs were branch offices. Companies had the right to decide where to put, or not put, their operations, the NFL said.

The judge tried to get the two sides to settle their differences. He even suggested that Davis be given an expansion team in Los Angeles and that the Raiders remain in Oakland. Davis and Los Angeles agreed to go along with this, and the NFL owners voted 17-10 in favor of it. But Rozelle, fearing the league's control over franchises was at risk, threatened to quit, and the owners later rejected the proposal.

There were also reports at the time of another intriguing offer by the league, designed to divide Davis from Los Angeles officials: The league would put an expansion team in L.A. and fight to keep Davis in Oakland. The owner of the new team, it was said, would be none other than Art Modell, who was at the time bedeviled with lawsuits in Cleveland and presumably looking to get out. Modell denied the reports, and the deal never materialized.

Before the case went to a jury, the NFL suffered a serious blow: The judge sided with Davis on a key issue, the league's structure, and issued a directed verdict on this point. This meant the jury had to accept Davis' contention that the league was a collection of competing businesses, not a single entity.

The first trial ended with a hung jury, but Davis prevailed in the second one, in May 1982. The team was allowed to move, and the rest of the NFL was ordered to pay its wayward partner $34.65 million and to pay the L.A. Coliseum Commission $14.58 million in damages.

Davis and Los Angeles then inked their deal. The city promised him a $6.7 million loan, tax breaks, 99 skyboxes and most of the money raised from tickets, concessions, parking, and stadium advertising.

It was a sweet deal and a bitter precedent. In 1983, the Raiders' first season in Los Angeles other than the strike year of 1982, the team had the highest revenue in the NFL — $29 million.

With this advantage, they were able to field the most expensive team in the league: Their 1983 player payroll was $16 million. The investment paid off immediately when the Raiders beat the Washington Redskins, 38-9, in Super Bowl XVIII.

Davis' move ended a long period of franchise stability. In fact, it had been 23 years since the last team move, when the Chicago Cardinals had relocated to St. Louis. The only move before that was in 1946, when the Cleveland Rams moved to L.A..

Davis' case was upheld on appeal two years later in a decision that still has an enormous impact on how American sports leagues work. Circuit Court Judge J. Blaine Anderson ruled, "To withstand antitrust scrutiny, restrictions on team movement should be more closely tailored to serve the needs inherent in producing the NFL 'product' ...." In essence, the judge said the NFL could have stopped the Raiders from moving had it acted to promote legitimate business reasons.

For example, the league has a legitimate interest in spreading its teams all around the country — attracting fans and network-television coverage. But protecting one team's turf from another's — as the league was doing in preventing a second franchise from entering Los Angeles — was not legitimate. In blocking the Raiders' move, the NFL had tried to shield the Rams from having to compete for fans, something that was bound to result in higher ticket prices, worse deals for suppliers, etc. That sort of monopolistic behavior was illegal, the judge ruled.

The decision was not a carte blanche inviting sports teams to move. But the stiff damage award took the fight out of the NFL.

Rozelle drew up some guidelines, tailored to the judge's directions, to govern team relocations. The new rules required a team to demonstrate a lack of governmental and fan support, as well as financial distress, before it could move.

But the legality of these rules wouldn't be known until the NFL went to court to stop another member club from moving. And there was little stomach to do that after the Raiders debacle. The door seemed to widen for team owners dissatisfied with their home stadiums and wanting to move.

When the Davis court decision was announced, Irsay said: "I don't think the implication is that every team is a free agent. As for myself, I'm happy in Baltimore ... I feel confident that there's a future for the Colts in Baltimore. I think we're all going to be sticking with the cities we've already got."

• • •

In 1980, at the height of the Raiders uproar, Schaefer brought the downtown stadium idea back to life briefly. He unveiled a scaled-down plan to build the Orioles a 45,000-seat, open-air stadium at Camden Yards and to fix up Memorial Stadium for the Colts.

But, like the first go-round, the idea went nowhere.

The election of President Reagan that year brought deep cuts in federal aid, essentially shutting off Baltimore's lifeline to capital and development grants. In the fall of 1980, Maryland Governor Harry Hughes, a former minor-league baseball player from the state's rural Eastern Shore, said he wouldn't support the use of public money other than low-interest, state-backed construction loans, for the building of a sports stadium.

The only hope was if one or both of the teams came up with their own money. Williams considered the idea and called a friend: Cleveland Browns owner Art Modell. The two talked about jointly developing a stadium; rumor had it that they liked Columbia, Md., in nearby suburban Howard County, as a site.

Modell, then operating Cleveland's Municipal Stadium, knew the pitfalls and potentials of stadium management. Early on, Williams told city business leaders that he and Modell could make money on a new stadium.

"I took a cursory look. It gave me a better feel for the area," Modell told a reporter in 1980. "It's very, very tentative. Nothing has been determined or even planned."

Williams said, "I have talked to Art, who is an old, old friend of mine. He's tremendously familiar with stadiums as a result of operating the Cleveland stadium, and I discussed various leases with him."

Williams apparently decided the numbers didn't work and announced later that he wasn't going to build the stadium himself.

The chances of funding a new stadium appeared remote.

After that, Schaefer modified his goal. Instead of trying to build a new stadium, he and his aides decided on what they considered a more cost-effective remedy: to fix up the existing stadium and cut the rent. In 1980, the state legislature, at Hughes' and Schaefer's urging, approved a $22 million package of improvements contingent on getting both teams to sign long-term leases.

But neither team would.

In 1981, the Colts and Schaefer signed a two-year lease that was one of the best in football: The rent would be 1 percent of the first $1 million in revenue, 2 percent of the second $1 million, 3 percent of the third $1 million, and 10 percent of revenues above $3.5 million. The signing seemed to avert disaster, and even Irsay said he expected it to result in a long-term lease some time in the coming year. The Colts would now have the lowest rent in the NFL, outside of Green Bay, Wis., though the lease was good only through 1984.

"The Colts are here to stay," Irsay said, adding reassuringly that Memorial Stadium was one of the "best built" stadiums in the country.

The Orioles, however, saw things differently. In 1982, they announced they would only sign one-year deals until their stadium situation was permanently improved. Williams didn't think much of the renovation plan then under consideration. Adding seats would help the Colts, but diminish the atmosphere for baseball, he figured. He continued to push for a new park.

The legislature's $22 million renovation package expired, unspent, after an extension.

Then, in 1983, Schaefer got the legislature to agree to pay for a scaled-down, $15 million renovation. He also tried to separate the negotiations. He offered each team up to $7.5 million for stadium work, and tried to get the teams to agree on what was to be done. The negotiations were arduous, with each team insisting on parity and resisting items demanded by the other.

After one meeting with Irsay and Williams on Dec. 19, 1983, Schaefer wrote notes to himself: "I had high hopes for the meeting. Beginning was awkward and tense, and, finally, I suggested we review possible areas of agreement … Irsay will not sign a lease, and I am of the opinion he will move the Colts from Baltimore …. Results of the meeting from my standpoint — totally unsatisfactory and there seems no possibility for continuation of negotiations."

In January 1984, the Orioles signed a three-year deal with the city. Schaefer maintained publicly that Memorial Stadium could be made to work.

"We're not going to build a new stadium. We don't have the bonding capacity. We don't have the voters or the taxpayers who can support a $60 million stadium. One-third of the people in Baltimore pay taxes. Unless private enterprise builds it, we won't build it," Schaefer said.

• • •

Over the next few months, Schaefer and Hughes endured one humiliation after another. The two ferried offers and counteroffers to Irsay, who was rumored to be cutting a deal elsewhere. Meanwhile, the Colts pointedly did not send out applications for season-ticket renewals. A receptionist was taking names for a waiting list.

Irsay's wanderlust grew so severe that the *Baltimore News-American* began running a daily "Irsay Watch" box with topics such as "What City Irsay's in."

In January 1984, Irsay opened negotiations with an Arizona real estate developer about moving or selling the club. At one point, he ordered Arizona Governor Bruce Babbitt and other top state officials to meet him secretly at a hotel in Bakersfield, Calif. The Arizona delegates left the meeting feeling they were "about 80 percent there."

But a few days later, on Jan. 20, 1984, another meeting was abruptly canceled by the team owner when word leaked out. Irsay instead flew to Baltimore aboard his private plane and convened a rambling, disjointed — many believe drunken — session with reporters at Baltimore-Washington International Airport. Schaefer stood by his side as Irsay swung his hands wildly in the air and alternately denied any talks with Arizona officials and accused reporters of "hanging" him.

"I have not any intention to move the goddamn team. If I did, I would tell you about it," Irsay said.

"If you love the Colts, why don't you treat me right? I'm going to send you some articles ..... You want me here, why do you hang me? Why do you hang me for?"

Irsay eventually disappeared into a meeting room, where he talked with Schaefer for about 10 minutes.

When he emerged, Schaefer was uncharacteristically reserved. "He's one of the most interesting men I've ever met. You never know what he'll say," the mayor said.

Despite the spectacle, Schaefer said he was encouraged by the meeting with Irsay and the prospects for keeping the team. The mayor asked, and the team owner agreed, that Irsay would call him personally before moving the team. It was a pledge they repeated each time they saw each other over the last few months of negotiations.

"We're going to work hard to keep the Colts here. And I'll tell you, if they go, trying to get an expansion team is one difficult thing. So don't think it's any easier if the Colts go," Schaefer warned.

Then he asked the reporters to lighten up on the team owner. "If we could just be a little more gentle, maybe it would work both ways," he plaintively suggested.

In February, a desperate Schaefer again asked local church and community leaders around Memorial Stadium to permit Sunday games to start at 1 p.m. The Colts' 2 p.m. kickoffs kept them off of a lot of network broadcasts, most of which were scheduled for 1 p.m. and 4 p.m. tune-in times. In Irsay's mind, the Colts' inability to be like the other teams symbolized Baltimore's inhospitality.

Schaefer proposed an ordinance to repeal the city's blue law and to change the game times, but eventually withdrew it in favor of state legislative action. That bill, submitted by a suburban Baltimore senator because of lingering opposition in the city, passed on March 19, 1984.

On financial matters, Schaefer for the city and Hughes for the state tried every which way to be flexible. But both said that every time they satisfied one of Irsay's demands, another one popped up.

"When you had a meeting with Irsay, it was like you never had the one before it. It was like starting all over again," Hughes recalled years later.

On March 11, Schaefer, Hughes, and Baltimore County Executive Donald Hutchinson even flew to Chicago to deliver in-person a package of inducements to Irsay. The team owner surprised them by asking for something new: a ticket guarantee, which, it turned out, Indianapolis had offered. A few days later, Irsay was in California, meeting again with the governor of Arizona.

Ten days after his West Coast session, in a secret meeting at Washington's National Airport, Irsay received a sweetened offer from the Maryland delegation. Hughes was represented by his economic development chief, Frank De Francis.

"Frank came back and reported to me optimism and confidence. His words were, 'We've got him. We've met all his demands,'" Hughes said.

The final offer called for spending the $7.5 million already approved on Memorial Stadium. It also gave the Colts ticket-sale guarantees equal to 43,000 and a $15 million loan at below-market interest rates (coming due was the loan Irsay took out to buy the team). The city also agreed to buy the team's suburban training complex for $4.4 million and rent it to the team for $1 a year.

But Indianapolis, a newly emerging city as hungry for sports as Baltimore had been 30 years earlier, had something better: a new, $80 million, domed stadium.

The Hoosierdome had 61,300 seats (colored, by coincidence, Colt blue), a fabric roof held aloft by giant electric fans, and, best of all, a ring of "skyboxes." These suites permitted corporations to host a dozen or so favored clients in a private, elegant setting. Each box resembled a luxury hotel room, with upholstered furniture, a small wet bar, private bathroom, and framed art on the walls Though not new, these corporate suites were still an oddity in sports. Some teams had convinced their landlords to retrotrofit them into their stadiums, generally adding them on top of the seating bowl high above the field — hence the name "skybox." A new stadium, like the Hoosierdome, could do a bit better. They were built right into the structure.

Their role in upending the sport's economics was not yet obvious. For Irsay, they would prove a nice source of additional revenue. In another decade or two, they would be seen as essential to a team as shoulderpads and lawyers.

The Hoosierdome had been in the works for years and was to be a centerpiece of the city's downtown redevelopment plans. Officials had met with Irsay as early as 1977 to discuss the project, but by early 1984, no tenant had been signed, and Indianapolis was planning to hold an NFL pre-season game there in 1985 to show it off. They were anxious to keep it from becoming a white elephant.

Colts officials secretly toured the dome on Feb. 13, 1984. Irsay himself visited on Feb. 23, less than a month after his volatile press conference with Schaefer in which he swore he was not shopping the team. The talks progressed on and off as reports surfaced that Irsay was also meeting with leaders in Phoenix and New York, where the Colts presumably would play in Shea Stadium.

By late March, Indianapolis and the Colts were close to a deal. Leading the talks for the Midwestern city was Mayor William H. Hudnut. He once had been a Presbyterian minister in Annapolis, Md., and used to sneak up Sunday afternoons to see the Colts play. He would buy an obstructed-view seat at Memorial Stadium and lean around a pillar to catch a glimpse of Unitas lining up a receiver.

But this was business.

"We didn't steal the Colts," Hudnut would later argue. "Baltimore lost them."

Indianapolis negotiators were anxiously awaiting the final signature of the team owner when an attorney for the Colts noticed in *The Sun* on Wednesday, March 28, a news brief headlined "Senate OKs eminent domain."

Baltimore city officials, growing pessimistic about the Colts negotiations, were trying to beef up the city's already substantial powers of eminent domain, which allow it to seize property deemed necessary for the public good. The proposed legislation would allow the city to seize the team the way it seized land for a highway — paying the owner "fair market value."

The bill passed the Senate on March 27, but still needed to clear the House of Delegates. But seeing it move from one body to the other was enough to spook Irsay.

Colts general counsel Michael Chernoff said Irsay called him that day and asked if he'd seen the news item. He had. Irsay told him: "Implement. We're moving to Indianapolis."

Irsay called Indianapolis' bargainers and said they had a deal.

The lease was for 20 years with optional extensions. The team would get all the revenue from ticket sales, except for taxes, and half the income from skybox rentals. Some game-day expenses, such as providing medical crews and post-game clean-up, would be picked up by Indianapolis. The team was promised $25,000 for moving expenses. (Mayflower, headquartered outside of Indianapolis, actually moved the Colts for free. The team kept the money.)

Stadium rent would be $250,000 a year, and the team would be guaranteed $7 million a year from tickets and local broadcast rights, equal to about 40,000 ticket sales per game. A $3-million-to-$4-million training complex would be built and rented to the team for $15,000 a year, and the team would get a $12.5 million loan at below-market rates.

By Indianapolis's official estimate, the deal would cost the city's stadium authority about $1.2 million a year, but the team would pay $2.6 million in rent and ticket taxes — netting the city a profit of $1.4 million.

The Colts did even better. The team went from $19.5 million in revenues in its last season in Baltimore to $26.3 million the next year in Indianapolis — a 35 percent increase.

Its operating profit, a robust $7.2 million, was the highest in the NFL that year. The owners of other NFL teams couldn't help but notice what a new stadium could do for the bottom line.

• • •

Once Irsay decided to move, team officials wanted to get out of town quickly, before a judge could slap an order on them to stop. So moving vans began pulling up at the Colts' Owings Mills, Md., training center late on Wednesday during a wet, spring snowstorm. On Chernoff's advice, the first van was loaded with the business records that he thought had the greatest legal weight. All of the trucks took slightly different routes out of the state to stay ahead of the long arm of Maryland law. They were met at the Indiana line by state troopers who escorted them safely into Indianapolis.

Most Colts employees and players had not been informed of the move and were not there when the gear was loaded and hauled out of town. Someone tipped off the media, however, and the ignoble scene of an NFL franchise sneaking out of its hometown was captured for posterity on videotape.

Among those who gathered by the side of the road to watch the strange scene was a teary-eyed "Loudy" Loudenslager, the Colts' No. 1 Fan.

"It is heartbreaking. I'm so hurt, so humiliated … ," Loudy said. "The removing of the equipment at night was so low class that it was ridiculous."

The next morning, Schaefer told reporters: "How can you do this to a city with a tradition like we have with the Baltimore Colts? To be able to just come in and take the team away from you, just take it away; there's something wrong with that."

Because there was no one around to heckle the Colts, many Baltimore fans took their frustration out on Mayflower. Though the company's local franchise had not been involved in the move, company' employees received telephone threats, and some company trucks and vans were stoned. Fans boycotted the line. To make amends, the company offered free service for years to the Colts band, which now would be marching without its team. It turned out to be a longer march (and a larger gift) than anyone expected.

Bumper stickers and T-shirts soon appeared in Baltimore saying, "Will Rogers never met Bob Irsay." A cartoon in *The Sun* compared the Colts' 1958 game against the New York Giants, "the greatest game ever played," with the moving trucks pulling out of town in the dark. "The dirtiest trick ever played," the cartoon said.

Unitas said of Irsay, "It's just what that sneaky guy would do. It's degrading to himself and puts him in a lot lesser position than he had. During the past 12 years, he ran the best franchise in football into the ground."

The city tried the predictable lawsuits and public persuasion, but to no avail. Hughes signed the eminent domain bill the day after the team left, and the city tried to condemn the team. But a judge threw out the case on the grounds that the team was already gone. Hearings were convened in Congress and calls made to tighten the antitrust screws on the NFL, but nothing came to pass.

Schaefer warned his colleagues across the country: "All mayors [with] professional football teams, baseball teams, beware." When the Colts suddenly departed for Indianapolis, the NFL was still reeling from the Raiders case. The verdict against the league had come back in May 1982, but the separate proceedings to calculate damages were still under way. The damage award came down about a month after the Colts departed. Irsay merely reported the move at the league's meetings and sat down, with no formal vote asked for or taken.

The Colts' relocation had a profound effect on Baltimore's

political leaders. Schaefer would spend the rest of his career trying to remedy the wrong. Support for the new stadiums' construction grew, and the seeds of Camden Yards were sown.

That fall, by a 62-percent to 38-percent margin, city voters repealed the 10-year-old charter amendment restricting stadium spending to Memorial Stadium. Leaders of the repeal movement, dubbed "Fans for a Plex," hailed the vote as the first step toward a new, multiplex stadium in Baltimore.

NFL historian Robert Barnett of West Virginia's Marshall University said Irsay will be remembered as the owner who brought to the NFL the wholesale relocation of franchises for profit.

"[Al] Davis was a football man, but Irsay ushered in the era of the entrepreneurial owner who wanted not only to make money, but make lots of it," Barnett said.

Among those complaining most loudly about Irsay's move was Art Modell.

"I feel for the Baltimore fans. I grew up in the era when Baltimore ruled the roost. It's a great sports town. I'm not sitting in judgment on whether Bob Irsay is right or wrong. What concerns me is where the league is going," Modell said.

"This is the legacy of the Raiders' move. Baltimore is paying for it now and others might in the future."

Browns owner Art Modell *slouches grimly at a Baltimore press conference on the morning of November 6, 1995. Thanks to a new state-of-the-art stadium promised for his team, he was now $75 million richer, but the longtime Browns owner looked anything but happy.*

Maryland Governor Parris Glendening, *usually quite adept at calculating action and reaction, grins and waves a Browns' mug on the morning of the press conference announcing the team's move to Baltimore. It was one of many actions that led reporters to dub him "Governor Gloat-dening."*

On the day of the big announcement, **Maryland's former governor, William Donald Schaefer, and Browns owner Art Modell** *shake hands like colleagues of old. No one, except Schaefer's successor, forgot how valiantly he, as Baltimore's mayor and as Maryland's governor, had fought to bring a football team back to Baltimore.*

Art Modell, Paul Brown, and R.J. Schaefer *laugh and smile in 1961 as they sign documents making them the new owners of the Browns. Less than two years later, Modell and Brown were no longer on speaking terms. Modell's unexpected firing of Brown forced the head coach to leave a team he'd loved and shaped for decades.*

Bernie Kosar passes to his nearest eligible receiver as the Cleveland Browns move downfield against archrival Pittsburgh Steelers. Kosar, an Ohio native and a favorite of many Cleveland football fans, was one of numerous Browns treated as tradable commodities during the team's final years in Cleveland. When Modell finally let Kosar loose, asserting that his quarterbacking skills had declined, a great many Cleveland fans were sure the owner had completely lost touch with them.

*The image of **Mayflower vans, packed with Colts' business records** and deserting Baltimore in the middle of the night in March 1984, would long haunt Baltimore's leaders and football fans.*

*Seated with **then-mayor Schaefer, owner Robert Irsay** angrily informs the press that his Colts have no intention of leaving their Baltimore home. Just two months later, despite repeated promises to "call his old friend Don" before taking precipitous action, Irsay pulled the trigger, accepting a lucrative deal from Indianapolis, Indiana.*

Photo originally appeared in The Baltimore Sun

lfred Lerner, a Cleveland businessman, played ajor roles in bringing the Browns to Baltimore. ecause of his Baltimore roots and his NFL ties, was Gov. Schaefer's reluctant, last minute andidate for expansion team owner presented NFL team owners displeased with Maryland's arlier owner selections. As Baltimore remained otball-less, though, Lerner turned his efforts to cting as an intermediary between Cleveland and altimore, and to encourage Art Modell, his friend nd business associate, to accept Baltimore's nd Maryland's lucrative stadium offer.

Baltimore Mayor Kurt Schmoke, a Rhodes scholar and high-school football player, backed state-led efforts to bring football back to Baltimore, despite his belief that Baltimore needed to spend more money on repairing a fallen city than on having a home football team.

AP/Wide World Photos

eveland gave the Indians **Jacobs Field**, later alled the "Jake." The new baseball-only stadium as so enriching to team owners that they quick- assembled a pricey but World Series-bound anchise. Modell, left with the decrepit Municipal tadium, felt great bitterness. The Indians played the spacious, state-of-the-art, publicly funded ke, while his team was still being offered "ren- ations only" to Municipal Stadium.

Ohio Governor George Voinovich was a longtime friend and ally of Modell. The team owner had contributed financially to Voinovich's various political campaigns, including several successful bids to be Cleveland's mayor. A concerned Gov. Voinovich made personal contact with Modell but failed to organize a plan to keep the Browns from leaving Cleveland and Ohio.

(From left to right) **Mathias J. DeVito, Gov. William Donald Schaefer, Mayor Kurt L. Schmoke, and Stadium Authority chairman Herbert J. Belgrad** head dejectedly to the airport after hearing the NFL's decision against them in November 1993. Of the many defeats these men faced in trying to bring footba~~ back to their hometown of Baltimore, this one was particularly bitter. They had counted on Modell and Lerner to push for Baltimore, but the Cleveland businessmen actually argued and worked against the city

Herbert Belgrad (left), chairman of the Maryland Stadium Authority, tries to discuss Baltimore's expansion chances with **NFL official Joe Ellis**. Ellis was one of the league executives to inform Baltimore an~ the other bidding cities that Jacksonville had won a much-coveted franchise.

Part 2

Adapting to Change

CHAPTER SIX

Modell
Flunks
Stadium Economics

During the 1980s, the National Football League that Art Modell had lovingly fathered through a difficult infancy grew into a strong but unruly adolescent.

The NFL was the richest sports league in the world and Modell's franchise one of the most valuable. But the league was bickering in court with its players, and some owners were suing other owners over the very principles that had made the league great. A shift in economics was also distorting the old order, forcing teams to think more about their stadiums than the fans seated in them.

In Cleveland, too, Modell's magic touch seemed to be fading. The Cleveland Stadium deal that he struck with the city proved to be a colossal mistake. His health began to fail. Even his son, David, fell into a serious drug habit, acknowledging a marijuana and cocaine problem in 1982 and checking into a rehab center in La Jolla, Calif.

But the NFL was still growing.

A 1983 survey by CBS and *The New York Times* showed that 53 percent of the nation's sports fans considered football their favorite spectator sport, compared with 18 percent who rated baseball their top choice.

By the mid 1980s, NFL games were averaging more than

59,000 people, and the league's stadiums were better than 92 percent full on Sunday afternoons. Total attendance was now more than 13 million a season.

Television ratings were also hitting new heights, as were broadcast fees. The networks shelled out $169 million in 1981, $211 million in 1982, $316 million in 1983, and $434 million in 1984. There seemed to be no end to the money.

But the riches of those deals only seemed to drive up expectations and to foster infighting within the closeted meetings of the once collegial team owners. The fight over relocation was especially bitter and costly.

The Raiders lawsuit had opened the floodgates, and the Colts were the first to take advantage of the legal ambiguity. Then, in 1987, the Cardinals abandoned St. Louis. Busch Stadium, one of the most ambitious of the two-sport stadiums built in the late 1960s and early 1970s, was proving itself economically obsolete. The fans, too, stayed away from the losing team and its ugly-duckling stadium — especially after owner Bill Bidwill made it clear he was thinking of moving. Game days saw the place half-full at best. And the stadium was run by the baseball Cardinals, a humiliation the emergent NFL need no longer accept. Bidwill, a member of one of the league's founding families, formally requested approval to move to Phoenix, which he obtained despite a hostile report from the commissioner. He was promised skyboxes in a renovated college bowl, and, he said, a new stadium eventually.

The implications to other cities weren't immediately obvious. But in all three cases — the Raiders, the Colts and the Cardinals — the teams were moving in search not of bigger cities or more enthusiastic fans, but of better stadiums. The playing venue had moved from a secondary consideration to the primary one.

The new cities offered skyboxes and facilities that wouldn't be shared with a baseball franchise. The era of dual-purpose stadiums and of the NFL's second-class citizenship was coming to an end. And taxpayers would soon be paying the price.

Davis and his Raider franchise remained in the vanguard of the movement. In 1987, Davis decided that Los Angeles had not lived up to its end of the bargain and declared his Coliseum lease void. He then talked with Oakland officials about returning.

That spring, Davis announced his intention to move his team

to the tiny L.A. suburb of Irwindale, which had parlayed tax revenues from the local gravel mining industry into vast riches and was now spending them liberally on economic development. Irwindale offered to build a stadium for the Raiders in an old gravel pit.

After Davis agreed to move, the city forwarded him a $10 million down payment on a larger loan to come. T-shirts were printed up, and local football fans celebrated. But the deal soon fell apart, and Davis legally kept the $10 million. Three years later, another announced move of the Raiders — this time back to Oakland — also collapsed.

Fans everywhere wondered if it was safe to love their team any more.

Meanwhile, the players were generating more worry for the owners. The NFL Players Association, seeking a larger piece of the league's enormous economic pie, grew more and more militant.

The owner-player relationship had always been testy. In 1964, when Colts defensive end Ordell Braase was elected the association's president, the owners refused to meet with him or other association officers. But Braase thought the players should at least have representation on the NFL's pension board, which at the time voted on whether to grant or deny an individual player a pension.

"We were fragmented to begin with, and the owners did a good job of keeping it that way," Braase said.

To get his nose inside the tent, Braase met with Baltimore labor attorney, A. Samuel Cook, and together they assembled a plan. Buffeted by increasingly public and embarrassing player complaints, Rozelle had invited the player association's representatives to join with him and team owners after the 1965 owners' meetings in Miami Beach.

Braase, on Cook's advice, accepted the invitation with an innocuous but legally significant telegram. The meeting, he wrote back, would be held to discuss the pension plan "and other matters affecting the employment condition of players."

Cook told Braase that under federal labor law, the association would automatically become recognized as a union if the owners merely negotiated a few points at the meeting.

When the player reps showed up at the Ivanhoe Hotel in Miami Beach, the owners were already there, seated around a

U-shaped table with spaces next to them reserved for their teams' player representatives. The obviously scripted meeting, chaired by Rozelle, began with Chicago Bears owner George Halas delivering a speech about how the game was bigger than all of them. Other owners, including Modell, followed up, urging cooperation.

Braase then spoke, proposing that a player replace Rozelle on the pension board. Several owners voiced outrage at the notion that players couldn't trust Rozelle to look after their best interests. The volume went up. Green Bay Packer player rep Dan Currie noticed that team executive and coach Vince Lombardi was writing "Currie" on his legal pad and crossing it out, over and over again. Two weeks later, Currie was traded to the Rams.

"It was an interesting time. I'm not going to say we got a lot accomplished, but we got our foot in the door," Braase recalled. According to his lawyer, the association could now claim bargaining rights, and the claim would stand up in court.

The owners, whether bowing to that legal certitude or just to inevitability, eventually agreed to negotiate. Modell, chairman of the NFL's labor committee, sent the Players Association a telegram in early 1968: "We will, of course, abide by the wishes of the players. We are prepared to meet with you and your associates at a mutually convenient time and place to discuss the procedures to be followed in determining the wishes of the players, regarding a representative for the purpose of collective bargaining."

In 1971, the Players Association became the first union of athletes certified by the National Labor Relations Board.

By the early 1980s, the players no longer concerned themselves merely with improving pensions. The teams were making big money, and the players wanted more of it. During 1982 discussions with the league, they demanded more freedom of movement; they wanted to be able to sell their services to the highest bidder. The players proposed a radical idea: that the team owners set aside 55 percent of their television and ticket revenue for player salaries, to be distributed according to seniority and incentives.

The owners rejected outright the idea of such revenue-sharing.

"The players want a bigger voice in the conduct of our sport, contrary to our view that management rights belong to management," Modell said.

"It was obvious that, when they first started talking about

wanting 55 percent of the gross, they wanted control," he continued. "Is that what we've come to, rewarding a player for longevity instead of achievement and production? If it is, it's the end of the game as we have come to know it."

A 57-day strike delayed the start of the 1982 season. When it was settled, the players had more money, but not revenue-sharing or any of the other structural changes they had sought. The new bargaining contract did establish minimum salaries based on experience, however, and also boosted player benefits.

In disgust over the dispute, fans stayed away from some games, but attendance soon revived and grew again.

Then in 1987, the NFL train lurched to another stop. Contract talks with the players again broke down, and the players walked out two games into the season. This time, though, the owners were ready. They hired replacement players, a ragtag collection of wannabes who were roundly derided by the public.

But the games counted in the standings, and the association got the message. After 24 days, enough players had crossed the picket line that the union gave up and went back to the drawing board.

If they couldn't win on the picket line, the players decided, they would try to win in court by attacking the league's fragile antitrust status. If the NFL truly was a collection of individual companies, as the judge had ruled in the Oakland Raiders case, then its systematic collusion to control salaries through a college draft and team trading rules must be illegal.

But the players struck out. Under antitrust law, even competing companies can jointly agree on what to pay employees so long as the workers give their OK through a collective bargaining agreement. This is commonly done in so-called multiemployer agreements. For example, competing construction companies can form an association to negotiate uniform wage rates for carpenters, masons, and other skilled workers. Bargaining takes place with the union on one side and the association on the other.

In 1988, a federal judge ruled that so long as the NFL players were represented by a union, they could not claim that team owners had violated antitrust laws. Subsequent decisions ruled that the players wouldn't have a case after the contract's expiration because a collective bargaining "process" would still be under way.

The players then settled upon an unorthodox strategy. If their union was shielding the NFL from antitrust violations, then they would eliminate the union. So, in November 1989, the NFL Players Association notified the NLRB that it was forfeiting its right to bargain collectively on behalf of the players. In essence, the association said it was no longer a union, but a voluntary professional association.

In 1991, the association filed yet another lawsuit, this time on behalf of New York Jets running back Freeman McNeil and seven other players. It charged that these players' salaries had been illegally depressed by the NFL's restrictions on free agency. In response, the NFL argued that players like McNeil were getting plenty. Though ranked 45th among running backs in 1990, McNeil received a base salary of $850,000. Over his 11 seasons in the league, he had been paid $7 million.

For a few sensational weeks in 1992, the NFL's most closely guarded financial secrets — from coaches' pay to the bonuses that team owners paid themselves — were laid out for the jury and the public. Experts hired by the union to cull through financial records said that the 28 teams' pretax operating profits had grown from $1 billion in 1989 to $1.3 billion in 1990 to $1.4 billion in 1991. The teams' actual combined profits, after taxes and interest on debt, came to $170 million, the union said.

Union experts also estimated that the team owners had paid themselves between $50 million and $60 million in salaries from 1987 to 1990 — an annual average of about $500,000 — and had disguised these payouts as operating expenses. This was on top of any team profit the owner wanted to claim.

Philadelphia Eagles owner Norman Braman, for example, paid himself $7.5 million in 1990 — the only money, he said, that he had ever made in seven years of ownership. Modell paid himself $195,000 that year, Irsay $312,000.

The league numbers in 1990 showed an average profit of $5.8 million per team, although Stanford University economist Roger Noll testified for the union that the actual profits were probably much higher — perhaps as high as $15 million, if expenses such as owner compensation were properly accounted for.

The McNeil jury deliberated for 16 hours over two days before ruling in favor of the players on Sept. 10, 1992. It awarded actual damages of $1.6 million.

U.S. District Judge David Doty delayed issuing a punitive-damage ruling and specific orders to restructure the game, urging the two sides to negotiate a settlement. He assured both that they would find elements of his judgment not to their liking if they left these decisions to him. Finally, in 1993, with Doty's gavel hanging over their heads, the league and the Players Association reached agreement.

The pact was a breakthrough, providing the Holy Grail that each side had sought for generations. The owners got a cap on salaries, so that no team could provoke a disastrous bidding war for players. And the players got much broader free-agency rights. After four years in the league, they could sell their services to the highest bidder.

Only the National Basketball Association had achieved a salary cap in professional athletics, and it had saved that league. The NFL's cap, like the NBA's, was tied to league revenues, thus guaranteeing players a share of the sport's revenue growth.

Here's how it works: The NFL annually adds up all the money it receives from ticket sales and network and local television and radio deals (their largest sources of income) and creates a pool of "designated gross revenue." To calculate an average amount per team, the pool is then divided by the number of clubs. A payroll floor and ceiling are then calculated by multiplying the average designated team revenue by 50 percent and 62 percent. Each team has to pay at least the lower figure, and cannot spend more than the higher one — in theory, anyway.

The agreement had a dramatic and immediate impact on the league. Although team owners no longer had to worry about an unrestricted salary spiral, they did have to bid against one another for top talent. Total salaries quickly climbed to the maximum allowed under the cap. Between 1990 and 1995, the average player's salary in the NFL nearly doubled. Though football players still lagged behind multimillionaire baseball players, they were getting closer.

The new rules also changed the way the NFL owners got rich and won games. No longer would bare-bones player payrolls — a specialty of the Colts' Bob Irsay — be the path to riches. Each team would have to meet the minimum payroll.

But neither would the clubs be locked into a spiraling arms race for free agents. In theory, the Green Bays of the football world would be able to compete on the field with the New York Giants.

• • •

Agreement or no agreement, Art Modell was feeling the squeeze from his stadium deal. Municipal Stadium had turned out to be a bigger money drain than he had imagined in 1974, the year he signed the 25-year lease with Cleveland.

The city came out OK. The deal saved it the expense of operating and improving the fast-deteriorating relic. Modell had agreed to pay a minimum rent that would equal at least the city's debt service and presumed property taxes. And he had to spend $10 million on stadium improvements.

The deal was also supposed to cut the city in on the profits of the Browns' good years. In practice, the complicated formula assured the team's retention of those extra revenues.

In a 1982 report to the city, consultants Coopers & Lybrand nonetheless figured that Cleveland came out ahead about $1.7 million a year — in taxes, rent paid, and savings on interest payments that it would have incurred had it paid for the renovations.

For a few years, Modell, too, seemed to do well under the arrangement. A year after taking over the stadium, he sold the Strongville land to his Cleveland Stadium Corp. for more than $3 million. This represented a substantial profit: He had paid only $625,000 for the suburban property two years earlier.

As chairman of both the Stadium Corp. and the Browns, Modell had significant control of both entities. But not all of the investors shared in both corporations. The team derived its revenue largely from ticket sales and radio and TV contracts. The Stadium Corp. paid for the construction of skyboxes and other structural improvements and drew its monies from stadium advertising, rents, and other stadium-related sources.

By the early 1980s, though, everything seemed to be coming apart. The Cleveland Indians, one of the worst teams in baseball throughout the 1970s and 1980s, were barely averaging 11,000 fans a game, thus cutting into the Stadium Corp.'s rental income. Other Modell investments were also failing in a hurry.

And the variable interest rate on Modell's fix-up-the-stadium loan had shot up to 21 percent. The debt service was now 100 percent of the stadium's cash flow, despite the additional income from the skyboxes he had installed.

Modell said his interest payments, repair bills, and operating costs on the stadium were so high that he would gladly hand over the lease for $1 to anyone willing to take over his debt.

There were no takers.

So Modell turned to his most valuable asset: the Browns. For $6 million, he sold the team his stadium corporation and its Strongville land title. Despite his earlier claims that the deal was costing him money, Modell later insisted the sales price was justified because of refinancing by the stadium's concessionaire.

The Browns' board of directors, stocked with Modell's employees and associates, approved the purchase in 1981.

Only one board member dissented: Robert Gries, son of Robert H. Gries, who had helped Modell buy the team. In 1966, when his father died, the younger Gries inherited responsibility for his family's Browns investment. A Yale graduate and investment banker, Gries enjoyed mountain climbing and long-distance running, and he didn't mind playing a quiet role in the Browns — at least until the stadium deal came up.

Because his family owned 43 percent of the team's stock, but had not invested in the Stadium Corp., Robert Gries complained that the team paid at least $3 million more than the deal was worth. But Modell stood by the $6 million assessment, made by a Cleveland investment firm whose top executives were among his close friends.

Gries was especially skeptical of the Strongsville purchase. He commissioned appraisals of the land that came in at less than $700,000, a fraction of what the team paid and less than one-fifth of Modell's $3.8 million valuation. Gries was also unhappy with Modell's new compensation package, which obligated the team to pay its owner more than $200,000 a year.

The low-key Gries, whose role in the team was a virtual secret in Cleveland, filed a series of blockbuster lawsuits in 1982. And all hell broke loose.

First, he challenged the $6 million purchase price of the Stadium Corp., accusing Modell of lining his own pockets and saddling the team with unbearable debt just as it was facing a players' strike.

Three months later, Gries accused Modell of failing to call regular board meetings and excluding the minority stockholder from the team's business decisions. Finally, he infuriated Modell by accusing him of improperly giving himself a big raise, tripling his base pay of $60,000, and of harassing Gries.

Gries termed Modell's management style "one man autocratic" rule and demanded an audit of the team's expense accounts.

Modell stood by his appraisal of the stadium corporation purchase, said the Browns didn't need regular meetings because he kept in touch with investors, and claimed his new compensation deal merely kept up with revenue growth.

In a letter to Gries in May 1982, Modell said, "I have no idea what your motivations are and, frankly, don't care .... You have chosen to create an adversary relationship and to publicize it to the hilt."

The Gries-Modell combat was the talk of Cleveland and the NFL. Several years of messy litigation tarnished Modell's carefully tended image of competency and honesty. Reporters who had once swooned over his glib quotes were now questioning his finances and his honor.

Not to be outdone, the Indians got into the act. The baseball team — which Modell years earlier had hoped would become a Stadium Corp. partner — began negotiating with the Browns owner to replace its 10-year lease.

The bargaining got ugly. Modell publicly accused the baseball team of trying to pry a subsidy out of him. An Indians executive replied by calling Modell's proposal "a sham."

The dispute landed in court in April 1983 when the Indians filed the first of several lawsuits. They accused Modell and the Cleveland Stadium Corp. of bilking the baseball team out of $1.25 million in concession revenue.

Modell refused an audit of the concessions and balked at negotiating a new lease until the Indians settled the suit and apologized.

Then, in a federal lawsuit, the Indians claimed that Modell was effectively barring them from the only stadium in town, and thus violating antitrust laws.

By settling the suits, the Indians ended up getting a better lease. But the fighting took its toll on Modell. He suffered a heart attack in June 1983 and was rushed into quadruple bypass surgery at the Cleveland Clinic Hospital, a prominent institution that he would later head as board president. Two days after his surgery, Modell had another operation to correct complications. He reduced his involvement in Browns' affairs and recuperated while his attorneys battled Gries all the way to the Ohio Supreme Court.

There they lost. Modell was forced in 1986 to buy the stadium corporation back and to hold regular stockholders' meetings. Under the judge's guidance, Gries and Modell settled their third case, setting up an arbitration procedure to handle future disputes.

Modell also had to pay Gries $1 million for legal expenses. Loan documents filed with the Ohio and New York secretaries of state at the time reveal heavy borrowing by Modell, with just about everything used as collateral, from NFL TV rights to camera equipment at the Browns' television studios. Although league rules limited how much he could borrow against the team, they didn't limit borrowing by the Stadium Corp. And the Browns and Modell took full advantage of the loophole.

Salvation for Modell came in the form of Alfred Lerner, a cigar-chomping, self-made millionaire who would play a major role in the future of the Browns and Baltimore. Lerner had bought some radio stations with Modell in the 1970s, and the two had become fast friends. In 1986, he bought half of the Stadium Corp. and 5 percent of the Browns.

Born in New York in 1933 to a pair of Russian immigrants, Lerner earned a bachelor's degree from Columbia University before signing up for a peacetime stint as a Marine pilot. He got his start in business in Baltimore as a $75-a-week factory sales representative for Ethan Allen furniture, where he impressed co-workers as smart and hard-working. He had a photographic memory, a voracious appetite for reading, and a flair for extravagance: He smoked expensive cigars and drove Cadillacs. He also told friends he would be a millionaire by the time he was 35.

Lerner moved from Baltimore to Cleveland and began dabbling in real estate. He formed Realty ReFund Trust, which specialized in debt refinancing of successful buildings, and made a bundle. He also became one of Baltimore's biggest landlords with a $180 million purchase of apartments in Maryland and

Pennsylvania through Town and Country Management.

In 1981, he and some partners made a run at Equitable Bancorporation, Baltimore's third largest bank. The bank fought back with a lawsuit impugning Lerner and his partners. In settling the case, the bank agreed to let Lerner, but not his partners, buy 27 percent of Equitable's stock for $29.5 million.

For the most part, Lerner stayed away from the bank he now partly owned, letting its president, H. Grant Hathaway, a Johns Hopkins graduate and longtime Equitable banker, run the show. The two men stressed simple banking fundamentals, and Equitable doubled in size and its profits hit new highs.

His taste for banking whetted, Lerner and Progressive Corp., a Cleveland auto insurance company, made a run at Ameritrust Corp., one of the Ohio city's biggest banks. Ameritrust — run by some of the bluest blue bloods in Cleveland — panicked. It ended up paying Lerner and his partners more than $30 million just to go away.

The next year, Lerner invested $75 million in Progressive and found himself on *Forbes* magazine's list of the 400 richest Americans, with an estimated worth of $230 million.

In 1989, Equitable agreed to a buyout by MNC Financial Inc., the parent company of the state's largest bank, Maryland National. The deal kept the bank locally owned and gave Lerner stock in MNC valued at $160 million. It also gave him a $45,000-a-month, 10-year consulting contract with MNC and the use of a corporate jet as long as he promised not to increase his MNC stake beyond his 8.9 percent. More than 1,000 employees were expected to lose their jobs in the merger as MNC set out to cut $100 million in expenses.

Hathaway became vice chairman of MNC and chairman of Maryland National Bank, and Lerner went back to Cleveland. A fast-rising MNC executive, Frank P. Bramble Sr., was assigned to oversee the Equitable assimilation.

A year later, however, the real estate market collapsed, and the bank was roiling in bad loans. Investors sued, and regulators, jumpy over the savings and loan crisis then under way, combed through MNC's books. With the bank headed for a $440 million loss that year, Lerner arranged an infusion of $180 million in capital through a special stock offer — half of which he would buy. In return, he was allowed to increase his share of the bank's stock to about 24 percent.

While the transaction was being finalized, MNC's chairman, Alan P. Hoblitzell Jr., a long-time civic leader, resigned. Lerner put himself in Hoblitzell's place, thus becoming Baltimore's biggest banker.

Local leaders were nervous about the new face. Reached by *The Sun*, Art Modell offered some assurances on behalf of his friend: "Obviously, he has a pretty good batting average in life. He's as honest a man as I've ever known and about the brightest man I've ever known. He should do a great job for MNC and its shareholders."

Lerner and his management team went quickly to work. They wrung out bad loans and sold off assets. In a bold stroke, they spun off MNC's profitable credit-card subsidiary, MBNA, into a free-standing, publicly traded company. The move raised $1.1 billion for MNC. Lerner himself bought 6.6 million shares of the new venture and cut a deal to save $8.4 million in underwriting fees. In 1991, Lerner named the 43-year-old Bramble MNC's new president. Hathaway retired the next year.

Then, in 1993, MNC agreed to a buyout by NationsBank. This deal, too, contained a special sweetener: MNC investors with more than 5 million shares could exchange their stock for NationsBank shares without paying capital-gains taxes. Those opting for cash would have to pay taxes. As it turned out, only two investors had more than 5 million shares: Lerner and Fidelity Investments of Boston.

"It's really outright greed," said analyst John Hershey Jr. of Ferris, Baker Watts.

Lerner was soon back in Cleveland, smoking his Cuban cigars, rubbing elbows with financiers and U.S. presidents, and bailing out Art Modell.

Stadium Corp.'s immediate crisis passed with Lerner's 1986 purchase. But the longer-term problem of Municipal Stadium was only getting worse.

• • •

Rumors soon began surfacing that Modell was looking to join the gold rush of team owners moving their teams. He denied it.

"I haven't given a thought to selling the team," Modell told reporters in 1984. "As to moving it, that's absurd. Pete Rozelle and

I led the fight to keep the Raiders in Oakland. I was also against the move of the Colts to Indianapolis. I want to see stability in the league. I repeat, I'm keeping the Browns and they are staying in Cleveland."

In October 1984, *Sports Illustrated* reported that Modell was ready to sell the team and, with former President Gerald Ford, to buy a stake in the Los Angeles Rams. According to the report, Modell would be the managing partner.

This, too, adamantly he denied. But he soon was displaying a more than a passing interest in owning an NFL team in Baltimore.

A typed memorandum in Mayor Schaefer's archives relates an "NFL contact" on Aug. 19, 1985. Addressed to Schaefer by his then-press secretary Pat Bernstein, it reports an encounter between Modell and former Colts marketing executive Bob Leffler, who was running a marketing firm in Baltimore:

"He [Leffler] was in the private box with Art Modell at this weekend's exhibition game and Modell peppered him with questions: reasons for low attendance at Colts games, chances of changing that, attitude of fans to baseball, financial probability of success, etc. Bob knows Modell is a fan of yours and that EBW [Orioles owner Edward Bennett Williams] contacted him [Modell] two years ago to inquire about their organization running a baseball stadium like the way they presently do in Cleveland. With the extensive questioning on both baseball and football, Bob felt the questions were more than just casual interest. He will be continuing to be exposed to Modell as the football season progresses and felt that if he could be of any help, he would like to."

An attached, handwritten message dated Aug. 6, 1985 noted Modell's friendship with Pete Rozelle and Modell's "unhappy arrangement" with a minority investor. It also mentioned Lerner's relationship to Modell and Grant Hathaway.

It adds: "Sell Browns. He may get franchise ... Must create a facility. Modell says no to our stadium."

Leffler, in a 1997 interview, recalled it differently. "He didn't pepper me. He was mystified about what happened to Baltimore, and what happened to all the sellouts," Leffler said.

Leffler said he contacted the mayor's office to learn what the city was doing so he could aid the effort to get a team back.

Shortly after this stadium conversation, Governor Harry

Hughes received a call from Hathaway. The two scheduled a secret meeting at Martin State Airport, outside Baltimore, for December 1985. Modell also attended, as did Lerner, Schaefer, Williams, Orioles executive Larry Luchino, and Frank De Francis, Hughes' secretary of economic development. The topic: an expansion team for Baltimore, to be owned by Art Modell, Hughes recalled in a 1996 interview.

"My recollection was Modell would come up with the expansion team. He was having problems with his minority investor," Hughes said.

A stadium, of course, was the big issue. Modell made it clear that a new one would need to be built.

"I remember something Art Modell said, which is ironic now. He said the NFL owners say they will never play another game at Memorial Stadium," said Hughes, who was encouraged by the meeting.

The governor's advisers told him that Modell, with his influence in the league, could pull off an expansion vote. One person involved in the talks said Modell discussed selling the Browns, possibly to Lerner, moving to Baltimore and heading up an expansion effort on behalf of the city. He would, in essence, become a "team owner in waiting" while he used his league contacts to steer a team Maryland's way.

A second meeting was held in Annapolis, but this one didn't go as well. Modell and Williams couldn't agree on sharing a stadium, even a new one. The matter was dropped.

Later, Lerner went to see Hughes. He brought a letter, written to Rozelle, in which he expressed interest in an expansion team for Baltimore and bragged that he wouldn't be an absentee owner. Lerner left him a copy of the letter and asked him to keep it confidential. Hughes never heard back.

In 1995, Modell said he had acted only as a friendly consultant on the city's efforts to build a stadium for the Orioles and get a new NFL team.

"As far as what can we do with that team or expansion or whatever, sure we discussed that. There's no question that football came up," he said.

But other participants recall Modell talking about selling the Browns and moving an expansion team into a new stadium with the Orioles.

Chris Hartman, then an aide to Schaefer, recalls later conversations between the city and Browns that involved the possibility of the franchise moving to Baltimore outright. He said he received a call from a Browns contact in late 1986, after Schaefer had been elected governor but before he was sworn in. The contact explained that the Browns might be interested in a move and that Modell's sons were particularly fond of the Baltimore market. Hartman discussed the call with Schaefer while the governor-elect was sitting for his official portrait. Schaefer gave the go-ahead for further talks but wanted to speak to George Voinovich, then the mayor of Cleveland. Voinovich and Schaefer were close, and Schaefer wanted to assure his Ohio ally that he wasn't going to do anything that would leave Cleveland without a team, Hartman said.

Among the scenarios discussed, according to Hartman, were Lerner buying a team and moving it to Cleveland, and Modell moving the Browns to Baltimore. At least one meeting was held on the matter, Hartman said, but nothing ever came of it. The league was embroiled in unrelated troubles and seemed to have little interest in adding more teams anytime soon.

When asked about the conversations in 1995, Schaefer said he didn't recall it but has been reminded by others that they took place. He was opposed to raiding another city of its franchise, he said. In 1987 he called Vincent Schoemehl, the mayor of St. Louis, before talking with the NFL Cardinals, and was told the team appeared headed out of town anyway. Schaefer said he was granted permission to try and lure the Cardinals.

"Everybody tells me that I did it, so I presume I did," Schaefer said of his consultation with Voinovich. "You can say I did. Our rule was never to steal a team from a city that was fighting to keep it."

Voinovich, through a spokesman, said he had no recollection of the conversation with Schaefer.

In 1995, Modell denied it all, saying everyone was mistaken, and insisting that he never thought about moving to Baltimore until ten years later.

CHAPTER SEVEN

Baltimore
Strikes Back

Herbert J. Belgrad was an unlikely sports standard-bearer for a city that came to prominence in the muddy age of Art Donovan and Johnny Unitas.

Five-feet, 9-inches tall, rail-thin, and balding, Belgrad looked more like an accounting professor than a powerful civic booster. He was excruciatingly honest, button-down steady, and vested with a bone-dry sense of humor. Although he didn't like to talk about it, the best bets were that he had never actually been to an NFL game.

He had, but just a few.

Belgrad grew up in a solidly middle-class, orthodox Jewish household in the city's Pimlico neighborhood, the son of a men's clothier. He avidly followed the sports of his schools, City College High School, and, later, Johns Hopkins University. But pro sports ranked low on his list of interests. He'd make a few Orioles games a year with friends and maybe see the Colts once or twice a season if tickets became available, but these were mostly last-minute social occasions.

After getting a psychology degree from Hopkins, Belgrad headed off to the University of Illinois at Urbana-Champaign for a master's degree in labor relations. His thesis: the psychogenics of labor leaders. He received his law degree in 1961 from the University of Maryland. It being the age of great labor conflict in

American industry, Belgrad hoped to represent corporations in their negotiations with unions.

His 1986 appointment as chairman of the newly formed Maryland Stadium Authority rankled some. The city's football god-fathers — powerful developers and civic do-gooders who had launched countless failed schemes to get the city back into the game — were none too pleased.

But the two-pronged job of saving the Orioles and replacing the Colts would be expensive, and one best not left to an aging jock. There would be huge contracts to negotiate and political shenanigans to avoid. Belgrad's background as a labor lawyer and skillful negotiator could only help smooth the choppy waters ahead.

It was Governor Harry Hughes who, in the waning days of his second administration, tapped Belgrad, then a partner with the Baltimore law firm of Kaplan, Heyman, Greenberg, Engleman for the Stadium Authority post. Hughes knew Belgrad professionally. For a while, Belgrad even had an office down the hall from Hughes in the governor's Baltimore office complex. Belgrad headed the state bar association for a time and served as the chairman of the state ethics commission, where he had been in charge of politically sensitive financial reports and disclosure forms. He also ran a group set up to use lawyers' client escrow accounts to raise money for charities. Laudable tasks all — but hardly preparation for a job that would soon make Herb Belgrad a household name in Maryland.

Hughes said he wanted Belgrad precisely because he would bring a dispassionate approach to the emotional issue of Memorial Stadium's future.

Belgrad agreed. "I have not been part of the stadium debate, so I'm approaching the entire issue with an open mind," he told reporters after being appointed to this critical, but unpaid, post.

Five months earlier, the Maryland General Assembly and Governor Hughes had created the Stadium Authority amid a panic that Baltimore was falling out of the major leagues. The Orioles were increasingly working on selling season tickets in Washington, and many people were convinced that owner Edward Bennett Williams had long intended to move the team to the nation's capital. Washington was the larger and wealthier of the two cities and had been pining for baseball since the Senators moved to Arlington,

Texas, in 1971 and became the Rangers.

The bill that created the Stadium Authority gave it a two-fold mission: Keep the Orioles and get the NFL back. But the legislature, recognizing the tenuous Orioles situation, added a deadline. It wanted a proposal on a baseball stadium from the Authority by Dec. 1.

Belgrad's appointment was announced Sept. 6, 1986, the day before Maryland's primary election for governor. It was an open seat. Hughes had served his legal limit of two four-year terms. The two Democratic contenders were William Donald Schaefer and Maryland Attorney General Steve Sachs.

Sachs, also a Baltimorean, was running a campaign based, in part, on portraying Schaefer as too parochial a city leader to run the state. Sachs favored building any new stadiums outside of the city, in a suburb south of Baltimore called Landsdowne, at a site selected by a Hughes-appointed commission.

Schaefer, of course, wanted the stadiums built in downtown Baltimore. As mayor, he had appointed his own stadium site task force, and it had favored the Camden Station area.

Schaefer easily won the primary, 62 percent to Sachs' 35 percent.

The day after Schaefer's convincing victory, the presumed governor-elect complained about the nominees for the Stadium Authority board. They included Janice Piccinini, a former head of the state's teachers' union, which had endorsed Sachs, and, most notably, Belgrad. Schaefer said he should have been consulted.

That he hadn't came as no particular surprise to political observers. Schaefer had long had a testy relationship with Hughes, a fellow Democrat, but a native of Maryland's rural Eastern Shore, where antipathy for Baltimore ran strong. Hughes had come into office riding a wave of reform after the scandals of former governors Marvin Mandel and Spiro Agnew. Schaefer himself was politically close to Mandel and Mandel's closest political allies.

And when it came to the Orioles and football, the two couldn't have been farther apart. Hughes was not about to send the state into bankruptcy for the sake of Baltimore or its sports. Schaefer despised him for political cowardice.

When told of Belgrad's appointment, Schaefer was both grumpy and tactful. "This was so long in coming," he told reporters, "and I'm a little disappointed in a couple of the appointments. They seemed to me to be very political," complained Schaefer, who pointedly refused to commit himself to listening to the Authority's advice.

Belgrad's swearing-in, which had been scheduled for the next day, was postponed. He and Schaefer met, and Belgrad was surprised to find Schaefer angry and edgy, rather than celebratory. Schaefer confided disappointment in a great many long-time friends who had supported Sachs in the primary. It soon came out that Schaefer thought Belgrad was on that list.

"I always thought of you as a friend," Schaefer moaned.

At the very least, the two men *had* known each other a long time. In the early 1960s, when Schaefer was an earnest city councilman, Belgrad served as an assistant city solicitor for housing, education, and labor. The two traveled together to New York City to study that city's innovative housing policies and returned to write legislation overhauling Baltimore's housing department.

But Belgrad's relationship with Sachs was closer and longer, dating back to their Baltimore childhoods. Belgrad even had a "Sachs for Governor" sign on his front lawn, and his car carried a "Sachs for Governor" bumper sticker. Schaefer didn't tolerate such disloyalty in his inner circle.

Belgrad explained that his wife had put the lawn sign up, and that although he had worked on previous Sachs campaigns, he had been neutral on this one — he contributed to both camps — and would be loyal to Schaefer now.

It was exactly what Schaefer wanted to hear. He promised to keep Belgrad on and support him in every way he could.

• • •

The new chairman set out immediately to learn everything he could about two topics he had virtually ignored his whole life: stadiums and sports.

His first step was firing up the grill and hosting a cookout at his Baltimore home for two of his closest counsels: former U.S. Attorney General Benjamin Civiletti and Jerry Sachs. Sachs, no relation to the gubernatorial candidate, was a top executive in Abe Pollin's sports empire. Pollin not only owned the NBA Bullets, but also the National Hockey League Capitals and their arena in Largo, a suburb outside Washington.

The three men sat at Belgrad's kitchen table and listed on a yellow legal pad the people whom Belgrad would have to meet — all of the politicians, business leaders, sports figures. They then made plans for Belgrad to visit stadiums and teams around the country.

Over the next three months, Belgrad and other Stadium Authority members devised their strategy. Baltimore, while a proud city with a solid history of fan support, hardly had the appeal of a major city like Chicago. The major leagues had grown beyond sentimentality, and Baltimore's pitch would have to be financial, not emotional.

Something else became apparent in Belgrad's talks with sports executives and consultants. In cities where sports teams shared stadiums, there inevitably was conflict. The sight lines for baseball were almost the polar opposite of those desired for football games. The best baseball seats were the ones closest to home plate and the players, whereas football's premier digs were midfield and high enough to see plays unfold on the turf. Teams sometimes felt slighted by the mere existence of their cotenants, and fights were frequent over which one obtained the best weekend dates. Scheduling games and practices and picking concessionaires became feats of diplomacy.

Belgrad asked his consultants to compare the cost of a multipurpose stadium, which could be shared by two teams, with the cost of building two separate structures. He was surprised by what he was told.

Building a baseball stadium adaptable to football would cost $41 million more than a baseball-only park and would spoil the sight lines and character of each park. Building another football stadium would add only another $16 million to that price tag, or $201.1 million altogether.

The possibility of renovating Memorial Stadium came up but was never seriously discussed. Belgrad's consultants said it would cost about $75 million to bring the 35-year old structure up to modern standards. But even then, compromises would have to be made on design, and conflicts were sure to arise in scheduling. And, because of its residential location, precious little could be done about the stadium's pre- and post-game traffic snarls.

Besides, the Orioles had made it clear that they would not sign a long-term lease at Memorial Stadium. Commissioner Rozelle, as well as other football officials contacted by the Maryland Stadium Authority, confirmed that the city's expansion chances would not be strong if the only stadium it offered was one an earlier club had abandoned.

"The decision made itself," Belgrad recalled later.

The Orioles would get the new, baseball-only stadium they desperately wanted. And the NFL would get its own stadium. Not only would it be leased at the cheapest possible amount, but it would be an open-air facility, which team owners preferred for the "ambiance" even though it was financially ludicrous. Domed stadiums at least could be used for large conventions, circuses, and other events that would bring money to the city and pay for the structures. But owners fought domes and, increasingly, were winning.

Fresh from the humiliation of Bob Irsay's midnight ride, Baltimore was desperate to pay the price.

• • •

With Schaefer now running the state, Camden Yards easily beat out Landsdowne as the stadium's site. Being on a rail line, Camden Yards offered mass transit; it also expanded by a few blocks west the Inner Harbor rejuvenation that Schaefer had begun as mayor. (Schaefer's transportation secretary had estimated that it would cost up to $120 million more to build ramps and widen roads for the stadium if it were built at Landsdowne.)

At the time of this recommendation, Camden Station was vacant and shuttered. The neighborhood was a mishmash of industry, employing about 1,000 people, all of which would have to be moved at public expense.

In announcing the two-stadium, Camden Yards proposal, Belgrad offered no hint about the sports palaces that would eventually emerge: "We're talking about cost-effective designs. That's a little bit more than no-frills, but we're not talking luxury either," he said. "We're all taxpayers on this authority."

The proposal ignited a firestorm of protest. Residents around Camden Yards fought the new stadiums. Their counterparts around Memorial Stadium opposed the loss of the Orioles and the prospect of a huge, empty nuisance in their neighborhood.

In the legislature, the issue was viewed as pork for Baltimore and folly from one of the nation's last brick-and-mortar politicians. Why should the taxpayers line the pockets of sports millionaires? asked opponents. Let them build their own stadiums.

Belgrad, in his soothing monotone, calmly answered the questions in hearing after hearing, talking up the economic benefits of an NFL franchise. His unflashy demeanor and unquestioned integrity put lawmakers at ease about turning over to him a major chunk of the state's capital budget.

Underscoring the debate was the politicians' reluctance to be blamed for losing the Orioles, especially three years after the Colts had left. That would be the equivalent of losing Florida to the Communists shortly after the fall of Cuba.

The issue came to a head at a legislative hearing in Annapolis in March 1987.

Orioles owner Edward Bennett Williams hadn't exactly volunteered to testify. He planned to spend the day in Boston, where he was to receive another in a series of painful chemotherapy treatments for an advanced case of cancer.

So Schaefer's staff had been surprised when the governor announced at a press conference that "EBW," as Williams was known, would appear at the hearing. So was Williams. He learned of it from a reporter and called the governor's office to complain bitterly and to threaten not to come.

But he flew in, immediately after his morning chemotherapy. Before the afternoon hearing, a concerned Belgrad suggested that the committee chairman have a signal ready to use if Williams became fatigued. Williams, who was trying to keep his illness a secret, nixed this idea immediately.

EBW, a veritable Perry Mason whose clients had included Teamsters chief Jimmy Hoffa and the Communist-baiting Senator Joe McCarthy, delivered a bravura performance. He never threatened to move the Orioles but made it clear that continued support of the team would factor into future decisions. There would be no long-term leases at Memorial Stadium, he said. (At the time, he was signing year-to-year contracts with the city.)

Populist Baltimore Senator Jack Lapides, an ardent foe of the new stadiums, opened the questioning. The idea was supported only by "fat cats," he said. Ordinary fans were satisfied with Memorial Stadium. Wouldn't it be cheaper for the state simply to buy 15,000 season tickets to ensure the Orioles' success? he asked. Williams waited for the applause from the gallery to die down, then calmly replied: "I didn't come here to ask for a subsidy. I don't think we should have a subsidy. I'm against subsidies for the private sector ... I can make this thing go in the private sector if I get the tools."

Williams said he would put a winning team on the field but expected the public to provide the stadium. Several times he held up the current issue of *Sports Illustrated*, with the three baseball Ripkens on the cover: Orioles manager Cal Sr. and his two sons, shortstop Cal Jr. and second baseman Billy.

"It was a masterful performance," Belgrad recalled later. No one watching could have guessed that Williams would be dead by the following year and the team sold two years after that. (EBW's heirs would sell the Orioles to a syndicate headed by New York financier and reclusive millionaire Eli Jacobs.)

When the stadium funding bills came to a final vote in the Maryland Senate on April 1, 1987, opponents filibustered for 18 hours. Schaefer and his lieutenant governor, former Senate president Mickey Steinberg, fought for every vote.

"We traded a lot of votes on things, but it [the victory-gaining number on the legislative toteboard] came down," recalled Alan Rifkin, Schaefer's chief lobbyist.

Belgrad and Rifkin listened to the proceedings over speakers in an office behind the Senate chambers. As questions came up, they ferried in the answers via telephone to Senator Laurence Levitan, D-Montgomery Co., the chairman of the Budget and Taxation Committee acting as floor leader for the fight.

The final margin of victory was close, but it was enough. Success in the House of Delegates was considered more certain.

After the Senate vote, Belgrad and Rifkin went to Schaefer's office, where the first-year chief executive, who had put his political reputation on the line, was ebullient. They tossed about a giant, inflated football and an oversized baseball and savored the victory.

"The city was blackmailed into building a new stadium. That's the despicable part," Lapides told reporters. "It's simply unconscionable that cities are forced to succumb to blackmail by

pro football and baseball."

The bills passed the Maryland House of Delegates on April 3.

For Senate President Thomas V. "Mike" Miller Jr., it was one of his early glimpses at the clout of the new governor. "I was one of the doubters," he said. "But this bill is an indication that his [Schaefer's] attitude can be contagious." Schaefer called it "one of the most important days in the history of sports in Maryland."

The legislation allowed Schaefer to claim, somewhat disingenuously, that no tax dollars would be used to build the stadiums. The Maryland Stadium Authority would float bonds and repay them with a special, sports-theme, instant lottery game that would be run as many as four times a year.

But the state already had a lottery, and there was no reason to think that merely designating four games as "stadium games" would attract new wagering money. It would merely redirect $16 million a year that would have come in anyway and gone to the general fund to pay for schools, police, and other public needs.

Work could begin immediately on the baseball stadium, first in negotiating a long-term lease with the Orioles, and then in turning dirt. No money could be spent on the football stadium, however, until a contract was signed with a team. Though the National Football League was then talking seriously about expanding, no firm timetable had been set. The site would be cleared for the football stadium and used, if only temporarily, as a parking lot for the baseball park.

Estimated cost for the twin stadiums: $201 million.

Opponents of the bill fought one final skirmish. A group called Marylanders for Sports Sanity collected 44,000 names on petitions to put the stadium issue onto the ballot, where polls showed it would likely fail. Schaefer fought this petition drive in the courts, arguing that the state constitution did not permit appropriations bills to be challenged by referendum.

A Baltimore Circuit Court judge ruled for the anti-stadium group. But Schaefer appealed to the state's highest court, the Maryland Court of Appeals, which agreed with the governor. The decision came down Sept. 7, 1987.

"This is terrible. It's a travesty. I'm sorry our leadership doesn't see there are other needs, like education, poor people, and the elderly. This fight is not yet over by any means," said William B.

Marker, head of the Marylanders for Sports Sanity.

But the fight *was* over, and Baltimore's strategy was set: Both the Orioles and an NFL team would get the best stadiums money could buy, built entirely at public expense. It was more than Irsay or Williams had ever asked for and was a 180-degree turnaround for a city that had spent years quibbling over how to renovate the concession stands at Memorial Stadium.

The twin stadiums would make their tenants rich by transferring millions of dollars from taxpayers to wealthy team owners and players. But they would also keep the city in both major leagues, at least for a few decades.

Baltimore and Governor Schaefer finally recognized the lesson that the city had ignored only three years before: No amount of heritage or history can keep a franchise from moving. Fan loyalty is a one-way street. Baltimore's appeal would have to be based on economics, not emotion. The city that entered the 1980s as naive as any in the country about the mobility of sports teams would enter the 1990s at the cutting edge of the new, stadium-powered politics of appeasement.

Belgrad led a triumphant delegation of community leaders to New York City in June 1987 to present the state legislation to Pete Rozelle.

The commissioner was duly impressed with the promised public investment. Baltimore, he noted, had meant a great deal to the league during its formative years and suggested that NFL expansion was imminent.

While there, Belgrad asked him two questions whose answers would form crucial parts of the city's strategy: Should we select an ownership group? Should we anoint a standard-bearer?

The last time the league had expanded — adding Seattle and Tampa Bay in 1974 — the NFL hadn't been shy about designating the cities and then rounding up ownership groups to its liking.

No, Rozelle told Belgrad. This time, leave that up to the team owners and the league. That's the NFL's business.

It turned out to be very bad advice.

• • •

Baltimore's new, honey-baited trap got its first nibble sooner than even Belgrad dreamed. Cardinals owner Bill Bidwill was frustrated with his secondary status in St. Louis, where he played in a stadium run by baseball's Cardinals. Attendance, too, had dipped to embarrassing lows as fans in the 1980s thrilled to a baseball team that made three trips to the World Series. The miserable football team was all but forgotten, with crowds sometimes topping out at 20,000.

A meeting between Belgrad and Bidwill was set up by Baltimore sportswriter Vito Stellino for October 1987, barely a month after the Court of Appeals' decision. It would take place during the NFL owners' meeting.

This was the first serious inquiry the city had received since 1984. Shortly after the Colts left, a group of Baltimore investors secretly negotiated for weeks to buy the New Orleans Saints. They were close to a deal in December when the NFL went to court to prevent the Philadelphia Eagles from following through on a threat to move to Phoenix. The group, sensing a new league stridency on stopping team moves, and unable to get everything it wanted from Baltimore's City Hall, dropped its plans. The Saints were sold to investors who kept them in New Orleans.

On Nov. 12, Bidwill came to town for a look-see. The bow-tied, roly-poly team owner received the red-carpet treatment. As talks progressed, Baltimore sat on the edge of its imaginary stadium seat. Bidwill had pitted Baltimore against Phoenix, the other city he was considering.

The city that had lost the Colts wasn't quite committing the same crime it had fallen victim to. Sensitive to St. Louis' position, Schaefer called its mayor, who said he thought that the Cardinals were going somewhere and that Baltimore may as well stay in the race.

That was good enough for Schaefer and Belgrad. The two had put together a three-part, anti-raiding test that they applied before talking to a franchise. First, the team had to have made an irrevocable decision to move. Second, it must have communicated this decision to the authorities in its hometown. And third, the league had to be aware of the talks. Belgrad assumed the expansion decision would be made primarily by the commissioner, with the owners going along. And he didn't want to anger Rozelle with a losing bid for an existing team.

"We made the judgment that he [Bidwill] won't be playing in

St. Louis, and nothing has happened to change that judgment," Belgrad said. "We don't want an NFL team so badly we'll raid another city for it."

About the same time, Belgrad received informal inquiries on behalf of the Houston Oilers and Atlanta Falcons, but did not pursue them because he didn't think those teams met the anti-raiding standard.

Bidwill seriously considered Baltimore's offer, but a family meeting called in the final days of deliberations tilted the scales toward Phoenix. It was a Sun Belt city full of promise, even though the team would be playing in a renovated college stadium.

When Bidwill announced his move to Phoenix on Jan. 15, 1985, Baltimore tasted a disappointment that would become familiar fare over the next decade.

"I'm disappointed, but certainly not discouraged," Belgrad said. "Our objective from the beginning was to return NFL football to Baltimore. We're not deterred at all from our initial objective. We're ready to vigorously seek an expansion franchise."

In this effort, Belgrad would find himself wooing a man more inscrutable than Irsay and Bidwill put together. A man named Paul Tagliabue.

CHAPTER EIGHT

The League Expands

L awyerly and pinstriped, Paul Tagliabue brought a new look to the National Football League.

Where Pete Rozelle was gregarious and clever, Tagliabue was stiff and dry. A high school high-jump champion and basketball star, Tagliabue stood 6-foot-5 and carried himself like a Marine honor guard unhappy with his assignment. He could be tough: In high school, he slammed his elbows against the cinder block walls of his parents' basement to improve his rebounding.

Tagliabue's co-workers swore he also could be funny and friendly, but he kept that side of himself out of the public eye as he prepared to lead the NFL into a decade of tumultuous change and historic growth.

Tagliabue's involvement with the league dated back to 1969, when he began serving as the NFL's outside legal counsel. While working for the powerful Washington law firm of Covington & Burling, Tagliabue had been Rozelle's trusted adviser on all manner of issues — everything from forcing Joe Namath to divest himself of ownership of a tavern of ill-repute to the antitrust wars against the players. He guided the league through its brutal, and ultimately losing, fights with Al Davis and the Raiders.

Earlier in his career, Tagliabue had been a policy analyst at the

Defense Department, helping to decide where NATO would aim its nuclear missiles. Intellectual challenge and achievement came easily to Tagliabue, a Rhodes Scholar finalist and former editor of New York University's *Law Review*.

But his ascension in the NFL, though difficult, proved to be a watershed for the league. The old-guard owners, led by Art Modell, favored a commissioner more like themselves, a so-called "football man" who would be faithful to the game's heritage and the compromises they had made. They wanted another Pete Rozelle.

These old-liners dominated the search committee to find Rozelle's replacement. With Modell at the table were the Giants' Wellington Mara, the Chiefs' Lamar Hunt, and the Buffalo Bills' Ralph Wilson. The committee spent four months poring over applications and eventually chose one of their own: Jim Finks, the likeable and able president of the New Orleans Saints. League history suggested that the other owners would go along with the committee's recommendation. After all, the owners on the committee were revered.

But at least 11 owners, many of them new to the league, had paid a fortune for their franchises and had debts to service — people like the Dallas Cowboys' Jerry Jones and the Philadelphia Eagles' Norman Braman. And they wanted a commissioner who would pay attention to their bottom lines, not to ancient handshake deals. They wanted someone more like David Stern, the "businessman-commissioner" and lawyer who had righted the listing ship of the National Basketball Association and almost single-handedly reestablished the primacy of professional basketball.

In a glimpse of fights to come, the "young Turks" blocked Finks' election and held out for someone who would recognize football as a multimillion-dollar business, not just a sport. They wanted Tagliabue.

Months of infighting ensued, and neither side could muster the necessary 19 votes. Finally, Rozelle appointed a five-man panel, headed by the nonaligned Dan Rooney of the Pittsburgh Steelers, to break the deadlock. On the panel with him were Mara and Modell, representing the old-guard stalwarts, and "newcomers" Pat Bowlen of the Denver Broncos and Mike Lynn of the Minnesota Vikings.

The debate raged on, with each side refusing to budge. Modell suggested they take Finks, then 62, and then have Tagliabue take over a few years later. This didn't fly. The newer owners were resolute. Finally, Rooney threw his weight behind Tagliabue, and Modell and Mara capitulated.

Tagliabue was elected Oct. 26, 1989, 228 days after Rozelle had announced his retirement.

After the vote, Modell told a reporter: "The truth of the matter is Paul Tagliabue is as much old guard as anybody."

Tagliabue, 49 when he took over the $800,000-a-year post, kept on most of Rozelle's lieutenants. And he retained many of his policies. For example, he took a hard line against drug use by players and favored minority advancement in team front offices and at NFL headquarters. But he and his lieutenants made it clear to Maryland Stadium Authority chairman Herb Belgrad and the other expansion hopefuls that theirs was a new regime.

At first, Tagliabue seemed, if only briefly, like Baltimore's best friend.

He lived in Washington's Maryland suburbs and had a bottom-line orientation to which Baltimore and its rich stadium deal might appeal. Belgrad actually thought he had a professional soulmate in Tagliabue, another lawyer schooled in rigorous ethics.

Tagliabue shared Rozelle's goal of increasing the league through expansion, and doing so as quickly as possible. In January 1990, in his first Super Bowl press conference, Tagliabue said the league wanted to add teams "well before the mid-1990s."

The only impediment, he said, was reaching a collective bargaining agreement with the players. (At the time, the NFL Players Association had decertified itself and was pursuing antitrust litigation against the league.)

But Tagliabue said he hoped he could get the two sides talking. Expansion — with its promise of 100 new player slots — would lure the players back to the table, he said. In the meantime, he appointed an expansion committee and seemed prepared to move ahead rapidly with what had been the subject of considerable foot-dragging.

In July 1990, Tagliabue released a statement outlining the league's initial expansion policy: The NFL would strive to add two teams by 1993, with selection of the cities made by 1991 or 1992 at the latest. Any U.S. or Canadian city could apply.

"This will fit our timetable very well," said Belgrad.

Then, in August, ex-commissioner Rozelle enunciated what some in the NFL considered an informal goal: To put one team in virgin NFL territory and one team in a city that had lost a team. Even Tagliabue voiced some early support for this notion, which, according to an NFL spokesman, was the early "working assumption" of the expansion committee.

The concept was pure Rozelle: "Grow in new areas, but remember where you've been." Under this thinking, Baltimore would be up against Oakland and St. Louis, and its prospects bright, at least in comparison. Oakland's stadium offer was unsettled, and St. Louis had been voted out of the league just three years before.

In May 1991, at a meeting in Minneapolis, the NFL team owners made expansion official. They approved a resolution, 22-4-2, to add a pair of teams beginning in 1994, and to consider the tricky issue of reapportioning all of the teams among the various conferences and divisions.

The debate had been long and emotional. Team owners were reluctant to carve out two more slices from their network TV pie, but Tagliabue convinced them that the sport's continued growth would depend on expansion. And franchise fees could be assessed to ease the short-term loss of shared revenue.

Among the four "no" votes cast was that of the Washington Redskins, Baltimore's longtime football nemesis. Though John Cooke, son of team owner Jack Kent Cooke, explained that the Redskins wanted a labor agreement first, Washington had a long history of opposing expansion. Before the emergence of league-wide contracts, the Redskins, as the NFL's de facto team of Dixie, had knitted together a string of TV contracts throughout the South. Clearly, they weren't keen on the inevitable expansion of the league into their region.

Baltimore had good reason to keep a wary eye on the team 30 miles to its south.

Canadian Jack Kent Cooke was a self-made billionaire who hadn't amassed a fortune by being patient or nice. In 1988, the year he emerged as sole owner of the Redskins, he was already a bona fide sports mogul.

In 1965, he had bought the Los Angeles Lakers for $5 million and inaugurated that franchise's golden era by signing both

Kareem Abdul-Jabbar and Wilt Chamberlain. Two years later, Cooke paid $2 million for an expansion NHL franchise, the Los Angeles Kings, and moved both basketball and hockey teams to the L.A. Forum, an arena he built for $16.5 million, after the commission overseeing the public arena refused him year-round exclusive use.

In 1979, he sold the two teams, the Forum, and some Nevada real estate for $67.5 million and headed east. That same year, he divorced his wife of 42 years and ended up in the *Guinness Book of World Records* by agreeing to a $41-million divorce settlement. The judge in the suit was Joseph Wapner, who would later preside over TV's "The People's Court."

Subsequent romances were less costly, thanks to prenuptial agreements, but also less successful. Cooke's second marriage lasted 10 months; the third, only 73 days long, failed when wife Suzanne Martin refused his demand to have an abortion.

His fourth visit to the altar proved to be the most colorful. Marlene Chalmers, a Bolivian-born beauty 40 years Cooke's junior, had served time in a federal prison for conspiracy to import cocaine. The marital relationship began to sour when she was arrested — after careening around Georgetown with a male acquaintance on the hood of her Jaguar convertible. Cooke's attorneys turned up evidence that Chalmers' prior divorce, granted in the Dominican Republic, may not have been legal, and for a time, Cooke contested the marriage. But the two later patched things up.

In 1960, the same year he received his U.S. citizenship through an act of Congress, Cooke began acquiring a percentage of the Redskins. He paid $350,000 for a quarter of the team, then still controlled by the original owner and chief share-holder George Preston Marshall. In 1962, Edward Bennett Williams, the future Orioles owner, stepped in and bought a chunk of the football team.

Marshall died in 1969. Squabbling over his will lasted for several years. Gradually, the Redskins bought back and retired most of Marshall's stock, and, by 1985, Williams' stock, too. Cooke apparently succeeded in gaining control of the team, piecemeal, by spending no more than $15 million.

In 1987, at the start of the NFL's expansion process, Gene McHale, a consultant for the Maryland Stadium Authority, visited the Redskins owner at his farm in rural Virginia. He wanted to feel him out on Baltimore's application. Cooke told McHale he had no problem with it.

"He didn't see it as a threat to him and he wanted to see Baltimore get a new stadium and thought the rivalry would be good," McHale recalled later.

Of course, Cooke could hardly say otherwise, in light of antitrust laws. Any opposition by Cooke to a team in Baltimore would be a textbook case of anti-competitive behavior and likely make some lawyers a lot of money.

To the uninitiated, Cooke would seem to have little reason to oppose a team in Baltimore. The Redskins had a season-ticket waiting list of 48,000 and had sold out every game at Robert F. Kennedy Stadium since 1966, the longest NFL streak. All of the seats were season-ticket sales. A single-game ticket hadn't been sold at RFK since 1965.

But the team was playing in one of the smallest venues in the league, with only 56,454 seats and no skyboxes. And Cooke was interested in a bigger and newer stadium, even though the process of creating one was just under way, and it focused on Washington, a city far removed culturally and commercially from Baltimore.

There was plenty of reason, however, to be skeptical that Cooke actually approved of a new competitor up Interstate 95. Selling skyboxes, for example, would be easier with two cities from which to draw fans rather than one. And in the event pay-per-view television ever came to the NFL, commanding the vast common market of Baltimore and Washington — by some counts the nation's fourth biggest metroplex, — would be lucrative.

In fact, former New England Patriots owner Victor Kiam alleged in a lawsuit years later that a Redskins representative told him in 1991 that the team would never permit another franchise to relocate to Baltimore. Kiam was unhappy with Foxboro Stadium, outside Boston, and was considering a move to Baltimore.

Belgrad talked with Kiam's representatives. But ever by-the-book, Belgrad then called NFL headquarters to ask if it would be all right for him to enter into negotiations. No, the league responded. It wouldn't be. The matter would be handled internally, Belgrad was told, and you won't be hearing from the Patriots any more. Obligingly, he cut off contact with the Patriots, and the talks ceased.

• • •

On May 22, 1991, NFL owners, meeting in a Minneapolis hotel, passed their expansion resolution. And, almost immediately, cities like Baltimore began lining up their representatives "like pitchmen at a carnival."

The Jacksonville, Fla., delegation, for example, was headed by Tom Petway and included Hamilton Jordan, a former Carter Administration insider, and Jeb Bush, son of President George Bush and a rising Florida politico. Group members bragged that they could provide a visiting team more than $1 million in gate receipts because the team would play in the Gator Bowl and not have any debt service to worry about. And their city was one of the fastest growing in the country.

Charlotte, N.C.'s backers, headed by former Baltimore Colts player and fast food magnate Jerry Richardson, promoted the regional nature of their application: Charlotte was a fast-growing city miles from any other NFL franchises. Memphis touted itself as the seat of a thriving "Mid-South" region.

Baltimore could make no such claim to an expansive, rapidly growing market. Instead, Belgrad emphasized Maryland's high median incomes and its enriching stadium offer, backed by the state's full faith and credit and the football fanaticism of its governor.

As normally self-respecting cities vied for the NFL's affection, the competition became garish at times. Subsequent owners' meetings became colorful bazaars with expansion contenders serving regional cuisine from booths set up in hallways and buffet tables in hospitality suites.

St. Louis once rented a hot air balloon with "Meet me in St. Louis" emblazoned across the side. City delegates had it tethered outside a meeting hotel and offered free rides to team owners and their spouses. At another meeting, the city dished out sundaes from a floating ice cream bar in the hotel pool.

Especially memorable were the 1990 meetings held in Orlando, Fla. Jacksonville boosters rented Disney's MGM Studios theme park one night and whisked NFL team owners and officials over in limousines for lobster and red snapper. That afternoon, the city brought in models and sponsored a fashion show for the owners' wives. (The only female NFL team owner was and is Georgia

Frontiere, owner of the Rams and widow of Carroll Rosenbloom.) Jacksonville nixed an earlier plan to hire Vanna White to conduct a mock "Wheel of Fortune" game when it discovered that taxpayers would be footing the bill. Private sponsors picked up the tab for the lobster and snapper event.

At the same meeting, Memphis' chief expansion delegate, Fred Smith, the chairman of Federal Express, arranged for Fed Ex to deliver daily gift packages to each owner. One day it was chocolate; the next, whiskey. The packages also contained messages from Fed Ex workers in each team owner's city, putting in a good word for their colleagues in Tennessee.

Belgrad, in keeping with his low-key style, confined most of Baltimore's activities to a traditional hospitality suite, where the city's famous crabcakes became a favorite. However, he did print up mock front pages of *The Sun* announcing: "Baltimore Awarded an NFL Franchise." These good-news front pages were wrapped around actual newspapers left each morning outside the 28 owners' rooms.

In 1991, Tagliabue formed a "Stage II" expansion committee with himself as chairman and, as members, the six team owners who headed the NFL's key committees: Cleveland's Art Modell; Philadelphia's Norman Braman; Tampa Bay's Hugh Culverhouse Sr.; San Francisco's Ed DeBartolo Jr.; Atlanta's Rankin Smith; and San Diego's Alex Spanos.

Braman was the most enthusiastic about Baltimore. Although he now lived in Miami, he had grown up in West Chester, Penn., a region cleaved by loyalties to the Colts and Eagles.

As the committee was getting underway, Tagliabue began to signal a shift from Rozelle's old-city, new-city concept. "I think basically we'll start with a level playing-field concept rather than pre-judging whether one will be an old city and one will be a new idea," he told reporters at the Minneapolis meeting.

The Maryland boosters were undaunted. The NFL was re-committed to expansion, they said, and that was all that mattered.

"What more positive sign can you have that the NFL is on the march?" asked Belgrad.

A few months later, during an interview with *The New York Times*, Modell gave the first glimpse of his franchise preferences: "It's two teams by 1994 and, in my view, there has to be a commitment to realignment, too. If I had to choose, I'd take Charlotte and St. Louis."

Belgrad didn't take the comment too seriously. "He's a good team player and I'm sure he'll read the analysis of the applications … I just don't give a quarter for any of these predictions. The process is just beginning."

Expressions of interest were due on Sept. 16, 1991, less than four months later, and 11 cities responded, including all 3 cities that had lost teams in the past decade: Baltimore, St. Louis, and Oakland. Also submitting applications were Charlotte; Raleigh-Durham, N.C., in a joint application; Honolulu; Jacksonville; Memphis; Nashville, Tenn.; and Sacramento, Calif.

Baltimore's application was nearly 100 pages long and included a number of demographic tidbits. *Fact:* The per capita income of the metropolitan area's 2.3 million residents is ninth in the nation. *Fact:* Baltimore has the 22nd largest TV market.

It also pointedly noted that the Washington Redskins hadn't captured the hearts and minds of Baltimore fans, despite concerted efforts by NFL programmers, who beamed the team's weekly games into the city. The Redskins' TV ratings were only half what the Colts' ratings had been during their final, lackluster year in Baltimore.

But it was the application's revenue projections that really got everyone's attention. When an expansion team moved into its new stadium in 1995, the Maryland Stadium Authority estimated that the franchise would earn $16 million a year from skyboxes and club seats; keep almost all of the money made on parking, concessions, tickets and stadium advertising; and pay only about $3 million in stadium operating costs as rent. This would give the team an eye-popping $31.3 million in operating profit.

Furthermore, the team would pay each visiting opponent $1.03 million in ticket receipts under the league's revenue-sharing plan, which split the box-office take for each game 66-34 between the home and away teams. That was twice the NFL average at the time and almost enough by itself to keep Baltimore in the running.

The figures made an immediate impression in the league's front office, which was teeming with MBAs. Neil Austrian, the NFL's president, was a Harvard Business School graduate and former managing director at Dillon, Read & Co., investment bankers.

Roger Goodell, the league's vice president of operations, had primary responsibility for the expansion effort. Viewed by many as future commissioner material, Goodell was the son of New York senator Charles Goodell and had grown up a Redskins fan in the Maryland suburbs of Washington.

Goodell started out by studying past expansions: In 1974, the league picked the cities first — Tampa and Seattle — and lined up owners afterward. This time, the NFL focused on ownership, deeming it to be a crucial factor in the eventual success of the franchise.

Goodell also identified three primary criteria, which came to be known as the three-legged stool: ownership, market, and stadium.

Baltimore listed five investors or groups that were "seriously considering" applying. They included novelist Tom Clancy, Florida-based financier Malcolm Glazer, Maryland developer and political heavyweight Nathan Landow, Colorado oilman J. Thomas Stoen, and iconoclastic retailer Leonard "Boogie" Weinglass.

In his application cover letter to Tagliabue, Belgrad wrote: "At this time our committee has made no commitment of support to any group/individual, but we are prepared to do so if it would be of assistance to the expansion committee or if we deem it appropriate to do so in the future."

On Oct. 1, 1991, 10 prospective ownership groups submitted their separate applications to the NFL. Honolulu, Nashville, and Raleigh-Durham, unable to attract any potential owners, dropped out of contention.

While only a single group filed for each of the remaining cities, Baltimore fielded three, all of which put down the required $100,000 fee — half of which was refundable. Belgrad's plan was to have the potential owners make their individual cases to the league while he made his case for the city.

The fan favorite was Weinglass, a gregarious, 50-year-old hippie who wore his hair in a ponytail. By correctly predicting the fickle fashion tastes of teenagers and catering to them through his coast-to-coast chain of Merry-Go-Round shopping boutiques, he had made a fortune.

Colorful and eccentric, Weinglass was as temperamentally and philosophically removed from the NFL's gray-haired oligarchy as the Grateful Dead's Jerry Garcia. But Weinglass, then residing in

Aspen, Colo., was fiercely loyal to his hometown, where he once ran the streets and squeaked through high school.

Among his childhood chums and co-investors was Barry Levinson, who had become a successful Hollywood director. Levinson's 1982 hit movie, "Diner," told of growing up in Baltimore during the Colts-crazy 1960s. Named for the place where a gang of teenage boys hung out, "Diner" had one memorable scene in which a bride-to-be is tested — more accurately, grilled — on Colts trivia by her football fanatical fiance.

Boogie's character, played in the movie by actor Mickey Rourke, was a lovable, somewhat sleazy schemer who routinely hatched outrageous plots to get dates, make easy money, and live for another day. Weinglass considered it a fairly accurate, and complimentary, depiction.

Tom Clancy, 44, a one-time insurance agent and military buff, had hit it big with *The Hunt for Red October*, his novel about a Soviet submarine run amuck. First published by the Naval Institute Press in Annapolis, the book rocketed to the top of best-seller lists like a laser-guided surface-to-air missile, especially after President Reagan publicly praised it.

Clancy's unabashed celebration of military ethos and high-tech hardware took root in the Reagan years of Pentagon buildups. Soon, this darling of the nascent right wing had become a very rich, extraordinarily successful novelist. But he still spoke fondly and loyally of his Baltimore upbringing — his father had been a long-time Colts season-ticket holder.

Like Weinglass, Clancy considered Irsay's move to Indianapolis a crime against humanity. But, as a potential owner, the novelist seemingly got off on the wrong foot with NFL officials. During presentations before Tagliabue in New York, Clancy boasted that many people with money could buy an NFL team, but he also had the brains to fix the league's many problems.

Asked for some examples, Clancy demurred, saying he preferred to get paid for his ideas.

The wild card in the mix was Malcolm Glazer, 63, a reclusive, full-bearded financier from Palm Beach, Fla. A man who looked more like a rabbi than a mega-millionaire, he had made a fortune in the 1980s, buying and selling stock in companies such as Harley-Davidson, Formica Corp., and Tonka Corp. Although he denied it, many viewed his tactics as "greenmail" — one of the more reprehensible innovations on Wall Street. Greenmailers buy large stakes in corporations, threaten to take them over, and then, after their stock zooms in value in response to the buyout talk, either quickly sell off the inflated stock or negotiate a lucrative sale back.

Among Glazer's early sporting interests was baseball expansion team. In a novel bid for an expansion team, he suggested putting a team in four different towns, which would then rotate its home games. Baseball summarily dismissed the notion. Glazer also looked at the New England Patriots, but when he walked away from the deal, the NFL executives in on it dismissed him as a "tire kicker."

Because his personality was seen as cold and his zip code distant, Glazer tried to compensate by buying new instruments for the still-marching Colts band, but the move was clumsy, and Baltimore fans were never really won over.

And, while he was immediately perceived as having the deepest pockets of all the potential Baltimore owners, he initially refused to contribute the $50,000 that Belgrad asked from each of the bidders to help with the city's sales campaign. Nor was Glazer's cause aided by his personal secretiveness. When he made his presentation to the league staff that winter, he didn't invite Belgrad and other civic representatives to sit in and observe.

Also significant were the men who didn't make bids. Modell's friend and associate Alfred Lerner, then chairman of Maryland National Bank, had been in touch for years with state officials. He seemed to have it all: great wealth, ownership of a piece of the Cleveland Browns and, as an NFL insider, rapport with the other owners.

"If Baltimore does get a team and Lerner surfaces as a prospective owner, he'd get a hearty endorsement from me. He'd be an asset to the league," Modell told the Baltimore *Evening Sun* in 1987.

But Lerner told Belgrad that he didn't want any part of a "beauty contest" pitting him against other owners in a public competition. Standing on Rozelle's assurances that the state should stay out of the owner-picking game, Maryland declined to express a preference. According to acquaintances, Lerner was put off by Maryland's refusal to back him.

P. Robert Tisch, a wealthy New York businessman and former U.S. Postmaster General, once had been considered Baltimore's strongest candidate for ownership. He was loaded with money, and his brother, Lawrence, ran CBS. Even rival Jacksonville tried to lure him away for its NFL bid in September 1990.

But Tisch dropped out of the running in February 1991 when given a chance to buy a 50-percent stake in his hometown team, the New York Giants, owned by old-guard member Wellington Mara.

His defection was a devastating blow to Baltimore's chances. The remaining potential owners were a quirky and varied lot — hometown characters and one out-of-towner. None seemed to fit easily into the NFL mold.

Still, Belgrad thought the three-way application was safer for Baltimore than just a single shot. "It's very risky to tie yourself to a particular owner of an expansion group," he said at the time. "My view is that St. Louis and Charlotte are taking risks we are not ready to take."

What Belgrad most wanted was to keep the state in control of its own application and spare it another crisis if another applicant dropped out.

Besides, NFL officials assured Belgrad that the multiple application was not a problem.

The league said the same thing to Jacksonville's contingent, which would suffer its own ownership turmoil. But Jacksonville wasn't reassured. Its delegates had received different advice from people in Atlanta, who had won the bid for the 1996 Olympics.

"They impressed upon us that Atlanta got the games for a lot of reasons, but one of them was they had built personal relationships," said Rick Catlett, a top strategist in Jacksonville.

"It is the most elite club in America. There are only 100 U.S. senators, but 30 NFL team owners. They are not going to have anyone in the club they do not want."

Down in Charlotte, strategist and consultant Max Muhleman was happy. He considered Baltimore, with its promise of a new stadium, a formidable contender. But he thought its application was bound to become muddied with all of the contending owners. Those voting on a franchise award want to know the people who will own the team, he reasoned, not the landlord.

Charlotte's prospective owner, Jerry Richardson, and his son

Mark, a godson of former Colts star Raymond Berry, quietly got to work calling on team owners, playing golf with them, and preparing them to accept an ex-player turned millionaire restaurateur as a partner.

.   Richardson, drafted by the Baltimore Colts in 1959, when he set a record for receptions by a rookie, played a second season with the Colts, then used his $4,674 bonus check from the 1959 championship to buy a hamburger joint. He built this business into a fast-food empire that now included Denny's and was the fourth largest food-service operation in the country.

In their quest for a franchise, the Richardsons even hosted pre-season games to bring voting owners to them. The Redskins and the Falcons played on Aug. 11, 1990, in the University of North Carolina's football stadium at Chapel Hill; the year before, the Jets met the Eagles in a contest in Raleigh.

When he first entered the expansion race in August 1989, one of Richardson's first calls was to Pete Rozelle; it was shortly after the commissioner had retired.

"Pete, if it wouldn't be awkward for you, now that you're no longer commissioner, would you mind if I came to see you and asked you to help coach us in trying to get this franchise?" Richardson asked.

"I don't even have to think about it," Rozelle replied. "I'll be glad to help you."

• • •

In March 1992, the NFL pared the list of city finalists to seven: Baltimore, Charlotte, Jacksonville, Memphis, Oakland, Sacramento, and St. Louis. Two months later, the committee dropped Oakland and Sacramento.

"The real favorites at the beginning of the process were St. Louis and Charlotte," Braman said.

On Sept. 17, Tagliabue announced that the winning cities would not be picked that fall, as initially planned, because of the continuing labor dispute with the players. To the franchise contestants, it was a frustrating delay.

The owners wanted to use expansion — with its promise of hundreds of new jobs for players — as an enticement to the NFL

Players Association. But the association wasn't buying. Instead, it was pursuing its antitrust claims in court.

And, while settlement talks in the Freeman McNeil case were then going on, progress was slow. On Jan. 6, 1993, after the judge pressured both sides, the NFL and the players emerged with a tentative agreement.

The deal ushered free agency and revenue sharing into the NFL. And more important for Baltimore, it put expansion back on track. The NFL had a new deadline: The cities would be selected in the fall of 1993.

Then, at their May meeting, the NFL owners made sure they could afford expansion. They set the highest franchise fee in sports: $140 million. Payment terms and restrictions on TV revenues in the first years pushed the total franchise package to a 1993 value of $170 million. Half of the money would have to be paid before the new teams even took the field; and they would get only half of their 1/30 share of the network TV revenue during their first three years. If a new owner found himself struggling early, he was further limited by a rule requiring any club sale profits to go to the league.

It was a steep price. Two years earlier, Major League Baseball had charged $95 million for a new franchise. The year before, the NHL had charged $50 million. In 1989, the NBA had asked for $32.5 million.

But the NFL was a league that thought a lot of itself.

"I think it says it's the No. 1-rated sport in the world," Neil Austrian told reporters.

"We've got more television viewers worldwide than any sport in history. We get better ratings on our pre-season games than the NBA does with its playoffs. We don't have some of the problems that other sports have. I think the price reflects that."

One potential investor wasn't so sure. A week before the fee was announced, Tom Clancy, complaining about the NFL's changing economics and rumored high franchise fees, dropped his bid and joined with local attorney Peter Angelos to buy the Orioles. Down to two potential owners, Baltimore geared up for a final push.

• • •

The campaign now got serious, and, at times, silly. The league asked the finalists to take one final test. During two months in the heat of summer, the applicants were asked to lease as many of their skyboxes and club seats as they could, taking deposits for each.

This would mean real fans putting down real money. Belgrad was apprehensive. He suspected that the plan was designed to help Charlotte. Having serious problems lining up funding for his stadium, Richardson had put together a plan to sell "personal seat licenses." Fans in the Carolinas, he hoped, would be so eager for football that they would buy the right to buy a season ticket. Under this scheme, each seat would have a license, and a fan would have to buy that license — good for 30 years — before he could buy an annual season ticket.

There was some precedent. The NBA Hornets had success selling "charter seat rights" in Charlotte, and Max Muhleman, who had helped land that team for the city, thought it might work for football, too.

It was a new twist on an old idea. Texas Stadium had been financed in part by the sale of interest-bearing seat bonds. And churches had been known to sell the rights to good pews in colonial times. But never had anything been done on this scale. Richardson was trying to sell $150 million worth of seat licenses, in prices ranging from $600 to $5,400. If he sold them all, he would have about $100 million, after taxes. This money, combined with land in Charlotte's "uptown" section promised by local governments, would allow Richardson to build and own his own palace.

Stadium financing had been the weak element in his application, but he was a successful and conservative businessman. With Muhleman's adroit use of maps and population projections, he had managed to create a sprawling region teeming with 10 million potential fans within a two-hour drive of Charlotte — a city with a population of just 452,000. But the bid still lacked money.

There was plenty of talk about the seat licenses growing in value, as had some Hornet seat rights. At one point, worried that the prospective NFL owners were peddling unregistered securities, North Carolina's security regulators stepped in with questions. The Charlotte group backed off from its claims of investment potential.

But the truth was the expansion team was likely to control the PSL resale value by, among other things, the prices it charged for season tickets every year, and by its performance on the field.

The league was intrigued. Not only could PSLs be a new source of revenue for team owners, but they would almost guarantee season-ticket sales down the road. Anyone not buying a season ticket would forfeit the license. And public funding of stadiums was getting harder and harder to achieve.

Richardson wanted to prove that the licenses would actually sell. His ownership group reasoned that the sales would go better if they were tied to a larger civic mission such as bringing an NFL team to town.

The NFL approved the idea and extended the premium-seat challenge to all of the finalists. Although it was technically a voluntary test, the cities knew they had to compete and turned the effort into a crusade. There were downtown rallies, arm-twisting sessions in city halls, and a frenzy of gushing media coverage.

In Baltimore, Schaefer rounded up his most loyal business supporters for a lunch at the Camden Club, adjacent to Oriole Park. He asked them to do their part. One guest impudently asked about the competition and the city's chances against St. Louis and Charlotte.

Schaefer pointed out the window, where the football stadium was going to be built, and promised, "There's going to be a hole in the ground before I leave office."

• • •

Just as the two-month premium-seat campaign was gearing up, Jacksonville quit the franchise chase. With ticket sales going slowly and stadium talks between the city and franchise investors going poorly, the ownership group dropped out.

The Gator Bowl had initially been slated for a $60 million overhaul. But with the NFL setting a higher-than-expected franchise fee, investors demanded more from the city, and the price rose to $145 million. Each side now wanted the other to cover potential cost overruns.

"It's just a huge disappointment and somewhat surprising in that it came over a glitch in the lease," said John Delaney, chief of staff for Jacksonville Mayor Ed Austin.

Strategists in several of the other cities expressed public disappointment over the loss. Privately, however, several smugly said they didn't think it mattered much. Jacksonville was the smallest city of the bunch. Its television market was tiny. And there were already two other teams in Florida. It was never really a contender, they reasoned.

In Baltimore, the Maryland Stadium Authority, which had been keeping current with the competition through local-newspaper clips, hadn't even bothered to monitor the Memphis or Jacksonville papers.

Then, a month later, at Tagliabue's urging, the Jacksonville parties patched up their differences and jumped back into the race. The city agreed to pay up to $121 million, but said any overruns would be the team's responsibility.

So, in early August 1994, the "final four" were five again, and none of the cities felt it had done poorly enough in the premium-seat drive to hurt its chances. Baltimore sold its 100 skyboxes and 7,500 club seats before anyone else — and several days before the campaign's official end.

"Every time there is a challenge that the NFL puts before us, we seem to meet and beat it," Mayor Kurt L. Schmoke said at a press conference convened on the site of the proposed stadium.

Suffering catastrophic flooding of the Mississippi River, St. Louis sold only 70 skyboxes and 6,169 of its 6,252 club seats. Memphis, with some last-minute improvements to its stadium, got into the race late, but managed to sell out its 100 skyboxes and 8,302 club seats.

On-again, off-again Jacksonville wouldn't say how it did with skybox sales, but reported selling 7,899 out of 10,000 available club seats.

Charlotte went 98 for 98 on suites and 8,314 for 8,314 on club seats. But it sold only 48,000 of the 62,000 seat licenses. Competitors snickered, but Richardson drew up a plan for the NFL that called for local banks and businesses to buy up the remaining PSL inventory, if that money were needed to get the stadium built.

In Baltimore, optimism was running high as the city entered the final stretch.

Fans even allowed themselves to get lost in a name-the-team

controversy. The league asked all five cities to pick names so trade-mark applications could be filed and designs drawn up. The mar-keting-savvy NFL wanted to hit the streets with caps, T-shirts, and other merchandise as soon as the winners were announced.

Memphis — home of Elvis Presley — picked the Hound Dogs, Bombers, and Showboats. Charlotte went with the Panthers; Jacksonville the Jaguars, and St. Louis the Stallions.

In Baltimore, the Glazer group liked the Cobras. Weinglass preferred the Bombers, for its alliterative value and also because it harked back to Baltimore's brief but significant contributions to military aviation during World War II. The league forced a com-promise: the Rhinos.

The fans stampeded.

The two investor groups agreed to cut the fans in on the action and cooperated in a mail-in/call-in poll coordinated by *The Sun*. The Bombers got 9 percent of the vote, the Rhinos 8 percent, and the Cobras 5 percent. "The Hons," a local term of endearment, received 2 percent.

The surprise winner came from one of the city's more bizarre, dead residents: Edgar Allan Poe. A Richmond, Va., native, the famed poet and short-story writer lived briefly in Baltimore, where he launched his ill-fated literary career. It was also where, under murky circumstances, he died and was buried. Every year on his January birthday, a red rose and a bottle of brandy mysteriously appeared on his grave.

Quoth the fans: The Ravens. They liked the connection with the other birds in town, the Orioles, and the brooding and menac-ing nature of the scavenger.

But Weinglass and Glazer weren't convinced. After more deliberation, the two went with the Bombers, largely because of the merchandise possibilities. Weinglass said he liked the Ravens, but thought the logos looked too much like crows.

A lot of back-room maneuvering went on in the final weeks of the summer. Heading into the final presentations and votes by the league, cities divined what they could from owners and league offi-cials and tried to shore up weak points in their applications.

Charlotte, still facing questions about its financial solvency, added a pair of multimillionaire investors: Donald Keough, the retired president of Coca-Cola Co., and Leon Levine, a retail executive estimated by *Forbes* magazine to have a personal fortune of $380 million. Memphis picked up Elvis Presley Enterprises as a minority investor.

St. Louis, a favorite among handicappers until then, simply imploded. The city had a large regional market, a new stadium under construction — or, more accurately, a convention center annex that doubled as a domed stadium — and an owner already in the NFL, James Busch Orthwein — *Busch*, as in Anheuser-*Busch*, the league's largest advertiser.

Orthwein stepped in when it became clear the city's application needed more money. Along the way, he picked up another team. In the spring of 1992, he bought the New England Patriots from Victor Kiam. Even in St. Louis, where Orthwein was seen as the city's great hope for an expansion team, his purchase of the hapless Pats was considered a plus. He had done the league a favor and gained St. Louis an entree to the NFL's back rooms. And Orthwein reassuringly declared that he would sell the Patriots if St. Louis got a franchise.

But in August 1993, just as quickly as he had joined the expansion drive, Orthwein dropped out. He had a falling out with Jerry Clinton, a gregarious beer distributor who had assembled the chief investment group, then shepherded the stadium plan through the state, city, and county governments.

Clinton faced some tough questions in Chicago on Aug. 21 when the five cities made their final presentations to committees of NFL team owners. He had to explain the city's lethargic response to the premium seat campaign, as well as the shifting composition of the ownership group.

Long the presumptive favorite, St. Louis was suddenly up against the ropes and gasping. Jacksonville was still bobbing and weaving. And Memphis was receiving blunt messages from the NFL that its partial renovation of the Liberty Bowl simply wasn't enough. But it couldn't do any more.

Baltimore couldn't have written a better ending.

The Maryland delegation arrived at the Chicago meeting armed with a short film. It began with shots of the city's Inner Harbor, before and after its conversion from rat-infested warehouses to tourist Mecca. Then the cameras panned to Oriole Park at Camden Yards, where the Orioles were setting new records for sellouts and had just been sold for a record price. There were interviews of Gov. William Donald Schaefer, local business titans, and ex-Colts star Lenny Moore. The film closed with a clip of Johnny Unitas moving the Colts downfield during the glory days.

Maryland Stadium Authority executive director Bruce Hoffman followed up with a presentation on the state's lottery-backed stadium financing. The team would get to keep all of the stadium revenues, he said.

"I'll take that deal," quipped San Diego Chargers owner Alex Spanos.

Weinglass and Glazer then made brief remarks before yielding to the delegation's "closer" — Schaefer himself. The governor's appearance had been a closely guarded secret. Baltimore's planners didn't want their competitors to respond in kind with their own chief executives.

The deception went so far as to have Schaefer attend a meeting of the Southern Governors' Association in Virginia that morning, then have a car whisk him from the meeting to the airport and a flight to Chicago.

He made an emotional pitch for the city he had rebuilt. Without saying so, he asked the NFL owners to remedy the wrong inflicted nine years earlier by Robert Irsay, and to erase the darkest blotch on his political resume.

"I was there when the team left, and I want to be there when they come back," Schaefer told them.

The Baltimore representatives came out of the meetings feeling confident. Weinglass termed the city, and himself, "a lock."

But warning signs soon started appearing.

Through their network of confidants and insiders, the Stadium Authority learned what they feared most: Weinglass and Glazer had fared poorly. Some owners liked one or the other, but neither was exactly considered NFL material.

Weinglass, with his ponytail and reputation for wildness, turned off conservative team owners. It also didn't help that someone was engaged in a smear campaign against Weinglass, sending anonymous packages to the team owners reminding them of his admitted history of high-stakes gambling. Or that his business was beginning to fail.

As for Glazer, he said and did nothing to dispel fears that he would run the team just the way he had run his other investments: as a profit center to be bought low and sold high. The owners also knew Glazer's history of conflict with his sisters over their parents' meager estate. As corporate as the league had become, its owners still wanted partners who showed some knowledge or affection for the game. Glazer showed neither, and boasted that he would turn the team over to his sons to operate.

A month later, Schaefer met with Weinglass and Glazer at the Maryland State House to get another read on them. He also made a secret visit to New York on Oct. 20 to feel out Tagliabue. The governor told the commissioner he could support either prospective owner, but was open to other candidates.

Tagliabue told him not to worry.

CHAPTER NINE

A
Sun Belt
Strategy

On Oct. 26, 1993, members of the National Football League's finance and expansion committees met to select the cities that would receive expansion teams. Gathered around a long table at the O'Hare Hyatt, a drab luxury hotel in the Chicago suburb of Rosemont, sat some of the league's heavyweights: Giants president Robert Tisch, Saints owner Tom Benson, and 49ers president Carmen Policy.

Commissioner Tagliabue chaired both the expansion committee and the day's joint meeting. After his staff gave a presentation heavy with demographics, Charlotte and Jacksonville bobbed quickly to the top. In a comparison of population and economic-growth rates, the two Sun Belt cities shined.

The fact was Tagliabue and his staff had internally developed a "Sun Belt strategy," their idea being to steer teams to fast-growing regions which could capture fans and dollars not otherwise committed to professional sports. The NFL commissioner's buzzwords had become "hot markets" and "virgin territory."

This was a radical departure for sports leagues. In the past, they had merely targeted the next largest cities for expansion. This gave the edge to already populated cities, not up-and-comers. Tagliabue not only ignored this tactic, but also dismissed the "old-city/new-city" approach Rozelle had discussed, thus depriving

Baltimore of credit for helping to get the NFL off the ground. Television network executives said they didn't care where teams were based. The NFL had become a national broadcast product. It would garner high viewership wherever the games were played.

Los Angeles even demonstrated the fallacy of the "big-market-is-better" theory: Its teams frequently failed to sell out, which meant — in accord with NFL rules — that home games were blacked out in L.A. The networks, which supposedly insisted on teams in the biggest cities, were thus frequently forced to skip broadcasts of home games in the nation's second-biggest market. Big-city fans were blasè about anything but a winning team, said the common wisdom. They had a myriad of entertainment options, from the latest movies to the hottest restaurants, to enjoy.

Large-population centers were more important to sports such as baseball and basketball, which had large ticket inventories. Each year, a baseball team plays 81 home games and has up to 4 million tickets to move. A football team, by contrast, only has eight regular-season home games and one or two pre-season games — 700,000 tickets at most.

Cities like Buffalo and Green Bay, where the NFL is the only game in town and its teams receive enthusiastic fan support, are the future of pro football, Tagliabue argued. A franchise could flourish in a city where it doesn't have to compete for corporate sponsors or season-ticket customers. And the league could be assured of sell-outs, giving the viewers at home the sense of a sport on the move.

Among the most devout Sun Belt apostles on the expansion committee was Art Modell, who spoke often in favor of valuable new markets and *against* old NFL cities like Baltimore and St. Louis. Returning to those cities was simply "not in the best interest of the NFL," said Modell, according to fellow committee member and Eagles owner Norman Braman.

To emphasize the point at the Chicago meeting, NFL staffers projected onto a screen a computer-generated map of the country. Circled were the cities with NFL teams and the cities that were potential expansion sites. The circle encompassing Baltimore pointedly overlapped those around Washington and Philadelphia.

After some initial discussion, committee members decided to take a straw poll, going around the room to allow each participant to nominate a pair of cities.

Charlotte, small but fast-growing, made everyone's top two list. It was a virtual poster child for Tagliabue's vision of an untapped, booming market. The month before, Charlotte's downtown had graced the cover of *Fortune* magazine, which rated it the nation's hottest city for business. Modell was especially supportive of Charlotte.

But there was so much disagreement about the second team that the polling didn't even make it around the table.

The committee members then tried a "one-and-one" strategy. The first ballot on a single city gave Charlotte nine votes, with Baltimore, Jacksonville, and St. Louis each receiving one. In discussions on the second city, interest in St. Louis picked up, although there was trepidation about its murky ownership situation.

St. Louis' newly constituted ownership group, now headed by the woefully dull Stan Kroenke, a Missouri developer and Wal-Mart heir, had not performed well in owner presentations earlier that day. A member of the former group, Fran Murray, had also arrived, bringing along additional investors, laying claim to the lease, and holding himself out as a prospective owner unsanctioned by the city.

Murray and his partner Jerry Clinton had led St. Louis' early expansion effort. They had lobbied city, county, and state leaders for stadium funding, and when the funding had been approved, had been given a lease, contingent on obtaining a team.

At the time, the deal made perfect sense: Lawmakers weren't about to approve millions of dollars in stadium money unless they had a commitment from a prospective team owner willing to put his own money at risk. The problem with the arrangement was now clear. Under the lease, Clinton and Murray retained exclusive use of the facility for football games. That meant they could keep out anyone else's team. Civic leaders put together an $8 million deal to buy the lease back from Murray and Clinton and give it to the Kroenke group, which Clinton joined.

But Murray, a former part-owner with James Busch Orthwein of the New England Patriots, rejected the proposed settlement. He now hinted at a lawsuit.

The league couldn't tell who would get the franchise if it was awarded to St. Louis. But it did seem clear there would be a lawsuit to settle the matter. The city had simply shot itself in the foot.

Because it offered the weakest stadium plan — a $60 million

renovation of the Liberty Bowl — Memphis was viewed as a non-starter. Its prospective owners were also haggling with the NFL over the terms of the expansion fee.

Maryland's stadium plan was universally praised, but Weinglass and Glazer failed to elicit the same enthusiasm that some of their competitors did. Weinglass' retail company was beginning to fail, raising questions about his ability to do the deal. There was even doubt about Baltimore's desire for football after the long absence of the Colts.

Baltimore won support from Tisch, Braman, and Atlanta Falcons owner Rankin Smith. For a time, it appeared to committee members that Baltimore and St. Louis had equal support, with Jacksonville trailing behind. Tagliabue himself was never asked for a formal recommendation.

The owners group couldn't agree on a second city. The commissioner's staff thought going into the meeting that it might be necessary to split the votes, and now Tagliabue suggested as much. Upon his recommendation, the joint committee voted 12-0 for Charlotte and postponed for a month their vote on a second city. The NFL ownership followed suit, by unanimous vote, and Jerry Richardson's Panthers became the NFL's 29th franchise.

"It was very difficult. One was easy, but the second one, you can tell by what we did, how tough it was," Braman said afterward.

Modell told reporters that Charlotte was "a growing, thriving, flourishing community with a lot of appeal. I think it's one of the great areas of the country."

Baltimore's NFL delegation, anxiously awaiting word of the owners' decision, passed the time in their hotel suite swapping gossip, practicing golf swings, and drinking Cokes. Governor Schaefer emerged occasionally to wander the concrete skywalks that crisscrossed the interior of the labyrinthine Hyatt.

When the knock finally came at Baltimore's door about 9 p.m., Schaefer, Mayor Schmoke and others were out to dinner. Only Herb Belgrad and two of the city's chief strategists were there: former Colts and Browns executive Ernie Accorsi, then a paid special adviser to the Stadium Authority, and Rouse Co. chairman Mathias J. DeVito. The knock was a surprise: The delegation had been told to expect a phone call.

The NFL executive wouldn't tell the Baltimore delegates what the decision was, instead ushering them down to a service elevator, where they found Weinglass. He whispered that he had seen the Charlotte delegation being led to another elevator — a development he considered a bad omen.

The elevator then went down a floor, and representatives from Memphis boarded. It finally arrived at the hotel's basement kitchen, where the Jacksonville delegation had already assembled.

To avoid the crush of reporters and camera crews, the entourage was guided down a series of back hallways stacked with furniture and mechanical equipment to a big, cold banquet room with chairs scattered about. It didn't take long for the city groups to figure out which cities weren't represented: Charlotte and St. Louis.

Belgrad deduced that Baltimore had lost and stepped to the back of the room to collect his thoughts. Weinglass huddled with his rival, Glazer, in a corner and made a joke about waiting for the gas to be dropped into the room, Holocaust-style.

Just then, St. Louis Mayor Freeman Bosley showed up, and relief spread throughout the room. Tagliabue appeared with NFL President Neil Austrian and Joe Browne, league vice president of communications. Tagliabue, explaining the decision, joked that he knew these owners so well that when they didn't quickly agree, they could spend another two weeks without reaching a decision.

Several of the prospective expansion owners asked questions about technical issues, such as the letters of credit being held pending the decision and their premium seat deposits.

Tagliabue asked for their patience, and Browne gave them a pep talk. Austrian said the league would pay the interest on extending the $20 million letters of credit each had been required to post. The league ended up giving each group $15,000 for this.

Jacksonville's prospective owner, millionaire shoe retailer J. Wayne Weaver, was the most assertive. He was angry that the NFL appeared to be accommodating St. Louis and its 11th-hour ownership entry. Surely, he asked, doesn't the league know by now which city is *not* in the running?

"If we are not going to be in the finals, tell us now. We don't want to know 30 days from now," Weaver told Austrian. He then demanded, and received, a meeting with Tagliabue the next day.

In subsequent weeks, Weaver spoke with Tagliabue and Austrian again. The conversations, he later said, were encouraging.

• • •

Given the chaos over the St. Louis lease, Belgrad's policy of keeping public control over the lease looked like sheer genius. But the strategy's downside was also becoming apparent.

Fairly or not, Glazer and Weinglass were considered the weak link in the city's application. And the day of the Charlotte vote, Glazer appeared to make matters worse. In his final presentation to the NFL owners, he sprang a surprise on Belgrad and the Baltimore officials by offering to eliminate the annual rent for skybox customers for the first five years and instead charge higher ticket prices. There would be no difference for fans, but the entire sum would become subject to the league's revenue-sharing distribution. Teams playing in Baltimore would thus leave with $1.5 million after every sold-out game. Glazer crassly underscored this point by flashing it on a screen with an overhead projector.

The ploy backfired. Some owners got the feeling they were being bought, while others, who either had or wanted club seats, didn't want to see a newcomer disrupting the delicate revenue-sharing balance then in effect.

Glazer merely succeeded in reinforcing his image as an awkward loner interested more in money than sport.

But Boogie Weinglass' jocular manner also left some owners worried that he would be a loose cannon in the conservative league. A few days after the expansion decision, he went to New York to meet with Tagliabue, who assured him he had passed muster. But Belgrad was hearing the opposite from his contacts.

Other cities had investors with international business reputations: Memphis had William Dunavant, the world's largest cotton merchant; Jacksonville had Weaver, who had made a fortune with Nine West Group Inc., Shoe Carnival, and other retailers.

Still, there seemed little room for improvement in Baltimore's financial offer. It had been constructed to be so overwhelmingly lucrative that the city's geographical shortcomings would be overcome. Baltimore was just a few hours' drive from five NFL franchises — the Redskins, Giants, Jets, Eagles, and Steelers — and it was hardly a Sun Belt hot spot.

On Nov. 3, Belgrad and the city's other strategists held a secret summit in the Greater Baltimore Committee's downtown Baltimore offices. Over catered dinner and a birthday cake for Schaefer, who turned 72 the day before, the group decided to do something drastic: Draft a new owner. They would essentially dump their longtime partners, Weinglass and Glazer. The men's status would remain officially unchanged, but Schaefer would endorse a new owner, making it unlikely the other two would be picked.

After word of Baltimore's disenchantment with its owners had leaked out, there had been some inquiries from prospective parties, including Houston oilman Bruce McNair, who had been referred to Baltimore by the NFL. Hollywood producer Jeff Lurie also called. His family had a longstanding business relationship with Bob Tisch.

Tisch mentioned Lurie to Baltimore banker H. Furlong Baldwin, a member of Tisch's old Baltimore investment group, who was working behind the scenes to try to salvage the city's bid. Lurie went to Baltimore on Oct. 8 and 9, 1993, to meet with the city's NFL-expansion leaders and, later, with Schaefer at the State House. In the ensuing weeks, Lurie concluded that Baltimore's chances were not good, and he stayed out. Not that Belgrad minded. He didn't think Lurie offered anything beyond what Glazer and Weinglass had provided. Lurie later bought the Eagles from Braman.

Meanwhile, the strategists also received feelers from intermediaries that Alfred Lerner was still interested in helping.

Lerner seemed the obvious candidate. *Forbes* magazine had placed his fortune at $770 million. He was an insider, having traveled with the Cleveland Browns and met many of the owners. His Baltimore connections were thin, but helpful. And his good friend Art Modell sat on the expansion committee.

Until now, Belgrad viewed Modell as someone who would observe the commissioner's wishes. Bringing Lerner aboard, he thought, could win over Modell and his considerable influence.

Lerner and the Maryland Stadium Authority then engaged in extensive negotiations on the lease. The banker was not satisfied with the general terms laid out in Belgrad's letter to Glazer and Weinglass — terms that called for the team to get all of the revenue from the stadium's NFL games in exchange for paying the costs of operation.

Working through his personal attorney, former U.S. Attorney General Benjamin Civiletti, Lerner won the right to control the stadium year-round. He would be able to book concerts and other events in exchange for a management fee and half of the profits. Belgrad took the tough negotiations as a good sign. Lerner was a winner and a fighter, he thought, and wouldn't be bothering with these terms unless he intended to get a team.

Meanwhile, Schaefer made another pilgrimage to Tagliabue's New York office. Later, he recalled the gist of their conversation:

"I said, 'Look, we've been battling a long time. It's costing us a lot of money. We've had the support of the business community. Are we wasting our time?'"

"He said, 'Absolutely, Governor, you are not wasting your time. Please, stay in.' He did not say we were getting a team. But he said, 'Your presentation was the best.' And it was. It was by far the best."

Schaefer called Lerner Nov. 15 to say he would give him his exclusive endorsement. Then he announced the switch.

"We supported Mr. Glazer and Mr. Weinglass, but we didn't win. We can't stand pat," Schaefer explained to reporters.

Glazer took the news quietly. But not Weinglass. He took out a full-page ad in *The Sun* headlined: "An open letter to the Football Fans of Baltimore from Leonard 'Boogie' Weinglass."

"I am shocked and hurt by the Lerner application," Weinglass wrote. Lerner's bank, Maryland National, had provided Weinglass' group with its financing and had access to its projections and plans.

"I am not a banker. I am not a lawyer. I do not have an MBA from a fancy school. But, I do know right from wrong. I also know that a person who takes a deal to a bank should not have to worry about the bank or its officers competing with him."

Charlotte won a team by presenting a united front, said Weinglass —something Baltimore was not doing because of the multiple-ownership scheme.

"The governor and mayor were poorly advised in thinking that multiple ownership groups were a strength," he concluded. "It proved to be a weakness ... It's the Baltimore Expansion Committee's game plan that failed — not me."

Weinglass vowed to fight on. But without the endorsement of the mayor or the governor, his chances of winning a team were virtually nil.

Belgrad and Schaefer prepared for an intense lobbying campaign during which they and Lerner would fly all around the country, meeting owners and making their case. Regarded now as moot was the commissioner's prohibition on contacting owners — and all of his other rules.

"We were all prepared to put on hold our professional lives and the government of Maryland to go to NFL owners with Al Lerner," Belgrad said.

Lerner called to say he had spoken with Modell, who advised against such a public campaign. The league, too, was worried about an all-out lobbying blitz by the remaining finalists. Leave everything to him, said the Browns owner, and he would line up Baltimore's votes.

Belgrad was stunned. He asked for a meeting, and Lerner flew into Baltimore on his private plane. Schaefer, Belgrad, Civiletti, Lerner, and the Rouse Co.'s Matt DeVito met with Lerner aboard his jet at BWI.

"Al Lerner said Modell was going to do this, and Modell was his friend, and we had to have confidence in him," Belgrad recalled.

Though Belgrad wasn't comfortable leaving the work up to Modell, and said so, Lerner countered that his relationship with Modell superseded his relationship with Baltimore.

Maryland's strategists began hearing indirectly that Modell and his wife were not happy about Lerner's sudden involvement with Baltimore. Aware that their family would have a hard time holding on to the Browns after Modell's death, when estate taxes would substantially reduce his fortune, they had hoped Lerner would buy the team and keep their son, David, in the business. NFL rules prohibit owners from having a stake in two competing teams, so Lerner couldn't be involved in both Baltimore's and Modell's teams.

A few months later, in an interview with *The Akron Beacon Journal*, Modell didn't mention the estate issue. He said he simply thought Baltimore's chances were not good, and he wanted to spare his friend humiliation.

"He asked me what I thought. I said, 'Al, you're a long shot, but you've got a better shot at getting it than some of the other groups in Baltimore, so come on in and I'll introduce you to the committee,'" Modell told the newspaper.

But Modell said he also advised his friend "to come in the

back way and go out the back way. I didn't want him to be exposed
to the media under the scenario that Jacksonville got it, and Al
Lerner came in on his white charger and failed.... I didn't want him
to be embarrassed in any way. He got into the picture at the behest
of the governor, reluctantly. He wasn't crazy about it. He said he
wanted to step forward if he could be of help to the city of
Baltimore."

Lerner, Modell said later, advised the Browns owner not to get
himself into a bind with the league by supporting him, and then
paid his $100,000 application fee.

Despite strategic disagreements, Lerner's role buoyed spirits
among the city's expansion committee. But a new and even bigger
problem was developing not far to the south.

• • •

When expansion rolled around, the Washington Redskins
were still publicly neutral on Baltimore's application. But Baltimore
still had ample reason to be nervous.

Despite years of negotiating with local D.C. government,
owner Jack Kent Cooke had been unable to get a new stadium built
for his football team. In 1988, he promised to invest $150 million of
his own money to build in the District. Then, four years later, with
talks still dragging on and Cooke's friend, Mayor Marion Barry,
headed to prison for smoking crack-cocaine, the Redskins
announced a deal to build in an old rail yard in Alexandria, Va.

The idea raised a loud outcry from residents of the tony, bed-
room suburb, and the deal was called off four months later. Then,
in February 1993, Cooke announced that he had settled his differences with then-Washington Mayor Sharon Pratt Kelly and signed
a formal agreement to build in the capital.

But those talks, too, soon faltered, and Cooke was on the
prowl again. Late in 1993, he connected with Joseph De Francis, the
embattled owner of thoroughbred racetracks in Baltimore and
Laurel, Md., a suburb off of Interstate 95, about halfway between
Baltimore and Washington.

A corporate lawyer, De Francis had been busily engaged in
mega-mergers and acquisitions while his popular father, Frank De
Francis, was reviving Maryland's moribund racing industry. The

elder De Francis, economic development secretary under Governor Hughes, died in August 1989. After his death, his lawyer son decided to run the De Francis tracks himself.

This took his father's partners, brothers John and Robert Manfuso, by surprise. As well-connected horsemen, they thought they would be running the show. Soon, they were battling in court with the younger De Francis. As part of a settlement, the two sides agreed to an arrangement whereby either one buy the other out; the would-be seller would then have the choice of taking the offer or matching it. This seemed to favor the Manfusos, who had made a fortune in pharmaceuticals.

But De Francis ended up buying out his hostile partners, agreeing to pay $8.2 million over five years with interest of prime plus a point. The Manfusos wondered where De Francis would come up with the money and demanded to hold the track's stock as collateral.

They thought they had the answer when Cooke announced plans to construct a new stadium on 100 acres adjacent to the Laurel racetrack, which he had optioned from De Francis. De Francis told the Maryland Racing Commission that Cooke had helped him with the financing to buy out the Manfusos. Just how, he didn't say. But, a few years later, the Manfusos had their suspicions confirmed: Responding to their inquiry about a tardy De Francis payment, a bank employee casually told them that past payments had all been preceded by a like-sum deposit from a Cooke account and that Cooke's latest payment had come in one day late.

This wasn't Cooke's first sign of interest in Laurel. In 1981, he spent six months negotiating to buy the De Francis racetrack for $9 million. His intention was to build a sports complex similar to the New Jersey Meadowlands, where the New York Giants play, but he did not complete the deal because, as he explained later, the NFL would not have looked favorably on his racetrack purchase.

• • •

Fortified with Lerner as their new prospective owner, and unaware of the talks between Cooke and De Francis, the Baltimore representatives gathered Nov. 30, 1993 at the same hotel where the league had voted in Charlotte a month earlier.

The scene was all too familiar. The same drab hotel with its exposed concrete architecture and overhead skywalks. Television trucks parked alongside the hotel with telescoping dishes fully extended, beaming live shots to four expectant cities. Reporters and scattered fans from applicant cities milling about in the hotel's lobby, forcing guests to walk a gauntlet of cameras and cables.

But Baltimore's delegates again had reason for relative optimism. Despite the extra time, St. Louis had not cleared all the clouds from its application and was seen as a litigation hazard. Memphis was still not considered a serious contender. Its ownership group had further turned off some league officials by offering to pay more of the expansion fee up front in exchange for a reduction in the final amount.

That left Baltimore, with 2.4 million metropolitan-area residents, slugging it out with Jacksonville, whose urban area encompassed less than 1 million residents and no major-league sports. Moreover, the Florida city's television market was ranked 54th in the country, compared with 18th for St. Louis and 22nd for Baltimore. If selected, Jacksonville would be the smallest city in the NFL except for Green Bay.

A few days before the meeting, Cooke wrote Tagliabue to say that he had given up trying to build a stadium in Washington or Virginia. Laurel was now his preferred option. And, he noted, about half of his season-ticket holders lived in Maryland.

Schaefer caught wind of the scheme and was furious. But the matter was kept quiet until Tagliabue, who had already decided to back Jacksonville and Wayne Weaver, read Cooke's letter to the expansion and finance committees the day of their second vote.

Cooke was hardly a league force, but the message had to be clear. Putting a team in his back yard, even his newly designated back yard, would violate whatever unwritten code of loyalty still existed among owners.

League staffers, who had met before the meeting and settled on Jacksonville, then reviewed the data again. They pointed out that the nation's southeastern quadrant had 65 million residents but only five NFL teams — the Atlanta Falcons, Miami Dolphins, Tampa Bay Buccaneers, New Orleans Saints, and now the Carolina Panthers. The "Northeast," they said, had 75 million people and nine teams — the Redskins, Jets, Giants, Patriots, Eagles, Steelers,

Bills, Browns, and Bengals.

During the 1980s, the South and West accounted for nearly 90 percent of the nation's population growth. While Florida gained more population than any other state, the North and Northeast were losing 3 million people to migration.

Other leagues were attentive to this trend. Since 1980, major-league baseball, football, hockey, and basketball had added 14 teams through expansion. Ten went to the South and Southeast, four to Florida. In the previous five years alone, the Sunshine State had acquired the National League Marlins, the NHL Lightning, and the NBA Heat and Magic.

As the owners went through the cities one by one, they discovered a problem with all of them but Jacksonville. Baltimore was now muddied with a third ownership candidate, one whose presentation that morning had not been exactly enthusiastic. Jacksonville, said Modell, was "the cleanest" option.

The Eagles' Norman Braman was skeptical of the demographic data and felt it was skewed in favor of Tagliabue's pick. Of course, Jacksonville had a faster growth rate, Braman said. It was starting from a smaller base. Giants co-owner Bob Tisch also defended Baltimore.

Ever the league man, Modell adamantly defended the commissioner's recommendation of Jacksonville. In fact, Modell used Lerner's bid as evidence that he was serious: He told the other committee members that his misgivings about Baltimore were serious enough and his support for Jacksonville strong enough that he would vote against his good friend.

Jacksonville also picked up support from other "Southeasterners": the Saints' Tom Benson, the Falcons' Rankin Smith, and the Oilers' Bud Adams. Each of their franchises had threatened over the years to move to Jacksonville and ended up winning concessions from their local authorities that magically cured their wanderlust.

The committee ultimately voted 10-2 in favor of Jacksonville, with Braman and Tisch voting for Baltimore. Chicago Bears president Michael McCaskey supported Baltimore initially, but switched to Jacksonville. St. Louis and Memphis received no votes.

Meanwhile, up in their hotel suite, Baltimore strategists were getting wind of their troubles. Initially, Lerner had refused even to make a group presentation to the league owners. Belgrad and others had persuaded him to change his mind. Lerner insisted, however, that he would not stay at the hotel like the other applicants. Instead, he would await the decision on his plane at nearby O'Hare Airport. He left a pair of phone numbers with Belgrad.

Lerner, who had never publicly acknowledged his application, slipped in and out of hotel back doors that morning — out of camera range of reporters in the lobby. He called Belgrad to say that his presentation had gone extremely well and that he would be waiting on the plane for the voting results. Belgrad and the other Marylanders were buoyant.

A few hours later, after the finance and expansion committees voted to recommend Jacksonville, Modell grabbed his coat and headed for the hotel exit. Baltimore *Sun* sports columnist John Steadman followed him into a cab for the ride to the airport, where he saw Modell get on Lerner's plane. The two then took off for a charity event scheduled that night in New York.

When Steadman reported this to Belgrad and Schaefer, the two men were shocked and humiliated.

"We expected Lerner to be at the airport, and Art Modell to lead the campaign for us," Belgrad said.

If Lerner thought he had a chance of getting a team, he would have stuck around for the vote of the 28 team owners, Belgrad figured. The fact that Modell wasn't even in the building after the vote made it obvious that Baltimore had lost again.

DeVito tried to call Lerner on his plane, but there was no answer. He then called the airport and confirmed that Lerner's plane had already taken off.

"It was as if the rug had been pulled out from under us," Belgrad recalled.

The Jacksonville recommendation was approved by the full ownership, 26-2. The dissenters were Braman, who argued passionately for Baltimore, and the Patriots' Orthwein, who backed St. Louis. The Giants' votes on such league matters were left to owner Wellington Mara, not Tisch, and Mara went along with the majority.

The Cleveland Browns voted for Jacksonville.

Afterward, owners cited several factors for their votes. The potential of the Jacksonville market was appealing, they said, but so, too, was franchise owner Wayne Weaver. Weaver was viewed as a strong addition to the league and a future leader. Also, putting another franchise in the crowded northeastern corridor didn't make sense, they thought.

"There was a very strong feeling that Jacksonville was a hotbed of football interest. It's a part of the country where there is tremendous interest in football and the NFL. Putting a team in Jacksonville puts the NFL in, if not the fastest growing part of the country, then one of the fastest," Tagliabue told reporters after the vote.

Asked about the possibility of a franchise moving to St. Louis or Baltimore, Tagliabue responded, "I can't say I've lost a lot of sleep over that." The league, he added, would enforce its relocation procedures, which he felt were legally sound.

It was a bitter loss for Baltimore, made all the more bitter by the experience with Lerner. There was no evidence that the investor did anything on behalf of the city, other than lull it into a false sense of complacency that prevented the recruitment of another, more motivated owner.

After moving to Baltimore, Modell explained his expansion vote by saying he thought Jacksonville was "another Green Bay" in the making. And he felt it unfair to support one former NFL city but not the other. Better to let both cities get teams from those interested in moving — which, at the time, he said, did not include the Browns.

But Modell never shared that thinking with the Maryland delegation. Neither he nor Lerner contacted Schaefer or Belgrad afterward.

"I've been hit twice — when the team left and now this," a seething Schaefer said to reporters in a hallway press conference immediately following the vote.

"I think the NFL ought to go back and seriously review the process. I don't think it's helped the league at all," said Baltimore Mayor Schmoke.

"Will we listen to people who want to move to Baltimore?" he wondered. "I don't know. We don't want to make any decisions right now. It's pretty emotionally charged. The strategy has always been if a team had made a firm decision to move and is not using us as a bargaining chip, then we would be foolish not to listen."

John Pica Jr., the Maryland state senator who had co-sponsored the eminent domain legislation that allegedly triggered Irsay's move to Indianapolis, launched a fiercer verbal attack on the NFL. Writing Dec. 2, 1993 to Commissioner Tagliabue on Maryland Senate stationery, Pica, head of the Baltimore City Senate delegation, said:

"One day we will have a football franchise in Baltimore. For one reason: The hardworking men and women who built and rebuilt this city as a Mecca of urban pride deserve it. And again, we will become the backbone of the National Football League. While our franchise marks its place in football history selling out game after game, I'll offer you some advice: Watch our home games on television because if you show up at our beautiful new stadium, you will not be able to hide in the crowd."

Belgrad called the selection of Jacksonville "the ultimate insult" and said he felt betrayed by the league and commissioner. If geography was a problem, he said, why was Baltimore kept in the running for so many years?

"What emerges clearly is that the owners have deferred to the commissioner through a process by which all kinds of standards and tests are set without regard to the time, effort, and cost involved, and in the long run, it doesn't matter, because it's what the commissioner wants," Belgrad told reporters.

Days later, when Cooke publicly announced his plans to build in Maryland, it only angered the Marylanders more. Cooke now got the treatment heaped on George Preston Marshall 40 years earlier, when he set out to annex Baltimore to Redskins country. Ironically, the men who had fought so hard to bring a franchise to the state now were arguing against one (Cooke's) moving there.

"I didn't work for nine years for Mr. Cooke all of a sudden to say, 'I'm going to move to Laurel.' We had always gone on the presumption that [a team] was going to be in Baltimore. Baltimore, period," Schaefer said.

The governor, saying he had been "conned" by the NFL, promised to make life hard on Cooke's project, blocking state spending on roads and raising environmental issues.

The Redskins project quickly became an issue in the gubernatorial campaign. Schaefer would be leaving office in a year pursuant to the state constitution's two-term limit. Some candidates suggested embracing Cooke and his stadium and giving up the

Baltimore pipe dream.

But the man who would ultimately win that office took another tack, one geared toward winning support in Baltimore.

"We should recognize without any hesitation that, if an NFL team goes into that area, neither Washington nor Baltimore will ever have a chance of getting their own team. I think our goal should be each city gets its own team," said Prince George's County Executive Parris N. Glendening, then a candidate for governor.

To Belgrad, the Laurel stadium appeared to be a sham from the start.

"The timing of the letter and the fact that he was within 15 miles of Baltimore was not coincidental," Belgrad recalled later.

But the Stadium Authority chairman, still hoping to land a team for Baltimore, received some encouraging signs. After the Jacksonville vote, a lawyer for Los Angeles Raiders owner Al Davis approached Belgrad, telling him, as he was getting into a cab outside the hotel, that he'd be hearing from her.

Belgrad met Davis at the Atlanta Ritz-Carlton in January, the day before the 1994 Super Bowl. They talked for three hours in the team owners' room. Davis, who asked specific questions about the stadium package, seemed to Belgrad to be genuinely interested while making it clear he hadn't decided whether to move or not.

The two were to speak on and off again in the coming year, and Davis would secretly visit Baltimore.

Two other teams were also in contact. Mike Brown, owner and president of the Cincinnati Bengals, called Belgrad after the Charlotte vote and requested details of the stadium package.

Belgrad agreed to fax the material but said the city was engaged in expansion and hoped Brown's interest in moving wouldn't cost Baltimore a vote. Brown assured him it wouldn't.

Also calling before the Jacksonville vote was John Shaw, president of the Los Angeles Rams and a friend of Braman, who was Baltimore's strongest supporter in the league. Braman had urged Shaw to contact Belgrad, as he had Davis.

Shaw, whom Belgrad met in New York in December 1993, seemed very keen about moving to Baltimore, and told Belgrad the Rams were frustrated in their efforts to obtain a better stadium deal in Southern California.

Belgrad left the meeting hopeful. But in subsequent discussions with Shaw, the Rams official brought up new concerns about Cooke and the Redskins blocking a move to Baltimore. This reaffirmed Belgrad's suspicions that Cooke, despite his public neutrality, had indeed worked against Baltimore.

Cooke would have every reason to try to keep a rival out of Baltimore — even more reason than Marshall had. In the new world of the NFL, corporate customers were the key to success. The Redskins planned nearly 300 skyboxes and 15,000 club seats for their new stadium. The last thing the team needed was a publicly funded competitor flooding the market with another 100 skyboxes and 7,500 club seats.

Eventually, Cooke's Laurel plans would be blocked by Maryland zoning law, and he would settle on another stadium site in Maryland — this one closer to Washington.

In late 1993, Baltimore officially went on the hunt, ready to pounce on any team it could convince to move — with or without the league's consent. Maryland's public stadium funding seemed just the tonic for teams tired of endless talks with their own city halls.

Schaefer even enlisted the help of Peter Angelos, who had bought the Baltimore Orioles in 1993 for $173 million. To the governor, Angelos seemed a can-do man with the cash to get the NFL job done.

"The governor has given us the green light to negotiate with teams that approach us. Instead of going to the NFL as beggars and dancing to their tune, we are now going to take control of our own destiny," Belgrad declared.

But, he added, "We're just not going to invade a city or collude to take away a franchise from a city that supported the franchise. We have to be convinced that there is a firm and irrevocable decision to change locales."

CHAPTER TEN

Cleveland
and the
"Jake"

O n opening day 1994, the glassed-in owner's box high above
Jacobs Field offered a panoramic view of the lush baseball
playing field *and* the stunning new order of sports in Cleveland.

No longer tenants of Art Modell's crumbling Municipal
Stadium, the Indians now commanded a spectacular park, built
with $175 million of mostly public funds. Next door to the luxuri-
ous "Jake" was the new $152 million Gund Arena, named for the
brothers whose team would play there: the National Basketball
Association Cavaliers.

In the battle for new or improved facilities, the Cleveland
Browns had dropped to third place. It seemed more than a little
ironic.

Before he bought the Cleveland Indians, multimillionaire
mall developer Richard Jacobs had distinguished himself neither in
baseball nor in Cleveland. He even bought the team by default.

After Indians owner Steve O'Neill died in 1983, O'Neill's
estate put the baseball franchise up for sale. The next year,
Cleveland lawyer David LeFevre formed an investor syndicate
which bid $41 million for the team. Jacobs signed on as a syndicate
participant, but the LeFevre deal collapsed when bickering among
the investors spilled over into court. Jacobs quietly assembled his

own investor group, including his brother, David, and 61 limited partners, and purchased the Indians in 1986 for $35 million. By insisting that each limited partner turn control of his stock over to him, he retained sole decision-making authority over the team.

When Jacobs took over, the Indians were the laughingstock of the American League East. They had finished the 1985 season in sixth place, 19 games out. They had posted winning seasons only four times in the previous 20 years, hadn't won a pennant in 30 years, or gone to the World Series in nearly 50 years.

Although they played different sports, the Browns and the Indians — like all teams in the same city — were very much competitors. They vied for fans' dollars, for local corporate sponsorships, and for media attention. Modell's long-standing control over Municipal Stadium gave him an important edge in the competition. He built the stadium skyboxes and the scoreboard and kept most of the revenue they brought in — a situation that didn't please the no-nonsense Jacobs.

Dick Jacobs presented a striking contrast to the string of community-minded men cajoled into buying the hapless Indians every few years in order to keep the team in town. He immediately recognized the need to liberate the team from its stadium and to get the taxpayers to foot the bill.

Though based in Cleveland, and quite wealthy, Jacobs was not well known in the city. He had grown up in nearby Akron, Ohio, where his father had worked in marketing for Goodyear Tire & Rubber Co. In fact, the Jacobses lived close enough to the Goodyear factory that they could sit in their living room and smell rubber burning.

After graduating from Indiana University in 1949, Jacobs gravitated toward real estate, and with his brother, David, and developer Dominic Visconsi, formed the firm of Jacobs-Visconsi-Jacobs. Within 10 years, the company was building shopping malls nationwide and riding America's post-war wave to the suburbs. The firm's fortunes multiplied quickly, and Cleveland political leaders soon were grumbling about the principals' lack of interest in the city.

That would soon change. In 1986, the Jacobs brothers bought Cleveland's Erieview Tower skyscraper. Later, they built a glass-roofed shopping mall adjacent to it called the Galleria. Then, in

1991, they opened the Society Bank Tower (now called the Key Tower), the tallest building in the city, built a new Marriott Hotel, and refurbished the old Society building, adjacent to the new skyscraper. This $330 million worth of construction changed the face of the city.

In his public dealings, though, Jacobs established a reputation for bluntness and an unwillingness to compromise. In an appearance before the Cleveland City Council — to seek tax abatements and the use of some city-owned parcels for parking — he let his lawyer explain the project details. Then he stood up and, instead of extolling what the project would do for the city, said simply that if the council didn't give him what he wanted, he would cancel the deal.

He got what he wanted.

Now, on this opening day eight years after Jacobs' purchase, the Indians — long merely tolerated by Clevelanders — were awash in adulation. More than 41,000 fans filled the hunter green seats of baseball's newest park despite the chilly 48-degree temperature. The club that had averaged only 15,204 people at its games over the previous 10 years had a sellout.

President Clinton attended, as did Modell, as did corporate leaders of the community, men and women with whom Modell had served on countless boards and civic groups going back more than 30 years. Some had canceled their leases on Municipal Stadium skyboxes to take advantage of the premium seating offered at Jacobs Field. Today, they all basked in the glory of the city's latest achievement, a stadium that resembled Municipal only in its sand-colored brick work.

Modell supported the plans that built Jacobs Field and Gund Arena. He stood aside, patiently waiting his turn. But now he was smarting from the inattention. He wanted action.

Despite a decade of talking, the Browns owner was no closer to getting a publicly funded facelift for his stadium than when he started. The politicians that he had bankrolled and courted over the years were no longer in positions to help. And their replacements were worrying about paying for the Jake and the new basketball arena.

Things would only get worse for Modell as his Browns fumbled through two more disappointing seasons with an unpopular coach. Fans began to jeer Modell at games, questioning his ability to field a winner. Meanwhile, the Indians, their coffers overflowing, reinvented themselves and shot their way into the hearts of local sports fans and the 1995 World Series.

• • •

Like the bevy of other stadiums opening around the country, Jacobs Field was a team owner's dream. Designed by the architects of Oriole Park at Camden Yards, the Jake fit like a manicured garden into Cleveland's pot-holed urban landscape. Exposed, oversized steel columns and beams matched the city's nearby bridges. Vertical light towers mimicked the gritty smokestacks and glittering skyscrapers.

Inside, a multimillion-dollar sound system boomed rock and roll hits between innings, and concession stands served up chocolate eclairs and boutique beers.

But most important, 123 skyboxes and 2,058 club seats bracketed the playing field, providing the most up-to-date revenue enhancement for millionaire team owners and their millionaire players.

The pricey seats demonstrated how far luxury seats had evolved from the early days of cramped, retrofitted skyboxes then ringing Municipal Stadium. Or even the modern boxes at the Hoosierdome that were constructed up in the rafters, above the upper deck and well back from the field. Jacob Field's boxes and club seats were blended right into the design, in their own level tucked between the upper and lower decks and jutting out close to the field — affording the gilded patrons both princely accommodations and a prime view. The extra-wide club seats came with waiter service, so a patron could have a glass of Chablis brought to him. Suite and club-seat holders had their own level of bars and restaurants built behind their seating sections and not accessible to the general fan. If the sun became a bit hot, or the noise a bit much for deal-making, the luxury seat renters could retire to this air-conditioned enclave that resembled the lobby of a five-star hotel. Ceramic tile floors were a tasteful maroon; the accents brass. Chilled shrimp was served.

These premium accommodations catered to a new class of

clientele: the corporation, the fastest-growing and biggest-spending target market of professional sports. Unlike fans who griped about $100 being tacked on to the cost of a season ticket, the Fortune 500 and Fortune 500 aspirants were more than willing to pay for luxury (and in some cases could even write off a portion of the costs on their corporate taxes). A premier "dugout" box at Jacobs Field — built behind the batter's box and putting a fan closer to home plate than the pitcher — cost a cool $100,000 a year in 1994. A club seat rented for $1,215, not including the required season ticket.

By comparison, Modell's skyboxes were tacky and cheap. In the 1980s, as part of his deal with the city, he had installed 108 suites under the edge of Municipal Stadium's upper deck. They were cramped, with circular staircases that linked the seating area with washrooms in an upper, loft level. They were decorated in a garish orange and were equipped with coffee makers, mini-fridges, and wet bars. Patrons reached the boxes via rusty, open-air staircases and catwalks. There was no exclusive restaurant/bar level that made the suites at Jacobs Field and Oriole Park such an attraction.

These shortcomings depressed prices. Modell's most expensive box rented for $59,000 a year (some NFL teams were commanding upwards of $200,000 by the mid-1990s). To keep renters happy, Modell even allowed them to bring their own food and drinks. Jacobs Field, and most other new stadiums, required the park's caterer to provide food and beverages, generating another revenue stream for the team.

Even regular seating at the Jake carried a premium over old Municipal Stadium. The Indians raised their ticket prices 39 percent for the inaugural season. And they sold as many tickets as they could print.

As a stadium operator, Modell was supremely aware of Jacobs Field's potential. From luxury seating alone, the Indians could generate $10 million a year — as much as some of their competitors earned from total ticket sales. Throw in specialized concessions with more than 60 menu items, a "Terrace Club" restaurant and team store, the world's largest free-standing scoreboard with plenty of advertising space, a "KidsLand" with the latest in Little Tikes equipment, and packaged sponsorships, and the Indians were well on their way to becoming one of the richest teams in baseball.

The Jake became a national phenomenon, just as Camden Yards in Baltimore had two years before. Wrote *Washington Post* sportswriter Richard Justice: "After 61 years at baseball's worst address, at a cavernous, old stadium that was dark and cold and utterly depressing, the Indians now have a home that can stand beside any of the game's other showcases ... Jacobs Field has the cozy feel of Wrigley Field, the urban backdrop of Camden Yards, and the nooks and crannies of Fenway Park."

The lease, too, was a gold mine. The Indians contributed to the stadium's construction, including $7 million for the right to name it, and were responsible for paying $2.95 million per year to help retire the construction debt. They also covered operating costs. Beyond that, the team paid rent based on a formula tied to the season's attendance: 75 cents for every ticket sold over 1.85 million tickets, up to 2.25 million; $1 for every ticket sold over 2.25 million, up to 2.5 million; and $1.25 for each ticket over 2.5 million.

Otherwise, the team kept all of the money collected on parking, advertising, concessions, tickets, and luxury suites.

The Indians had indeed come a long way.

When they originally signed their lease with Modell in 1973, the baseball club agreed to turn over 8 percent of its ticket revenues, with a guaranteed season minimum of $100,000. The Indians front office had no control over skyboxes in Municipal and received none of their proceeds, except for the revenue from baseball season tickets that renters had to pay for each skybox seat.

Even though they provided most of the stadium entertainment, the Indians received only $25,000 from scoreboard advertising. Modell likewise controlled the concession contracts and paid the Indians 20 percent of the sales revenue. The baseball team had the right to sell Indians hats and shirts, but had to pay Modell $50,000 in order to do so or else allow Modell to operate the novelty concessions and negotiate a division of revenues.

Municipal Stadium clearly belonged to Art Modell, not the Cleveland Indians.

A stadium's immense impact on a team's profitability and value had been amply demonstrated in Baltimore. In 1993, Peter Angelos, then a little-known but strong-willed labor attorney, led a group of civic-minded investors into bankruptcy court to buy the Orioles from their foundering owner, New York financier Eli Jacobs (no relation to the Indians owner). When the bidding was over, Angelos had paid a record $173 million for a franchise Jacobs had bought five years earlier for $70 million. The profit was quickly divided up among Jacobs' creditors.

Oriole Park became a national phenomenon and revived the fortunes of the Baltimore franchise. Figures released by Angelos for 1993 showed the Orioles generating an astounding $93.9 million in revenues and a profit of $25.5 million, reportedly the highest in Major League Baseball. A mere five years earlier, playing at Memorial Stadium, the Orioles generated $34 million in revenues and just $1 million in profit.

Longtime fans griped about the "new" Orioles look, of Brie cheese being munched by Washington lawyers with cellular phones. But the turnstiles kept spinning. During the Orioles' last decade at Memorial Stadium, attendance hovered around 2 million per season. It hit 3.56 million in the first year at Oriole Park. Sixty-five straight games sold out between 1992 and 1993, breaking a record established by the Toronto Blue Jays.

No one in sports — including Art Modell — could miss the significance. Camden Yards had transformed the Orioles. And Jacobs Field was going to do the same for the Indians.

• • •

Progress on renovating or replacing cavernous, old Municipal Stadium had been halting, to say the least. Since 1984, both the Cleveland political leadership and Modell had reversed course several times.

The first proposal was a new, $150-million domed facility to be used by both the Indians and the Browns and funded by a property tax levy. Though the teams embraced the idea, the voters rejected it 2-to-1. Cleveland-area voters were little swayed by the $1 million pro-stadium campaign, nor did they care much that Baltimore had lost the Colts just a few months before. For good measure, they even tossed out of office Vince Campanella, the county commissioner who had promoted the stadium plan.

This upset sent a chill through the political leadership. Campanella, who appeared to have a promising career ahead of him, had hoped that the stadium issue would propel him upward politically. Instead, it pushed him out.

The 1984 campaign opened some ugly political fissures, too. Although he said he supported a domed stadium, then-Mayor George Voinovich came out against the referendum. He said he didn't like using property taxes in such a manner. But he also knew that Campanella was a potentially dangerous rival who could ride something like a new stadium to higher office. The mayor supported Mary Boyle, the anti-dome candidate who took on Campanella and beat him.

Angry that the political and civic establishment had not supported the dome, Modell lashed out on election night. "I don't need a dome. I play nine games a year. It's the city and baseball team that need a dome," he told reporters.

As they had in Baltimore a decade earlier, stadium plans sprouted like weeds over the next few years, then quickly withered. One idea called for an inflatable top on Municipal Stadium. Modell didn't much care for that. Another proposed a six-sided, multi-sports facility. Voinovich scotched that idea, refusing to sell the city-owned land needed for its development.

By 1985, a group of the city's business and civic leaders had formed the nonprofit Greater Cleveland Domed Stadium Corp. At Voinovich's urging, the group began buying land in what was known as the Central Market, a blighted neighborhood of rotting markets and boarded-up buildings on the southern edge of downtown.

As the name suggested, the corporation's initial plan was to resurrect the domed stadium idea. It dubbed the project "Gateway" because the Central Market property was the first thing many motorists saw as they exited the highway and headed into town.

By 1986, GCDSC had received $2 million from the state, borrowed another $22 million, and gained control over about 80 percent of the property it needed.

Meanwhile, business leaders — many of them also active in the GCDSC — were beginning to exert more and more influence over the issue. A number of chief executive officers from around Cleveland banded together in the 1980s to raise $30 million for a revolving loan fund. They focused squarely on economic development, favoring projects with a strong potential for drawing jobs and visitors to the center city. To qualify for the group's financial aid, a hotel, for example, needed to have at least 500 rooms and a 10,000-square-foot ballroom.

Among the CEOs' primary development goals was a new baseball stadium that would end the frequent threat of losing the Indians. Baseball officials and other major-league team owners had grown increasingly harsh in their assessments of Municipal Stadium, warning city leaders that the Indians needed a new home, or else.

Patrick O'Neill, nephew of the late Indians owner Steve O'Neill, showed early interest in the dome project and was even a member of the dome corporation. But when the hardscrabble Jacobs took over in 1986, the team's attitude — and the dome's future — changed.

"My brother and I watched the All-Star game in Houston this year," Jacobs told a reporter in December 1986. "That's the only domed stadium I've seen. I'm still collecting information on it."

Jacobs quickly concluded that the Indians needed their own park. In talks with city leaders, he said his first choice was a baseball-only park. His second was a joint football/baseball stadium that would be controlled by the Indians.

He knew then what baseball was rediscovering after a dalliance with multipurpose behemoths. If fans could get tickets at the last minute, they wouldn't buy season tickets. Smaller parks, like Camden Yards, created the kind of contrived urgency and scarcity that guaranteed sellouts. Besides, Jacobs saw where the revenues at Municipal Stadium were going. Not to him.

On Nov. 2, 1987, as community leaders continued pressing the teams to commit to the dome, Jacobs announced that the Indians would move to a stadium at Gateway. But, he said, it would have to be a small, intimate ballpark with real grass. No dome.

This was the beginning of the end for shared sports facilities in Cleveland, though the idea would gasp a few more times before dying altogether.

In 1988, Voinovich invited himself over to lunch at Modell's office and asked if there was any way to renovate Municipal Stadium for both the baseball and football teams. Modell said he was pretty sure there wasn't, but agreed to commission a conceptual plan from Hellmuth Obata Kassabaum (HOK), the architects who later designed Camden Yards and Jacobs Field.

Voinovich and Modell then came up with an interim agreement to extend the Browns' lease for two consecutive, 10-year
terms in exchange for higher rent and the team's cash infusion of $8
million. The money would be used to overhaul the stadium
restrooms and build a new scoreboard. The extension would allow
Modell to borrow the money to renovate and then wait for a credi-
ble stadium plan to emerge from Cleveland's fractious politics.

But the measure drew criticism from community leaders, who
feared it would reduce support for new taxes to fund *new* sports
facilities. Modell asked to have the proposed ordinance withdrawn.

"We have been here 28 years. We like the city and want to stay,
but I want to be treated fairly. I have to look out for my own interests and realize the value a National Football League franchise is to
some communities who don't have one," Modell said at the start of
the 1988 football season.

Public attention then turned back to Gateway, but now the
Browns had decided they didn't want to share space there. Modell
was concerned both about losing seating capacity and playing in a
jerry-rigged baseball park. And both teams were wary.

"We tried to get Gateway to be one stadium with both teams,"
said James Biggar, chairman of Gateway in its start-up years. "But
neither wanted to be tenants of the other or of the mayor," added
Biggar, a former chairman of Nestle USA Corp. and co-founder of
the CEO group trying to revitalize Cleveland's downtown.

Still clinging to the hope that they might bring the two teams
together, Cleveland's leaders went ahead and began striking a solo
deal with the Indians, the team that seemed most at risk of leaving
town. A baseball stadium also meshed nicely with the economic
development orientation of the business group: With its 81 home
dates, a baseball team could draw 4 million visitors downtown.

Architects drew up designs for a natural-grass, baseball-only
stadium, but included provisions for later adding retractable seating along the left-field wall for football games. It seemed a cheap
way of keeping both teams happy; it would also free up valuable
lakefront property for something other than a stadium.

Jacobs resisted the plan, but reluctantly said he would go
along. Then Biggar went to see Modell.

"I said, 'Art, the difference between Jacobs Field and your
existing stadium will be the difference between the concierge level

of a hotel and a warehouse,'" Biggar recalled. But Modell wasn't persuaded.

On Aug. 2, 1989, with Modell and the Cleveland Browns in London for an exhibition game, Jacobs called a press conference and proposed a new baseball park that would seat 44,000, but could be expanded by 28,000 for football. Jacobs said he wouldn't contribute to the financing of the project, an estimated $150 million cost.

A few weeks later, Modell held his own press conference at Municipal Stadium, releasing the results of the HOK study that Voinovich had recommended. It suggested an $85- to $90-million overhaul of Municipal with retractable seating to accommodate both sports. Modell even unveiled a scale model of the proposed facility. But virtually every politician, including Voinovich, snubbed the event, as did the Indians ownership.

Modell fumed.

"I can understand why the Jacobses want their own baseball stadium. Hey, 44,000 seats, a grass field, open air. That's great. If I were the owner of the Cleveland Indians, that's what I would pursue," Modell said.

"That's what it will be — a baseball stadium. The Browns are not interested in a baseball stadium where they add 28,000 more seats for football. That isn't a stadium for football. It's just an expanded baseball stadium."

Modell also expressed concerns about traffic jams and reduced parking at Gateway. And, as decrepit as it was, Municipal Stadium had a long history.

"The money for expandability in the new stadium should be used in the old stadium," Modell proposed. "If the new stadium costs $150 million — and these are just figures, I have no way of knowing — and if an additional $50 million is needed to turn it into a stadium for football, too, I'm suggesting that money should be put to use in Cleveland stadium."

Build the baseball stadium, he said, just give the Browns "fair and equitable" treatment.

Mike White, then mayor of Cleveland, insisted on the baseball stadium's expandability and harbored hopes of eventually talking Modell into the plan. But, in private conversations with White, Modell was just as adamant as he had been in public.

In fact, there wasn't enough space on the 24-acre Gateway site for both a football and a baseball stadium. Nearby land had been optioned, but building there would require a new plan with its own financing. And it would have to wait. Community leaders now had their eyes on another prize that would fit on the site: Cleveland's pro basketball team, the Cavaliers.

• • •

From the beginning, it was obvious that the Gateway plan would have to be sold to the community as an economic-development project, not as a program for lining the pockets of millionaire sports moguls. A simple calculation showed that merely moving the Indians a few blocks south was unlikely to produce a bonanza, even though it might keep the team from leaving the city.

Mayor White, too, was aware of the math. Shortly after his election, he told Gateway's executive director, Tom Chema, that he would support the project only if it provided an economic boost to the city, not just to the sports teams. *The solution:* add an arena that would draw millions of visitors downtown each year for basketball, hockey, circuses, and other attractions.

White was immediately enthusiastic about this idea. Not only was it a good investment, but it would bring back to the city a team now playing in the suburbs. The Cavaliers had fled to Richfield in the dark days of 1974, when the city was rife with conflict and unable to build a new arena.

The Cavs were quite happy in their suburban arena. The team owners, brothers George and Gordon Gund, were a pair of old-line, old-money Clevelanders who had dabbled in other sports teams — Gordon owned a piece of the NHL's San Jose Sharks, and he and his brother had previously owned a stake in the Minnesota North Stars. But both men now lived out of town. They had bought the Richfield Coliseum in 1981 and the Cavaliers two years later. The location was a bit removed from downtown, but the team played to better than 90 percent capacity in the 20,000-seat arena.

"We really talked the Cavs into coming down," Biggar recalled.

It was a tough sell, and the Gunds held out for the very best possible terms. They ended up with a $152-million arena, built mostly at public expense. The Gund Arena, as it came to be known, was another example of stadium economics: It had 92 skyboxes, leased annually for $85,000 to $150,000, and 3,000 club seats, each of which cost fans $3,150 a year. The team kept all of the proceeds from parking, advertising, and concessions. For rent, it agreed to pay 27.5 percent of the skybox revenue and 48 percent of the club-seat receipts, as well as a per-ticket fee similar to what the Indians paid.

Going after the Cavaliers was a logical, if fateful, policy decision. It meant that the Browns weren't going to be part of Gateway. Modell says he accepted assurances that he would be taken care of after Gateway was completed — a decision some of his aides at the time considered a mistake. He even contributed $10,000 to efforts to win voter approval for Gateway's funding.

To bolster that campaign, Jacobs brought baseball commissioner Fay Vincent to town to make it clear that the Indians would be allowed to move out of Cleveland if the team didn't get a new stadium.

"Should this facility not be available in Cleveland, should the vote be a negative one, we may be finding ourselves confronting a subject that we want to avoid," Vincent warned darkly in 1990, on the eve of the stadium-funding vote. In May 1991, voters approved a special tax on alcohol and tobacco sold in Cuyahoga County — by the narrow margin of 52 percent to 48 percent.

The city then broke ground just off of East 9th Street.

Cleveland leaders didn't seem worried about Modell, the owner who had been left out of Cleveland's sports renaissance. The Browns seemed safe. Modell was building a lavish, $13 million training center and corporate headquarters in the Cleveland suburb of Berea planned for opening the next year. In his usual style, Modell had spared no expense: The 10-acre complex consisted of a 76,000-square-foot administrative building with parquet floors; a 60,000-square-foot field house; four natural-grass fields and a 70-yard artificial-turf field; a 6,000-square-foot weight room; two racquetball courts; a Jacuzzi, whirlpools, and cold-water plunge; and a television production studio.

Such a healthy investment hardly hinted at a Modell departure from Cleveland.

"The main focus was on keeping the Indians," recalled

Richard Pogue, a civic leader who served on a mayoral stadium task force. "Everyone assumed the Browns had a lease and would be there forever… . It was, 'We'll get around to that when the time comes.'" Pogue, a senior adviser with the powerhouse Cleveland public-relations firm of Dix & Eaton, had previously been a senior partner at the law firm of Jones, Day, Reavis & Pogue, which counted the Browns among its clients.

It wasn't long after groundbreaking that Modell cryptically complained about the pace of talks for his stadium. In the fall of 1993, as Jacobs Field was taking shape, he told reporters, "We've got five years left on our lease. Beyond that, I don't know."

But, he added, he would never leave before his lease was up in 1998. "A deal's a deal," he said. "We'll live with it."

• • •

Just as Major League Baseball was being transformed by luxury ballparks like Camden Yards and Jacobs Field, the National Football League was undergoing its own economic upheaval. Mostly, this was due to the league's 1993 collective bargaining agreement with players and the agreed-to salary cap.

The salary cap, based on NFL revenue-sharing, required each team to maintain a minimum and maximum payroll, including salaries and benefits. In 1995, the salary cap was no less than $31.4 million, but no more than $38.8 million. Unfortunately, the new NFL salary system came with peculiar, easy-to-abuse accounting rules. To take advantage of them, teams soon were employing their own "cap-ologists."

Under the salary cap system, signing bonuses became especially important because they could be prorated over the length of a player's contract. For example, a player could sign a five-year, $10-million deal and get, say, $6 million in his first year and $1 million in each of the next four years, but the team's books would only reflect $2 million each year against its cap account.

Over time, the entire value of a player contract would indeed be counted, but the spread-out accounting procedures were anything but trivial. Paying big bonuses up front proved a powerful team weapon in the bidding wars for top athletes. Unlike major league baseball, where they are common, the NFL frowns on so-called "guaranteed" contracts — payable whether players play or not. Most NFL players and their paychecks can be dropped at any time. The smart player opts for a deal that pays the most up front.

Paying for all of those signing bonuses soon became an expensive proposition. Teams and their owners either had to have the revenue coming in or sufficient credit with banks, which demanded repayment in real dollars, not cap dollars. Cash quickly became king. And there was no better place to find extra cash than in a new stadium. Money generated through concessions, stadium advertising, and skybox rentals was not included in the league's gross-revenue formula, and thus did not push up the salary minimums. And this revenue did not have to be shared with visiting teams, as did ticket receipts. Moreover, important categories of expenses, such as coaches' salaries and training facilities, were excluded from the salary cap's spending limits and could greatly affect a team's ability to lure players and win titles.

Stadiums and the money they could generate were now more important than ever. The sweetheart deals given to owners Al Davis, Robert Irsay, and Bill Bidwill in Los Angeles, Indianapolis, and Phoenix, respectively, were obsolete. The prototypical beneficiary of the new order was Dallas Cowboys owner Jerry Jones.

In 1995, a season in which the Cowboys won the Super Bowl, Jones paid out $22 million in salaries and $40 million in signing bonuses, but managed to stay *under* the $38.8 million salary cap. Only $15 million of the bonus pool was counted against the cap, though his actual payroll that year was $62 million, more than $1 million a player, and nearly 50 percent above the league average. How could he afford it? He controlled Texas Stadium, its 370 skyboxes, its controversial "identity rights," which he sold to Nike, and the stadium's other money-making elements. *Financial World* magazine estimated Jones' stadium revenue in 1995 at nearly $40 million, more than six times the NFL average.

Despite controlling Cleveland stadium, Modell, by *Financial World*'s estimate, generated only $8.3 million from luxury seats, stadium advertising, concessions, and other stadium revenues.

"It used to be that what was important was market size. Now the determining factor between the haves and the have-nots isn't market size. It's stadium economics," Chicago Bears vice president Ted Phillips complained in 1995.

Suddenly, the one-for-all and all-for-one philosophy of Rozelle — and Art Modell — was coming apart. The NFL had been spared the pressures of inequality suffered in other sports, chiefly baseball, where a huge local TV deal enriched a big-market team like the New York Yankees while small-market teams like the Pittsburgh Pirates were forced to dismantle contending teams to cover their bills.

Football had been different, by design. In 1990, NFL team owners were sharing more than 90 percent of their sport's revenues. Baseball was sharing only a small fraction of that: In 1991, baseball owners' shared income from broadcast fees and sales of licensed goods totaled only 26 percent of total revenues. That same year, baseball club revenue averaged $56 million, but ranged widely — from a high of $98 million for the richest team to a low of $39 million for the poorest. Some of the more affluent clubs spent more on payroll than other, less well-off teams were taking in.

By contrast, the most successful NFL teams in 1990 were generating an average of $47 million in revenue. The least successful made do with about $43 million — a variance of only 10 percent. This meant there were no small-market NFL teams, as there were in baseball, clamoring for an overhaul of the sport's economics and a dramatic — and ultimately strike-provoking — change in the relationship with players. Franchise relocations were thus few and far between.

By the mid-1990s, however, the new stadium economics were rewriting the NFL's rules. Some teams with lavish stadium deals prospered, and those without them faltered, creating a baseball-like world of "haves and have nots." *Financial World* estimated the revenue gap between the richest and poorest NFL teams was more than 33 percent by 1996. And it was growing wider.

Financial documents that came to light as part of the players' 1992 lawsuit against the NFL showed that the Cincinnati Bengals, the Tampa Bay Buccaneers, and the Philadelphia Eagles were the three richest teams of the 1980s. By the 1990s, all three were threatening to leave their cities if they didn't get new stadiums.

Not surprisingly, team owners began leaning on their local governments for new or renovated stadiums, claiming, quite literally, that they needed them to keep up with the Joneses. The Jerry Joneses, that is.

Modell's loge rental-rate fell from 100 percent in 1993 to 76 percent in 1994, when Gund Arena and Jacobs Field opened and their 225 skyboxes were immediately sold out. Even after the Indians moved out of Municipal into the Jake, Modell offered only a $4,000-a-year discount for suite renters.

Although fans who remembered the great games played at Municipal had a powerful bond with the old hulk of a stadium, it had little pizzazz to attract the next generation of fans. It was hardly a place for the stylish to congregate, not in a city with two glistening new sports venues, as well as the soon-to-open Great Lakes Science Center and the nationally acclaimed Rock and Roll Hall of Fame and Museum.

Falling concrete had left the stadium with gaping holes and exposed, rusted girders. Moisture seeping through the concrete was producing a chemical reaction with the imbedded steel reinforcing bars. Chunks of cement had popped off. Although no fans ever got hurt, workers, for safety's sake, had to hammer out loosened cement between games to protect people. The plumbing system's supply lines had never been upgraded to accommodate the additional loge washrooms and other modern demands, so toilets wouldn't flush during peak periods, such as half-time. The electrical and other systems were in serious disrepair.

Engineering studies performed in 1993 and 1994 uncovered alarming deterioration: "The carbonated condition of the concrete, which allows reinforcing steel to corrode, is comparable to a creeping cancer," they concluded. A mayoral task force in 1995 reported that 91 percent, or $141 million, of the renovations then being considered for the stadium would be spent merely trying to meet "structural, safety, code, and Americans with Disabilities Act requirements." (Critics, however, said this figure was exaggerated to make the stadium work seem less of a boondoggle for Modell).

Whether Modell did enough to get a better stadium deal from the city remains the subject of bitter disagreement. City leaders say they knew he wanted improvements but insist he never communicated his sense of urgency. According to his critics, he intentionally lulled Cleveland into a false sense of security about the Browns.

Modell said he was afraid of being labeled an extortionist if he made threats the way Jacobs had. It wasn't his style. Many longtime friends and associates thought Modell was waiting for community leaders to recognize his contributions and return the favor. He didn't want to beg or badger.

Whatever one believes, the threat of losing the team was obvious — just as it had been in Baltimore a decade earlier.

On Dec. 31, 1993, the Cleveland *Plain Dealer* ran an ominous headline: "Several cities trying to lure away the Browns, White says."

In the newspaper's report, Mayor White acknowledged the economics of the new National Football League.

"It's just a reality," he said. "NFL teams are mobile. I know that. I know what that does to the set of discussions that I've got to have with Art Modell."

The mayor had his work cut out for him.

CHAPTER ELEVEN

A Stadium Hangover

On Jan. 8, 1994, Art Modell and Cleveland Mayor Mike White sat down for breakfast at the city's Ritz-Carlton. They had a lot to discuss.

The two were not natural friends or political allies. Modell was a lifelong Republican and a major contributor to the GOP, both locally and nationally. He was close to the former mayor, Republican George Voinovich and had supported him in 1990 in his successful bid to become governor of Ohio. Modell had given hundreds of thousands of dollars to Voinovich's various campaigns.

But now Voinovich had to be careful not to appear to favor his old home city. Ohio was host to five major-league teams, several minor-league ones, and a raft of successful collegiate programs. Anything done for one team would have to be done for the others. The Browns' future would be in White's hands, not Voinovich's. And that was OK with the governor.

White, a Democrat, was a scrappy product of inner-city Cleveland. Although a strong booster of Jacobs Field and Gund Arena, he saw the Gateway project more from an economist's perspective than a sportsman's. Ten years earlier, during a budget debate in the Cleveland City Council, then-Councilman White opposed Voinovich on a domed baseball/football facility, calling it "a sports palace for the Republican privileged."

The grandson of two preachers and the son of a union organizer, White had been exposed to politics at an early age. As a teenager, he marched for civil rights alongside his machinist father, and, at age 14, joined the campaign of Carl Stokes, cleaning latrines and handing out literature for the man who in 1967 became the first black mayor of a major American city.

Inspired by Stokes, Robert Kennedy, and Martin Luther King Jr., White, an African American, headed off to Ohio State University to earn a degree in public administration. It was his first extended stay away from Glenville, his nearly all-black, working-class neighborhood in Cleveland. On the day when four student protesters were shot by National Guardsmen at Kent State University, a sister campus up Ohio's Interstate 71, he was marching in a similar demonstration against the Vietnam War at his college in Columbus.

"In those days, government was the engine of change, it was on the edge, it was the provocateur of creative thought," White recalled in a 1996 interview.

After college, he became an assistant to the mayor of Columbus, then to Cleveland's City Council. In 1978, he won his own seat on the council and six years later was elected to the state Senate. There, he developed a reputation for fiery oratory and confrontational, unapologetic politics.

But it was the mayoralty of Cleveland that he coveted, and in 1990 he won as a long-shot candidate campaigning on the themes of racial healing and fighting crime.

The city's business elite, including Modell, backed White's opponent, George Forbes, but soon came to view the new mayor as someone with whom they could work. To their relief, White continued Voinovich's emphasis on downtown development and fiscal discipline.

This was important to a city humiliated in the 1960s and 1970s by environmental and fiscal disaster. The city's Cuyahoga River had been so polluted that it caught fire; the city's treasury was so depleted that it defaulted on loans.

Although he kept his residence within a few blocks of where he grew up, White as mayor disappointed the city's neighborhood leaders. While they hoped for a major shift in government priorities and especially more dollars going toward community-based developments, he cut the ribbons on a variety of expensive public projects, from Jacobs Field to the Rock and Roll Hall of Fame and Museum. The city was gaining a comeback reputation similar to the one enjoyed by Baltimore in the 1980s.

Bearded and bespectacled, the 5-foot, 7-inch White played football for a community league in his youth but described himself as the team punching bag. Though he attended a few Browns games each year, he reserved his passion for more intellectual topics like school financing reform and Urban Development Action Grants.

Like Baltimore's William Donald Schaefer, White also demonstrated a legendary ability to hold a grudge and an inability to work with opponents, even leaders in the city council. This message permeated City Hall, where department heads wouldn't even take the calls of council members unfriendly to the mayor. Despite his personal brand of politics, Clevelanders returned White to office in 1994 with 85 percent of the vote.

Privately, Modell had good things to say about the mayor and his efforts on behalf of the city. At first, the Browns owner was even optimistic that his needs would be met.

Their breakfast meeting at the Ritz was cordial. Jacobs Field was scheduled to open in a few months, and anticipation was running high. Gund Arena would open a few months later.

But there were no plans in place for Municipal Stadium. Modell, a Gateway supporter, had "stepped aside," as he would often say, at the request of community leaders. He had waited his turn. Now he thought his time had come and he told the mayor so.

Modell complained to White that the Browns were losing skybox renters to the Jake and that something needed to get going soon. He also said he couldn't afford to contribute to the costs of his own stadium.

White didn't say so, but he assumed then that, after the usual negotiations, the team would eventually agree to contribute to stadium costs. The Indians and Cavaliers had both started out saying they wouldn't pay for anything, but eventually agreed to do so. White considered this the nature of bargaining. Responding to Modell, he acknowledged the urgency of the situation and promised a proposal — and the political consensus to get it passed — within 120 days.

White then asked Modell to deal only with him, putting the mayor squarely at the center of a controversy sure to rage for months. White told Modell that he had appointed an attorney, Fred Nance, and his economic development aide, Steve Strnisha, to lead the talks, and that the city was "ready to go."

Modell was pumped up by these promises.

Before they parted, the Browns owner reassured the mayor that the team would never move as long as he owned the franchise. It was a pledge he would repeat in many ways and in many forums over the next few months — in words that would come back to haunt him.

"I'm not about to rape this city as others in my league have done. You will never hear me say, 'If I don't get this, I'm moving.' You can go to press on that one. I couldn't live with myself if I did that," said Modell a few weeks after his breakfast meeting with the mayor.

But he added: "The Cleveland Browns as an organization will expect only fair treatment. There will be no demands made. If they can't give us fair treatment, which means that we can't be competitive, then that's something we have to take into consideration."

• • •

Modell already doubted that a third sports facility could be built from the ground up in Cleveland, both because of the costs and the scarcity of downtown real estate.

The city was bursting with high-priced public projects, most of them opening a few hundred feet from Municipal Stadium. Jacobs Field and the Gund Arena were just up the street. The Rock and Roll Hall of Fame, a monstrous project that would become a major tourist attraction for the city, was going up to the east of Municipal. Next to it, in what had been Browns' parking lots, was the new Great Lakes Science Center. Connecting many of the attractions was a sleek, new trolley line.

The Browns owner resolved to settle and push for a massive fix-up of Municipal Stadium, but he was concerned about the time frame. Working around his team's playing schedule, the renovation would take a year to design and three years to accomplish. In Modell's mind, there was no time to waste. He was now an old man

and not in very good health. He was also in the process of convert-
ing his team to a trust to lessen the expected blow of estate taxes following his death. And he desperately wanted to win a Super Bowl
before he left the game. But it wouldn't be easy.

Throughout the 1980s, the Browns were notorious both for
front-office intrigue and for rapid turnover of coaches and popular
players. Even the media, once Modell's most reliable boosters, had
grown immune to his charm and increasingly were portraying him
as a meddlesome manager and sore loser.

Much of the change had to do with the Browns' playing performance, and the irony of rising expectations.

Seven times the team made it to the playoffs, and seven times
it lost, often by heartbreakingly close margins. Second-guessing
Modell became a municipal sport nearly as popular as football.

Cleveland's decade of frustration began with the "Kardiac
Kids" of 1980, a collection of talented Browns players who came as
close as any athletes can to winning it all without actually doing so.
They won and lost games with seconds to spare, often on freak mis-
takes or Herculean performances.

The time was right for the emergence of a Cleveland dynasty.
The Pittsburgh Steelers, the Browns' arch-rivals who had dominated the 1970s with four Super Bowl victories, had grown stale. And
the Browns had been reinvigorated with players like quarterback
Brian Sipe; wide receivers Reggie Rucker and Dave Logan; running
backs Mike Pruitt and Greg Pruitt; and tight end Ozzie Newsome.

In 1980, the Browns finished 11-5, winning five games by
three points or less and capturing their division. In the first round
of the playoffs, they faced the Oakland Raiders at a frozen
Municipal Stadium. The wind chill was a frosty 36-below.

The weather and the home field favored them, but typical of
their come-from-behind style that season, the Browns were trailing
14-12 when they muscled the ball from their own 15-yard line to the
Raiders' 13 in the final minute of play. It was then that Coach Sam
Rutigliano called a second-down play that would go down in
infamy: Red Slot Right Halfback Stay 88.

In Cleveland lore, the code has been shortened to simply
"Red Right 88." Sipe, who led the NFL that season with 14 touchdowns and earned its Most Valuable Player Award, was supposed
to hit Newsome in the end zone. If the tight end was covered, Sipe

was to throw the ball away and on the next down, hand off to Mike Pruitt, who would either score a TD or set up what would be the game-winning field goal.

But the Raiders' Mike Davis intercepted Sipe's pass to Newsome, sealing the win for Oakland. The Raiders, who were then in the early stages of their dispute with the NFL over moving to Los Angeles, went on to win Super Bowl XV, beating the Eagles, 27-10.

The Browns' next season was the polar opposite. Instead of winning 11 and losing 5, they won 5 and lost 11, including seven of their last eight games. The 1982 season was shortened by a player strike, but the Browns still fell below .500, finishing 4-5.

In 1983, they began to show some life again, ending the season 9-7 and outscoring their opponents, 356-342. They actually tied for a wild-card playoff spot but were denied it by NFL tie-breaker rules.

The next year, optimism ran high, but the team got off to a bad start with consecutive losses to the Seahawks, Rams, and Broncos. The Browns then beat Pittsburgh, 20-10, before losing to the Chiefs, Patriots, and Jets. Questions about Rutigliano's future arose, but Modell dismissed them. He and the coach had not only become close friends, but next-door neighbors. They and their wives frequently socialized after games.

Modell's reluctance to fire Rutigliano gave rise to criticism that the owner was too loyal to nonperforming or low-performing Browns' employees. He allowed emotions to cloud his business judgment, critics said. But Modell was adamant, telling reporters that he wasn't another Bob Irsay. Besides, the Browns had just extended Rutigliano's contract.

Thirty minutes before a 1984 game against the Cincinnati Bengals, Modell assured his friend that his job was safe. After the game, with the scoreboard showing a 12-9 Browns loss, he fired his the coach. Now critics chastised the owner for being impatient and impetuous, traits even friends admit were ingrained in Modell.

The team ended the season a very disappointing 5-11 but acquired one of its more endearing and enduring symbols: the "dawg."

For years, Cleveland's All-Pro cornerback Hanford Dixon fired up his defensive line teammates by barking at them like a dog.

What better way to inspire the sacking of opposing team quarter-backs? But soon he and fellow cornerback Frank Minnifield were barking at opponents, too.

Then the fans got into the act. Dog yelps began to echo through Municipal Stadium, especially when Minnifield or Dixon charged up a small hill in front of the end-zone bleachers. An especially enthusiastic group of fans sat in these cheap bench seats, which had been added for the 1981 baseball All-Star game. Dixon dubbed the section the "Dawg Pound."

Fans brought dog biscuits to the games, tossing them onto the field in celebration and in anger. During one game, the fans pelted the Broncos with biscuits as they approached the goal line. Officials had to stop play and reverse field.

One group of fans took to every game an actual dog house, which soon became a fixture of the Dawg Pound. Stadium officials eventually discovered a keg of beer inside the house and made the owners sign statements promising not to bring any more in. They were allowed to keep the dog house, though.

Particularly moved by Dixon's barking was John Thompson, who, in 1984, was a 22-year-old office equipment salesman. On a visit to the team's pre-season training camp at Lakeland Community College, he and his friends chuckled at the on-field barking and, after practice, stopped by a tavern. On their way out, they noticed that a costume shop next door was having a grand opening. Dog masks were only $10.

"I thought it would be a good addition to the game," Thompson later recalled.

Was it ever. Soon Thompson, with his ample physique and long-faced, brown, rubber dog mask, was leading canine cheers on Sundays and getting more TV air time than ABC commentator Al Michaels. Thompson added a jersey to the outfit, assigning himself the unused number 98. "Big Dawg" was born.

Also in 1984, the team hired ex-Baltimore Colts General Manager Ernie Accorsi, a former sportswriter, as its head of football operations. Accorsi oversaw some of the team's best years and best moves.

In a maneuver that has since been outlawed by the NFL, Accorsi convinced a promising young quarterback and Cleveland-area native, Bernie Kosar, to declare for the supplemental college draft in his junior year. After Kosar was selected first by another team, Accorsi traded for him, landing the curly-haired home boy in the spring.

The team went 8-8 that season, won the division again, and faced Miami in the playoffs. The Browns took a 21-3 lead, but a disputed pass-interference call and a wrong-way run by Browns' running back Earnest Byner on a crucial third-down play allowed quarterback Dan Marino to bring the Dolphins back. Cleveland lost, 24-21.

In 1986, the Browns went 12-4, winning the most regular season games in their franchise history, and scoring their second consecutive American Football Conference-Central Division title.

In the playoffs, the Browns found themselves at a packed Municipal Stadium trailing the New York Jets by 10 with a little more than four minutes left. It looked like yet another first-round loss. But the Browns rallied to tie the game with seven seconds left on a run by Kevin Mack and a field goal by former Redskins kicker Mark Moseley.

The teams played one overtime period, but neither side scored. Two minutes into a rare double overtime, Moseley kicked a 27-yard field goal, winning the game for the Browns, 23-20. Kosar, now a proven hero at home, set an NFL playoff record by passing for 489 yards. The defense was credited with nine sacks.

The next week, the Denver Broncos came to town for the AFC championship. A fourth-quarter touchdown pass by Kosar, whose 62-percent completion rate led the league that year, put the favored Browns up, 20-13.

The Browns' Super Bowl chances looked even better when the Broncos misplayed the ensuing kickoff and started their next possession on their own 2-yard line, heading into the wind. In the Denver huddle, the Bronco players laughed at the futility of their position. But, on the first play from scrimmage, Denver quarterback John Elway launched what has come to be known simply as "The Drive."

Running himself for 11 yards, then passing to Steve Sewell for 22 yards, the four-year NFL veteran promptly threw again, this time for a 12-yard gain to Steve Watson. On second down at the Cleveland 40, the Browns' pumped-up defense finally caught up with Elway, sacking him for a loss of eight.

But Elway responded with a 20-yard pass to Mark Jackson, and a 14-yard first down gainer to Sewell at the Browns' 14. A nine-yard Elway scramble put the ball at the 5. With just 37 seconds remaining, the Bronco QB dropped back and hit Jackson for the touchdown.

The 98-yard, 15-play march sent the Browns into their third overtime in eight days. This one started propitiously, with Cleveland winning the coin toss, but the offense couldn't get untracked, and was forced to punt. Elway then engineered a 60-yard drive that ended with a field goal.

Denver won the game, 23-20.

The next season (1987), the Browns captured their third straight division title, and this time it was a fumble that took them out of Super Bowl contention. It was Denver again, at home, for the AFC championship. Kosar had rallied the Browns from an early deficit, putting up 30 Cleveland points in the second half. Then, during a play that should have resulted in the tying touchdown, Earnest Byner fumbled the ball near the goal line. The Broncos recovered and won, 38-33. This heartbreaker became known simply as "The Fumble."

In 1988, the Browns went 10-6 and earned a wild-card playoff berth, only to lose to the Houston Oilers, 24-23, on Christmas Eve.

In 1989, Modell hired Bud Carson, his third coaching change in five years. Carson led the team to its fourth division title in five years with a 9-6-1 record. A come-from-behind, 24-20 win over Houston in the last week of the season put the team into the play-offs. The Browns even beat the Buffalo Bills, 34-30, in the first round when linebacker Clay Matthews intercepted Buffalo QB Jim Kelly's pass at the Cleveland 1-yard line with nine seconds left to play.

But the Browns lost the conference championship, 37-21, to their nemesis, Elway and the Broncos, at Denver's Mile High Stadium.

Then everything fell apart. Early in 1990, Modell underwent his second heart bypass surgery, the ailing Browns posted their worst season in franchise history, finishing 3-13, and Carson was fired.

The fans, spoiled by the string of winning playoff seasons, got cranky, and began flashing a variety of anti-Modell signs in the direction of the owner's skybox. One popular message read:

"Jump, Art." Another said: "Art Steinbrenner."

One man hired a plane to tow his banner over the field: "You can't touch this. Jump, Art," it read. Modell, showing little tolerance for dissent, had stadium guards seize the signs. Now, fans had one more thing to complain about.

"It was the worst of my 30 years here, but I'd rather have the hostility than apathy," Modell said after the season was over.

But friends said the criticism hurt him deeply.

He reacted by pushing even harder to win games. Modell announced a Kremlin-style five-year plan for the Super Bowl. Clearly exasperated, he said, "If we don't get the job done, you won't have me to kick around any more in three years. I will get out of football and Cleveland."

Later, he explained, "The Super Bowl is my obsession because it's been so elusive."

By now, fans had caught on to Modell's bad habit. He would often issue inflated pledges with certitude, only to back down weeks or months later. Sometimes, he would even deny making the pledge in the first place.

Accorsi, a congenial and effective executive, quit the Browns in 1992, further stirring a roiling stew of front-office intrigue.

The next year, the Browns, now led by colorless and terse Coach Bill Belichick, released Kosar, claiming he was suffering from "diminished skills." Fans were outraged. The front page of the Cleveland *Plain Dealer* led with a one-word headline: "Sacked."

Kosar was both a crowd pleaser and a game winner. In his five years with the Browns, he gained 16,450 yards and scored 85 touchdowns, giving him the third best quarterback numbers in team history, just ahead of Otto Graham's NFL record. Kosar was second only to Sipe in total yards and 300-yard games.

The firing was a turning point for fans still supporting Modell. Their anger was palpable five months later, when Jacobs Field opened. It only added to Modell's sense that his adopted hometown had forgotten all he had done for it. A deeply emotional man, he felt betrayed.

Friends could see it in his eyes, along with the realization that winning a Super Bowl might not be possible. Although the Browns were successful by most objective measurements, they were one of only 10 teams that in 1994 had failed to ever make the Super Bowl.

• • •

On Jan. 27, 1994, a city/county "working group" met to discuss Municipal Stadium. Mayor White appeared to be moving ahead with his pledge to have a proposal for Modell within six months.

Next, the Browns agreed to pay for an engineering study which confirmed that the stadium's basic structure was sound. Architects then came up with an innovative plan: Essentially, the cement would be hacked off and rebuilt on the stadium's original steel skeleton.

Further, the field would be lowered eight feet to improve the view from the stands, and a new deck of seats would be built along the sidelines, filling in the oval gap and bringing the mid-field fans closer to the action. The existing lower deck would be torn out and replaced by the section behind it, which would be brought forward to create space underneath for restaurants and restrooms. The roof would be removed, concessions would be rebuilt, and posts would be taken out of the way of spectators.

Modell was enthusiastic. "It's a fantastic architectural plan. It will be the talk of the industry. The sight lines will change. There will be no obstacles. Double the capacity and number of men's rooms. Triple the number and capacity of the women's rooms. Right there, we'd have anybody who urinates voting for us in the next poll," Modell quipped.

At the same time, the Browns hired a Washington consulting firm to review stadiums around the country. The resulting three-volume study was eventually turned over to the city by team officials.

Unfortunately, Modell's optimism didn't last long. The mayor's 120 days came and went with no plan produced. City officials continued to meet with Modell's representatives, but the county and state were conspicuously absent from many of the sessions.

The city/county working group met 15 times — including another one-on-one session between Modell and White at the Ritz — but little progress was made. Browns officials began to worry that the mayor was merely buying time while figuring out what to do. A Sept. 1 target date to announce a stadium plan also came and went. Frustrated, the Browns cut off talks in late September.

The mayor, meanwhile, was getting concerned. Though he hadn't asked county commissioners for help or involved them closely in the negotiations, he had counted on Cuyahoga County to pay for much of the work, as it had with Gateway. The city couldn't afford to go it alone. Its schools were in state receivership. Its police cars were falling apart. Its bridges and roads were crumbling. And, by now, the estimated cost of the Municipal Stadium facelift had swelled to $130 million.

"It became very clear in September that a solution on the renovation of the stadium went beyond the ability of the city to meet the need; that is, we didn't have $130 million we could just get out of the bank and fix the stadium," White recalled later.

But by the fall of 1994, Cuyahoga County was facing its own financial problems.

Although it was winning design awards, Gateway was going way over-budget, and the county was on the hook to make up the shortfalls. The project had fallen victim to a number of problems, most driven by a fast-track construction timetable where some work was being performed, then torn out as the design was altered.

Jacobs Field came in $6 million over-budget. Gund Arena was even worse: $22 million over-budget, thanks to the open-ended contract negotiated with the Cavaliers to get them to move back downtown. Because the lease allowed them to demand the best, the Cavs could stick Gateway with a $10 million penalty, payable to the team, if the arena was not ready in time for the 1994 season.

Even after both facilities opened, Gateway began running a $1 million-a-year deficit. Workers were laid off, and contractors sued to get paid. Sony was even threatening to foreclose on the Jumbotron scoreboard. And if that weren't bad enough, the county was rocked by an investment scandal.

In October 1994, amid allegations of mismanagement, Cuyahoga County closed down a pooled investment fund it had operated for area governments. The Secured Assets Fund Earnings program, known by the acronym SAFE, proved to be anything but. Employees who allegedly had little financial expertise made risky investments, and the county spent more than $100 million cleaning up their mess. County commissioners had to slash the county's budget by 11 percent. Dozens of workers were laid off, and the rest had their wages frozen. The county's bond rating was temporarily downgraded. And its elected treasurer, Francis E. Gaul, was convicted of dereliction of duty and sentenced to 90 days in jail.

Helping the city with another gold-plated sports project was clearly not on the county commissioners' agenda.

"I wish them well," said Timothy F. Hagan, president of the commissioners. "Maybe the mayor has a rabbit he can pull out of his hat."

Even if the county's finances had been healthier, Hagan wasn't sold on a large public investment in a new football stadium. Paying off $130 million in bonds would cost $10 million a year for 30 years, he figured. "That's a $1 million subsidy per game. I don't think the taxpayers in Cleveland want to subsidize the Browns like that," he added.

To win converts opposed to sports stadiums, White tried to tie the stadium financing to other projects, to make it part of a giant development program like Gateway. But his $285 million lakefront plan, which included the stadium, a new aquarium, and improvements to the city's port, was dead on arrival. When he suggested a property or sales tax increase to pay for the plan, he might as well have suggested a community skinny dip in Lake Erie.

"We are obligated, as elected officials, to focus attention on projects that will help benefit the community," Hagan said. "But our first order of business is to put order in the business. We're not there yet."

City Council President Jay Westbrook said the mayor was "way out on a limb" with his ambitious lakefront plan.

"The council is going haywire over this," said Westbrook. "The theme song for this ought to be the *William Tell Overture* because the mayor is certainly the Lone Ranger."

To Modell, nearly a year after their January meeting, the mayor's efforts to achieve consensus had gone nowhere. Nearly a year had elapsed since their January meeting. Then, in December, White shifted gears. He invited the region's top business leaders to a meeting to hear Modell make his case directly.

Those who heard the presentation called it vintage, upbeat Modell. Though he played a slick videotape showing what the renovated stadium would look like and made a strong argument for fixing up the aging structure, he never threatened to leave town or suggested that he was experiencing any financial duress.

Some in the audience were puzzled as to why he was pushing for an overhaul and not a new stadium. The team owner said he preferred the nostalgia of Municipal Stadium and its lakefront location.

"That struck me as odd," stadium task force member Richard Pogue said later. But he agreed with Modell's assessment of the financial impediments to getting a new structure. "We just finished Gateway and Gund, and for the community to go out and raise another $300 million seemed daunting."

On Dec. 9, White convened a press conference as the "first step" toward educating the city about the money needed to keep the Browns from moving.

He tried to sound the alarm. Investors from both Baltimore and St. Louis, he warned, had contacted the Browns and were offering "tens of millions of dollars" to lure the team away. He called Municipal Stadium "an old, decrepit stadium that other teams don't want to play in" and said its owner — the city — does "bear a responsibility."

Building a new park would cost $280 million, he said. Modell, "in all probability, will begin looking at other options in January."

Then he hit Clevelanders wh ▲ e it was beginning to hurt *him*.

"I will not sit idly by and then wake up one morning to see the moving vans out my window.... I don't want to wake up with a Baltimore hangover," he said.

Reached for comment, Modell denied talking to other cities. But he did vow not to play in the stadium after the lease expiration — unless Municipal was refurbished.

Privately, however, Modell was less diplomatic. Later that month, at a Republican fund-raiser in Orrville, Ohio for Newt Gingrich, Modell pulled Governor Voinovich aside.

"You can lose the Browns," Modell said he told him. "We can't make it unless something is done with the stadium."

But the governor, who had his eye on higher office and had just watched a wave of fiscal conservatism sweep Gingrich into the speakership of the U.S. House of Representatives, didn't want to jump into the quagmire.

"It's a local matter," he responded, according to Modell.

Publicly, the governor's spokesman Mike Dawson explained: "The Governor believes there has to be local public and private financial support before the state should be asked to participate."

Hagan knew the lack of state help was the kiss of death. He told reporters that Modell would have to cut the stadium price tag in half. Then the Browns and the state would have to split the cost.

"There's no local money," he said. "The honorable way to deal with this is to say publicly what a lot of people are saying privately, and that is that the citizens are unwilling to pay taxes for it and the governor has to take the leadership role… . Keeping an NFL franchise in Cleveland is important, but I think there has to be a realistic assessment of that cost and a clear understanding that the people of Cuyahoga County are not going to support a tax on property or sales to refurbish the stadium.

"He can't have a state-of-the-art stadium for eight days. It's just impossible. Modell cannot drive that discussion," Hagan said.

"We have to call upon the mayor to join with the county to call upon the governor to make this a statewide rule."

But instead of taking Hagan's advice, White did what most politicians would do under the circumstances: He appointed another task force to study the issue.

Chuck Crow / Plain Dealer Photographer

The stadium that Baltimore promised Modell was fresh, lush, friendly, and replete with skyb es and club seats — all the things he'd wante in Cleveland, but never had gotten.

Modell stands with a model of his $80 million plan to renovate Municipal Stadium. He called this 1989 press conference to discuss stadium improvements, but hardly anyone came, including Cleveland Mayor Mike White and Ohio Governor George Voinovich. Their "snub" and this model exemplify the string of broken promises that fueled Modell's resentment towards the Ohio city.

Photo by: John Makely, The Baltimore Sun

Ravens fans behind the end zone congratulate running back Earnes Byner after he scores the game-winning touchdown in the team's Baltimore debut. Baltimoreans wept, screamed, and shared utter joy as they watched an NFL home team play football again in their c after a nearly 13 year absence.

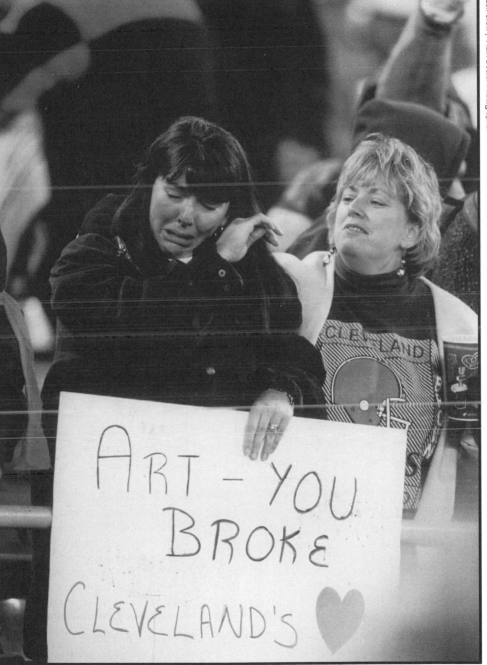

Browns' fan couldn't hold back tears in December 1995 after the Browns lost to the Pittsburgh
eelers, 20-3, in what was thought to be the team's final game in Cleveland. The NFL later promised to
t a team in the abandoned city by 1999. It most likely will be called "the Browns."

*In response to media questions, **Cleveland Mayor Michael White** outlines his plans to keep the Brown from moving, but development official **Fred Nance and County Commissioner Tim Hagan** (right) can't hide their frustration or their sense of doom.*

Art Modell *reveals his stunning surprise at the November press conference in Baltimore, surrounded by the politicians and leaders who helped bring the team to the East Coast.*

Part 3

"Browns" Up for Grabs

CHAPTER TWELVE

Modell Drops the Bomb

The new task force's mandate was to submit its stadium proposals by the end of January 1995, just six weeks away. It missed the deadline — badly.

The report came down in May, with an unmistakable air of urgency. It frequently mentioned tight deadlines and the need to start design work by June, in order to complete the stadium overhaul by the end of the Browns' lease:

• The engineering and design work would take 13 months. If the refurbished stadium were to open by 1999, this initial phase would have to be completed by June 1996, the report said.

• Working around the team's playing schedule was a tricky and time-consuming process.

• Fans would have to be protected from falling concrete; and season-ticket holders assured of access to their seats.

"Cleveland City Council needs to consider, debate, and pass legislation enabling a flat parking tax rate as soon as possible, preferably before the summer recess," the report concluded. "Failure to do so, or to identify and approve an alternative source of funds, would seriously jeopardize the community's ability to retain the Browns."

The report raised the specter of Gateway-like overruns and

strongly prompted public officials to come to agreement with the Browns "in the very near future."

City leaders, pointing to the Browns' $125,000 contribution to task force expenses, concluded at least that the team was serious about staying in place.

"This is a major advantage for Cleveland, contrasting with many other teams and owners who have gained tremendous benefits at other cities' expense, choosing to relocate franchises in exchange for enticements that make little economic sense for the communities granting them," the report said.

"Cities that have lost teams, such as St. Louis and Baltimore, are the most desperate to get back into the game."

The task force essentially went along with the Browns' request for a massive overhaul of Municipal Stadium, which it estimated would cost $154 million — $141 million just to bring the facility up to federal code standards.

It called for replacing the concrete, rebuilding the concourses, and otherwise redoing the aging structure almost from the ground up. Seats would be added along the sidelines, moving them 57 yards closer to the sidelines. The aluminum roof, blackened with age, would be torn off. A new scoreboard would be installed, the playing field lowered eight feet to improve the view from the stands, and new bleachers constructed with player clubhouses and offices underneath.

New food and novelty concessions would also be installed, loges renovated, and club seats added. Space would be left for a restaurant to be developed later.

As for the contentious issue of paying for the work, the task force settled on an artful burden-sharing formula: 55.5 percent for the city, 12.6 percent for the county, 15 percent for the state, and 16.9 percent for private businesses, including the Browns.

The task force recommended that the city finance its share of the deal by imposing a 15 percent tax on parking. (Cleveland had no parking tax at all.) A tax, said the task force, would not only transfer the fund-raising burden to mostly higher-income, non-resident commuters, but raise $13.3 million a year, enough to back $128 million in bonds.

Cuyahoga County's share would not be due for a few years, after its financial bleeding was stanched. Beginning in 1998, though, it would be expected to pay $1.8 million a year, the money drawn from whatever revenue source it chose. The 15 percent state share — about $2 million a year for 20 years — was consistent with what Governor Voinovich had said was acceptable for all sports facilities in Ohio.

The team's contribution — $10 million up front and another $20 million in forgone revenue — was consistent with Gateway's financing. Both the Indians and the Cavaliers had bought the naming rights to their facilities, to be purchased over time at a cost equal to about $7 million in 1994 dollars. The Browns could do the same, or sell the naming rights to a corporate sponsor, then toss in a few million dollars from other sources.

The task force also suggested that the revenue from 2,000 to 2,500 club seats, income that the team wasn't now getting, could be dedicated to repaying $10 million in construction loans. This meant the Browns would forego about 30 percent of the stadium's luxury seating revenue, on par with what the Indians and the Cavs had done.

The report's recommendations, released at a May 3 press conference, were immediately opposed.

The county commissioners, still wrestling with the SAFE fiasco, were adamant that they couldn't contribute. "It's simple. We don't have the money," Hagan said.

Downtown property owners complained that the parking tax would drive businesses to the suburbs and vowed to fight the plan in court, if necessary.

Art Modell, too, was bothered by several aspects of the plan, especially the size of his team's contribution. The city hadn't put any money into Municipal Stadium since 1966, but was still getting back $2.5 million a year in rent and taxes. He, on the other hand, had invested $18 million in the stadium.

Furthermore, Modell thought the team's contribution had already been made in the form of pared-down demands for the stadium, like club seats. The club would do without these pricey accommodations *only* if he got credit for the sacrifice. It angered Modell to see club seats included in the task force plan, but the revenue from them going elsewhere. This diverted fan money otherwise directed to his team.

Publicly, Modell was restrained. In a written statement issued the day the report was released, he said: "The task force's recommendations are a positive step toward meeting the challenge of making Cleveland stadium competitive and a safe, comfortable, and convenient home for fans of the Cleveland Browns.

"Nevertheless, we are concerned with political opposition to the task force recommendations — opposition which surfaced even before the task force recommendations were finalized."

Despite these objections, there was no hint of the coming disaster.

• • •

Mayor White's reaction to the task force recommendations was perhaps the biggest surprise of all. James Biggar and other members of the task force briefed White a few hours before the release of their report and came away thinking he agreed with the recommendations. Earlier in the process, he had favored a parking tax as a way for the city to spread the burden beyond its borders. It would essentially be a commuter tax on suburbanites, Biggar said.

The mayor had no immediate public reaction to the report, but the next day convened a press conference and dropped a bomb. He wasn't so sure about the parking tax, he said, but if there was to be one, he wanted it approved by voters first, even though the city council had the authority to institute the tax without a referendum.

He also said that the city could not afford to pay $438,000 for a special election, so the matter would have to wait until November's general election — six months away.

Furthermore, he considered the stadium cost estimates to be too low. Having shown the plan to a few engineers, he now believed the work would more likely cost $172 million. Though he didn't say so then, he thought that it would be politically safer to start with a higher cost estimate and have the project come in below-cost, rather than the other way around, as had happened at Gateway.

He then announced another "working group" — the third stadium task force in less than two years. This group was to study the recommendations of the previous committee, headed by David Hoag, and to resolve cost and funding issues by early June. The new group would be comprised of representatives from the mayor's office, three members of the Hoag committee, and five city council representatives.

Some of the current task-force members thought that the mayor had pulled the rug out from under them. But White said the job was large and the players disparate.

"That plan called for the actions, significant actions, expensive actions to the public by three different governments.... My belief was we had to try to reach some point of consensus so that we would be able to get this issue resolved," he recalled later.

In a telephone conversation with Modell the day the report came out, White asked to start lease negotiations right away, while work on funding issues went ahead. Modell put him off. He said he didn't want to bargain for a lease until the mechanism was in place to pay for the stadium work. White viewed this as a bad omen.

He was right.

Modell and the Browns were furious. The practical effect of White's actions was to add another year to the stadium timetable, pushing it beyond the expiration of the lease.

Cleveland City Council president Jay Westbrook suggested extending the team's lease by a year or two to continue working out the details. The team said no. "We've been getting guarantees since 1989 that something's going to be done," David Hopcraft, a governmental affairs consultant for Modell, told reporters.

Meanwhile, the newly appointed working group began meeting in private. But public statements from some of its members suggested a rough start. One councilman, James Rokakis, said he was pessimistic that the group could agree on a solution because city voters were unlikely to approve a new tax. Another, Gary Paulenske, raised anew the issue of renovations. Perhaps, he said, it would be smarter to build a new stadium elsewhere and turn the lakefront parcel over to developers.

White gamely tried to corral the stampeding interests. Over the next few weeks, he advanced idea after idea. He suggested new taxes on parking, retail sales, cigarettes, and alcohol. But each idea sank quickly under the weight of fierce opposition.

On June 1, White unveiled his fourth proposal in 30 days. This one called on the City Council to impose a 10 percent tax on parking and an additional 2 percent tax to pay for a midnight basketball league and extracurricular school programs. Gone was the idea of going to the voters with proposals for new taxes. Now being pushed was a Cuyahoga County extension of its sin tax, thus creating new bonding authority to pay for Municipal Stadium and Gateway overruns.

The mayor's plan, sprung on the city council only a few hours before its public announcement, created an uproar. It caught White's own "consensus group" by surprise, and several members opposed it outright. Councilman Rokakis said he thought owners of downtown buildings and parking decks might go along with an 8 percent parking tax, but not 12 percent. Meanwhile, a new group threatened to take any tax to referendum. Cuyahoga County commissioners, then leaning on the Cavaliers and Indians to cover Gateway overruns, said they opposed more taxes for that project.

Furthermore, extension of the sin tax would require state legislative approval, something White said he hoped to have by Sept. 1.

White acknowledged both the financial and political uncertainties. "We're literally putting one brick in at a time," the mayor told reporters. "We believe we've come to a point where action is necessary and we must move rapidly."

He didn't know how right he was.

Modell was repulsed by the divisive tenor of the debate. Eighteen months after his breakfast meeting with White at the Ritz-Carlton, the team appeared no closer to getting the stadium renovated than it had when the first dome proposal was rejected 10 years before. Ribbon-cutting now looked like it would take place in 2000 at the earliest, when Modell would be 75.

On June 5, Modell dropped his own bomb. He wrote a letter to Mayor White, at the same time forwarding a copy to *The Plain Dealer*. In it, the Browns owner spelled out his position:

"… the Browns organization cannot condone, support, or participate in a continuation of the divisive and disruptive dialogue concerning Stadium renovation. Nor are we willing to endure a campaign associated with either an initiative or recall referendum on the November ballot."

Instead, said Modell, the team had to turn its attention to the upcoming season. The Browns had gone 12-6 the year before and were a pre-season pick of some sports magazines to win the Super Bowl. Modell didn't want distractions. Internally, team officials had decided they would be better off drawing up their own plan and taking it back to the city with a firm deadline *after* the 1995 football season.

Modell asked for a moratorium on the debate, writing:

"We hope a moratorium until the end of the season will allow the political and economic environment to stabilize.... . For many years we have been told by community leaders that 'now' is not the right time for the community to address the responsibility of repairing the stadium. At this time then, I hope you will understand that 'now' is not the right time for the Cleveland Browns and their fans to address this issue given the negative atmosphere being fostered by special interests and resulting intense divisiveness within the community."

Minutes after receiving the letter, White called the team owner. "Art, I'm on top of City Hall. I'm getting ready to jump. What are you doing to me?" he joked.

Modell laughed, and the two talked agreeably for a few minutes. Modell, the eternal optimist, said he thought he had a good shot at the Super Bowl and assured the mayor that Cleveland would have a chance to put its financial package together. The Browns would not negotiate with any other cities, he promised. Though he didn't say so, Modell assumed White would continue working behind the scenes; he himself preferred that such maneuvering be done quietly.

But White was shaken and suspicious. "... what I didn't tell him was that I was deathly afraid that if we didn't put a package in front of him before the end of the season, we would be out of the ball game."

The mayor had said as much to council president Westbrook and stadium task force chairman David Hoag. They needed to have something by the end of the season, he explained to them, "or it was all over for us."

Like Baltimore a decade earlier, Cleveland was engulfed in a crisis atmosphere, groping to save its team. Communication broke down between the parties, and suspicion grew. Like Mayor Schaefer, White feared the game was already lost. But he plunged ahead.

The next day, White sent a letter to Modell in which he stated that his administration could not, "in good conscience, let our efforts to assure that there is a viable home for the Browns in Cleveland wane."

Wrote the mayor: "It is regrettable that the tenor of the public debate on Stadium renovation financing plans has, on occasion, included commentary which is neither productive, nor geared towards a constructive solution. However, it is critically important the Browns organization understand one thing even if it takes nothing else away from the public debate. The City of Cleveland is irretrievably committed to making certain the Cleveland Browns have a competitive lease arrangement for the next twenty-five to thirty years that is fair to both the people of the City of Cleveland and the legitimate economic interests of the Browns."

Two weeks later, on June 21, White wrote to NFL Commissioner Paul Tagliabue: "We are aware of speculative reports in the media concerning other cities being interested in our team. I want you to know in the strongest possible terms that the City of Cleveland, joined by significant efforts from the business community, is doing everything within its power to provide the Browns with a competitive economic package ..."

The next day, White and Westbrook sent a letter by messenger to Modell, announcing an agreement between the mayor and city council. This plan called for an 8 percent parking tax, a 2 percentage-point increase in the city's stadium-admission tax, $25 million from the state, $10 million from the Browns, $10 million from club seats, and $6 million from stadium naming rights.

The plan also specified a 20-year extension of the county's sin tax, a matter that had to be put on the November ballot and approved. White expressed confidence that Cuyahoga County would appropriately follow through.

In fact, at White's urging, the Ohio General Assembly passed legislation permitting the Cuyahoga County Commissioners to extend the Gateway sin tax without referendum. The bill, signed by Governor Voinovich on July 19, 1995, would allow additional bonds — backed by the expected tax proceeds — to be sold, raising about 15 percent of the money needed for the work. But the county would have to act within 45 days or its powers would expire.

Some of the county commissioners, up for re-election in 16 months, were not at all sure they wanted to act. One immediate foe was Mary Boyle, who had defeated Vince Campanella and his dome tax 10 years earlier. The region's political establishment was splintered on the issue. Jimmy Dimora, the county's Democratic Party chairman and the mayor of suburban Bedford Heights, favored letting the voters decide on the tax extension.

"We've always stood for making people part of the process," said Dimora, who was feuding with White.

White wasn't sitting still. He pushed the 8 percent parking tax through the city council. He strongly urged the county to act or to risk losing the beloved Browns.

But there he encountered a big stumbling block. County commissioners didn't want to extend the sin tax until they had reached agreement with the Indians and the Cavaliers on the Gateway overruns.

It didn't help that Modell and the Browns were playing it coy, making it unclear whether they wanted the matter submitted to a vote or even if they would stick around if the tax passed. This left the commissioners with the unappealing choice of risking their political futures on a vote that might not even save the team.

"We find ourselves in a terribly awkward position because the owner of the Browns hasn't given us any indication that this isn't an exercise in futility," Hagan said at a commissioners meeting.

Instead, the team, through Hopcraft, publicly questioned whether the financing plan then coming together would be sufficient. It was supposed to raise $154 million; White himself had estimated the work would cost $175 million. Hopcraft bemoaned the fact that some of the sin and parking tax proceeds were to be siphoned off for sports programs in the city's schools and for Gateway.

"Don't do it in the name of the Browns," he implored.

When he pointedly declined to promise that the team would stay in town if the tax plan was enacted, the plan appeared doomed.

"I know that Modell finds it inconvenient that we have a democracy," said Hagan. "The voters cannot be sold on 'maybe they'll stay or maybe not.'"

On Sept. 1, the commissioners unanimously decided to put the measure on the ballot. They also changed the number of years that the sin tax would be extended. Now, instead of expiring in

2005, it would run until 2015. But, even if passed, the extension would not take effect until an NFL team committed to the city. And, the commissioners agreed, no sin tax money would cover Gateway's overruns.

"We have tried to fashion a proposal we think can keep an NFL franchise in Cleveland," Hagan told reporters. "We all wish Mother Teresa owned the Browns. It'd be an easier sell."

As with Baltimore and the Colts, Cleveland and the Browns had now switched positions. Modell had spent years clumsily trying to get the city's attention and its dollars. Now he was on the run, and the city was chasing him.

Meanwhile, early in September, Tagliabue quietly visited Cleveland to meet with Modell. The Browns owner set forth his dilemma and told the commissioner that he didn't think things were going to work out in Cleveland. But Modell didn't mention Baltimore, specifically. He gave the commissioner a stack of photocopied local newspaper stories, including a section of letters to the editor that opposed the use of Cleveland public money for a football stadium. It was headlined: "No, No, No. Proposed Stadium Tax Sacked."

On the top of the stack, a cartoon from *The Plain Dealer* depicted a forlorn Browns fan in a knit cap. The slogan on his shirt read: "Go Browns! But leave the Indians here."

According to Browns officials, Tagliabue advised Modell not to overlook Sacramento, Calif., a one-time expansion candidate. This sent Modell and his aides scrambling for a map to find out where Sacramento was.

As White and Hagan tried to raise the money for a campaign to extend the sin tax, Modell remained silent. He viewed the leaders' plan as a no-win situation. If voters rejected the tax, then the team's hopes for a renovated stadium would be dashed. If the tax passed, it would be inadequate to do the job. Either way, the team would be plunged involuntarily into a public debate on its value to Cleveland.

White would later view the team's reaction to the plan as proof that the Browns had already decided to leave Cleveland. The moratorium, he thought, had been the set-up for the eventual sucker punch.

In Modell's view, all bets were now off. Some of his advisers had been nudging him for months about leaving. A few had gone so far as to explore a move to Summit County, to land near the Richfield Coliseum that the Cavaliers had vacated. Some of Summit County's heavyweights, smarting at the city's nabbing of the basketball team, viewed a run at the Browns as fair play. A county poll was quietly conducted, asking residents if they would support a small increase in the sales tax to pay for various projects, including a stadium. The response was not encouraging.

Meanwhile, as White suspected, the Browns' financial situation worsened.

The team was making money, but its cash flow had been damaged by Modell's pursuit of a Super Bowl. In 1995, *Financial World* magazine listed the Browns among the top five most valuable franchises in sports, but its estimate did not reflect the team's monstrous amount of debt.

The team had done so well in the 1994 season that Modell had decided to go for broke and convert some money, budgeted for long-term salary obligations, into signing bonuses. The San Francisco 49ers had done this same thing very successfully in 1994, essentially buying their way to Super Bowl XXIX. (The ploy is akin to a contending baseball team borrowing in July from the next season's budget to pick up one more hot bat down the pennant stretch.)

In 1995, Modell and the Browns spent $23 million in guaranteed signing bonuses, the second highest total in the NFL, where the average was only $15 million. Eight Browns players signed for bonuses exceeding $1 million, including wide receiver Andre Rison ($5 million); quarterback Vinny Testaverde ($2.85 million); safety Eric Turner ($2.75 million); linebacker Pepper Johnson ($2.2 million); offensive tackle Tony Jones ($1.66 million); and running back Leroy Hoard ($1.5 million).

Other teams could have easily carried this load on their books. But Modell and the Browns were already saddled with extraordinary debt for stadium improvements, the Berea facility, and operating cash. And there were outside constraints. To keep teams from going bankrupt, the NFL limits an owner's borrowing to a total of $50 million. Modell had already borrowed this amount, then put up both the Cleveland Stadium Corp.'s assets and his own personal assets to borrow even more. Even if, as Cleveland's lawyers would later contend, the Browns were earning more from their stadium than the league average, it was not enough to fund Modell's spending spree or to sustain the team in the future.

Moreover, Modell ran one of the NFL's most expensive off-field operations. His front office had a reputation for innovation and quality, but also for keeping hangers-on whom Modell was loathe to dispatch. The 91-person administrative staff was considerably larger than the league average.

• • •

NFL teams, as private companies, don't have to disclose their finances and almost never do. But there have been a few tantalizing glimpses inside the team's books.

Freeman McNeil's and the NFL Players Association's 1992 lawsuit against the NFL forced the clubs to turn over their financial statements from 1980 to 1990. The Browns showed a 1990 operating profit of $1.38 million — the third-worst in the NFL, ahead of only the New England Patriots and the San Francisco 49ers, who actually lost money. The average club earned $5.8 million in operating profit, which doesn't include interest paid on loans or taxes.

The financial documents showed the Browns losing $9 million in the 1980s — the fifth-highest loss by a team. During this time, the team paid Modell an annual salary of about $200,000, which was average for the league.

Had things worsened in the ensuing five years? The team said yes. After he announced the team's move to Baltimore, Modell claimed that the team suffered a $21 million "cash loss," though he wouldn't specify what the team's actual profit or loss was. He said he had borrowed all he could from the banks to sign free agents and was having a hard time paying his bills.

According to a report obtained by the Cleveland *Plain Dealer*, Modell's Cleveland Stadium Corp. turned a respectable $2.4 million profit in 1994, even after paying interest on more than $30 million in debt. This was on revenues of $8.2 million.

"I don't think he has a plausible case that he has had financial difficulties in the past. Relative to the behavior of the typical NFL owner, Modell is just fine," said Roger Noll, a Stanford University economist who reviewed the league's financial statements and testified on behalf of the players' union in the 1992 court case.

The NFL, too, was skeptical of Modell claims of losing money. In a 1996 report to the other owners, Commissioner Tagliabue wrote, rather clinically, "When the Stadium Corporation is included, the Browns have not incurred net operating losses, exclusive of depreciation and amortization, sufficient to threaten the continued viability of the team. The Browns have, however, experienced substantial cash flow problems that raise issues about the team's continued competitive viability under current circumstances in Cleveland."

The Browns finances had ranked the team low enough to qualify for special league assistance the year before. The NFL, in a half-hearted effort to lessen the widening revenue gap between teams, instituted a new distribution plan in the mid 1990s for club seat rental receipts. Under this plan, the visitor's share of seat licenses and the annual fee charged for club seats was diverted to a central fund and split up among the bottom-third grossing NFL franchises. The Browns were in this group.

Even if the team had managed to make money in Cleveland, its ability to continue doing so, while remaining competitive on the field, depended on getting a better stadium arrangement.

"In the NFL of the future, you need at least $20 million a year of stadium economics to remain competitive. In the old stadium, Cleveland would have been left in the dust," said Paul Much, a sports-team financial consultant and senior managing director of Houlihan Lokey Howard & Zukin, a specialty investment banking firm in Chicago.

In addition, Modell desperately wanted to keep up with the other team owners, who hadn't paid half his dues.

Georgia Frontiere, the former lounge singer who inherited the Rams after the death of her husband Carroll Rosenbloom, snagged one of the NFL's sweetest deals. In 1994, her Rams agreed to move from Anaheim, Calif., to St. Louis and a new, $260 million, domed stadium that doubled as a convention center annex. The city's lease called for the Rams to pay $250,000 annual rent — less, the city figured, than it would cost to run the stadium. The Rams also demanded and received another $86 million worth of inducements, from a new practice facility, to help in paying off the NFL's relocation fee and the Rams' debt on the Anaheim stadium. It was enough money to make the Rams dangerous on Sundays.

Meanwhile, the owner who had started franchise roulette in the NFL, the Raiders' Al Davis, was poised to make a fortune and assemble a fearsome contender, thanks to the taxpayers of Oakland, Calif. Davis in 1995 returned his once-championship team to the city he had earlier abandoned. And the Houston Oilers' owner Bud Adams, an NFL stalwart whose team was only occasionally a threat on game day, pulled off a deal with Nashville, Tenn. that he hoped would radically improve on-field performance.

Then there was Modell, a builder of the NFL, trying to squeeze out a few more wins in a stadium that barely provided enough toilets for fans, let alone cash for players. He was falling far behind team owners who enjoyed the league riches he had helped to amass, but who were contributing nothing in return.

"The fact is, he was just getting deeper and deeper into hock every year. He was getting tapped out," explained his friend and business associate, Alfred Lerner. "And he is a proud man. It was very hard for him to say that.

"Art just kept getting more and more discouraged and finally said, 'We need to start talking to Baltimore.'"

Even the league itself was growing unfamiliar to Modell. New, younger owners were replacing familiar, older ones. Modell was now the longest tenured team operator in the league. The new NFL was now driven by a harsher mentality, by men who had acquired their wealth independent of football and had paid a fortune for their franchises.

In 1992, when the TV networks claimed they were losing money on pro football, Modell, who viewed the broadcasters as partners, went to his fellow owners with a plan to give back $210 million of the rights' fees in exchange for a contract extension.

"For 30 years, we have had an amicable partnership with the networks, and it is one we want to continue," Modell argued. "With the state of the economy and the TV market, they need our help. And I think it's an issue where we would also be helping ourselves."

The other owners, led by the Cowboys' Jerry Jones and the Eagles' Norman Braman, vehemently disagreed, and they made sure Modell's rebate proposal fell a few votes shy of the 21 needed to pass. The next year (1993), Modell gave up his 31-year chairmanship of the broadcast committee, and the NFL did the unthinkable: It dropped CBS, its oldest broadcaster, in favor of the glittery upstart Fox and a record-breaking $1.6 billion contract.

On Sept. 5, 1995, Modell convened a meeting of some of his top aides and confidants in the offices of his chief law firm, Jones, Day, Reavis & Pogue. Attending were his executive vice president, Jim Bailey; his son David; his government relations consultant Hopcraft; his friend Lerner; and Jones, Day's managing partner Patrick F. McCartan.

The meeting lasted from 10 a.m. to 1 p.m. Over Caesar salads, the men reviewed the team's situation.

Hopcraft noted that the Browns and Modell were getting beaten up in the media. This, he felt, was significant. Despite the wholehearted support of most elected officials, Gateway funding had passed by a narrow margin. In fact, city voters had rejected the measure; suburbanites carried it to passage. But their interest in bailing out projects in downtown Cleveland was now surely strained by the Gateway funding debacle.

The Browns, Hopcraft said, were unlikely to do as well in a second vote, given the divisions among community leaders and the Gateway outcome.

Lerner gave a report about Baltimore and what he knew of the city's timetable for keeping stadium funding in place.

Bailey went over the team's financial situation. A discussion of the Browns' legal options concluded that the team could probably get out of its lease but that the local courts would be loathe to side with the team. Final victory would come only on appeal.

Finally, Modell, his face ashen, said to no one in particular, "I have no choice."

Lerner concurred. "You have no choice," he said.

There was a brief silence in the room as the decision's ramifications sank in. The Browns were leaving Cleveland. Modell volunteered that he could sell the franchise. But the group agreed that, given the stadium problems, it would be hard to find a buyer who would pay enough to cover the team's debts and the capital-gains taxes and leave anything for Modell's family.

Among the NFL's increasingly corporate owners, Modell was an anachronism. His franchise did not reflect his wealth; it *was* his wealth, his sole source of significant income.

To Hopcraft, the meeting represented a crossing of the Rubicon. Modell had "been stonewalling us for six years," he recalled later. "He wouldn't pull the trigger. That was the first time he came to grips with it."

Modell seemed so shaken by the meeting that both Hopcraft and McCartan called him at home that night to check on him.

Explaining his decision months later, Modell pointed to the accumulation of factors and events, from Cleveland's fractious political climate, to the superior accommodations afforded the Cavaliers and the Indians, to the readiness of business leaders to align themselves with the Indians' rising star.

"What got to us was the treatment basketball and baseball were getting.... We were fifth man on the totem pole. That bothered me more than the government's reaction," Modell said.

Friends find that very plausible. Modell was famous for making impetuous decisions and filling in the facts later.

"He's a very emotional guy. He makes decisions based on emotion," said James Biggar.

It hurt Modell that people were continually making comparisons between him and Dick Jacobs, often concluding that the baseball team owner was smarter and more effective.

"I think one of the things that bothered Art was he was always the King Arthur of sports," Biggar said. "Art always wanted to be loved. Dick preferred to be quietly respected."

In interviews months later with *The Plain Dealer*, Lerner said, "You sort of have to see the climate that was going on.

"He was not being viewed very favorably in the media. When he said what he wanted, he was being labeled as an extortionist and a blackmailer. When he didn't say what he wanted, he was being labeled as not being forthcoming, and he felt kind of trapped between those two lines."

A week after these comments, Lerner put it even more succinctly to another reporter: "Art was yesterday's hero, and Dick Jacobs was today's hero."

CHAPTER THIRTEEN

Darth
Vader

Until 1995, Baltimore's National Football League quest had largely been a gentlemanly affair. When the league asked the city to stay away from the New England Patriots, a team briefly smitten by wanderlust, Baltimore diligently obliged.

When the league told the city to stop contacting team owners individually during expansion, Baltimore — and perhaps *only* Baltimore — complied.

And when the league said to sell 100 skyboxes and 7,500 club seats in a stadium that didn't exist, and 50,000 seats to a pre-season game that didn't count, Baltimore did so with barely a blink.

That all changed with the appointment of John Moag, Jr. as chairman of the Maryland Stadium Authority. Where Herb Belgrad had been the good guy of expansion, honest as a Boy Scout and as businesslike as the MBAs and lawyers running the NFL, the chain-smoking Moag was Darth Vader.

Moag was little interested in ingratiating himself with the league heavyweights. He felt, as did Belgrad at the end, that the city's attempted appeasement had been wasted on team owners using Baltimore's financial package to drive up the bidding in other cities. Moag didn't want any part of that kind of embarrassment.

Though he had spent a lifetime in politics, this was Moag's

first time squarely in the public eye, and he didn't intend to lose. At 41, he was a hard-working, hard-partying lobbyist on Capitol Hill, where results mattered more than methods. His rise through the ranks had been swift, and his reputation was that of a brash young man in a hurry.

John Moag was born in Chicago but as a youth moved to Baltimore with his parents and five younger siblings. He spent his early years in a home near Memorial Stadium, where he hustled money by parking cars on the family lawn during Colts games — a time-honored Baltimore tradition.

His first taste of politics came in 1972, immediately after he graduated from the Jesuit Loyola High School in Towson, Md. He went to work for George McGovern's unsuccessful presidential campaign, eventually heading the Democrat's Kent County organization while attending classes at Washington College in Chestertown.

In 1977, Moag received his political science degree from the small Eastern Shore institution and, four years later, a law degree from the University of Baltimore. From there, he headed to Annapolis, where he worked as an aide to then-Senate President Steny Hoyer, a job that introduced him to Maryland's burgeoning Washington suburbs, Parris Glendening's turf. When Hoyer ran for lieutenant governor in 1978, Moag served as his driver for $25 a week. Hoyer lost but won a seat two years later in the U.S. Congress. He took Moag with him as legislative director and associate staffer to the House Appropriations Committee.

Six years later, Moag, then 33, was brought in as full partner at the powerful Washington law firm Patton, Boggs and Blow, which had deep connections and influence in the national Democratic Party. Among its one-time partners was Ron Brown, the former party chairman who went on to serve as Secretary of Commerce in the Clinton Administration (he died in a plane crash over Bosnia in April 1996). Tom Boggs, son of Hale Boggs, the Louisiana lawmaker who won a team for New Orleans in exchange for shepherding Pete Rozelle's AFL-NFL merger legislation through Congress, was a firm co-founder.

Moag became managing partner of Patton, Boggs and Blow's Baltimore operation, with oversight of its branch offices in Denver, Dallas, Seattle, and Greensboro and Raleigh, N.C. Among his

Baltimore office mates was former Maryland Governor Harry Hughes.

Six feet tall and trim, Moag was not much of an athlete. His sport was his work. He developed a reputation for tenacity, as well as for revelry. He was just as likely to be ducking into a U.S. senator's office as going back stage at a Grateful Dead concert.

But make no mistake: Moag was effective. He helped win federal funding for the Christopher Columbus Center, a marine research facility in downtown Baltimore that resurgent congressional Republicans targeted as pure pork. And when the University of Arizona, another Moag client, was blocked from building an observatory outside of Tucson, he cleared the way. According to environmentalists, the planned site was home to the Mount Graham Red Squirrel, a rodent which they had succeeded in listing as an endangered species. Moag pushed through an act of Congress that made the squirrel the first species *exempted* from endangered species protection.

It was just this sort of tenacity that Governor Parris Glendening was seeking when he named Moag head of the Maryland Stadium Authority.

• • •

When he first met with Glendening in Maryland's State House in February 1995, Moag had already drawn some strategic conclusions that meshed with the new governor's 1994 campaign. Glendening had vowed to continue the city's NFL fight, at least for a while. Other gubernatorial candidates, and even Baltimore Mayor Kurt L. Schmoke, were beginning to talk about giving up. Glendening also opposed the Redskins' plans to build a stadium in Laurel, Md. Among Baltimore's NFL faithful, it was a litmus test of sorts for Glendening, a longtime Redskins fan whom they viewed suspiciously.

For Moag, Glendening, and Maryland, the situation was anything but encouraging. The state had just suffered a pair of defeats. Despite intense wooing by Marylanders, both the Tampa Bay Buccaneers and the L.A. Rams chose not to move to Baltimore. Glendening did not want to set himself up for the same humiliation to which Schaefer had been subjected. He asked Moag for a frank analysis of the state's chances, and Moag, in response, was equally blunt: The odds were long of getting a team, and it was nearly inevitable that more teams would come sniffing — if only to scare their politicians back home into cutting a better deal.

The men agreed on some basic strategy. First, talks with any teams would be kept secret; neither wanted the state or the Maryland Stadium Authority to be used. Moag's and Glendening's predecessors had also tried to keep contacts discreet, but expansion was a beauty contest that required public displays of support, such as selling out an exhibition game and premium seating. Now, even key figures in the city's long battle would be kept in the dark.

Baltimore Orioles owner Peter Angelos, in particular, was angry about being shut out of the process. After the expansion set-back, Schaefer went to Angelos to enlist his help in bringing a team to Baltimore. Angelos had the investors and the money, and he thought that an NFL team owner would rather deal with him than with a bureaucrat like Moag. Angelos also felt strongly that any football team coming to town should have local investors and a mechanism by which it would eventually pass to local control.

Angelos, who had paid $173 million to acquire the Orioles, didn't take kindly to his landlord using his tax dollars to lure a competitor to his backyard. The new stadium would be built adjacent to Oriole Park at Camden Yards.

But Moag, overlooking Baltimore's horrific history with out-of-town mercenaries, told prospective owners that if they moved to the city, they'd never be forced to give the locals franchise control.

There was a further problem with Angelos. Just a few months before, at the height of the major league baseball players' strike, Angelos, a labor lawyer, had been the only team owner to refuse to field replacement players. This stance made him persona non grata in baseball and would not endear him to NFL owners. By insisting on eventually taking over the team, Angelos also ruled out teams whose owners were interested in moving to Baltimore, but not in selling —which is to say most prospects.

Angelos was so upset about the snub that he approached Glendening and asked that Moag be fired. The governor refused.

As the second part of their strategy, Moag and Glendening agreed to cut their losses. They imposed an end-of-the-year dead-line, both to spur prospects and to avoid involving the new governor in a humiliating and, very likely, losing effort. Besides, Glendening didn't think he could hold on to the stadium funding much longer.

The 1987 legislation that had established funding for the twin-stadium Camden Yards project contained no expiration date and conceivably could be left in place forever. It wasn't as if there were $100 million lying around in a bank account. Most of the money would come from bonds that wouldn't be sold until a team signed a contract to move to Baltimore.

But there was pressure to eliminate the funding. Some city officials, including Mayor Schmoke, were already thinking of alternative uses for the bonds. Some were interested in building an indoor arena for basketball and hockey teams now that Abe Pollin's NBA Bullets and NHL Capitals were moving into a downtown Washington forum. Before committing to D.C., Pollin had offered to bring his teams to an arena at Camden Yards, but Baltimore was then still in the NFL hunt.

Some powerful lawmakers from the Maryland suburbs of D.C. were hoping that the Redskins would build a stadium in their region. Shut out of Laurel, the Redskins were now looking at a site in Landover, in Prince George's County, closer to the District. Glendening himself wanted to use the designated stadium lottery money for school construction but gave Moag permission to explore alternatives, such as an arena.

Moag told Glendening that NFL expansion wasn't likely to happen in the next year. If Baltimore was going to get a team, it would have to steal one from another city. Neither Moag nor Glendening raised the ethics of NFL team raiding or the other gentleman's rules of engagement that Schaefer and Belgrad had espoused. This was not going to be an operation performed through the auspices of the U.S. Conference of Mayors.

When the Colts moved out of Baltimore in 1984, Glendening couldn't have known personally the emotions such franchise relocations can engender. He was both resident and county executive — essentially the mayor — of Prince George's County, a populous, predominantly black suburb of Washington that was in the Redskins' orbit. He was just beginning his slow, steady climb upward in politics, one that was consistent with his bookish, cautious manner.

After becoming the youngest student at Florida State University to earn a doctorate in political science, Glendening taught at the University of Maryland in College Park. He became a recognized authority on government finance, writing several textbooks that were used by more than 400 colleges.

In 1973, the professor won a seat on the Hyattsville [Md.] City Council and, the next year, on the Prince George's County Council. In 1982, he was elected county executive, an office in which he developed a reputation for innovative, conciliatory government, aggressive fund raising, and limitless ambition. According to friends, he quickly began plotting his move to Annapolis, weighing the competition, issues, and timing. The 1980s belonged to Governor Schaefer, Glendening concluded, so he would wait until Schaefer's second term to begin making his move to the Governor's Mansion.

At the end of their meeting, Glendening patted Moag on the back and wished him luck. The governor was not optimistic.

Moag then set in motion a plan that was the opposite of the city's expansion strategy. He focused primarily on NFL team owners and totally ignored Tagliabue and the league office. An owner in financial trouble, he reasoned, would have to consider the city's lucrative stadium offer.

But he also put the league on notice, through a newspaper interview, that he was talking to lawyers and seriously considering filing an antitrust suit against the NFL — one that would accuse the league of colluding to keep competitors out of Baltimore and away from the Redskins' territory. Moag's lawyers told him he had a strong case. He hoped his threat would shake up the league. It did.

"We'd tried the carrot long enough, and I wanted them to know we were going to have another approach," Moag explained later.

He then began calling and visiting team owners and useful pro football insiders. He invited Charlotte-based consultant Max Muhleman to Baltimore. The two talked football and arenas. At the time, Moag thought the latter more likely than the former.

Moag flew to Charlotte to meet with Carolina Panthers owner, and former Baltimore Colt, Jerry Richardson, chairman of a new NFL committee formed to cure the league's now-chronic stadium problem. Despite its success on television, the National

Football League was falling behind Major League Baseball in the race for fan-friendly stadiums. It had no Camden Yards, let alone a Wrigley Field.

Minutes from a 1995 meeting show Richardson's stadium committee (and other NFL owners) uneasy about facilities: "The stadium issue is a priority for the NFL. At least 16 teams are faced with significant stadium concerns, and the NFL trails other sports leagues in the number of new facilities that have been built or are under construction in recent years."

Citing his fond memories of Baltimore and his playing days there, Richardson promised Moag he would do whatever he could to help the city. Moag told Richardson that the stadium funding was going to disappear, and with it, the Richardson committee's chances of enjoying at least one quick success. Richardson himself, confirming that league expansion was unlikely, predicted that some teams would be moving. He asked if there was any way to save the Maryland funding, short of getting a team to the city. Moag said he would need a binding commitment from the league to put a team in Baltimore.

Moag returned home and began drawing up a list of teams that might need a new stadium. He worked the phones, contacting team owners or those familiar with team owners. He subscribed to a clipping service that collected newspaper stories from around the country about NFL teams in distress.

He came up with 10 teams that he thought might be ripe for the plucking. *Among the clips that caught his eye*: an article covering the faltering stadium negotiations between Cleveland and the Browns. He read with interest Art Modell's expressed frustration with the progress of his talks.

The Baltimore Browns? It seemed a long shot, even to the scrappy Moag. The Browns were one of the most respected teams in the league, a franchise rich in history and fan support. And Modell, who opposed relocations by other teams, seemed the least likely team owner to abandon his city. But the league was buzzing with the problems Modell was having getting a new stadium.

Informed by former Governor Hughes of Modell's earlier interest in Baltimore, Moag made his first contact with the Browns in the spring of 1995 through an intermediary: Robert Leffler, a Baltimore-based marketing man who not only had contacts in

Cleveland, but was an NFL insider with both an encyclopedic knowledge of the business and a long familiarity with Baltimore's travails.

Leffler had been the Colts' marketing director — resigning mere months before their move — and now ran his own agency. Among his clients were Alfred Lerner, who owned an apartment complex that the Leffler Agency publicized, and the Cleveland Browns. Leffler's agency handled the international Browns Backers fan-club network, responding to requests for club membership and merchandise. Leffler himself had once represented Malcolm Glazer, the failed Baltimore expansion bidder who now owned the Tampa Bay Buccaneers.

Moag asked Leffler to contact the Browns to see if the Cleveland team had any interest in the city. Leffler did, but the initial response was not encouraging. Browns executive vice president Jim Bailey didn't think the team was interested, he said, but he would check. A few days later, he called Leffler and told him Modell was not interested. Furthermore, Leffler reported, when Modell heard Moag's name, the team owner had inquired: "Isn't that the guy who's talking about suing the league?"

Other prospects appeared more hopeful.

The most immediate was the Cincinnati Bengals, owned by Mike Brown, the son of Cleveland Browns founding coach and namesake Paul Brown. The Bengals were locked in a debate remarkably similar to the one going on in Cleveland. They shared Cincinnati's Riverfront Stadium with the National League baseball Reds. Both teams thought the stadium was obsolete. And, as in Cleveland, the community's stadium-related efforts had been largely devoted to baseball.

But unlike Modell, Mike Brown insisted on being at the front, not the end, of the stadium line.

In May 1995, when city leaders announced plans for building the Reds a new ballpark, Brown was publicly dour on the prospects for his team. He vowed to accept nothing less than "a new, grade-A facility." Among his options, he said, was moving to Baltimore.

This was not news to Baltimore officials. They had been in contact with the team on and off for several years, and things had heated up in recent months. In 1994, when Peter Angelos was bidding on the Tampa Bay Buccaneers, Tagliabue told him it was too bad that Angelos wasn't interested in the Bengals, suggesting that Cincinnati was a less strategically coveted market than Tampa.

Moag flew to Cincinnati on March 29, 1995, and met with Brown, who was candid about his allegiance to his city. Moag came away feeling that Brown had a "very high threshold" for moving and would probably take just about anything the community offered him to stay.

On June 14, Brown traveled to Baltimore for a "secret" visit with Moag. Several camera crews from Cincinnati TV news stations followed Brown off of his plane in Baltimore.

Angry that he was being used, Moag nonetheless went through the motions, taking Brown to a baseball game at Camden Yards and showing him the site, just to the south, where the football stadium would be built. Brown told reporters he was pursuing all options but hoped to stay in Ohio.

The gambit worked. Within weeks, the city and county governments around Cincinnati had put together a sales tax plan to pay for new baseball and football stadiums. The issue would have to be put to the voters, and not until after Glendening and Moag's deadline had passed. By then, said Moag, Baltimore would have attracted another team or dropped its stadium funding. Brown reluctantly told Moag that, to keep his franchise in the city where his father had founded it, he was willing to take that risk.

In a telephone call to thank Moag after the visit, Brown said he had talked with Commissioner Tagliabue about Baltimore and felt good about its chances. "I think you have a very good shot at landing an NFL franchise in your city," he said.

The Houston Oilers were also looking that summer. Unhappy with the Astrodome and its sparse attendance, they made contact with the Maryland Stadium Authority but soon struck a deal with Nashville.

The Chicago Bears, then talking with both Chicago and Gary, Ind., popped up from time to time, but it seemed to Moag that team executives interested in a move had not convinced the person who counted: Virginia McCaskey, daughter of the late owner, George Halas. McCaskey, who inherited her father's team share, traveled to Baltimore that summer and sat silently in an empty Camden Yards.

The L.A. Raiders' Al Davis, again on the move, visited Baltimore in early May. Peter Angelos and an investors group he assembled offered to buy a 40 percent stake in the Raiders. It also wanted the right of first refusal if the controlling share were ever sold. Angelos surmised, however, that Davis preferred the climate and culture of California to his industrial East Coast city. He was right.

On June 23, Davis signed a letter of intent to return his team to Oakland. It was another loss for Maryland, and it ran the state's score for the year up to 0-4.

The Buccaneers seemed a better prospect. When Glazer outbid Angelos Jan. 16 to buy the Florida franchise, he vowed to keep it in Tampa forever. "I sure as heck would rather own a team in Tampa than I would in Baltimore," the Florida financier told reporters.

But only a few months later, as efforts to build a new stadium in northwest Florida progressed slowly, Glazer was back in touch with Maryland. The NFL thought Glazer's purchase agreement, which contained a multimillion-dollar penalty for moving, effectively prohibited the team from picking up stakes. But Glazer decided that the contract's performance guarantees on attendance and other matters had been abrogated by Tampa, and he was free to go. Moag met several times in Florida with the Tampa team owner.

Arizona Cardinals owner Bill Bidwill, who passed over Baltimore in 1987, came by for another visit that summer of 1995. He was unhappy with Phoenix and considering yet another move. Moag thought both Glazer and Bidwill offered some hope.

Meanwhile, at a party for the Orioles, Moag bumped into H. Furlong Baldwin, head of Mercantile Safe Deposit and Trust Co., an old-line relationship bank in Baltimore. Baldwin, who had taken part in Bob Tisch's short-lived expansion bid, chewed Moag out for threatening to sue the NFL and accused him of ruining the city's chances of getting a team.

A few weeks later, Moag got a call from Glendening. The governor said he would be attending a fence-mending session with Tagliabue, hosted by Giants co-owner Robert Tisch in one of Tisch's Washington hotels. Moag wasn't invited. And the governor suggested cooling the talk of lawsuits for a while. Moag urged Glendening not to back down.

Glendening, Tagliabue, and Tisch met secretly on July 13.

Glendening said he told the commissioner he would decide in December whether to keep the stadium funding in his budget. But, he warned, "we will not be brides-in-waiting forever." Keeping the funding would require a team, or at least the written promise of a team, tied to a financial penalty — about $15 million or so — if such a promise were made and not carried out.

Tagliabue spoke of Baltimore's abiding passion for football but expressed concern over its geographic shortcomings relative to faster-growing markets. Further expansion, he said, was not likely before the end of the decade. Glendening left the session neither encouraged nor discouraged.

The Cleveland Browns now resurfaced as a real prospect. In June, during the heat of the Bengal talks, Moag went to see Frank Bramble, president of the First National Bank and chairman of the Greater Baltimore Committee, an influential local business group that had long played a major role in the city's NFL quest. Bramble wanted Moag to brief him on the status of the state's effort, and Moag obliged.

Most of their conversation centered on the Bengals and Moag's belief that Mike Brown would not pull the trigger. But Moag, the consummate lobbyist, knew he had a contact to play here. At the end of their meeting, he asked Bramble, an Alfred Lerner protogé, to let Lerner — and his friend Modell — know that Baltimore was interested in the Browns. Bramble said he would. There was very little discussion.

The timing was remarkable.

Browns officials had looked at several options: Toronto, San Antonio, Memphis, and Los Angeles. No formal talks had been held with any of them, although Modell, while visiting his musician son John in Los Angeles, talked to some friends knowledgeable about efforts to build a stadium in nearby Anaheim. The plans were still unformed, and any ground breaking was well off in the future.

The Browns quickly determined that only Baltimore had funding in place for a first-class stadium that could transform the franchise's fortunes overnight. But they would have to move fast: Maryland's deadline was seven months away, and several teams were known to be talking to the state.

As a member of the NFL's expansion committee, Modell was

already familiar with Baltimore's offer. Now he dispatched Lerner to find out if the state's end-of-the-year deadline was as firm as Moag had asserted, and if the deal had changed. Lerner called his old friend Bramble, and they set up a meeting for a week later, July 28, when Lerner would be in the area for a wedding.

Lerner met with Moag at BWI Airport aboard the business-man's private jet, a white, 14-seat plane with maroon stripes and leather interior. The last time his jet had intersected with Baltimore's football future, Lerner himself had been living on the plane to avoid close contact with city and state delegates trying to bring an expansion team to Baltimore.

Lerner cautioned Moag and Bramble, who came along to make introductions, not to read too much into his presence. He was not speaking for Modell. His friend did not want to leave Cleveland. And Lerner himself didn't want him to leave. But Lerner felt the process in Cleveland had not worked and wouldn't work. He could delineate the list of reasons but didn't want to bore his guests, he said.

Moag explained that the governor needed to get the state budget together by December. Pressure from legislators was build-ing to de-authorize the bonds, possibly to help the Redskins build in Maryland. In order to keep stadium funding in place, he would need either a lease with a franchise or a legally binding resolution from the NFL promising a team, he said.

"Obviously, if you don't feel things are going to work out for you in Cleveland, we would be very interested in talking to you, and I hope that you will convey that to Mr. Modell," Moag said.

Lerner was noncommittal, not even letting on that Modell knew he was in Maryland that day. But Lerner did urge Baltimore to pursue the resolution with the league. Despite Lerner's caveats, Moag came away encouraged. Lerner was a no-nonsense billion-aire not given to wasting his time or engaging in frivolous conver-sations on airport tarmacs. And he didn't need to be sold on the merits of Baltimore's offer. He had negotiated much of it before becoming a short-lived expansion candidate.

Indeed, before the meeting ended, the two men exchanged a long list of fax and phone numbers for New York, Cleveland, and Delaware — as if to suggest there would be reason for further, maybe immediate, communication. Moag was on his way to a

Delaware beach, his Land Rover loaded with vacation gear. Lerner was headed to Wilmington, Del.

Moag stopped by the State House, unannounced, to brief the governor, who hadn't known in advance of Lerner's visit. Moag told Glendening he thought the team was "real serious."

Glendening responded coolly. "Don't worry about this over your vacation," he joked. "It's only your career."

Faced with such unexpected bounty, Moag and Glendening picked their team favorite: the Browns, a team with a strong tradition and a reputable owner. Talks with the Buccaneers and the Cardinals had slowed to a crawl as Moag, through carefully placed calls to intermediaries from Phoenix and Tampa, subtly gave notice to the Browns that they weren't alone in their affections for Baltimore.

On Sept. 1, Moag and Glendening wrote Tagliabue asking that the league pass a binding resolution guaranteeing Baltimore a team through expansion or relocation. In exchange, the stadium funding would be preserved.

"The [Maryland Stadium Authority] offers perhaps the most lucrative football venue in the Nation. And Baltimore offers a dedicated, football-hungry fan base that yearns to be reunited with the NFL family," they wrote.

Suddenly Baltimore was the player calling the shots.

• • •

Over the next several days, Moag spoke frequently with Lerner by phone, and the two conferred at a reception before the Sept. 6 Orioles game when star shortstop Cal Ripken broke Lou Gehrig's consecutive-game streak. (Lerner was a guest of his friend, Benjamin Civiletti.) Moag told Lerner that the NFL was looking at the Baltimore resolution, which could complicate matters by giving the commissioner control over the market. Moag also reminded Lerner of the deadline and suggested there was no reason why a deal could not be signed and hidden in a vault until after the season ended. The timing of the comment was quite coincidental.

Just the day before, while meeting with his lawyers in the Jones, Day offices, Modell had concluded a move was necessary.

Lerner called Moag the next day and scheduled a Modell-

Moag get-together on Sept. 18.

The meeting was held in Lerner's New York offices, a posh complex taking up the entire top floor of a building overlooking Central Park. With its dark wood and rich art, the office had the reassuring feel of a living room. Windows along one wall offered a breathtaking view of the park and a sunny fall day.

Moag arrived at 11 a.m. with Maryland Stadium Authority executive director Bruce Hoffman, an engineer, and Allison Asti, the Authority's general counsel. Modell was already there with his son, David; Browns executive vice president Jim Bailey; and friend/partner/intermediary Lerner.

The two groups congregated in a lounge area off to one side of Lerner's desk, exchanging pleasantries. Moag offered an elaborate get-acquainted gift: two boxes of very exclusive Dominican Davidoff "Double R" cigars, for which he paid $870 at a Washington tobacco shop. He had never tried them, but asked the shopkeeper for the best in the house.

He handed a box to Lerner, whose penchant for cigars was legendary despite a bout with throat cancer. The billionaire was appreciative but unimpressed — he preferred an even more exclusive Cuban brand. He gave the box to David, also a cigar aficionado, but Moag said that wasn't necessary. He had brought one for the younger Modell as well.

Modell told the Marylanders that he knew they had been used by other teams, which had feigned interest in Baltimore just to get the attention, and tax dollars, of their local officials. Modell assured them that he was "at the end of his rope" in Cleveland. They all agreed to hold the meeting in the strictest of confidence.

Moag related again the tenuousness of the Baltimore stadium financing: He was under pressure from other teams interested in it, and the governor wanted a deal by the end of the year. (This was only partly true. By now, Moag and Glendening had discussed extending the funding because they seemed to be close with a couple of prospects.)

The group retired to a round table on the other side of the office, where they enjoyed a catered buffet of salmon, roast beef, and chicken. The conversation topics ranged from stadium cleaning — something with which Modell, as the operator of Municipal Stadium, was familiar — to Colin Powell's presidential aspirations.

Moag contributed his Washington insider's view, predicting correctly, as it turned out, that Powell would not enter the race.

From this genteel setting emerged, with surprising swiftness, the basic structure of a deal that would wrench the sports world. Lerner fondly retold the story of a real estate venture his father had lost because of a trivial dispute over a case of toilet paper. *The moral:* Don't get hung up on minutiae.

Moag said that he didn't plan any major enhancements to Baltimore's already rich expansion deal, and that he opposed selling the right to the stadium name to a corporate sponsor. The team would get a $200-million, open-air stadium, along with a renovated training complex at Owings Mills in neighboring Baltimore County, which had been used by the Colts. Rent would consist of the operating costs of the stadium, estimated at about $4 million a year. The state would tax each ticket 10 percent, raising about $2.5 million more.

Moag expressed some reluctance about charging season-ticket buyers an up-front fee — the personal seat licenses introduced by the Panthers' Richardson in the expansion race — but said he understood they were being used elsewhere. However, he didn't want to make the deal contingent on selling a minimum number of tickets or seat licenses, major components of the deals that drew the Rams to St. Louis and the Oilers to Nashville.

Modell said he didn't expect guarantees, that if he couldn't sell football tickets in Baltimore, he should be in another line of work. Modell also agreed to limit the PSL proceeds to specific, moving-related expenses. Both sides agreed that secrecy was crucial.

"I can't believe it's come to this," Modell said after the Maryland delegation left. To Lerner, the decision to move was regrettable, but not illogical.

"We're talking about a 70-year-old guy, 35 years in the community, serious financial problems, all of this weight on his shoulders…. He's not a human computer, he's a very, very emotional guy and at some point he throws in the towel and says, 'That's it, I got one place to go, it isn't worth it here, here I go,'" Lerner recalled later.

As they flew back to Maryland, Moag and his entourage thought they were close to a deal. The fax machines were soon humming.

Stadium Authority officials met later in Washington with

Browns executives. Allison Asti told them that Maryland wanted a binding lease with the team itself, not just with a stadium operating corporation like the Browns had in Cleveland. They were counting on this multilayered arrangement to void the lease in Ohio, and the Marylanders didn't want to set themselves up for the same trick.

At one point during the exchange, Moag jokingly faxed Lerner a proposed lease amendment, promising the Browns a case of toilet paper.

Modell's refusal to negotiate a lease with Mayor White had convinced Cleveland political leaders that the worst was at hand. Governor Voinovich called Modell at home one night to see if he could figure out what was going on. Modell unloaded an angry diatribe on his old friend, who alerted White, who then fruitlessly stepped up efforts to see the team owner.

A few weeks later, on Oct. 12, Voinovich wrote Modell a letter.

"Many of us suspect you have decided there is no way we can possibly meet the opportunity you have in some other part of the country," Voinovich wrote. "It would be terrible, Art, if at the end of the season you were to sneak out of town like the Baltimore Colts did ...."

The Ohio governor didn't know it, but the Browns were sneaking into Baltimore. Within days of the letter, Moag called Lerner and said they had a deal. Moag called Glendening, who, in a reaction that anticipated his state's initial disbelief, said: "Are you sure?"

A clandestine meeting was set for Oct. 27 so Modell and Glendening could sign and seal the agreement aboard Lerner's private plane at BWI Airport. Only a few pieces of unfinished business remained.

To Moag's surprise, Tagliabue faxed on Oct. 20 a draft of the NFL resolution Glendening had requested six weeks earlier. The commissioner said the resolution would be considered Nov. 7 at an owners' meeting in Dallas. This resolution being the last thing he now wanted or needed, Moag assumed the league knew something was up and wanted to exert control. Moag faxed Tagliabue a request that the resolution be put aside for a while. The league refused.

Meanwhile, the Browns board of directors, in Cleveland, took up the proposed move at a secret meeting on Oct. 20. Because he owned 51 percent of the team, Chairman Modell controlled the board. Occupying board seats were his wife, son, Bailey, and Lerner, who owned about 5 percent of the team.

Robert Gries, the flamboyant Cleveland venture capitalist and adventurer whose father was a founding investor in the Browns, controlled a bloc of family-owned stock that comprised about 43 percent of the team. During the 1980s, he sued Modell to reverse the team's bailout of the Cleveland Stadium Corp. The men shared little affection for one another.

At the board meeting, Gries protested that this was the first he had heard of a move, and he didn't like it. And yet, he couldn't stop it. The meeting was adjourned, and papers were drawn up over the weekend to transfer all of Gries' stock to Modell. Modell agreed to pay the minority stockholder with team revenues over a period of 10 years, beginning in 1997. (If the team didn't move, the deal would be canceled, and Gries would get his stock back.)

The board met again the next Tuesday, without Gries, and the relocation was approved.

Two days before the meeting in Baltimore at which the franchise-moving papers would be signed, Modell dropped his old friend Voinovich a line. He neither confirmed nor denied the governor's suspicions. But he made clear his view:

"... no resolution that even remotely approximates the benefits afforded the local teams at Gateway and our NFL competitors is in sight."

CHAPTER FOURTEEN

The
Deal

As the tiny jet lifted off the runway Oct. 27 on its fateful mission, the passengers caught a view of Cleveland Municipal Stadium in the pre-dawn light — a great hulking structure between glistening skyscrapers and inky black Lake Erie.

Most of the city was still asleep, recovering from celebrations the previous night. At a packed Jacobs Field, the Indians had eked out a 5-4 win over the Atlanta Braves to remain alive in the 1995 World Series. Little could Clevelanders have imagined that a clandestine mission was then under way to steal their football team from them.

On the private plane were four men who had spent much of their lives at Municipal Stadium and knew it better than the masons who had built it: Browns owner Art Modell; his son, David; and two of his closest advisers, Jim Bailey and the jet's owner, Al Lerner.

Among this tight-knit group of confidants and partners, the mood was unusually subdued, like the overcast autumn sky. Even Modell, known for his clever quips, was reflective. No one mentioned the stadium below.

Modell assumed that he had probably spent the last of more than 300 Sundays at Municipal. For days now, the 70-year-old team owner had not had a full night's sleep. And here he was, headed to

Baltimore, where he would sign papers transferring his franchise and, for all practical purposes, his family to a new city. The deal would make him a much richer man, adding $50-75 million to the value of his franchise. But it would also make him a pariah in his home of 35 years and, for a time, in the National Football League which he so loved.

His son retrieved some bagels and rolls from the galley, but few were eaten. Sitting across from Modell, Bailey shuffled papers on a fold-out table. Lerner tended to his business.

Meanwhile, hundreds of miles away, John Moag was leaving his home in the exclusive Ruxton suburb of Baltimore, where skies were sunny. Chairman of the Maryland Stadium Authority for less than a year, Moag was about to achieve, almost single-handedly, a victory that had eluded Maryland's richest and most powerful people for 11 years.

But bragging rights would have to wait.

The deal was top secret, and the state had agreed to pay the Browns if word leaked out prematurely and depressed the team's ticket sales in Cleveland. Only a handful of Moag's associates and Governor Parris Glendening knew.

And, of course, Moag's wife, Peggy, who had secretly filled his green Lexus that morning with orange and brown balloons — the Browns' colors.

The irony of the situation was not lost on Moag. He remembered the Colts' heyday, and he knew the pain Baltimoreans suffered when the team suddenly bolted for Indianapolis in the middle of the night. Now, at dawn's early light, "Charm City," cheated by the mercenary Bob Irsay, would be tearing the heart out of another city, one even more attached to its franchise.

Moag arrived first at BWI's private-plane terminal, a secluded building around the back of the airport. It was in this terminal where, 11 years before, Irsay had insisted to reporters and to then-Mayor William Donald Schaefer that his Colts were not leaving Baltimore. A few months later, the team was gone.

At last, Baltimore's revenge was at hand.

Glendening arrived next, shortly after 8 a.m. Minutes later, after it touched down, the governor boarded Lerner's plane and greeted its owner with a handshake. Lerner escorted Glendening and Moag to the rear of the plane and a pair of leather-upholstered couches.

A somber Art Modell spoke first, expressing the difficulty of his decision. He had not met Glendening before, and in about 45 minutes of general conversation, discovered that both of their wives were active in the hospice movement. Glendening praised the state's education system. The two talked about getting together socially. Politically, they were from opposite worlds: Glendening, a FDR Democrat, and Modell, a Reagan Republican. But neither one was about to let that get in the way of this deal.

David Modell, who didn't want to interrupt his father and the others by walking between them, stood in the galley and kept their coffee cups full. At one point, he spilled milk on the governor's shoes, but Glendening took it in good humor. How could he not? He was about to score a major political coup.

Finally, Modell turned to Moag, who was sitting next to him, and asked: "You have some papers for me to sign?"

Moag produced two copies of the "Memorandum of Agreement among Maryland Stadium Authority and Cleveland Browns Inc. and BSC, LLC."

Despite its bulk, the 28-page agreement, with 30 pages of exhibits and side letters, represented only the outline of a lease. The full agreement would come later, after further negotiations.

The terms were as good as any sports team owner could get: To bring football back to Baltimore, the state of Maryland was obligating itself to spend $200 million. The construction of a 70,000-seat, open-air stadium was expected to cost $190 million. The remaining $10 million would go toward additional land acquisition, a new football training complex, and perhaps a parking deck if needed to meet a 4,000-space minimum parking guarantee given to Modell.

The state would "use its best efforts" to have the new structure up and running by the start of the 1998 NFL season.

An additional $2 million would be spent renovating Memorial Stadium, the old home of the Colts and the Orioles, which the Baltimore Browns would play in while the new structure was being built. About half of this sum had already been spent to prepare the field for the Canadian Football League team then playing on 33rd Street.

Modell would pay no rent at Memorial Stadium, and he

would keep all revenues from it, other than admission taxes paid by ticket buyers. The state would maintain and operate the facility, and the team would cover game-day costs. The team would also get to use the old Colts' training facility at Owings Mills, the site of the famous midnight ride of the Mayflowers, at a cost of $1 a year.

Once in the new stadium, the team would pay no rent, but reimburse the state for all operational costs, estimated to run about $4 million a year. The state would spend up to $200,000 each year of the lease on capital improvements, keeping the stadium up to modern standards.

The Browns would have year-round use of the stadium and keep all profits from parking, concessions, tickets, skyboxes, and advertising, passing along only a 10-percent ticket tax to the state. Pursuant to a clause Lerner had negotiated three years earlier, the team would also have the right to book and promote concerts and other events at the stadium and to keep a 10-percent management fee and half of the profits.

The state would have access to two free stadium billboards to advertise the Maryland lottery, which was funding the deal. The mayor and governor would each get a free skybox. The state would also retain the right to hold trade shows, banquets, and other occasional events in the stadium's club-level lounges, though not on the field nor in the stadium seats.

Importantly, the team also received the right to sell up to $80 million in personal seat licenses. The final $5 million of this amount, which would be turned over to the state, represented the team's only contribution to stadium construction costs. The remaining $75 million could be used only for specified "relocation-related" purposes, but those purposes were so broadly defined that the money could be spent — and quickly — on any NFL-imposed relocation fees, construction of a new training complex, severance pay for Cleveland employees, moving costs, legal bills and legal claims in Ohio, and the payoff of bonds or other debts related to the team's Ohio training center and its investments in Cleveland Stadium.

Rights to name the new stadium, to be jointly held by the state and the team, would not be sold to a corporate sponsor.

For the Browns, the deal's potential profitability was staggering. A dozen years after losing the Colts in a fight over how to renovate old Memorial Stadium, Baltimore and Maryland were about to build a luxurious, state-of-the-art football arena to a team owner's specifications and then hand him the keys. In this new facility, projections showed, the team could generate more than $30 million a year in pre-tax profits.

But the cost to the taxpayers would be equally staggering. The $87 million in bonds sold to finance the deal would incur $92 million in interest over their 30-year terms. That was on top of the $295 million in principal and interest already being paid for Oriole Park at Camden Yards, and another $130 million for the land under both stadiums. Paying off roughly $517 million in stadium-related construction and long-term debt would cost the state about $20 million a year for 30 years, roughly the annual operating budget of the Enoch Pratt, Baltimore's municipal library. (The annual debt service would be met through yearly payments from the Orioles and the Browns, the state's instant lotteries, and ticket taxes. The city of Baltimore also had to kick in $1 million a year.)

John Moag signed the memorandum of agreement for the state, with Glendening serving as a witness. Modell signed for the Browns, with his son witnessing.

Lerner and the younger Modell then broke out victory cigars. Glendening, an anti-smoker who was tightening Maryland's already light restrictions on tobacco, declined, grew uncomfortable in the haze, and was the first to leave the plane. The others remained for another 45 minutes.

Art Modell was adamant about keeping the deal secret. The 1995 season was only half over; early word that the Browns were skipping town would be deadly for ticket sales. The agreement with Maryland not only contained extensive confidentiality clauses, but also called for the team and the state to jointly announce the move in Baltimore on the Monday after the Browns' last home game in Cleveland.

Within days, however, tips flowed into newspapers and television stations in both cities. A few days after the contract signing, Moag even heard about it on a Baltimore radio sports talk show. A caller to the program reported hearing the news from one of the governor's bodyguards. Another report had the governor's teenage son bragging about it to classmates at school.

Modell was panicked, but he wasn't surprised. Browns employees, though not told about the deal, had caught on, although few were saying anything about it in the office.

"The secretaries knew about it. We were getting three calls a day from the Maryland Stadium Authority. They couldn't be for season tickets," Modell recalled. "It didn't take a Phi Beta to tell something was afloat."

One day, out at the Browns' Berea practice facility, Ozzie Newsome, a former Cleveland tight end then director of professional personnel, caught up with a haggard Modell and assured him, "Whatever happens, Boss, I'm with you." He was promoted the next season to vice president of player personnel.

Although each blamed the leaks on the other, Modell and Moag decided to move the announcement up to Nov. 6, the day before the planned sin-tax referendum for stadium funding in Cleveland. Modell said he was concerned that voters would be duped into thinking they could save the team with a "yes" vote; Cleveland officials, however, claim Modell was trying to dash the referendum's chances to maintain his case for relocation.

There was another reason for premature disclosure: On the league agenda Nov. 7, scheduled for a vote no less, was the Moag-inspired resolution promising Baltimore a team.

To get ready for the planned announcement in Baltimore, Art and David Modell rounded up their families and sent them to West Palm Beach, Fla., where the team owner had a $1.7 million penthouse condominium.

Olwen Modell, David's wife, remembered: "When David called me that day, he said, 'Things are getting a little out of control. It's going to become public knowledge, and we'd like to have a press conference before it all leaks out. Art and I think you guys should be out of town before then.'"

Olwen and the couple's children received a police escort to the airport.

● ● ●

At 9:29 a.m. on the Monday of the noon announcement, Cleveland Mayor White launched a public relations jihad. The city filed a lawsuit in Cuyahoga County Common Pleas Court alleging that the Browns were breaking their contract with Cleveland and that the city would suffer irreparable harm as a result. Cleveland asked a judge to block the move.

White flew to Baltimore to meet with his friend and political soul mate, Mayor Kurt L. Schmoke, for breakfast. Schmoke, who would coast to reelection the next day against a token Republican opponent, offered White some advice about getting Cleveland back into the NFL: Follow Baltimore's lead. Focus on getting stadium funding into place.

But Cleveland, like Baltimore a dozen years before, wasn't ready to concede it was out of the NFL yet.

"What does it say of an organization to kick a city in the teeth that has been so supportive?" White asked reporters.

At the same time, the Cleveland mayor's aides acknowledged what they were up against. Baltimore had revolutionized stadium economics; matching its offer would be nearly impossible for their cash-strapped city.

"We're not even going to come close to that," said Frederick Nance, White's chief counsel and the man who would eventually lead the city's various lawsuits against the Browns.

"We've got to make the Browns economically competitive. We're not going to give them windfall economics," he said.

Cleveland went from a frenzied, behind-the-scenes appeasement of Modell to an all-out war of vilification. All announcements of upcoming city events, which normally scrolled on electronic signs at the airport, in downtown tourist kiosks, and at the convention center now carried two simple exhortations: "Stop Art" and "Save Our Browns!"

The national reaction to the move was equally swift and vicious. National Football League fans may have grown accustomed to team moves. Over the previous two seasons, the Bucs, Cardinals, Seahawks, Oilers, Bengals, Raiders, and Rams had all either moved or were openly flirting with doing so.

But this was the Cleveland Browns. This was different. Those other team owners had driven the fans away before moving their teams. The Browns were beloved at home like no other team in sports.

In each of the previous nine years, the team's game-day attendance had been among the best in the NFL, averaging more than 70,000. Local TV ratings for Browns telecasts were also among the league's highest: In 1993, they were second only to the Dallas

Cowboys, and the next season, they were first.

Bare-chested fans with rubber dog masks waving dog biscuits in the Dawg Pound had become a staple of NFL highlight films. The team had a worldwide network of 310 Browns Backers fan clubs registered in 39 states, 9 countries, and 5 continents — stretching from Ohio to Japan to Australia.

After the announcement, Art Modell went overnight from being the NFL's elder statesman to its Benedict Arnold.

Ohio Governor Voinovich, hardly given to extreme statements, put it this way: "Up until this time, Art Modell has been an honorable man … I believe this was extremely unfair to a town that had demonstrated its support for the Cleveland Browns for decades. Ohio is the cradle of football."

Lou Groza, the Hall of Fame Brown, broke down in tears at an appearance with Mayor White. "This is an All-American town, and this is not an All-American happening," he said.

He described the experience as "just like saying your old girl friend is going out with some other guy. It's a sad state of affairs when they can't get a new team established in Baltimore, they had to go and take a team from an existing city."

In Baltimore, the reaction was divided. Fans who had waited so long for a team and who had come to blame the league, and especially Commissioner Tagliabue, for their travails, registered conflicting emotions. They were happy to have a team but knew the pain the move caused Clevelanders. They were somewhat pleased, however, at the trouble the move would cause Tagliabue and other NFL officials who had skipped over Baltimore in expansion and — many believed — steered other teams elsewhere.

Baltimore *Sun* columnist Michael Olesker suggested changing the name of the team to "The Revenge" to make "those lowlifes, the Irsays and the Tagliabues and the Cookes, read the name in the newspapers the rest of their miserable lives and be reminded of what they've brought to a business that once claimed to have some honor."

Olesker also had reservations about the deal: "Yeah, it'll be nice to have football again," he wrote. "But it feels like somebody else's football. It's not a move to Baltimore, it's just a move to luxury boxes and $1,000 tabs to buy licenses for the right to buy season tickets. It's a cash deal, no heart involved."

Publicly, Schaefer said he sympathized with the citizens and leaders of Cleveland. Losing a team, he said, was like "a kick in the stomach."

But privately, in a letter dated Nov. 9, 1995, he wrote to Lerner: "You said you would bring a team here, and you did. Not exactly in the way we all planned it, but the results are still the same."

He also offered Modell advice, through Lerner, that the Browns leave their name behind in Cleveland.

"Believe me, you are a marvelous banker," the former governor wrote, "but I know a little about public relations. Mr. Modell would remove some of the 'sting' of the Cleveland fans, and I believe he would be a great hero in Baltimore, by this simple gesture of good will."

A week later, Schaefer jotted off a few other notes. One, to Tagliabue, opened with the adage, "What goes around, comes around."

"You could have avoided all this turmoil if you had only played fair with the people of your state and the citizens of Baltimore, who know the pain and embarrassment of losing a team," Schaefer wrote.

In a letter to Voinovich, he said, "The elation Baltimore felt in getting an NFL franchise was tempered by the loss to the people of Cleveland. I know how it hurt when Ersay [sic] slipped out of Baltimore in that early snowy morning."

He ended with, "Well, George, you continue to be a great governor and are still my candidate for Vice President."

Others, regarding it as a small act of reparation by a guilty city, soon joined the drive to leave the Browns' name in Cleveland. *Sun* sportswriter Ken Rosenthal wrote of Modell: "Even if you give him every benefit of the doubt, even if you assume city, county, and state officials in Ohio blew it, the *least* he can do is give Cleveland back the name.

"This is a new beginning, a new day, a new age. But like it or not, this team will be forever tainted by its past. Modell can remove the scarlet letter, or add to his former city's misery."

Another *Sun* columnist, John Eisenberg, was harsher in his criticism: "It was Irsay arriving in Indianapolis all over again, only in Baltimore of all places. You could smell the hypocrisy in the chilly air."

He also rebuked Glendening's seemingly callous performance at the Monday announcement, writing on Nov. 7:

"And so, there was one final hardship for us to endure yesterday before we could celebrate the return of the NFL to our city. There was the part where the politicians congratulated themselves and took all the credit.

"The part where an owner turning his back on 70,000 fans a game was cheered like a rock star.

"The part where we rubbed it right in Cleveland's face on national television. Just what no one here wanted to do.

"Congratulations if you made it through yesterday's announcement ceremony without becoming nauseated."

Even Modell, who had stoked the flames of fan anger over other team moves, was unprepared for the ferocious reaction. To fans everywhere, already angry over player strikes, outlandish salaries, and fast-rising ticket prices, Modell instantly became a symbol of greed.

"The contemptible Cleveland Browns owner has the spine of a jellyfish, the scruples of a grave robber, the greed of a drug dealer, and the character of a repressive third world thug," wrote columnist Bob Hunter in *The Columbus Dispatch*.

"He says he is doing this because he has no choice, because the Browns have lost money the last few years and because the city hasn't been cooperative with him. He is lying. Modell is doing this because he has a chance to make a bundle, and because of his ineptitude as an owner, money is about the only thing that still matters in his wretched cesspool of a life."

This being the dawn of the information age, fury over the move spilled onto the Internet. Newspapers, fan groups, and others created a number of Worldwide Web pages seeking to block the move. Their titles hinted at the content: among them, the "FYouModell Page," "Greedwatch," and "Dawgs in Cyberspace."

So Browns fans could personalize their protests, some webmasters dutifully transmitted news of the Browns' fight and spread the phone and fax numbers of both NFL headquarter officials and individual team owners across the country.

Other Internet protesters turned to uglier tactics. One offered photos depicting a mock execution of Modell, his son David, and Browns coach Bill Belichick, staged in front of Municipal Stadium by a local radio station. Another, reproducing a photo of a grinning Glendening and Modell at the announcement, urged visitors to click first on a drawing of an egg box, and then onto the Glendening/Modell photo, to produce a cathartic simulated splat.

An "Internet Day" was scheduled so that fans could clog the computers of Baltimore media outlets, the Maryland Stadium Authority, and the NFL with anti-move messages, such as "No team, no peace."

"Art Modell cannot be allowed to move our beloved Browns to Baltimore. Join the Jihad. Do what you can to STOP ART" opened the "Save our Browns" Website.

In shutting down his Cleveland Browns' Web page, Keith Mahoney issued an open letter to Tagliabue, Modell, and other NFL team owners:

"You have made the biggest mistake in the history of the National Football League. The underhanded move by Art Modell to move the beloved Browns from the city of Cleveland to Baltimore has stunned, angered, and disgusted Browns fans in Northeast Ohio and around the world. We fans have cheered for our team for as long as we can remember. We have lived and relived every highlight and lowlight of this franchise. THIS IS ONE EVENT THAT WE WILL NEVER FORGET OR FORGIVE. I regret to inform you that because of this incident, I have decided to give up on NFL football and will not support it in any way."

Cleveland's Huntington Bank, which had been a major Browns lender, saw an opportunity. Within two weeks of Modell's announcement, the bank issued a special stadium Visa card. For every dollar charged on the new cards, it promised to contribute a half-penny to a fund aimed at attracting a new team to Cleveland or fixing up Municipal Stadium. It also called in its loans to the Browns.

Browns Backers urged fans everywhere to cut up any credit cards issued by Lerner's companies.

Art Modell received death threats and, in response, hired Henry Gomez, an ex-Marine and ex-counter-intelligence specialist, as a bodyguard. But even the stern-faced Gomez, who saw duty inside Cuba during the Cuban Missile Crisis, couldn't keep the enraged Browns fans at bay. About 35 lined Flagler Drive in West Palm Beach on Nov. 26, barking at the team owner's penthouse and shouting "Jump, Art, Jump." An airplane flew overhead, towing a banner that read "MODELL YOU CAN'T HIDE HERE!! WOOF. WOOF."

The national media also responded with outrage. Conservative commentator and sometime baseball philosopher George Will noted indignantly in his *Newsweek* column that "average folks are building suites for rich fans so rich owners can pay rich players."

Wrote Will: "If litigation in Cleveland and indignation in Maryland do not derail the deal, it will make Modell the latest proof that there often is no penalty for failure in America. Maryland's role in this farce is the latest proof that government often is the servant of those strong enough to wheedle it cleverly."

Ohio's senior U.S. senator, Democrat John Glenn, introduced in the Senate the "Fans' Rights Act" to shield sports leagues from antitrust lawsuits, provided that well-supported teams were prohibited from moving.

A Cleveland congressman, Republican Martin Hoke, drew up and introduced the "Fan Freedom and Community Protection Act," which would require leagues to replace departed franchises with expansion teams in markets with proven fan support.

Neither bill went anywhere.

The Browns' move also became a lively topic of conversation at the autumn meeting of the nation's Republican governors in Nashua, N.H.

"I don't have to tell the people in Cleveland that this has really gotten out of hand," said Massachusetts Governor William Weld.

Worried about his Chicago NFL team, Illinois Governor James Edgar said, "We've made it clear with the Bears that we'll be happy to work on infrastructure improvements like we would with any business. But we'll not get involved in a cash subsidy to build a stadium because a football stadium is used 12 days a year, if that. And it's difficult to justify using tax dollars on that.

"Unfortunately, some communities are willing to spend tax dollars to do that, like Baltimore."

At the height of the furor, John Moag checked some newspaper archives. What he found surprised him: The things being said and done in Cleveland mirrored almost exactly what Baltimore had done and said after the Colts left. Both cities went to court. Both cities got congressional representatives to submit bills and to convene hearings. The leaders of both cities gave high-minded speeches and issued threats. But, ultimately, both cities lost their teams and did precisely what their predators had done: They pledged stadium riches to get a new team.

• • •

The day after the announcement in the Camden Yards parking lot, Modell was in Dallas at a scheduled meeting of NFL team owners. The Browns' move, although not on the agenda originally, dominated the talk outside of the meeting. Reporters swooped in from around the country and dutifully recorded the plaintive appeals of Browns fans, who had been mobilized by the Browns Backers organization.

The crisis splintered the league. Even longtime Modell loyalists expressed disgust.

"This is wrong, and I am against it," said Buffalo Bills owner Ralph Wilson, a close friend of Modell. "The credibility of our league has taken a beating in the last year. Tampa Bay wants to move. Houston wants to move. Now one of the all-time great franchises is ready to pick up and leave. It's all crazy."

Other owners resigned themselves to the inevitable.

"I think the validity of our bylaws is in the scrap heap, as far as moves are concerned. I voted against the Rams' move two times. They did not fulfill the requirements for a move, and they moved," said New York Giants co-owner Wellington Mara.

But, he added, "I'm real close to Art, and my reaction is, for him to take this step, I have to realize what pressure he's been under and what a difficult step it is for him to take. I have to sympathize with him."

Cincinnati Bengals owner Mike Brown, who had spoken to Maryland officials about a team move to Baltimore, said, "It seems to me we've reached the point of absurdity if it means the Cleveland Browns and the Los Angeles Rams are the teams that are moving."

A straw poll of team owners conducted by NBC in the weeks after the announcement recorded at least seven "No" votes, enough to block Modell's move to Baltimore. They belonged to Buffalo,

Pittsburgh, Minnesota, Denver, Chicago, New England, and, predictably, Washington.

Paul Tagliabue was guarded in his public comments. The commissioner could not appear to be prejudging the outcome of the owners' deliberations. Nor did he want to show his own hand.

"I can't say that it's all over," the commissioner said during a halftime interview on "Monday Night Football" the day of the announcement.

"In a sense, from the league's perspective, it's just beginning. We have our procedures. We have our policies. We don't want to see any team leave when there is support from rabid fans such as there is in Cleveland. Pete Rozelle didn't want to see the Colts leave when there was support from those rabid fans in Baltimore in 1984. In a sense, the quandary here is that we have two of those franchises that have been marked through history, two of those cities, Baltimore and Cleveland, where the fans have been so rabid they've been the envy of the whole sports world. That's our quandary, and that's what we're going to have to work through in the next 30 to 60 days before we reach a decision."

An NFL vote on the move was now scheduled for January. Tagliabue promised to deliver, before then, a report to the owners on whether the Browns met the league's nine-point relocation guidelines.

• • •

Immediately after the Baltimore announcement, the Browns team went into a tailspin. Despite Modell's free spending, they had been only 4-4 before word leaked out about the move. They promptly lost six straight and seven of their last eight games. No-shows replaced loyal fans at Municipal Stadium, and fans started booing the team. Season-ticket holders skipped games to stand at stadium gates, collecting signatures on petitions to force the team to stay.

Though John "Big Dawg" Thompson continued to attend Browns home games, he left his trademark dog mask inside a "bone bag" tucked under his Municipal Stadium seat. "You wouldn't wear a dog mask to your brother's funeral, would you?" he asked rhetorically.

The relocation controversy took an obvious toll on the players, both on and off the field. It certainly didn't help that the unpopular Belichick, in a game of musical quarterbacks, even benched team leader and quarterback Vinny Testaverde.

"They were booing after we completed a pass," commented receiver Andre Rison after a 31-20 loss to the Packers. "Frankly, I'm ready to get the hell out of here. Because I don't deserve it, nor do the other players. We didn't make the [expletive] move … I'll be glad when we get to Baltimore, if that's the case. We don't have any home field advantage. I've never been booed at home. Baltimore's our home. Baltimore, here we come."

Said linebacker Pepper Johnson: "Everything ugly that can happen to us is happening right now. The shots are coming from all over."

Both highly paid players would finish the season with the team, but then be released. Rison would end up in Super Bowl XXXI, playing for Green Bay.

On Dec. 19, the last Browns home game at Municipal Stadium, the listless Cleveland squad beat Cincinnati, 26-10.

"Words can't express how I feel about this city and the support they've given our team and me," said Testaverde after the game. "We wanted to go out with a win and show the fans the appreciation they deserve for standing behind us all year long."

But the game attendance — 55,875 — was the second worst of the season. And the fans were angry. They chanted obscenities about Modell, booed the Browns, trashed the bathrooms, and vandalized the concession stands. And they helped themselves to souvenirs. After the crowd thinned, some fans removed about 3,000 stadium seats. Police, anxious to avoid aggravating an already hostile crowd, chose not to interfere.

● ● ●

The crisis focused the efforts of Cleveland City Hall as nothing ever had. Suddenly, Mayor White was everywhere — from NFL owners' meetings to ABC's "Nightline" — and everyone was solidly behind him. Politicians who had bickered over the details of stadium renovation now rallied around an unambiguous goal: Stop Art Modell.

White first turned to the sin-tax extension on the ballot the day after the announcement. He told voters that the item was no longer about stadium funding but was now a referendum on Cleveland football itself.

The voters responded resoundingly. The sin tax was approved by 72 percent of those who voted. The next day, White bundled up the city's latest offer to the Browns and visited the team's suburban headquarters in Berea. There, with television cameras rolling, a grim-faced White left the documents with a security guard. No one from the Browns would come out to talk to him.

In subsequent weeks, White would pursue a two-track strategy. He would aggressively push the city's lawsuit, even appearing in court and testifying about the team's value to the city. At the same time, he would quietly open behind-the-scenes negotiations with the league aimed at resolving the dispute and keeping his city in the NFL.

"We want our team, our colors, and our name," he would say over and over again. He even hired "Big Dawg" Thompson to do publicity for Cleveland's cause.

And he would adroitly play on the sympathies of Browns fans worldwide. They responded by holding rallies and maintaining blistering pressure on the NFL.

The city printed up special Christmas cards, which it sent to NFL team owners, league officials, and reporters. Appearing inside the card was a red and green Christmas tree, decorated with dog bones and Browns helmets. The card's inscription read: "All Cleveland Browns Fans Want for the Holidays is their Football Team in Cleveland."

Also neatly scripted inside was a quote from Art Modell, uttered years before: "We can't hopscotch franchises around the country. We have built this business on the trust of fans. If we treat that as if it doesn't count, it isn't going to wash."

At a City Hall rally on Jan. 2, 1996, Mayor White wore an orange ribbon (one of the team colors) and urged fans to call "523-DAWG" for daily instructions on which NFL team to call to protest the move. Mail Boxes, Etc., offered free fax services to Browns supporters who sent messages to NFL headquarters in New York. Artwork by Cleveland schoolchildren protesting the move was tacked up at City Hall. Area McDonalds restaurants aided the city's petition drive by positioning petitions on their counters for fans to sign.

"I have a message for Art Modell. We have a message for the NFL. You ain't seen nothin' yet," White declared.

The city won the early legal rounds. A judge, up for reelection in a few months, issued an order preventing the Browns from moving until the team's current contract could be settled at trial, a process the city was clearly in no hurry to move along.

White and his representatives continued to hold meetings with NFL officials and to make presentations to other team owners. Alfred Lerner also got involved, saying he wanted to try to help the city get a team. The bottom line that emerged, however, was that, although Cleveland's financing might be sufficient to renovate Municipal Stadium, it made little sense to spend $175 million on such a job.

Finally, Tagliabue pulled White aside at a meeting and told him to cool it. He also asked him to restrain the Browns Backers. The two then settled in for serious negotiations. The Browns were obviously going to leave, though Modell had decided, well before, that the team name and colors would be left behind, provided the city dropped its lawsuits. The NFL now added a third component to the settlement: an unprecedented guarantee of a team for Cleveland.

It was a far greater accommodation than was offered Baltimore. But then Cleveland was a market no one could doubt, and it fit Tagliabue's vision of a regional franchise territory uncluttered by other teams. And Cleveland did have $175 million on the table.

Talks dragged on for weeks. Modell and his lawyers gave their own presentations to other NFL team owners, projecting slide after slide of decrepit Municipal Stadium. They also distributed news clippings which, they said, demonstrated Cleveland government's incompetence and disinterest.

Not to be outdone, Cleveland added Glendening and Moag to its lawsuit, alleging that they had illegally interfered with the team and the city's lease and demanding that Glendening testify under oath at a deposition.

When an NFL owners' meeting, convened on Jan. 17 to address the Browns crisis, broke up without a vote, Moag added his own threat. He filed suit against the NFL, charging it with illegally keeping a team out of Baltimore to protect the Washington Redskins' turf. The suit promised to raise embarrassing questions related to the NFL's expansion process and the league's intervention with the Patriots and other teams interested in moving to Baltimore.

• • •

On Wednesday, Feb. 7, at a hotel adjacent to Chicago's O'Hare airport, the NFL's 30 team owners convened another meeting to talk about the Browns.

The broad outline of a deal had come together in the previous weeks. Modell and his franchise would be allowed to move to Baltimore but would have to pay off Cleveland's legal bills and stadium debt and leave the Browns' name, history books, and colors behind. The NFL would promise, in writing, that a franchise would be in Cleveland by 1999. The league would also contribute tens of millions of dollars to Cleveland to help build a stadium — an unprecedented concession to one of its cities. In exchange for all this, Cleveland and Maryland would drop their lawsuits.

The parties seemed resolved to the deal, although an alternative was kicked around for a few weeks — keeping the Browns in Cleveland, to be operated by an NFL trust, while Maryland built its stadium. When the new ballpark opened, Modell would move and rename his franchise, and Cleveland would get a new team, called the Browns. Under this proposed arrangement, Modell would have to sit out football for a few years, but be spared the capital-gains taxes he would otherwise pay after selling the Browns and bringing a new team to Baltimore. And fans would keep going to games in Cleveland because Modell would no longer be involved.

The idea won some support among NFL moderates, who thought Modell should suffer the inconvenience of the crisis he had caused. But Modell and Moag were resolutely opposed. Modell's life was football. And his age and ill health put a premium on each year. Though Moag deferred to Modell, both realized that delaying the arrival of a team in Baltimore increased the chances that something would go wrong, that the league would renege, that stadium funding would be lost, that somehow the deal would be undone.

Negotiators spent a February day in Chicago reaching accord on the final details and, when they broke for dinner, thought they were close to agreement. At about 9 p.m., the NFL's top brass — Tagliabue, president Neil Austrian, and operations vice president Roger Goodell — reported to a joint meeting of the league's finance and stadium committees. They explained the deal that was coming together but also laid out the option of keeping the Browns in Cleveland and promising owner Art Modell and Baltimore an expansion team after Maryland built its stadium.

The two committees, comprised of 12 of the league's most influential owners, were not shy about expressing their opinions, according to several participants. Some members, led by Jacksonville Jaguars owner Wayne Weaver — who beat out Baltimore for his expansion franchise little more than two years before — aggressively argued for making Baltimore wait. He was joined by Steelers owner Dan Rooney, who urged the storied Browns franchise to stay where it had been supported by fans for 50 seasons.

"There were some owners who were uncomfortable with it on principle, who wondered if it was fair to move the team," said committee member and new Philadelphia Eagles owner Jeffrey Lurie.

The meeting dragged on for two hours, deeply dividing the committees. Although Weaver spoke against Baltimore, expansion victor Jerry Richardson, owner of the Carolina Panthers, took the opposite position. He argued that the deal could bring the league four new stadiums. Cleveland and Baltimore would begin stadium construction immediately, thus enhancing legislative support in Annapolis for the Redskins' stadium in Landover, Md. And even Cincinnati, where voters were to decide the following month if they wanted to raise taxes for a new Bengals stadium, would get the message.

Richardson and the Giants' Robert Tisch argued that Modell, a pillar of the league for 35 years, was now 70 years old and in ill health. Depriving him of football — his passion and occupation — for even just a few years would not be fair, Tisch said. New Orleans Saints owner Tom Benson, who was chairman of the finance committee, was ambivalent, but clearly uncomfortable with the league precedent of paying for a stadium.

The owners agreed to approach Modell one last time to see if he would accept a football hiatus.

John Moag was not in the room for the owners' debate. He was staying at another hotel with Modell and the Browns delegation. All planned to be on hand for the meetings in case the committees had questions. But at dinner time, the deal seemed close, and the league told them they needn't come over. They left to eat.

Moag, of course, knew of the festering split within the league and its front office. The weekend before, Browns officials had engaged in some blunt conversations with NFL officials, saying they would not accept a deal that did not result in the Browns playing in Baltimore in 1996.

Just the previous Friday, however, Seattle Seahawks owner Ken Behring had shocked the football world, and Los Angeles, by announcing that he was moving to L.A. This was a frontal attack on the NFL and its commissioner, who a year before had won a formal owners' resolution giving the league control of the L.A. market. The NFL desperately wanted a team in the nation's second largest market, but it needed to keep bidders out of the neighborhood if it was going to have the leverage to win public funding for a stadium.

The Seahawks incident emboldened owners opposed to Modell's move. They said the league needed to make a stand in Cleveland if it hoped to maintain even the illusion of control over franchise moves. The notion of keeping the Browns in Cleveland through an NFL-operated trust, while Modell waited in Baltimore for a new franchise, thus came back to life.

On the Monday before the Chicago meetings, a distraught Moag called Richardson to ask if he could offer any assurances that the uproar wouldn't endanger the Browns' move. Richardson, who had been advising Moag, said he couldn't, that Maryland and the Browns had some serious difficulties. Browns officials spent the next few days trying to beat back the trust idea and thinking they had made progress.

Late Wednesday night, however, longtime NFL spokesman Joe Browne told reporters that Baltimore or Cleveland could end up with a promise and no team. And he said a vote might *not* be taken at the Chicago meeting.

Fred Nance, Cleveland's chief negotiator, was equally surprised when the NFL returned to the bargaining table at about midnight. The trust had been Cleveland's first preference, but its chances seemed to have faded hours earlier.

The NFL, earlier in the day, had increased its offer of stadium assistance, coming up with "real numbers" for the first time, Nance said. Under discussion for weeks was the concept of a league loan to be repaid by the team that eventually moved to Cleveland. In exchange, the city offered to ease its demands for reparations from Modell, Nance said.

Cleveland had $182 million in local and state funds in place and another $10 million in loans from a private business group, Cleveland Tomorrow. But a new stadium would cost at least $220 million, city officials figured. The city wanted the $28 million gap closed without any more public money.

The NFL's response, according to Nance, was that keeping the Browns in Cleveland would not endanger the city's stadium money but most assuredly would mean less money from Modell. On Wednesday, Modell formally offered Cleveland $2.5 million to compensate for rent he would have paid over the final three seasons of his lease. Cleveland wanted tens of millions of dollars for legal fees, consultants' reports, and lost tax revenue.

The offer to keep the team in town threw the talks off, and the NFL bargainers stayed at the table until 3 a.m. Thursday, haggling over various money issues.

At midmorning, Modell, his attorney, and top advisers met with Moag and NFL representatives Tagliabue, Austrian, Goodell, Jerry Richardson, and Tom Benson. Browne's comments the night before prepared Moag and the Modell group for what was coming.

"It wasn't pressure per se," Moag explained later, "but it was pressure in the sense that you've got the heavyweights of the NFL saying, 'Why would it be a problem if the team didn't arrive for a couple of years?'"

"I wasn't the least bit interested in assuming the risk of having the team play elsewhere, and we build a stadium and God knows what would happen."

In a passionate style familiar to his fellow team owners, Modell said he wasn't going to part with his team, even temporarily, even under the terms that the NFL was offering — no liability for losses and no capital-gains taxes. League officials said they were worried that the Maryland legislature would kill the stadium deal, leaving the NFL with its first homeless franchise. Moag assured them the deal was solid and said he was not going to change the contract that he and Modell had signed Oct. 27, 1995.

The notion of the NFL extending Baltimore's long wait, and Cleveland being spared a football hiatus, was finally dead.

That hurdle cleared, the rest of the package came together fairly quickly. Modell increased his offer for reparations, agreeing to compensate the city for millions of dollars in lost admissions taxes. His final offer was about $12 million — a few million more than he had hoped for, but still acceptable.

Modell also agreed to the unprecedented step of giving up the Browns' history and heritage, essentially parting with a team identity he had owned and honed for more than three decades. The record books, trophies, and other elements of the franchise's identity would not even be allowed out of Ohio. They would be boxed up and sent to the Pro Football Hall of Fame in Canton, Ohio for safe-keeping.

And finally, Modell agreed to pay the league a $29 million relocation fee and to forego his share of the expansion fee if a team were created for Cleveland.

The NFL said it would front Cleveland $28 million to $48 million for its stadium construction, as well as accept a key restriction sought by the city: Cleveland would consider as a replacement team only those NFL franchises not in violation of their home stadium leases and which met the league's guidelines for relocation.

"We were not willing, frankly, to do what Baltimore did," said Nance.

The league also agreed to an outline of a lease, which it would transfer to a new Cleveland team owner by 1999. (The lease called for the construction of a Dawg Pound bleacher section in the new stadium.) In exchange for dropping its lawsuit against the Browns and the Maryland Stadium Authority, Cleveland agreed to put its football future in the NFL's hands. It would not seek a team on its own, thus sparing the league another embarrassing situation like the Seahawks' proposed move to L.A.

Cleveland realized the limitations of its leverage. If successful, its lawsuit could have forced the Browns to stay for only three years. But that would have humiliated the NFL by holding one of its teams hostage.

"They made it clear that under those circumstances, the likelihood of us getting [another] football team was nil," Nance said.

The final handshake came at about 9 p.m., on Thursday, Feb. 8, after a long day of diplomacy by NFL officials shuttling between the Cleveland and Browns delegations, which never actually met in the same room, even after the deal was consummated.

The league ratified the final agreement late Friday morning after several hours of sometimes emotional, sometimes tedious debate about the NFL's power to control its franchises and its obligations to loyal fans, like those in Cleveland. Looming darkly over the proceedings were the upcoming debates over the Seahawks, the Oilers, and probably the Cardinals, Buccaneers, Patriots, and Bengals.

Tagliabue delivered a four-page report on the relocation, concluding, "The Browns meet some, but not all, of the league's relocation guidelines." Fan support for the team was unquestionable, the report said. And, financially, the team and affiliated stadium corporation were not suffering operating losses that threatened the team's future, as Modell had claimed. Tagliabue skirted the issue of whether the city and team owner had engaged in good-faith negotiations, but he agreed that Municipal Stadium was not adequate for the future.

"Like Cleveland, Baltimore is an important and substantial element of the league's history and tradition, even though the league's presence there was fundamentally changed by the Colts' departure a decade ago," Tagliabue wrote in his report.

Given the potential cost of Maryland's lawsuit, Tagliabue said, he supported the agreement reached with Cleveland.

Even the Redskins, long an enemy of Baltimore's football aspirations, voted for the deal. John Kent Cooke, son of Redskins owner Jack Kent Cooke and the man who represents the team at most league functions, delivered a 45-minute speech about NFL loyalty to fans and the ruination caused by relocations. But he voted for Modell. His father had received a call a week earlier from Glendening, reminding him of Maryland's intention to invest millions of dollars in the new Redskins stadium. A "no" vote from the Redskins would be problematic, Glendening said.

Arguing vigorously in favor of the deal was another member of the same 1993 expansion committee that had bypassed Baltimore: Alex Spanos of the San Diego Chargers.

"I don't like all the moving that's going on. I don't think any-one does. But it does pay off," Spanos said after the meeting, noting the sweet deal that a team can get from a jilted city like Baltimore.

The final owner tally of 25-2 was two votes more than the Browns needed, a testament, several owners said, to Modell's NFL contributions over the years. But the fissures were clear: The two "no" votes came from Modell's closest friends in the league, the Bills' Ralph Wilson and the Steelers' Dan Rooney. Three teams abstained from the vote. All had either moved recently or were flirt-ing with the idea of moving and disputed the league's control over relocation: the Arizona Cardinals, the Oakland Raiders, and the St. Louis Rams.

"The whistle has blown on this game, and it is time for a new life in Baltimore, my new hometown," Modell told reporters after the vote.

Modell had just given away one of the proudest franchise his-tories in sports, and with it the legacy of Jim Brown and Paul Brown, Lou Groza and Dante Lavelli. But he immediately latched onto another one.

"I lived through the '60s and early '70s of the Baltimore Colts. I fully intend to bring back and then some, the legacy of Unitas, Marchetti and Berry and Donovan," he vowed.

After signing the documents at a short ceremony with Tagliabue, Mayor White struck a conciliatory tone, one that was in sharp contrast to his months of Modell-bashing.

"It's time for us to let the past go and for us to look with clear-er eyes, to look with kinder eyes and maybe softer eyes at the future," White said. "I'm hopeful that we can commence a period of healing and a period of building."

White and Modell conducted back-to-back news conferences and left the hotel without appearing together.

But shortly after Modell's departure, his old nemesis Al Davis rounded up reporters and took them out to a hallway, where he highlighted the rich irony of the occasion in an angry, 20-minute diatribe.

"He's the one who spoke out adamantly against the Rams," said Davis, referring to Modell. "Spoke out adamantly against the Raiders. Put a lot of obstacles in our way in Los Angeles, and it's deja vu. Here he is standing up, changing everything he has said over 15 years in about one month."

CHAPTER FIFTEEN

The Ravens Kick Off

It was nearly 90 degrees on Sunday, Sept. 1, 1996, as the Ravens took the field in Baltimore for their first regular season game — and the city's third National Football League debut. Despite the blue skies, the throngs of fans marching into Memorial Stadium were clearly divided on the painful price of their city's football redemption.

The team name had been selected by fans through a telephone poll organized by the team and *The Sun*. Team officials, who were not wild about it, knew in advance that the "Ravens" would beat the other finalists: the Marauders, named for a World War II-era bomber made in Baltimore, and the Americans, a class of locomotives once manufactured in the city. Focus groups and polls showed fans identified with the menacing black bird, the raven, and liked both the literal connection to the Orioles and the literary connection to Edgar Allan Poe, the one-time Baltimorean, and his most famous poem, "The Raven."

After extensive discussions within the team and with the NFL, the franchise bowed to overwhelming public support for the name. The newly christened Ravens sold all but 15,000 tickets for the entire season.

The Ravens' purple and black uniforms featured a winged

"B" and elements of the black, red, and yellow Maryland state flag, designed to project permanence and hometown loyalty for an NFL era which boasted neither. More appropriate, perhaps, was the red and white Greek cross incorporated into the Ravens' logo. Part of the crest of one of Maryland's founding families, the Calverts, the cross had been adopted by Maryland's Confederate military units during the Civil War. The Ravens would now be the NFL's rebels.

Hours before the opening kickoff, fans too young to remember the Colts' years of greatness gathered in the stadium parking lot for tailgate parties, firing up charcoal grills in the beds of pickups and toasting the return of the NFL with cans of Budweiser. Some wore beaks. One group of fans mounted a man-sized bird cage on the top of a truck and took turns sitting inside and cawing at passersby.

"I was born a raven, but was raised by humans," explained 23-year-old Steve Lehner.

Nearby, solemn Browns fans mingled, some openly rooting for the opposing Oakland Raiders, despite that franchise's much longer history of trading cities for more lucrative stadium deals.

A man dressed as Poe, with stick-on sideburns and a black cape, wandered the crowd crowing, "Nevermore."

The public address system played the Rolling Stones' "Sympathy for the Devil" when Al Davis, wearing his trademark white and black outfit, slicked-back hair, and dark sunglasses, strolled onto the field before the game. Fans gave him a rousing round of boos.

Davis' frequent moves seemed to be catching up with him. Although his return to Oakland had been enthusiastically received by longtime Raiders fans, he discovered that many in the city had pledged allegiance to the cross-bay rival 49ers. And the prices he set — an average of more than $51 per seat — were the highest in the NFL. Community leaders had found it tough to sell seat licenses to pay Davis' dowry. Only 35,000 of the 55,000 10-year licenses had been sold.

But Davis wasn't concerned: He had already received the first $22 million he was owed. The taxpayers were obligated to make up any shortfalls for the stadium work.

Memorial Stadium looked much as it had in 1984 when the Colts declared it unsuitable for modern football and headed to

Indianapolis. The state put the required $2 million into fixing it up. But it was a minor repair in the world of modern stadium economics, remarkable considering Memorial would be abandoned again in two seasons when the new Ravens park opened.

Longtime Colts fans would recognize some of the changes: The field had been shifted 10 yards north, thus moving the legendary "Orrsville" out of the baseball dugouts. A spot near the third base line, Orrsville was the end-zone corner where Colts receiver Jimmy Orr (1961-70) often got open for a score. Aluminum bleachers were installed close to the end zones; and the corners of the horse-shoe shaped structure were boxed off with additional seating to bring crowd capacity up to almost 65,248 — about 5,000 more than during the Irsay era. Mezzanine seats were renamed "Premier Seats" and sold as faux club seats, with buffet food and waiters in each section.

Unimaginable during the prior incarnations of Baltimore football were the ticket prices: They ranged from $17 to $75 and had a weighted average (total value of tickets sold divided by the number sold) of $40.54, fourth-highest in the NFL that season. Parking, too, was dear: $15 for the right to be hemmed in, bumper to bumper, with no hope of escape until all surrounding cars had departed. And fans knew the worst was yet to come. Ticket prices and seat licenses still hadn't been worked out for the new stadium.

But none of that stopped anyone on the Ravens' opening day. The crowd of 64,124 was the largest in Baltimore's pro football history. Only the 80,000-plus attendance for Army-Navy games in old Municipal Stadium topped its size. Rival camps of "Raven Maniacs" and "The Bird Cage" set up in the bleachers, hoping to replace Cleveland's Dawg Pound.

The Colts Marching Band and conductor John Ziemann were on hand, too, bringing the crowd to its feet with the Colts' still-familiar fight song. Art Modell had agreed to adopt the band, and it was to be renamed the "Ravens Marching Band" during halftime of the team's last home game at Memorial Stadium in 1997.

The kickoff was a sweet moment for Ziemann, who had kept the band going for 12 years without a team, serving as a sometimes off-key but always passionate ambassador of a city's unrequited affection. Mayflower, the vilified mover that had carried the Colts out of town, tried to make amends by transporting the band to its out-of-town engagements for free. It had also proposed to move the new Ravens from Cleveland to Baltimore but hadn't gotten the job.

Ironically, during Baltimore's long football winter, it was Art Modell who flew the Colts band up to Cleveland for 10 halftime shows, underscoring the crime he felt had been committed against Baltimore. Modell's friend Ralph Wilson also brought the band up to Buffalo to play during the 1993 Colts-Bills game. The halftime show, billed as "Circus of Clowns," was widely interpreted as an insult aimed at Bob Irsay.

Bereft of any history of their own, the Ravens didn't miss a chance on Opening Day to envelop themselves in Baltimore's football heritage. For a pre-game ceremony, they invited onto the field 40 former Colts players, including Hall of Famers Art Donovan, Ted Hendricks, John Mackey, and Lenny Moore. The players and the Colts band lined up in two columns. On cue, the retired players donned "Ravens" jackets over their Colts T-shirts, symbolically uniting the two franchises and eras. The new Ravens then poured out of the dugout and ran through the column of Colts legends and band members.

Johnny Unitas, again wearing No. 19, appeared from the opposite side of the field. Sixty-three and stooped, Unitas carried over his head the game ball, which he delivered to the head referee.

Unitas had some reservations about the Ravens name, and the means by which the team was acquired. It certainly was a different league from the one in which he had played. In 1996, an *average* NFL player was earning about $750,000, *three times* the top annual salary he earned in uniform. Ravens QB Vinny Testaverde, whom many thought had not lived up to his advance billing, was pulling down $1.3 million a year.

But the old quarterback was happy to take part in the celebration. After his symbolic hand-off, he ran to the Ravens' sideline and, in one of the ceremony's few spontaneous moments, hugged the team's new head coach, Ted Marchibroda. Just the previous season, Marchibroda had coached the Indianapolis Colts to the AFC championship game, which they lost to the Pittsburgh Steelers, 20-16.

Unitas and Marchibroda shared a long history. Marchibroda had been the first draft pick of the Steelers in 1953 and was still there as a backup QB in 1955 when the Steelers drafted, then dropped, Unitas. Twenty years later, after Unitas had retired from playing, Marchibroda became the Baltimore Colts' head coach and led them to the playoffs three consecutive years. He signed on with the Indy Colts in 1992, engineering a last-to-first turnaround season (they finished 9-7), just as he had with the Baltimore Colts. The team went from 2-12 in '74 to 10-4 in '75.

The coach seemed happy to be back in Memorial Stadium.

Unitas had not been as lucky. In the early 1970s, he and one of his ex-high school coaches invested in Florida real estate — including what turned out to be swampland outside Orlando. The venture dissolved in lawsuits, acrimony, and steep losses. A courier service that he and some other investors operated in Baltimore flourished for a few years, but failed in 1984 when an accountant allegedly absconded with $250,000.

For many years, the Golden Arm restaurant, which Unitas and former Colts teammate Bobby Boyd owned and operated in Towson, Md., a suburb of Baltimore, made money. But Unitas sold it in 1983 when another partner — not Boyd — was charged in an insurance scam against the city. Also in 1983, Unitas allowed his name to appear in advertisements for a football gambling sheet called "All Pro Football Report."

In 1984, Unitas bought a Reisterstown, Md., electronics firm, National Circuits Inc., for $3.5 million. Six years later, with the Internal Revenue Service seeking back taxes, National Circuits was sold for $1 million. But Unitas retained much of its massive debt and, in 1991, he filed for personal bankruptcy, listing assets of $1.4 million and liabilities of $3.2 million. By 1996, under the watchful management of his son, John Jr., who allowed no autographs to be given away for free, Unitas was rebuilding his finances.

As old No. 19 jogged off the field, a team of Air National Guard jets streaked over the stadium.

Later, several planes trailing banners competed for attention: "Welcome to the relocation bowl," said one. "Jump, Art, and Land on David," said another. A smattering of hand-held signs outside the stadium contained the same sentiment. One read: "In from Cleveland, Luv those Raiders. Art you filthy Stinkin Traitor."

But inside the stadium, the crowd was more hospitable. Spontaneous chants of "Art, Art, Art" brought an occasional hand-wave from the team owner, seated prominently in a 50-yard-line skybox with his wife, son, bodyguard, and top team officials.

The Friday evening before the game, Modell had hosted a party for 500 invited guests in a giant, air-conditioned tent on the parking lot where his new stadium was being built. He and his wife personally greeted the early arrivals, including the governor, a senator, and titans of the state's corporate and government elite. Each table had a white chocolate box filled with candy and adorned with a dark chocolate Ravens football. Over a buffet of tenderloin, lamb, and sauteed lobster, Modell began the long process of courting his new community.

Noticeably absent from the festivities and opening game was Alfred Lerner. Having endured widespread public scorn in Cleveland for his role in moving the team, he sought to distance himself from Modell and the Ravens, touching off a chilly phase in their relationship. He would attend no Ravens games that first season. He would also talk to Modell about selling his Ravens shares, to free himself up to pursue a team for Cleveland — something he hoped would resurrect his image in his hometown. But the break may have been beyond repair. Cleveland fans were rooting not for Lerner, but for a Bernie Kosar-led ownership group.

First Maryland, the bank Lerner had put Modell in touch with originally, also walked away from the Browns deal and relationship. The NFL was concerned about the team's crushing debt and in coming months would reject Modell's first restructuring plan.

Watching from his owner's box, Modell was not in the best of health. Still unsteady from a blood infection that nearly killed him that spring, he thought he had contracted the infection from a cut suffered in a fall in Florida. Stinging from a rough CNN interview in the week before the first Ravens game, Modell canceled a planned pre-game interview and refused all interview requests from reporters, even local ones.

Commentator Bob Costas, who was to have interviewed Modell for NBC, instead delivered a blunt, 10-minute, pre-game monologue in which he noted that without the new, cash-generating stadium under construction downtown, "the average NFL owner would have as much use for Baltimore, and all its fans and tradition, as he would for East Hoboken, N.J."

"So, even amid the excitement here," Costas intoned, "there is reason to remain unmoved. Which is how the Cleveland Browns should have remained, instead of becoming the place where some of the last illusions about loyalty and tradition in sports were trashed. And all the cheering today, much of it from people who cried when the same thing was done to them, can't change that."

NBC's on-air analyst for the Baltimore game was equally outspoken. And biased. Bob Trumpy, a former Pro-Bowl Cincinnati Bengals tight end, wrote the week before in *Inside Sports* magazine: "I despise the whole concept of the Baltimore Ravens ... see nothing but doom and gloom for this franchise ... I wish the Ravens high winds and muddy fields; I wish them empty roads to and from the ball park; I wish them cold hot dogs ... I wish them nothing but bad."

Drafted out of Utah by Bengals founder Paul Brown, Trump had loyalties that dated back almost 30 years. From 1968 to 1977, he played for Cincinnati, all but two of the years under Coach Brown himself. Twice he led the Bengals in receptions and reception yardage. After his football retirement, he became a Cincinnati radio and TV sports commentator.

Ravens fans, stewing over his remarks for several days, eagerly waved "Dump Trumpy" signs printed by a local radio talk show host and handed out at the stadium gates.

Among the veterans of Baltimore's down-and-dirty football wars, retired Colts defensive tackle Art Donovan weighed in with a double-sided opinion of the Browns' move. "Yeah, I do feel sorry for the people in Cleveland," Donovan told a reporter. "Baltimore did this the way Irsay did it to us. But now that they're here, we have to support them."

Former Colts tight end John Mackey, a member of Tom Clancy's short-lived expansion ownership group, agreed. "The important thing is we have football back here," he said. Mackey, who played in Baltimore from 1963 to 1972, warmly recalled the riotous crowds that used to rock Memorial Stadium.

Former Governor Schaefer, wearing Ravens purple and exuding supreme satisfaction, commented diplomatically on his way to the opening game: "It's not vindication. It's a new day. We never gave up hope."

Schaefer, Glendening, and Schmoke, all Democrats, had never been close, so it was no surprise when they watched the Ravens' first game in separate sections. Besides relegating Schaefer to a ringside seat at the Nov. 6 announcement, Glendening had not invited the former governor to the ground breaking for the new football stadium, which many thought should be named for Schaefer. A Glendening spokesman offered a tepid excuse for the snub, saying that inviting one former governor meant inviting all of them — four were then living — and there might not be enough room at the event, which drew about 500.

Schaefer, who attended anyway, was conspicuous in the crowd.

Schmoke watched the opening game from the mayor's box and remembered his own Memorial Stadium memories: He quarterbacked City College High School in its 1964 and 1965 games against arch-rival Polytechnic High School. The first game, which both teams entered undefeated, was especially fulfilling. "We blew them out. It was great," Schmoke remembered. Thirty thousand fans watched from the stands. And the young City and Poly players even got to use the Colts' locker room.

For Schmoke, the Ravens' opening day in Memorial Stadium was more than he once expected. The city mayor had helped Schaefer win legislative approval for stadium funding. And he had backed him in the losing battles for an expansion franchise. But he had also been among those quietly suggesting in 1995 that it might be time to look for other uses for the stadium funds.

"Obviously, I'm thrilled for the whole community and very pleased I didn't approve the demolition of Memorial Stadium," Schmoke said.

Governor Glendening, watching the game with his wife from a mezzanine seat, declared himself "a Ravens fan," seemingly suspending his long-standing support of the Redskins — at least until the Washington team made its move into Maryland.

Assessing his own role in luring the Browns to Baltimore, the governor was suddenly charitable: "Maybe it was the one-two punch. Schaefer softened them up, and we went in for the kill."

The carnage was well spread. After Modell signed the contract with the Stadium Authority, Glendening had to fight to retain stadium funding. To secure support from wavering state legislators, who were stunned by the negative public reaction to the Browns' move, Glendening had Modell agree to a modification of the agreement: The team owner would contribute $24 million to the stadium construction over the course of the 30-year lease.

The team made one other change. Although it had the contractual right to sell up to $80 million in seat licenses — with the state collecting the last $5 million — the Ravens chose, after studying the market, to sell only $68 million worth. The state would get none of the proceeds.

Though the Stadium Authority denied it, some Browns officials privately admitted that Modell informally gained one more concession from the state to cover his $24 million contribution — the right to sell the stadium name to a corporate sponsor. This was another money-making trend sweeping sports. Familiar names such as Candlestick, Joe Robbie, and Jack Murphy were being stripped from stadiums in favor of commercialized monikers: 3-Com Park, Pro Player Stadium, and Qualcom Stadium.

Baltimore's twin stadium complex ended up costing far more than the Stadium Authority's initial project estimate of $201 million. Buying the land, relocating the businesses and clearing the site cost $99.9 million. Relocating railroad tracks and rehabbing the Camden Station and the signature warehouse (work that would be repaid by rent-paying tennants) cost $18.6 million. Baltimore city contributed $18.2 million of its federal highway funds to rebuild a street and construct a new highway access ramp. Accommodating the Oriole's desire for a "retro" ballapark pushed up the construction cost of the baseball stadium to $106.5 million (the team contributed $9 million for construction of its skyboxes). The Ravens stadium began with a construction budget of $190 million; another $10 million was put aside to add parking, either by purchasing additional land or building a parking deck.

All told, the project would cost close to $500 million — not including several hundred million dollars in interest on the bonds.

Glendening survived the legislative brawl and also won funding for the new Redskins Stadium infrastructure. Yet, by the Ravens' kickoff, he was facing widespread discontent, even in his own party. Supporters hoped that the opening of the Redskins' facility in the fall of 1997 and that of the Ravens' stadium in the fall of 1998, just before his re-election bid, would provide the boost he needed with voters.

Already underway was fierce competition among the region's sports teams. The Washington Bullets and Washington Capitals had announced a move from Largo, Md., to Washington's

Chinatown and the new MCI Center. This, and the expiration of many three-year leases on Orioles boxes, produced an unprecedented regional luxury glut of 30,625 club seats and 573 skyboxes, the highest such concentration in the nation; it gave the Baltimore-Washington area a club seat for every 219 residents and a skybox for every 11,693.

The teams were not shy about prices, either. The Redskins wanted $59,950 to $159,950 a year for a skybox and $995 to $1,995 in annual fees for a club seat. Not to be outdone, Ravens officials priced their 1,000-square-foot boxes at $55,000 to $200,000, but offered some extras: chartered flights to road games, pre-game field passes, and round-the-clock use of suites for office parties.

The competition was just what Redskins owner Jack Kent Cooke had sought to avoid. He had already reduced the number of suites from his initial stadium design, but was still planning 280 skyboxes to the Ravens' 108. Just to be sure the markets remained detached, the Redskins insisted, through the league, that their new NFL neighbors be called the Baltimore, not Maryland, Ravens.

To compound Cooke's competitive difficulties, his team was falling apart. After Coach Joe Gibbs retired in 1992, the Redskins compiled a won-loss record of 13-35. The irascible Cooke spent the Ravens' opening day in Washington's no-frills Robert F. Kennedy Stadium, enduring a 17-14 defeat by the Eagles. (The Redskins would rally to win their next seven games, but then fade down the stretch and finish 9-7.)

Cooke died less than a year later, on April 6, 1997, just a few months before he would have witnessed the opening of the stadium he had spent the last several years struggling to get built. His heirs, despite offers from corporations to pay to name the stadium, opted to call it "Jack Kent Cooke Stadium."

John Moag attended the Ravens game with his wife and daughters. His eyes welled with tears at the opening kickoff. Later, accompanying the governor, he paid Modell a visit in the owner's box.

"It was intense. Look at this crowd, it's a real Baltimore crowd," said Moag, whose 50-yard-line seats were a far cry from his youth, when he snuck into Colts games and sat wherever he thought he could avoid getting thrown out.

In his youth, that had also been the preferred means of entry for longtime Colts fan Leonard "Boogie" Weinglass. Though troubled by the circumstances of the Ravens' arrival, Weinglass bought season tickets anyway and planned to attend the team's opening game. At the last minute, however, he was called away on family business at his Aspen, Colo., home.

"Naturally, I would have loved to have bought the new franchise. But I found out in life you can't always get what you want," said Weinglass. "I'm now a Ravens fan."

Though still living in a luxurious mansion overlooking the Rocky Mountains, Weinglass had fallen on tough business times. He had tried to reorganize his company, Merry-Go-Round Enterprises, under bankruptcy court protection, but had failed. Merry-Go-Round was liquidated, and its assets, including the Harley motorcycles and other symbols of Weinglass' eccentric reign, were auctioned off.

Weinglass came out OK, though. The company had paid him tens of millions of dollars in dividends over the years, and his personal fortune was substantial. Now, instead of overseeing his own NFL franchise, he was filling his time as a volunteer assistant basketball coach at an Aspen high school.

Former Stadium Authority chairman Herb Belgrad went to the game as an unheralded civilian. Again practicing law full-time, he gave Moag credit whenever he could for landing the team.

Former Governor Harry Hughes was on a beach vacation in Delaware when the game began. A few days before the opener, he said: "I think it's great that they are back and we have a team and look forward to building the kind of tradition we had with the Colts. I think it's going to take time, though."

Tom Clancy planned to watch the Ravens' first game from his Calvert County, Md., estate. He was "in recovery" from the publication of his ninth novel, a soon-to-become best-seller called "Executive Orders." He could have watched the game from the Orioles' courtesy box, but opted not to. He hoped to catch a Ravens game later in the season.

"In an ideal world, I would have done it," said Clancy of his aborted pursuit of an NFL franchise in Baltimore. "But it's not an ideal world."

Baltimore's other prospective owner at one time, Malcolm Glazer, also missed the Ravens' game. Glazer attended his

Buccaneers' season opener in Tampa, where the team was battered, 34-3, by the Green Bay Packers, eventual Super Bowl champs. Better news was right around the corner, however. The next Tuesday, voters approved a measure to raise tax dollars to build a new stadium for the Bucs, thus continuing the expensive stadium wars then under way in the league.

The Bucs, considered a potential Cleveland team, would stay in Tampa "forever," Glazer promised.

Baltimore advertising consultant Robert Leffler, who worked for both the Browns and the Bucs and was Moag's initial go-between in the deal with Cleveland, was at Memorial Stadium for the game before heading off to Tampa for the stadium vote. He found the Ravens' debut moving.

"I never thought it would happen," Leffler said. "I thought it would be like Brooklyn. I was part of the old team and saw it die, and now to be part of the new one, it's cause for great personal satisfaction."

NFL commissioner Paul Tagliabue chose to spend the day in Charlotte, N.C., where the Panthers opened their new stadium. At Modell's suggestion, Tagliabue decided against a visit to Baltimore in 1996. But his office did issue a statement for opening day. "Baltimore's NFL fans have always been among the most knowledgeable and passionate in the country," it read. "The Ravens' future looks very promising."

Though he may not have been wanted in Baltimore, Tagliabue was having a pretty good year for the NFL and for himself. In 1995, he grappled with a league whose franchises seemed so mobile they might just as well have been mounted on wheels. By 1996, he seemed to have a grip on the wanderlust. The Seahawks had been turned back from the gates of Los Angeles by last-minute deals to sell the Seattle team and to build a new stadium. The Bucs were on their way to winning security in Florida. The Bears had rejected an offer from Gary, Ind., and were talking again with Chicago officials. And with Cleveland's lease under the NFL's control, an attractive nuisance for migratory team owners was removed.

Whether his luck would hold in the new era of franchise free agency and stadium economics was anybody's guess.

He would soon be publicly criticizing teams such as Modell's

— although he didn't name them — for bad salary cap management.

"There were some examples...of people who've done foolish kinds of contracts, front-loading, back-loading, voidables where they're [being charged] $7 million or $8 million of $41 million of cap room for players who are no longer playing," Tagliabue said at a subsequent owners meeting after the season was over. The Ravens, with $7 million in commitments to prior players, were used as an example.

"So people who thought they could outsmart the system, I think, are learning you can't," Tagliabue said. Soon he would even be hinting that the entire collective bargaining agreement needed to be reworked.

Tagliabue's predecessor, Pete Rozelle, had planned to spend the Ravens' opening day at his home in Rancho Santa Fe, Calif., with his daughter. Rozelle, 70, had been in and out of hospitals, fighting cancer and a brain tumor. He said he'd have three television sets going, one of them carrying the Ravens' game.

"Anyone who knows me is aware of how I was personally distressed when the Colts left Baltimore, and the league was powerless to do anything about it," Rozelle told *The Sun*.

"I was in Memorial Stadium so many times, going back to when I was with the L.A. Rams. The band playing, and listening to the most partisan press box in the league is a special memory. It would be nice to have the city have a winner," Rozelle said.

The former commissioner would not live to see that, however. He died Dec. 6, before the team's first season ended.

On opening day, former Philadelphia Eagles owner Norman Braman was wrapping up an extended summer stay at his home in France, outside Monaco. "I'm really happy for the [Baltimore] fans and the community. It took a long time," said Braman, who sold the Eagles after the NFL expansion.

"I will admit when I heard the announcement, I felt it was a hollow victory for you all," he added.

Another Baltimore supporter, Bob Tisch, spent the day at his home in New York's Westchester County before heading to the Meadowlands to see his Giants lose a night game to the Buffalo Bills in overtime, 23-20.

"I wanted personally to see Baltimore in, and the football

league is thrilled. We know the team in Baltimore will do well," Tisch said.

Former Indianapolis Mayor William Hudnut was in the midst of a personal move on game day. He had just left a job with a Chicago taxpayer watchdog group and taken a job as a fellow with the Urban Land Institute, a Washington trade association for developers. On Sept. 1, he was in a car driving his family to a new home in Bethesda, Md., just 30 miles from Baltimore.

"I'm happy for the city," Hudnut said.

Robert Irsay was gravely ill on opening day. After his move, he had become more active in the Indianapolis community than he had been in Baltimore and had yielded control of the team to his son, Jimmy. As general manager and senior vice president, Jimmy Irsay had brought the Colts some stability and respectability. On the field, however, the Indianapolis Colts were still a shadow of their former Baltimore glory. It took 11 years for the Indianapolis team to make the playoffs, and game attendance was hovering near the low levels left behind in Baltimore.

In November 1995, a few weeks after Modell's Baltimore announcement, the elder Irsay suffered an incapacitating stroke and was ruled legally incompetent, his assets transferred to a trust fund. As he moved in and out of consciousness, his son and his second wife, Nancy, whom he had married in 1989, fought over control of the team.

Modell approached Jimmy Irsay about buying back the Colts' name, but bidding, he was told, would start at $25 million.

"I suddenly became a bird lover," Modell says.

The Colts, who had come within a game of the Super Bowl in the 1995 season, won their 1996 opener against the Arizona Cardinals, 20-13.

The team claimed its 12-year-old lease, which helped set off the flurry of subsequent team moves, was no longer competitive. Deals such as those being offered in Baltimore had rendered the Hoosierdome — now known as the "RCA Dome" — inadequate. Despite repeated denials by Jimmy Irsay, speculation continued during the season that the Colts might move to Cleveland, thus bringing the Baltimore story full-circle.

Bob Irsay died Jan. 14, 1997, of heart and kidney failure.

John "Big Dawg" Thompson planned to watch the first

Ravens game on TV at his Cleveland home and to root for the Raiders.

"I'm working real hard to keep the Cleveland Browns' fires burning," Thompson said. "We lost what we tried to build for 35 years."

Some of his cohorts maintained their Cleveland traditions, driving to Municipal Stadium on Opening Day and holding a tail-gate party. Browns Backers, some wearing "Baltimore Sucks" T-shirts, turned up outside the darkened stadium with coolers and grills. Several cheering fans rushed and kicked their regular gates at 1 p.m. They were locked. "We wanted to show them one thing: You can take the Browns out of here, but you can't take the spirit," remarked one fan, John York.

Mayor Mike White, then wrestling with a thorny teachers' revolt, had his hands full when the NFL season opened. White had recently won City Council approval of the stadium funding deal struck with the league. Now, before the demolition of Municipal Stadium would begin, he planned on holding a festive "Final Play" auction and a series of related events. Everything would be auctioned off, from old ticket booths to wooden bleachers. (The toilet from Modell's offices would go for $2,700 to a nightclub owner who planned to make it an attraction.)

For Baltimore fans, the Ravens did their part that sunny first Sunday, beating a poorly regarded Raiders team playing without its starting quarterback, the injured Jeff Hostetler. Halfway through the first quarter, Baltimore QB Vinny Testaverde scored the first Ravens touchdown on a nine-yard carry up the middle. He then presented the ball to some bleacher fans who turned out to be wearing Raiders' black and silver. For its headquarters, the team commissioned a painting of the inaugural touchdown.

Oakland played a sloppy, penalty-marred game — at one point they were penalized for having too many men on the field — but still managed a 14-7 lead at half-time. In the second half, the Ravens came roaring back, taking advantage of turnovers and engineering a no-huddle offense that left Oakland dazed.

Up by a single point as they entered the fourth quarter, the Raiders lost the lead when Ravens journeyman running back Earnest Byner, the goat in the Cleveland Browns' notorious playoff "Fumble" against the Broncos, put the Ravens ahead to stay. His one-yard TD plunge over the left side capped an 83-yard, no-huddle drive. It may not have reminded fans of the Unitas heyday, but at least it accomplished the win. *Final score:* Ravens 19, Raiders 14.

On the day, Testaverde completed 19 of 33 pass attempts for 254 yards. Impressively, he also fell just a yard shy of Byner's rushing total of 43 yards.

The Ravens quarterback would finish the season with a career year and lead an offense ranked among the NFL's best. But a porous defense would hold the Ravens' debut season to a disappointing 4-12.

Other than Testaverde, who would make the Pro Bowl, the blockbuster players whom Modell signed during his 1995 spending spree proved a bust. Andrew Rison and Pepper Johnson were waived before the season 1996 started, and Leroy Hoard was cut shortly thereafter.

The impact of the ill-fated signings would be felt for years to come, though. The team would start the next season with $7 million of its $41 million salary cap consumed by players no longer on the roster. Cash-starved and chastened, the team would pledge new fiscal discipline as it sought to restructure contracts and return to playoff contention.

In the locker room after the first, glorious game, Ravens Coach Ted Marchibroda was in notably high spirits. "I asked the players: 'Where would you rather be than Baltimore today?'

"It was such a great game, it's a shame we have to play 15 more."

I f professional sports were any other industry, Americans would swell with pride over their success. By Wall Street standards — revenue growth, profitability, franchise value — sports are businesses worthy of envy.

But they're not like any other industry and never have been. Sports are about triumphs of the human spirit, community bonding, and family memories. They're about taking a break from the pettiness that divides us. They're about celebrating some of the things that make society whole: competition, victory, redemption.

Sports are about Alan "The Horse" Ameche crashing over a goal line to win an NFL championship in overtime. They're about Lou "The Toe" Groza, with only seconds to spare, splitting the uprights for a championship-clinching field goal. They're about yellowed newspaper clippings that recall both big games on the field and loved ones in the bleachers. About guts and glory, fathers and sons.

At least, they once were.

Even the hardiest football fans were left more cynical by the Browns move to Baltimore. Some even turned away from the sport completely. In 1996, NFL attendance fell by 3.6 percent, to just over 15 million — the first such decline in eight seasons. An average NFL game drew 62,682 fans, 2,278 fewer than in 1995. Television ratings also dropped by nearly 7 percent.

The NFL dismissed the drooping numbers as an aberration made inevitable by years of record growth. And why not? Business, from the perspective of the financiers then running the league, had never been better.

In 1996, *Financial World* magazine valued the average NFL franchise at $174 million, compared with $127 million for the average NBA club, $115 million for the average Major League Baseball franchise, and $74 million for the average NHL team. In what supposedly was a down year, consumers spent $3 billion on NFL hats, jerseys, CD-ROM computer games, and other team-related merchandise. On average, more than 12 million viewers tuned into an NFL regular game telecast; and 130 million watched the Super Bowl. Budweiser gladly paid up to $400,000 a minute to broadcast its ads on a football Sunday, knowing for certain that one out of every 10 American males ages 21 to 34 would be watching. No other sport delivered such a captive audience.

But football's profiteers depend on the local fans' willingness to give their hearts to their teams, and the Browns' move imperiled that relationship. Recognizing this, NFL Commissioner Tagliabue, who had thrown up his hands over previous relocations, began to bear down on wayward franchises. He became both a goodwill ambassador for the league and a mediator between the teams and their cities.

A year after Tampa voters rejected one stadium-funding plan, Tagliabue persuaded them to pass a nearly identical one under threat of losing their team. Fearing the loss of their own pro football teams, voters in Cincinnati, Detroit, and San Francisco followed suit. With NFL help, new investors were found to buy the Seattle Seahawks, thus ending a crisis that began when the team moved its weight lifting equipment to Los Angeles. (Seattle voters rejected stadium funding for both the Seahawks and the baseball Mariners, but legislators funded the baseball stadium anyway and voters went along with a second football referendum.)

In the calendar year following Modell's announcement, no NFL teams threatened to relocate. To some extent, this inactivity was due to the simple law of averages: Only so many teams want to move, and only so many cities are willing to pay their price. But the league, too, deserves some credit. It kept under control the NFL's two most attractive nuisances: Cleveland and Los Angeles.

Several years earlier, the NFL passed a resolution to prevent a team from moving to Los Angeles without league approval. As for Cleveland, the lease Tagliabue signed with the city not only guaranteed it a new team by 1999, but also prohibited Cleveland from trying to lure a team on its own. The NFL would choose which team did or didn't move there.

But franchise movement remained an ad-hoc process, with top league officials flying from one fire to the next, trying to smother the flames.

Far from reassuring host cities, the NFL continued to threaten the loss of their franchise if cities didn't provide the best stadium terms possible. And the league wasn't offering to help pay for the stadiums. In this sense, the Browns' relocation to Baltimore actually upped the ante. No longer could a city like Chicago, with generations of loyal fans, hope to keep the Bears in town with just a rehab of old Soldier Field, with new, luxury structures — new gold mines to be exact — popping up in Maryland and Ohio.

Directly or indirectly, the Browns' relocation caused new stadiums to be built for the Ravens, the Redskins, the Bengals, the Browns, the Buccaneers, the Lions, the 49ers, and the Seahawks. The impact of the Browns' move on taxpayers nationwide was thus staggering.

Over the past few years, $7 billion was spent or committed to build or rehab 30 major-league sports facilities, making sports one of the most highly subsidized industries in the United States. Add up all the residents of those cities and the total tops 100 million. By some estimates, another $5 billion to $7 billion would be committed for sporting venues within another five years.

But are the relative benefits of all these new stadiums clearly understood? Probably not.

More and more, as stadium costs climb, stadium construction money is coming from taxpayers. Some indoor arenas are still being privately financed, but they're versatile enough to attract a range of events that can make money. Not so for a 70,000-seat, open-air football stadium. A handful of circuses or mega-concerts may be staged in such facilities, but booking enough acts to be profitable is iffy.

At one time, all sports teams built their own parks. No more.

Consider the two most recently built privately-funded football parks: the Washington Redskins' stadium in Prince George's County, Md., and the Carolina Panthers' stadium in Charlotte. Redskins owner Jack Kent Cooke paid for his own $180 million stadium, but demanded and received $70.5 million in state-funded roadwork and infrastructure improvements. The Panthers, too, paid for their own stadium, but they built it on land donated and cleared at public expense (a jail and nursing home had to be moved). Panthers fans themselves kicked-in $100 million by purchasing costly personal seat licenses. Few experts think PSLs can be counted upon to raise that much money in most cities.

Once a sports league accepts public subsidies, it's hard for it to break free. Art Modell found himself in the unenviable position of competing against teams luxuriating in new parks and concluded that a new palace of his own was required. Increasingly, teams playing in outdated facilities have a hard time competing for players and, as a result, suffer in the standings. This sets off a spiral of slumping attendance and revenues.

If they pay for football stadiums, what do local communities get for their "investment"? Very little, at least very little in dollars and cents. Leaders championing stadium projects inevitably produce studies, performed by government analysts under their employ or by friendly economists for hire, to prove that taxpayers get a big return. But their ciphering is inexact at best and highly misleading at worst. During the 1993 expansion race, Maryland estimated that a Baltimore football team would bring $86 million a year and the equivalent of 1,170 full-time jobs to the local economy. A closer look suggests some mathematical hocus-pocus.

Maryland's study actually shows the team employing only 71 people, but, through the magic ripple of economics, another 397 jobs are "created" directly, and hundreds more indirectly. The theory is that whenever a single new worker is hired, other workers must be employed to service him (or her): people such as waiters and waitresses, launderers and dry cleaners, home builders, car mechanics, and so forth.

The Maryland study attributes 161 jobs, many admittedly part-time, to stadium concessions and associated service jobs. Fans staying at local hotels, buying beer and lunch on their way to and from games, and consuming other products, supposedly create the need for 396 jobs — 586 when "rippled." Reporters and broadcasters covering the game generate six new jobs, as do the visiting teams that pass through town, mostly in the hotel and restaurant trade.

Through elaborate figuring, it is thus possible for 71 NFL team employees — including the 50-man player roster — to beget more than 1,000 jobs, even though the team only plays 10 home games a year.

Naturally, independent economists raise some questions about such studies. Chief among them is how many of the dollars spent at football games are actually new to a community?

It seems likely that fans who pay $350 for Baltimore Ravens season tickets are spending $350 less on other things, thus depriving other local businesses of that revenue and eliminating jobs. Most people have a limited budget for entertainment, amusement, and recreation. What one "venue" doesn't get, another will. During the 1994-95 baseball strike, bowling alleys and movie theaters nationwide reported a business upturn.

"New money" may well be spent by fans who live out of town and come in only for game days. But those may be the only exception to the economic rule: Football teams simply redistribute millions of dollars in spending, adding little to local economies.

A large chunk of an NFL team's expenses goes to player payroll. In this era of free agency, a football player is as likely as not to send his paychecks to an off-season home in another state (Florida and Texas, two states with no income taxes, have become meccas for athletes). And many of the goods bought in stadiums, from hot dogs to ball caps, are made out of town or overseas.

"The statistical evidence ... indicates that professional sports as a golden goose ranks among the most enduring and greatest sports myths," concluded Robert A. Baade, chairman of the economics department at Lake Forest College in Lake Forest, Ill., in a 1996 study.

A frequent critic of public-stadium building, Baade did an overview of municipal economic performance for 47 U.S. cities between 1958 and 1988. Because cities don't have "gross national products," he charted each city's economy using federal estimates of its personal income, that is, all wages and salaries paid. He then looked for some evidence of an upswing when a city acquired a sports team, or of a downswing when it lost one. He found no meaningful impact or correlation. In fact, he found that Baltimore's economy actually *improved* after the Colts left in 1984, for reasons that had nothing to do with the team.

But stadiums do afford urban planners a unique opportunity to steer development to a desired location and to enhance an otherwise drab skyline. Camden Yards has clearly extended the range of Baltimore's Inner Harbor and funneled state money into the city — even though the city was forced to pay $1 million a year for the privilege.

In Indianapolis, the acquisition of the Colts and the construction of the downtown stadium were part of a carefully mapped-out economic development strategy. The city chose to focus on amateur and professional sports and succeeded in attracting an impressive array of associated businesses and events. Former Mayor William Hudnut credited the Colts with saving Indianapolis' downtown from the ills befalling other cities' commercial centers.

"Bob Irsay did as much for this city as anyone in its history," Hudnut contended.

But a 1994 study by Indiana University's Mark S. Rosentraub questioned these benefits to Indianapolis. Rosentraub concluded that the jobs created for the city were so low-paying, and the spin-off from development so sparse, that the investment may not have been worth the trouble. Other strategies, he said, may have created more jobs.

"Given how small sports is as an industry and the low pay associated with the numerous service-sector jobs created by sports activities, sports is not a prudent vehicle around which a development or redevelopment effort should be organized," his study asserted. "A sports strategy (even one as pronounced as Indianapolis' and connected to a downtown development emphasis) will not be an economic stimulus for a community or region."

Without question, communities willing to put up $200 million to attract a new company can do better than a football team, which employs 71 workers and annually earns $80 million to $100 million. Compare: In 1993, the state of Alabama pledged to Mercedes-Benz AG a package of tax cuts and incentives worth an estimated $300 million in order to land one of its factories. The plant is expected to employ 1,500 people directly and result in a spin-off of another

13,000 jobs.

Using a pair of economic-impact studies, the Congressional Research Service estimated that each job created by the Ravens and their stadium will cost Maryland from $127,000 to $331,000. By contrast, the service said the state's "sunny day" fund, used to help attract and retain conventional businesses, creates jobs at an average cost of $6,250.

Moreover, spending on sports teams promotes an unintentional redistribution of wealth. To fund stadiums, mainly middle-class citizens pay taxes that benefit millionaire players and team owners. But ticket prices in new stadiums are often priced out of the reach of middle-class fans. Not just prices for the skyboxes and club seats. The average cost of a ticket to an Orioles game doubled during the first five seasons in the team's new park.

As Baade noted: "Constructing a stadium at public expense creates a reverse Robin Hood effect — taking from the poor and giving to the rich.

"Taxpayers in general end up increasing the wealth of franchise owners and players and subsidizing the entertainment of fans who fill the stands on any given Sunday. And we know without question that owners, players, and NFL season-ticket holders are more affluent than the public at large."

The NFL seems an especially poor investment for a city. The teams play only eight regular season and two exhibition games at home each year. And the new stadiums are uniquely ill-suited for other purposes. Researchers at the University of California at Los Angeles even claimed, in a study released in 1997, that the sports industry had actually grown in L.A. after the Rams and Raiders bolted. Other sports, including a slew of minor league ones, flourished with the diminished competition.

But sports teams, because they aren't just about jobs and economics, shouldn't be judged as such. They are first and foremost cultural assets, like art museums and symphony orchestras. Baltimore is a better place to live because of the Orioles and Ravens. Cleveland is a better place to live because of the Browns, Indians, and Cavaliers. Hosting a World Series is no substitute for operating a successful school system or fielding an effective police force, but it shouldn't have to be. A major-league sports team, even a losing one, can be a wonderful community enhancement, like a bustling waterfront or a historic site. A team can be, in Frank Deford's words, a "mucilage" in a society sorely in need of cohesion.

Viewed this way, it's easier to justify some spending for sports teams, but it's still hard to justify the massive outlays now being proffered.

The language found in most new stadium leases reflects the inescapable fact that team owners still have the upper hand in negotiations with municipalities. The Orioles, for example, in their deal with the state of Maryland, worked out a complicated revenue-sharing formula under which they would pay rent. But even for blockbuster years of numerous sellouts, the team payment has failed to cover the state cost of operating the stadium.

In recent years, sports leagues have "capped" player costs in order to prevent competitive bidding from spiraling out of sight. After the Browns' move, it bears asking if communities can do the same thing — that is, prevent the intense competition for NFL franchises from bankrupting them?

Houston Mayor Robert Lanier showed that a city could just say no. To try to keep them in town, he made an offer to the NFL's Oilers. When they rejected it, Lanier decided that putting anything more on the table would be a bad investment. So Houston is losing the Oilers to Nashville. The same thing happened to the NHL Whalers in Hartford, Conn. Is that a solution?

And what's to keep the Oilers — or the Ravens — from leaving their new cities in a few years? No one really knows for sure. Increasingly, cities are demanding, and receiving, 30-year leases, the time coinciding with the term of bonds issued to build the stadiums. Several cities, including Baltimore and Cleveland, have negotiated lease terms that obligate a team to stay in town for the length of the lease and to waive its rights to buy out of it.

The concept is a significant departure from the legal doctrine that limits to money the damages awarded to plaintiffs in most civil cases. When it can be proved that money alone will not compensate plaintiffs for the breach of their contract, judges can order defendants to render "specific performance."

Cleveland tried to force the Browns to "specifically perform" their contract by continuing to play in Cleveland. The city argued to the courts that, even if the Browns actually paid off the final years of their lease, as they offered to do, it would not compensate

Cleveland for the team's loss. But the lawsuit was settled before the issue was legally tested.

Baltimore's lease with the Ravens contains a clause giving the Maryland Stadium Authority the right to demand that the team remain in town. For its new stadium, Cleveland has similar language in its 1996 lease with the NFL. Any team that moves to Cleveland by 1999 will be assigned the lease, including this specific performance clause. If these clauses hold up in court — and there is some debate in legal circles about their enforceability — they could prevent team relocations down the road. This assumes, of course, that a team with high-priced legal help can't concoct some city infraction of the lease that would nullify it.

• • •

In the NFL's new era of stadium economics, what role, if any, should the federal government play? Or, in sports in general? It was the feds, after all, who created this monster by clearing the way for the AFL-NFL merger and joint broadcast contracts.

After Modell left Cleveland, U.S. Representative Martin R. Hoke, a Republican from Cleveland, introduced the "Fan Freedom and Community Protection Act of 1995." The bill required a relocating franchise to give six months' notice to its home city before any move. It also charged the league with replacing the lost franchise with an expansion team if the city couldn't find suitable investors within three years.

Predictably, the bill went nowhere. It was opposed by the sports leagues, as well as by lawmakers from states that were getting relocated franchises, including Maryland.

Maryland Stadium Authority chairman John Moag Jr. testified against the bill before a U.S. Senate subcommittee, even going so far as to excuse Bob Irsay for his sneaky, late-night getaway — a first for a Marylander.

"It was the failure of our local and state elected officials in Maryland to provide the Colts with a firm proposal for a new stadium that led Mr. Irsay to accept an offer from Indianapolis to play in a new dome in that city," Moag said.

Moag argued in favor of the "free market at work" and recommended that Congress keep its nose out. Of course, it wasn't the free market that enabled him to lure the Browns. It was massive government spending.

Sen. Daniel Patrick Moynihan, a Democrat from New York, introduced a bill that would very much insert that Congressional nose. He proposed to strip a federal tax exemption from bonds used to build stadiums. If state bond buyers have to pay taxes on their earnings, then states have to pay higher interest rates to keep their bonds attractive investments. In the case of the Ravens' stadium, the state would be forced to pay, roughly, an additional $36 million over the 30-year term.

Backers of the Moynihan bill argued that federal taxpayers — such as those in Cleveland — shouldn't have to subsidize the "theft" of sports franchises. The federal subsidy is not insignificant. The Congressional Research Service estimated in 1996 that having a tax exemption on stadium bonds saves state and local stadium authorities from 17 percent to 34 percent of their stadium-building costs.

But like the fan protection act, this bill languished, too.

Perhaps a better idea would be to use the federal subsidies to impose broader policy restrictions on cities and states. Withholding federal highway aid is routinely used to coerce states into lowering their speed limits, raising their drinking ages, or cleaning up their pollution. The U.S. government could insist that no public money be spent on a sports stadium without holding a local taxpayer referendum first. (Of course, teams have demonstrated repeatedly in recent years that a multimillion dollar political campaign can swing a vote their way.) Teams could also be required to make minimum contributions to their stadiums and that their rent at least cover stadium operating costs. Or, teams could be compelled to share the wealth of a new stadium with the taxpayers: the Minneapolis Twins' owner Carl Pohlad offered to contribute $15 million and 49 percent of the team's stock in exchange for a new stadium. Such an equity stake could be structured in such a way that the people who paid for the stadium at least share in the value it adds to a team (remember the Oriole's Eli Jacobs, who made $103 million on a $70 million investment over five years?).

Other potential solutions surfaced at a Nov. 29, 1995 hearing before the Senate Judiciary Committee's subcommittee on Antitrust, Business Rights, and Competition. Among the more radical: Congress busts up the National Football League just like the courts broke up AT&T and the Standard Oil Trust.

University of Illinois law professor Stephen F. Ross suggested that Congress simply rescind approval of the AFL-NFL merger. The leagues would disconnect, he said, but still be allowed to continue cooperative interleague play and to preserve the Super Bowl.

"If two or more rival major leagues made their own independent determinations concerning expansion and relocation, the result would be the end of 'franchise free agency' and the end of massive exploitation of taxpayers," Ross predicted.

Forced to compete, the leagues would rapidly expand into open markets to keep these markets from falling into competitors' hands. Conversely, Ross testified, the leagues would be reluctant to abandon markets that have performed well, such as Cleveland and Baltimore. The leagues might even try harder to resolve problems by contributing money for stadiums or disciplining owners clearly not performing in the best interest of the game.

Not surprisingly, the NFL took the opposite tack. Tagliabue pushed instead for an expansion of the league's limited antitrust immunity. If Congress were to pass a law shielding the NFL from antitrust lawsuits over franchise relocations, he said, the league would be far more likely to prevent relocations.

"A review of the NFL's operations over the past forty years demonstrates the league's firm commitment to competitive and geographic balance in the location of its franchises, to franchise stability, and to the protection of fan and community interests," Tagliabue testified.

But Ross and others pointed out that arming the league with additional legal weaponry would do little to strengthen the cities. The league itself would just threaten to desert cities, the way its teams once did. After all, the Chicago White Sox won funding for their new stadium by signing a deal with St. Petersburg, Fla., that called for the team to move if Illinois didn't meet his demands. More recently, baseball's executive committee gave the Twins permission to explore a move. And baseball has an antitrust exemption.

If it really wanted to reduce the number of relocations, the NFL could include in its team revenue-sharing pot all the money generated by stadiums. Such a move would reduce the "edge" team owners gain from moving to a new stadium, Ross testified.

Gary Roberts, a professor at Tulane Law School who worked with Tagliabue on the Raiders case, suggested a middle ground: give the league the antitrust immunity it wants, but only for relocation decisions. Congress then could regulate the NFL as it does other monopolies — by creating a sports regulatory commission that would issue rules governing team behavior.

Baade gave the Senate subcommittee another solution: prohibit the use of state or local government funds to attract a franchise from another city. And he suggested that Congress pass legislation to encourage local ownership of teams, similar in structure to the Green Bay Packers. The Packers, the prototypical beneficiary of the NFL's revenue sharing and salary cap, ran away with the Super Bowl in January 1997.

One of the more endearing oddities in sports, the Packers play in the smallest city in the NFL: Green Bay's population numbers only 96,000. But, even more unusual, the Packers are a nonprofit, stock-issuing corporation, not a for-profit business. Their unique financial status was established in 1923 as the team teetered on the brink of insolvency.

Today, 1,915 people, mostly Green Bay-area residents, hold 4,464 shares of the Packers' stock. The shares pay no dividends and cannot be sold except with the permission of the board of directors, which prohibits prices higher than face value. No one stockholder can accumulate more than 200 shares, so a Wall Street-style hostile takeover is impossible.

So, too, is a move to another city. The Packers' corporate charter specifies that the team plays in Green Bay and "shall be a community project intended to promote community welfare and that its purposes shall be exclusively charitable." Putting on football games, the charter says, is "incidental to its purpose."

The team donates to charity all profits that it doesn't retain. If the team ever dissolves, the proceeds — which would top $200 million — would have to be used by the local American Legion post to build a hospital, clubhouse, or other edifice dedicated to fallen soldiers.

No sports team is more closely associated with its city than the Green Bay Packers. Mothers giving birth at area hospitals have the choice of taking their babies home in knit caps colored blue, pink, or Packer green and yellow. Most opt for the green and yellow. Each football season, children pedal their bicycles to the team's practice complex hoping that a player will borrow their two-wheelers for the short ride across the street to Vince Lombardi's Lambeau Field. Sighting a star Packer pedaling a comically undersized bicycle, with a youngster jogging alongside lugging a helmet, is a rite of fall in Green Bay.

Packers' games have been sold out since Dwight D. Eisenhower was president.

Because of its public ownership, the team voluntarily reports its finances each year at an annual stockholders' meeting that is as much pep rally and community reunion as business. No other NFL teams open their books, not without a court order.

In 1995, the Packers posted a profit of $5.4 million on revenues of $70.29 million. The team hasn't lost money since the 1983 players' strike. It's nearly debt free and pays for the upkeep of its stadium. It built its own skyboxes.

For many of us, the Packers define football. Open-air stadium, natural grass, the Lombardi tradition, manic fans. A team that belongs to its town. A town that loves its team.

But current NFL rules prevent the creation of another Green Bay. According to the league's constitution, "No corporation, association, partnership or other entity not operated for profit nor any charitable organization or entity not presently a member of the League shall be eligible for membership."

There have been suggestions, like Baade's, that Congress push the NFL to modify the league's prohibition. A community willing to buy a team would be allowed to raise $200 million from investors, but they would have to accept the fact that they could never make any money on their investment. The likelihood is remote that fans would be so inclined. But even if they were, it's even more unlikely that NFL team owners, given how much money they're now making, would tamper, on their own, with rules that now keep other Green Bays from happening.

With the chance for real reform so remote, fans may just have to make their own calculations about whether to continue supporting professional sports. There are alternatives, after all. We can take up the local minor-league team or college squad. There are two new women's basketball leagues as of this writing. The growth in cable programming has spawned a number of new upstart sports, many in the same vulnerable position as the NFL was when some of us first began rooting for it.

Probably the most enduring legacy of the Browns' move is the disillusionment of the fans. Our final loss of innocence. Old-guard team owners like Art Modell were supposed to be the conscience of sports, the last line of defense. The 70,000 fans who painted their faces and rocked Cleveland's crumbling Municipal Stadium for decades of Sunday afternoons were supposed to be proof that a team could still thrive on hometown pride. In recent years, the Browns had been playoff contenders. They were thriving.

But as beloved as they were, the Browns and their owner weren't immune to the times. When the team moved, the precious bond between sports teams and fans was already fraying. We live in an age of $40 million baseball players and $100 million NBA rookies. An age of season-ticket holders being bumped to make way for skyboxes and of corporate salesmen looking for a climate-controlled alternative to the golf course. Of quarterbacks too busy to sign a kid's football, baseball infielders spitting at umpires, and pro basketball players slugging cameramen. Of strikes, lockouts, and lawsuits.

After the Browns' move, even "Big Dawg" Thompson, Cleveland's biggest fan, cashed in. He sold limited-edition prints of himself in his copyrighted No. 98 jersey.

The NFL's brief desertion of Cleveland clearly didn't create the public cynicism that now infects professional football. But it did underscore two simple and irrefutable truths. NFL teams mean a great deal to many fans in many cities, but those emotional connections mean far too little to some team owners. In the new age of stadium economics, the Cleveland Browns' transformation into the Baltimore Ravens reminds us all of today's commercial reality: The priceless glory of NFL football remains very much for sale to the highest bidder.

John "Big Dawg" Thompson walks slowly out of the stadium where the Browns played for almost five decades.

APPENDIX

On sources: This book is the result of hundreds of interviews conducted in Baltimore, Cleveland, New York, Chicago, Cincinnati, Tampa, St. Louis, Atlanta, Dallas, and other cities over a period of six years while I was covering NFL expansion and relocation for *The Sun* and while researching this book. Unless otherwise noted, each quote or fact attributed to a source is the result of an interview conducted by me. Where sources requested anonymity, I corroborated the material with others familiar with the facts, whenever possible. Among the key players who declined to be interviewed for the book were Alfred Lerner and Paul Tagliabue.

FOOTNOTES

Note: The name of the city where a newspaper or magazine is published appears in a citation only when the publication's name does not make it clear.

PROLOGUE

p. 17: ...underachieving likes of Bernie Kosar and Vinny Testaverde.
The "dawg" became associated with the Cleveland Browns during the 1984 NFL season when Browns cornerback Hanford Dixon fired up his teammates by barking at them. Browns fans got into the act by tossing dog biscuits onto the playing field. An especially vocal group seated in the end-zone bleachers became known as the "Dawg Pound." For the full history, see page 221.

p.18: ..."a doormat to cut a better deal."
"Browns Bolt," by Timothy Heider, Tom Diemer and Evelyn Theiss.
The Cleveland *Plain Dealer*, Nov. 7, 1995.

CHAPTER ONE, "THE UPSTART LEAGUE"

p. 22: ...its coveted Cleveland Rams franchise.
Like most businesses, sports leagues are not supposed to drive their competitors out of business with the intention of establishing a monopoly. But a controversial Supreme Court ruling years earlier gave Major League Baseball an exemption from the so-called antitrust laws. Congress enacted these laws to break up conglomerates, called "trusts," that had cornered the market on steel making, railroading and other vital industries. The National Football League assumed it had similar protection until 1957, when another court decision limited the antitrust exemption to baseball. See page 27 for more on antitrust law.

p. 23: ...the league's debut would be delayed.
John F. Steadman, *The Baltimore Colts Story* (Baltimore: Press Box Publishers, 1958), pp. 21-22. Hereinafter referred to as *The Colts Story*.

p. 23: ...someone suggested the name was too long.
"Birth of the Big Leagues," a narrative based on interviews with Robert C. "Jake" Embry, a leader in the effort to build Memorial Stadium, conducted by Huntington Williams III, *Baltimore Magazine*, December 1991.

p. 24: ...ran it back 95 yards for a touchdown.
"Baltimore Colts Defeat Brooklyn, 167 in Opening Conference Game,"
by Robert Elmes, *The Sun*, Baltimore, Md., Sept. 8, 1947.

p. 25: "...a great day for me despite miserable weather."
Ibid.

p. 26: ...whose post-game parties were eating into receipts.
"Birth of the Big Leagues," note 3.

p. 26: ...the rival NFL (28,691).
James Quirk and Rodney Fort, *Pay Dirt, the Business of Professional Team Sports* (Princeton, N.J.: Princeton University Press, 1992), p. 344. Hereinafter referred to as *Pay Dirt.*

p. 26: ...developing a following in the city.
The Colts Story, note 2, p. 14.

p. 27: ...the Browns vs. Everyone Else.
Bob Carroll, *When the Grass was Real: the Ten Best Years of Pro Football* (New York: Simon & Schuster, 1993), p. 17.

p. 28: "...the total was deemed satisfactory."
Jesse A. Linthicum column, *The Sun*, Baltimore, Dec. 3, 1950.

p. 28: ...turned Watner down.
The Colts Story, note 2, p. 54.

p. 30: The Sherman Antitrust Act, he decided, did not apply.
Federal Baseball Club of Baltimore, Inc. v. National League of Professional Baseball Clubs et al., 259 U.S. 200 (1922).

p. 31: ...it has so far demurred.
Toolson v. New York Yankees, 346 U.S. 356 (1953).

p.31: ...Radovich v. National Football League.
Radovich v. National Football League, 352 U.S. 445 (1957).

p. 31: ...had to conform to the antitrust laws.
Ibid.

p. 31: ...forced to pay hefty damages.
All money judgments in antitrust cases are tripled, thus making for some hefty damages.

p. 32: "...Home Territory of the Washington Redskins."
The clause remained in the NFL's bylaws until 1978 when it was deleted in house-cleaning prompted by the antitrust scrutiny of the Oakland Raiders case. Also eliminated at the time was a provision requiring all team relocations to be approved by every other team. This requirement was changed to 75-percent approval.

p. 32: "...national and international prominence."
Stadium Committee Report to the Mayor, May 1, 1945.

p. 33: ...recalled in 1991.
"Birth of the Big Leagues," note 3.

p. 34: That deal fell through.
Ibid.

p. 35: ...baseball's cherished antitrust status.
James Edward Miller, *The Baseball Business: Pursuing Pennants & Profits in Baltimore* (Chapel Hill, N.C.: University of North Carolina Press, 1990), p. 35. Hereinafter referred to as *The Baseball Business.*

CHAPTER TWO, "THAT OLD COLT FEVER"

p. 37: ...a competitive spirit.
David Harris, *The League: the Rise and Decline of the NFL* (New York: Bantam Books, 1986), pp. 48-49. Hereinafter referred to as *The League.*

p. 38 ...still working for the Browns — theoretically.
Paul Brown with Jack Clary, *PB: the Paul Brown Story* (New York: Atheneum, 1979), p. 234. Hereinafter referred to as *PB.*

p. 38: ...*The Baltimore News-Post.*
"Ewbank, Donovan and McCormack, common threads in shared history," by Mike Klingaman, *The Sun*, Baltimore, Nov. 10, 1995.

p. 39: ...he flunked the admissions test.
Johnny Unitas and Ed Fitzgerald, *Pro Quarterback: My Own Story*, (New York: Simon & Schuster, 1965), pp. 29-31

p. 40: ...hollering and screaming 'Colts! Colts!'"
"Catching up with Johnny U.," by Kevin Cowherd. *The Sun*, Baltimore, March 23, 1996.

p. 45: ...on the frozen turf.
Vince Bagli and Norman L. Macht, *Sundays at 2:00 with the Baltimore Colts*, (Centreville, Md.: Tidewater Publishing, 1995), p. 16. Hereinafter referred to as *Sundays at 2:00.* Much has been written about the 1958 game, and details have become confused in the retelling. This book collects first-person accounts by famous Colts players, who authoritatively fill in many of the gaps.

p. 45: ...all across the Baltimore area.
Other widely circulated accounts provide a darker version of the game's conclusion, including that Rosenbloom, famous for his highstakes gambling, had a lot riding on the game and needed a touchdown to beat the point spread. See *The League*, note 1, pp. 45-46. Rosenbloom always denied betting on games that involved his team, and Ewbank has maintained that he made the decision not to kick because his kicker was erratic. His account can be found in *Sundays at 2:00*, *ibid*, pp. 43-44. Ewbank acknowledges suspecting that Rosenbloom was gambling in other instances.

p. 45: ...and the Colts' four recoveries were also records.
John Steadman, *The Greatest Football Game Ever Played* (Baltimore: Press Box Publishers, 1988), p.138. Hereinafter referred to as *The Greatest Game.*

p. 46: "...a great Cleveland team."
"The Best Football Game ever Played," by Tex Maule, *Sports Illustrated*, Jan. 5, 1959.

p. 50: ...the post-season.
When the Grass Was Real, pp. 158-59.

p. 50: ...with bruised ribs.
Ibid.

p. 51: ...the ball sailed wide.
"Chandler's admission helps take the sting out of a 31-year-old bad call,"
by John Steadman, *The Sun*, Baltimore, Nov. 3, 1996.

p. 51: ...the Hall of Fame.
Ibid.

p. 52: "...I'll guarantee you."
National Football League Properties Inc., *The Official NFL Encyclopedia of Pro
Football*, (New York and Scarborough, Ontario: American Library, 1982), p. 326.

p. 52: ...27-yard field-goal attempt.
When the Grass Was Real, p. 244.

p. 54: ...a part of Colts lore.
"He watched it all roll away; Cheers: Leonard Burrier," by Kevin Cowherd.
The Sun, Baltimore, July 14, 1996.

p. 54: ...suffering from heart problems.
William Gildea, *When the Colts Belonged to Baltimore*, (New York: Ticknor & Fields,
1994), p. 185. Hereinafter referred to as *When the Colts Belonged*.

p. 54: ...avoid the draft.
"Loudy's relics are up for grabs," by John Steadman. *The Sun*, Baltimore, Dec. 16,
1994.

p. 54: ...course of 30 years.
Florence Loudenslager obituary, *The Sun*, Baltimore, Nov. 22, 1995.

CHAPTER THREE, "THE LEGEND OF PAUL, JIM, AND ART"

p. 57: ...drafting all of the players.
National League Football, *The Official NFL Encyclopedia of Pro Football* (New York:
New American Library Books, 1982), p. 116.

p. 58: ...AAFC moved forward.
Ibid.

p. 58: ...his junior year.
Bill Levy, *Return to Glory: the Story of the Cleveland Browns*, (Cleveland, Ohio: The World Publishing Co., 1965), p. 24. Hereinafter referred to as *Return to Glory*.

p. 58: ...recalled years later.
Ibid., p. 44.

p. 58: ...a notable runner and passer.
Ibid.

p. 59: ...supporting Brown for the job.
Ibid., p. 46.

p. 59: ...in the National Football League.
The Official Encyclopedia of Pro Football, note 1, p. 154. This official NFL history contradicts assertions by the Browns under Modell. The team's history guide then claimed that the origins of the team name were ambiguous. In their view, it might have been a tribute either to Joe Louis, the African-American boxer known as "The Brown Bomber," or to coach Paul Brown. Paul Brown, in his autobiography, says the team was named for him.

p. 59: ...NFL title that year.
James A. Toman, *Cleveland Stadium: Sixty Years of Memories*, (Cleveland, Ohio: Cleveland Landmarks Press, Inc., revised, 1994), p. 17.

p. 59: ...only about 200.
Ibid., p. 20.

p. 59: permission to move to Los Angeles.
Ralph Hickok, *A Who's Who of Sports Champions* (New York: Houghton Mifflin Co., 1995), p. 575.

p. 60: ...the team's already famous coach.
Jack Clary, *Pro Football's Great Moments* (New York: Bonanza Books, 1989, pp. 25-29.)

p. 60: "...a half-mile excursion..."
"Gries family has preferred a quiet role with Browns," by Peter Phipps, *The Akron Beacon Journal*, Akron, Ohio, Jan. 16, 1983.

p. 61: "...a structure like this."
"Bitter End: How Art Modell's On-Again, Off-Again Love Affair with Cleveland Finally Ground to a Halt," by Bonnie DeSimone, the Cleveland *Plain Dealer*, Dec. 24, 1995.

p. 62: ...Graham's helmet.
PB, pp. 232-33. Otto Graham wore the piece of plastic for several games. After the season, Paul Brown asked his friend Jerry Morgan, who worked for Riddell, a sporting goods equipment company, to come up with a special face protector. The coach wanted something that was lightweight, wouldn't fog up or break in harsh weather, and allowed players to spit. The Browns were the first team to use the single-bar protective face device. Later, Riddell came out with the double bar system, which became the standard. Brown received royalties for many years.

p. 63: ...money until the end of the war.
Ibid., p. 124.

p. 66: ...during Bill Veeck's regime.
Return to Glory, note 3, p. 117.

p. 67: ...value to the organization.
Ibid., p. 119.

p. 69: ...take its profits and get out.
"Gries family has preferred a quiet role with Browns," note 12.

p. 69: ...porch of his home.
PB, note 14, p. 285.

p. 69: "...management through the media..."
Ibid., p. 262.

p. 70: ...his ability to heal from injuries was weakened.
Ibid., p. 275.

p. 70: "...why not let him have a little fun?'" Brown wrote.
Ibid.

p. 70: ... "the deep freeze," Brown recalled.
Ibid.

p. 70: "...only one dominant image."
Ibid., p. 262.

p. 70: ...he stood by his account.
"Paul Brown book draws criticism," by The Associated Press, *The Evening Sun*, Baltimore, Oct. 19, 1979.

p. 70: ...give Davis a chance to play before he died.
Ibid.

p. 71: "...without a bit of humor in him."
Notes column, by Cameron Snyder, *The Sun*, Baltimore, Nov. 20, 1979.

p. 71: "...the year he wanted, this was it."
Ibid.

CHAPTER FOUR, "THE MODELL DYNASTY"

p. 73: "...pleasure of being thrashed by Baltimore on Dec. 27."
"How the West Has Won," by Edwin Skrake, *Sports Illustrated*, New York, N.Y., Nov. 23, 1964.

p. 75: ...direction of his intended receiver.
When the Grass Was Real, pp. 125-26.

p. 77: He died at 6 p.m. that evening.
"Salesman Found Dying in Tourist Cabin Here," *The Austin American Statesman*, Austin, Texas, May 19, 1949.

p. 77: ... "toxemia ... probably related to alcoholism."
"The Modell Story," by Peter Phipps, *The Akron Beacon Journal*, Akron, Ohio, Jan. 17, 1983. Art Modell said the publication of this story was the first he had heard about the circumstances of his father's death. He refused to believe the report.

p. 78: ...precisely where he liked to be.
The League, p. 34.

p. 79: ABC kept the show on the air another six years, until 1954.
Ibid., p. 36.

p. 79: ...former Grand Union executive William Brady.
"The Modell Story," note 4.

p. 80: ...New York champagne maker.
Ibid.

p. 80: ...the CBS president backed out...
For more information, see "Chance, and others' money, opened the door to fortune," by Peter Phipps, *The Akron Beacon Journal*, Akron, Ohio, Jan. 17, 1983.

p. 82: ...$2.5 million loan to Modell.
"Gries family has preferred a quiet role with the Browns," note 12.

p. 83: "...Why should we be bothered by the other league?"
"Modell," by Cameron Snyder, *The Sun*, Baltimore, Feb. 18, 1965.

p. 84: ...$370,000 in New York.
Pay Dirt, p. 510.

p. 86: ...high-quality stereo tuned to classical music.
"The Modell Story," note 4.

p. 87: "...only bright spot in town."
"Of Time and Table 14," by Michael Roberts, *Cleveland Magazine*, June 1990.

p. 87: "...There has to be some resentment," Modell said.
"Modell," note 11.

p. 88: Walking to Schramm's car...
David A. Klatell and Norman Marcus, *Sports for Sale* (New York: Oxford University Press, 1988), pp. 141-42.

p. 90: ...keep its ad rates up.
Ibid.

p. 91: ...NFL's TV take to $57.6 million.
Pay Dirt, note 12, at 509.

p. 93: ...was clearly enjoying the ride.
"The building of the Modell dynasty from an electrician's helper to owner of the Cleveland Browns," by a staff writer. *The Akron Beacon Journal,* Akron, Ohio, Nov. 4, 1995.

p. 93: ...Gerald Ford and George Bush all came calling.
"Bitter End," Ch. 4, note 13.

p. 94: ...$500,000 a year beyond what it was taking in in revenue.
Cleveland commissioned the December 1988 lease analysis from Laventhol & Horwath. It was entered into the court record in the city's 1995 breach-of-contract lawsuit against Modell and the Browns.

p. 94: "...a long-term lease," the report concluded.
The League, note 5, p. 41.

p. 95: "...a fight all the way," Gries said.
Ibid., p. 40.

p. 95: ...he noted a "liquidity problem."
Ibid., p. 94.

p. 96: ...a community leader and friend.
"Many in the area will miss the Modells," by Mary Strassmeyer, the Cleveland *Plain Dealer,* Nov. 17, 1995.

p. 96: ...the Human Relations Award.
"Bitter End," note 20.

CHAPTER FIVE, "THE IRSAY WATCH"

p. 99: "...great mayors never travel well."
"Can the Best Mayor Win?," by Richard Ben Cramer, *Esquire,* New York, N.Y., October 1984.

p. 100: "...it degrades a great city."
"Team sneaks off to Indianapolis; Schaefer bitter," by Ken Murray and Jeffrey W. Peters, *The Evening Sun,* Baltimore, March 29, 1984.

p. 101: ...even during football games.
The Baseball Business, Ch. 2, note 17.

p. 102: "...anything that is big, new and progressive," he told reporters.
"Mayor, Hopkins Like New Stadium Idea," by Peter Marudas, *The Sun*, Baltimore,
Aug. 30, 1965.

p. 102: "...No matter what, we're wrong."
"The Morning After," by Bob Maisel, *The Sun*, Baltimore, Nov. 5, 1971.

p. 103: ...two franchises owned by such close relatives.
The League, Ch. 3, note 1, at 50-51.

p. 103: "...I ended up owning 100 percent," Irsay recalled years later.
"Bob Irsay. Fortunately for Indianapolis, neither the Colts owner nor his team has
lived up to its advance billing from Baltimore," by John Bansch, *The Indianapolis
Star*, May 7, 1989.

p. 103: ...Irsay figured he had paid $13 million.
Ibid.

p. 104: "...things are going so well."
"Robert Irsay: New Colt Owner," by Jim Walker, *The Sun*, Baltimore, Sept. 17, 1972.
Walker's first impression of the new team owner: "He has a firm handshake and
you soon gather, from talking to his friends and associates, that his word is bond.
He's honest, they say. For a millionaire, they say, he's a helluva guy."

p. 104: "...great sports town where there have been sellouts. Why move?"
"Colts traded; new head vows to stay in city," by Cameron C. Snyder, *The Sun*,
Baltimore, July 14, 1972.

p. 105: ...surprised his GM, Thomas, by naming *him* coach.
"Irsay's 12 years with the Colts: Untold Misery for Fans," by Ken Murray,
The Evening Sun, Baltimore, March 2, 1984.

p. 105: ...called in plays to Mike McCormack, his sixth head coach.
Ibid.

p. 105: ...Colts head coach Frank Kush.
Ibid.

p. 106: ...a total profit of $4 million that year.
Financial data submitted by NFL to the United States District Court in
Minneapolis, in Freeman McNeil et al v. The National Football League (case filed
April 1990). The trial was held in 1992.

p. 106: ...native Baltimorean Frank Deford in *Sports Illustrated* in April 1984.
"The Colts were ours ... they were one with the city," by Frank Deford, *Sports
Illustrated*, April 7, 1984.

p. 107: "...He was a bad boy."
"Truthfully Speaking ..." by E.M. Swift, *Sports Illustrated*, New York, N.Y., Dec. 15, 1986. Reprinted by permission, *The Evening Sun*, Baltimore, Dec. 15, 1986.

p. 108: "...he's a real sweetheart, all right."
Ibid.

p. 108: ...he never served overseas.
"Just who is this guy Irsay?" by Michael Wentzel, *The Evening Sun*, Baltimore, Feb. 16, 1984.

p. 109: "...the stadium has served a satisfactory economic life," the report said.
Report of the Ad Hoc Committee of Governor Marvin Mandel and Mayor William Donald Schaefer, March 15, 1972. Prepared by consulting firm Larry Smith & Co.

p. 109: "...related facilities in the greater Baltimore region."
The Baseball Business, note 3, at 204.

p. 109: ...rebuked the fledgling Authority for "not doing a thing."
"Stadium plans proceed," by Ken Nigro, *The Sun*, Baltimore, June 28, 1972.

p. 111: ...55,000 for baseball and 20,000 as an arena.
"Sports Complex Advisory Unit Favors Domed City Stadium," by Nick Yengich, *The Evening Sun*, Baltimore, July 3, 1972.

p. 111: ...season-opening series in Detroit.
Peter Richmond, *Ballpark: Camden Yards and the Building of an American Dream* (New York: Simon & Schuster, 1993), p. 24. Hereinafter referred to as *Ballpark*.

p. 112: ...he told reporters at a 1972 press conference.
"Mayor Wants Camden Site," by Nick Yengich, *The Evening Sun*, Baltimore, Aug. 4, 1972.

p. 112: "...city's firm commitment to proceed with these plans."
"Baltodome would aid 2 teams, city's image," by Jack Chevalier, *The Evening Sun*, Baltimore, Aug. 15, 1972.

p. 112: "...Memorial Stadium except on a short-term basis," the report said.
Report to the Governor of the State of Maryland and Mayor of the City of Baltimore, by the Maryland Sports Complex Authority, May 30, 1973.

p. 112: "...other needs that have to be met."
"Mandel move stalls plan for a new stadium," by James D. Dilts, *The Sun*, Baltimore, Feb. 28, 1974.

p. 113: "...they don't want a club."
"Complex delay disappoints Hoffberger," by Ken Nigro, *The Sun*, Baltimore, March 2, 1974.

p. 113: "...for conventions and other things besides football."
"Colts still optimistic about new stadium complex," by a staff correspondent,
The Sun, Baltimore, March 1, 1974.

p. 113: "...the team will stay in Baltimore."
Ibid.

p. 113: ...measure passed 56 percent to 44 percent.
"Voters bar use of funds for new stadium," by Richard Ben Cramer, *The Sun*,
Baltimore, Nov. 6, 1974.

p. 114: "...We can move if we want to."
"12 Years of Irsay Denials," by Eric Siegel, *The Sun*, Baltimore, March 30, 1984.

p. 114: "...problems will ever be solvable at that location," Williams suggested.
"Stadium would be smaller, less costly than in '72 plan," by John Schidlovsky,
The Sun, Baltimore, Aug. 31, 1980.

p. 115: ...had once considered it for an expansion franchise.
The League, note 6, at 308.

p. 115: ...didn't have standing to bring a suit.
Los Angeles Memorial Coliseum Commission v. NFL, 727 F.2nd 1381 (9th Circuit, 1984).

p. 116: ...earned profits of $2 million in 1978 and $1.5 million in 1979.
Testimony of NFL Commissioner Pete Rozelle before Senate Judiciary Committee
on Aug. 9, 1982. Portions of the transcript are reprinted in Robert C. Berry and
Glenn M. Wong, *The Law and Business of the Sports Industry* (Dover, Mass.: Auburn
House Publishing Co., 1986), p. 26. Hereinafter referred to as *The Law and Business*.

p. 116: ...a Senate committee a few years later.
Ibid., pp. 27-28.

p. 116: ..."an increase in its profit potential," Rozelle said later.
Ibid., p. 26.

p. 117: "...I'm sorry. I feel that very deeply."
Deposition of Art Modell, Sept. 24, 1980, in litigation involving the Los Angeles
Memorial Coliseum Commission, the Raiders, and the NFL. This was included in
the material collected and distributed by Cleveland during its public relations war
against the Browns in 1995.

p. 118: ...owners later rejected the proposal.
Written testimony by Los Angeles City Councilman David Cunningham before
Senate Judiciary Committee, 1982. From *The Law and Business*, note 36, pp. 34-35.

p. 118: Modell denied the reports and the deal never materialized.
The League, note 6, at 511. Also: "NFL gathers for key meetings," by Gerald
Eskenazi, New York Times, March 22, 1982.

p. 118: ...L.A. Coliseum Commission $14.58 million in damages.
See Ch. 2, note 12.

p. 118: ...tickets, concessions, parking, and advertising.
Charles C. Euchner, *Playing the Field: Why Sports Teams Move and Cities Fight to Keep Them* (Baltimore: Johns Hopkins University Press, 1993), p. 87. Hereinafter referred to as *Playing the Field*.

p. 118: Their 1983 player payroll was $16 million.
In McNeil v. The National Football League, the NFL had to turn over 10 years of internal, confidential financial data that detailed the profits and losses of its member clubs. The Raiders' payroll comes from these financial statements. In 1983, Al Davis' team showed a loss of $1.2 million, but many teams reported losses related to the player strike.

p. 119: ...acted to promote legitimate business reasons.
NFL financial data submitted in McNeil case. See notes 14 and 43.

p. 120: ...sticking with the cities we've already got.
"12 years of Irsay Denials," note 32.

p. 120: ...for the building of a sports stadium.
"Governor says stadium idea is fine, if ...," by Michael J. Himowitz, *The Sun*, Baltimore, Sept. 5, 1980.

p. 120: "... Nothing has been determined or even planned."
"Talks held on building stadium," by John Schidlovsky, *The Sun*, Baltimore, March 11, 1980.

p. 120: " ...discussed various leases with him."
"Leases discussed" by a *Sun* staff correspondent, *The Sun*, Baltimore, March 12, 1980.

p. 121: ...long-term lease some time in the coming year.
The League, note 6, at 402.

p. 121: ...lease was good only through 1984.
NFL financial data submitted in McNeil v. NFL, see note 44.

p. 121: ..."best built" stadiums in the country.
Ibid.

p. 121: ...renovation package expired, unspent, after an extension.
Playing the Field, note 42, p. 107.

p. 121: "...no possibility for continuation of negotiations."
Ibid., p. 106.

p. 122: ...we won't build it," Schaefer said.
"Colts' future worries Mayor," by Ken Murray, *The Evening Sun*, Baltimore, Feb. 22, 1984.

p. 122: ..."about 80 percent there."
"The Seduction of the Colts," by Jeffrey Kluger, *The New York Times*, Dec. 9, 1984.

p. 122: ...I would tell you about it," Irsay said.
"12 years of Irsay denials," note 32.

p. 123: "...maybe it would work both ways," he plaintively suggested.
"Transcript of press conference held by Irsay and Schaefer," *The Sun*, Baltimore, Jan. 21, 1984.

p. 124: ...rent it to the team for $1 a year.
"Md.'s offer to Irsay revealed as most lucrative," by Eileen Canzian, *The Sun*, Baltimore, April 1, 1984.

p. 124: ...pre-season game there in 1985 to show it off.
"Colts 'play by play' told," by Patrick J. Traub, *The Indianapolis Star*, April 1, 1984.

p. 125: ..."Senate OKs eminent domain."
"Senate OKs eminent domain," by Karen Hosler, *The Sun*, Baltimore, March 28, 1984.

p. 125: ...was enough to spook Irsay.
Schaefer maintains that the bill not only had been in the works for a long time, but that Irsay was kept informed of it all along. In any case, Irsay seemed as good as gone by then. He had lined up moving vans a few weeks earlier when talks with Phoenix appeared close to a settlement. He did the same in Indianapolis, contracting with the Carmel, Ind. based Mayflower company. That's why the trucks could move so quickly.

p. 125: ..."Implement. We're moving to Indianapolis."
"The Seduction of the Colts," note 55.

p. 126: ...$12.5 million loan at below-market rates.
"Colts' deal sweet for both sides," by Eric B. Schoch, *The Indianapolis Star*, April 1, 1984.

p. 126: ...netting the city a profit of $1.4 million.
"Indianapolis OKs 20-year Colt Lease," by Russ Robinson, *The Sun*, Baltimore, April 1, 1984.

p. 126: ...the highest in the NFL that year.
NFL financial data submitted in *McNeil v. The NFL*, note 44.

p. 126: ...long arm of Maryland law.
"Colts 'play by play' told," note 59.

p. 127: "...so low class that it was ridiculous."
"Oldtimers call 'sneaky' move typical," by Cameron Snyder, *The Sun*, Baltimore, March 29, 1984.

p. 127: "...here's something wrong with that."
"Irsay's 'friend,' the mayor, is still on hold," by Richard Berke, *The Evening Sun*, Baltimore, March 30, 1984.

p. 127: "...best franchise in football into the ground."
"Oldtimers call 'sneaky' move typical," note 67.

p. 127: "...professional football teams, baseball teams, beware."
"City Judge Bars Colts Transfer," by J.S. Bainbridge Jr. and Sandy Banisky, *The Sun*, Baltimore, March 31, 1984.

p.128: "...What concerns me is where the league is going," Modell said.
"NFL looks to high court, Congress for help," by Vito Stellino, *The Sun*, Baltimore, March 29, 1984.

CHAPTER SIX, "MODELL FLUNKS STADIUM ECONOMICS"

p. 131: ...acknowledging a marijuana and cocaine problem in 1982 and checking into a rehab center in La Jolla, Calif.
"Still a Fan of Art Modell; Pat Modell Insists her Husband Shouldn't be Hated in Cleveland," by Mary Strassmeyer, the Cleveland *Plain Dealer*, Dec. 24, 1995.

p. 132: He then talked with Oakland officials about returning.
Playing the Field, Ch. 6, note 42, pp. 100-101.

p. 134: "...to discuss the procedures to be followed in determining the wishes of the players, regarding a representative for the purpose of collective bargaining."
"NFL players, owners to meet," by The Associated Press, *The Sun*, Baltimore, Jan. 16, 1968.

p. 135: "...If it is, it's the end of the game as we have come to know it."
"Modell claims NFLPA wants 'control of game,'" by The Associated Press, *The Sun*, Baltimore, Oct. 4, 1982.

p. 136: The teams' actual combined profits, after taxes and interest on debt, came to $170 million, the union said.
"McNeil trial opens with battle of words," by Mike Freeman, *The Washington Post*, June 17, 1992.

p. 136: This was on top of any team profit the owner wanted to claim.
Ibid.

p. 139: The debt service was now 100 percent of the stadium's cash flow, despite the additional income from the skyboxes he had installed.
Testimony by Art Modell in an unrelated lawsuit; quoted in "The Modell Story," Ch. 5, note 4.

p. 139: ...hand over the lease for $1 to anyone willing to take over his debt.
Ibid.

p. 139: The low-key Gries, ... filed a series of blockbuster lawsuits in 1982.
"Gries no longer a low-profile money man," by John F. Hagan and W.C. Miller, the Cleveland *Plain Dealer*, Sept. 5, 1983.

p. 141: ...Indians claimed that Modell was effectively barring them from the only stadium in town, and thus violating antitrust laws.
Ibid.

p. 141: He got his start in business in Baltimore ... where he impressed co-workers as smart and hard-working.
"Fast Lerner," by Patrick J. Kiger, *Baltimore Magazine*, October 1990.

p. 141: He also told friends he would be a millionaire by the time he was 35.
Ibid.

p. 142: It ended up paying ... more than $30 million just to go away.
"Your average billionaire: Alfred Lerner," by Jay Greene, the Cleveland *Plain Dealer*, July 18, 1993.

p. 142: More than 1,000 employees were expected to lose their jobs in the merger as MNC set out to cut $100 million in expenses.
"Fast Lerner," note 11.

p. 143: "He should do a great job for MNC and its shareholders."
"Brilliant Lerner remains little known to analysts," by Timothy J. Mullaney, *The Sun*, Baltimore, Sept. 25, 1990.

p.143: Lerner himself bought 6.6 million shares of the new venture and cut a deal to save $8.4 million in underwriting fees.
"Al Lerner's Big Deal: greatness or greed?" by David Conn, *The Sun*, Baltimore, June 6, 1993.

p.143: "It's really outright greed," said ... John Hershey Jr. of Ferris, Baker Watts.
Ibid.

p.144: "...I'm keeping the Browns, and they are staying in Cleveland."
"Browns to Stay Put," by The Associated Press, *The Evening Sun*, Baltimore, Aug. 8, 1985.

p.144: ...Modell would be the managing partner.
"Modell denies that Ford is in ...," by Chuck Heaton, the Cleveland *Plain Dealer*, Oct. 13, 1984.

p.144: "...Modell says no to our stadium."
The letter is in William Donald Schaefer's City Hall files, now stored in Baltimore's official archives. Mr. Schaefer granted the author access.

p. 146: Modell talking about selling the Browns and moving an expansion team into a new stadium with the Orioles.
In his book, *Ballpark*, Ch. 6, note 23, p. 65, Peter Richmond offers this account: "It was Schaefer's idea: the state would donate the land, private capital would be raised, and Art Modell, a friend of Williams, would buy an NFL team, put it in Cleveland, and bring the Browns in."

CHAPTER SEVEN, "BALTIMORE STRIKES BACK"

p. 148: ... so I'm approaching the entire issue with an open mind," he told reporters after being appointed to this critical, but unpaid, post.
"Hughes appoints Belgrad, four others to stadium panel," *The Sun*, Baltimore, Sept. 7, 1986.

p. 148: Schaefer himself was politically close to Mandel and Mandel's closest political allies.
Mandel, a Democrat, was convicted in 1977 of accepting bribes from friends who owned a race track and sought his influence with state regulators. While serving as vice president under President Richard Nixon, Agnew pleaded no contest to charges that he took bribes from contractors doing state work when he was governor of Maryland.

p. 151: ...complained Schaefer, who pointedly refused to commit himself to listening to the Authority's advice.
"Schaefer Criticizes Governor," by John W. Frece, *The Sun*, Baltimore, Sept. 8, 1986.

p. 151: Building another football stadium would add only another $16 million to that price tag, or $201.1 million altogether.
The state Department of Fiscal Services reported cost estimates of $134.1 million for a baseball-only stadium, $201.1 million for two stadiums, and $185.2 million for a multipurpose stadium. Fixing up Memorial Stadium for baseball only would cost $56.1 million; for football only, $70.7 million; and for both, $75.3 million, according to the consultants.

p. 152: "We're all taxpayers on this authority."
"Two stadiums urged for Camden Yards," by Sandy Banisky, *The Sun*, Baltimore, Dec. 5, 1986.

p. 154: Wouldn't it be cheaper for the state simply to buy 15,000 season tickets to ensure the Orioles' success? he asked.
Ballpark, Ch. 6, note 23, p. 96.

p. 155: "... cities are forced to succumb to blackmail by pro football and baseball."
Ibid., p. 97.

p. 155: Schaefer called it "one of the most important days in the history of sports in Maryland."
"Legislature gives final OK to 2 stadiums," by Sandy Banisky, *The Sun*, Baltimore, April 4, 1987.

p. 156: ...William B. Marker, head of the Marylanders for Sports Sanity.
"Stadiums safe at home," by Thomas W. Waldron, *The Sun*, Baltimore, Sept. 8, 1987.

p. 157: ... the Saints were sold to investors who kept them in New Orleans.
"Local group nearly made offer for Saints football club," by Vito Stellino, *The Sun*, Baltimore, Feb. 3, 1985.

p. 158: "We don't want an NFL team so badly we'll raid another city for it.
"Belgrad won't undercut a St. Louis bid," by Ken Murray, *The Evening Sun*, Baltimore. Dec. 14, 1987.

p. 158: "... We're ready to vigorously seek an expansion franchise."
"Cardinals head to Phoenix," by Ken Murray, *The Evening Sun*, Baltimore, Jan. 15, 1988.

CHAPTER EIGHT, "NFL EXPANSION FRENZY"

p. 160: ...Tagliabue, a Rhodes Scholar finalist and former editor of New York University's *Law Review*.
"The Face of Sweeping Change," by Rick Telander, *Sports Illustrated*, New York, N.Y., Sept. 10, 1990.

p. 161: Modell suggested they take Finks, then 62, and then have Tagliabue take over a few years later.
"League-builder Modell never the maverick type," by Vito Stellino, *The Sun*, Baltimore, Nov. 10, 1996.

p. 161: "...The truth of the matter is Paul Tagliabue is as much old guard as anybody."
Column by Don Pierson. The *Chicago Tribune*, Oct. 27, 1989.

p. 161: (... NFL Players Association had decertified itself and was pursuing antitrust litigation against the league.)
"Tagliabue plans expansion before mid-90s," by Vito Stellino, *The Sun*, Baltimore, Jan. 27, 1990.

p. 161: "This will fit our timetable very well," said Belgrad.
"NFL to pursue expansion in '93 by 2 teams," by Vito Stellino, *The Sun*, Baltimore, July 27, 1990.

p. 162: ... To put one team in virgin NFL territory and one team in a city that had lost a team.
"Rozelle wants one old, one new city," by Vito Stellino, *The Sun*, Baltimore, Aug. 13, 1990.

p. 162: ... according to an NFL spokesman, was the early "working assumption" of the expansion committee.
"Tagliabue hints old city favored for team," by Vito Stellino, *The Sun*, Baltimore, June 14, 1991.

p. 162: ... fees could be assessed to ease the short-term loss of shared revenue.
"Expansion end zone now in sight," by Ken Murray, *The Evening Sun*, Baltimore, May 23, 1991.

p. 162: ...Washington had a long history of opposing expansion.
"NFL approves two-team expansion," by Vito Stellino, *The Sun*, Baltimore, May 23, 1991.

p. 163: ... an arena he built for $16.5 million after the commission overseeing the public arena refused him year-round exclusive use.
"Cooke: Man of Accomplishment," by Ken Murray, *The Sun*, Baltimore, Dec. 12, 1993.

p.163: In 1979, he sold the two teams, the Forum, and some Nevada real estate for $67.5 million and headed East.
Pay Dirt, Ch. 2, note 7, at 454.

p. 163: But the two later patched things up.
"Redskins owner boots marriage," by The Associated Press, *The Sun*, Baltimore, Feb. 8, 1994.

p. 164: ... Victor Kiam alleged in a lawsuit years later that a Redskins representative told him in 1991 that the team would never permit another franchise to relocate to Baltimore.
FWM Corporation v. VKK Corporation and VKK Patriots, Inc, Court of Chancery of Delaware, 1992 WL 87327 (Del. Ch.)

p. 164: Obligingly, he cut off contact with the Patriots, and the talks ceased.
Kiam alleged that the NFL illegally prevented him from considering a move of his team to Baltimore and other cities.

p. 165: ... cities like Baltimore began lining up their representatives "like pitchmen at a carnival."
"Expansion end zone now in sight," note 8.

p. 166: "I think basically we'll start with a level playing-field concept rather than prejudging whether one will be an old city and one will be a new idea," he told reporters at the Minneapolis meeting.
"Tagliabue hints old city favored for team," note 7.

p. 166: "What more positive sign can you have that the NFL is on the march?" asked Belgrad.
"Expansion end zone now in sight," note 8.

p. 166: "If I had to choose, I'd take Charlotte and St. Louis."
"Modell has always taken risks and doesn't plan to stop," by Thomas George, *The New York Times*, July 21, 1991.

p. 167: "The process is just beginning."
"Contenders undaunted by Modell's 'choice' of Charlotte, St. Louis," by Vito Stellino, *The Sun*, Baltimore, July 28, 1991.

p. 168: …had grown up a Redskins fan in the Maryland suburbs of Washington.
"Guru knows it all — About expansion," by Jim Thomas, *The St. Louis Post-Dispatch*, March 2, 1993.

p. 168: "…we are prepared to do so if it would be of assistance to the expansion committee or if we deem it appropriate to do so in the future."
Baltimore NFL Expansion Application, Sept. 16, 1991.

p. 170: "…He'd be an asset to the league," Modell told the Baltimore *Evening Sun* in 1987.
"City's fight for NFL franchise has heavy hitters," by Ken Murray, *The Evening Sun*, Baltimore, April 8, 1987.

p. 171: Even rival Jacksonville tried to lure him away for its NFL bid in September 1990.
"Jacksonville's expansion draw play goes for no gain as Tisch remains in Baltimore," by Ken Murray, *The Evening Sun*, Baltimore, Oct. 12, 1990.

p. 172: "My view is that St. Louis and Charlotte are taking risks we are not ready to take."
"Expansion end zone now in sight," note 8.

p. 172: "…would you mind if I came to see you and asked you to help coach us in trying to get this franchise?" Richardson asked.
"Pete Rozelle helped Charlotte make NFL," by Charles Chandler, *The Charlotte Observer*, Charlotte, N.C., Oct. 26, 1994.

p. 173: "I think the price reflects that."
"Expansion fee in NFL is set at $170 million," by Jon Morgan, *The Sun*, Baltimore, May 26, 1993.

CHAPTER NINE, "THE SUN BELT SHINES"

p. 184: "One was easy, but the second one, you can tell by what we did, how tough it was," Braman said afterward.
"Baltimore's offer doesn't excite owners," by Vito Stellino, *The Sun*, Baltimore, Oct. 27, 1993.

p. 184: "I think it's one of the great areas of the country."
"NFL expansion drill," *The Florida Times-Union*, Jacksonville, Fla., Oct. 28, 1993.

p. 190: "'… I'll introduce you to the committee,'" Modell told the newspaper.
"Browns at a Crossroads," by Ed Meyer, *The Akron Beacon Journal*, Akron, Ohio, Jan. 2, 1994.

p. 196: "… it doesn't matter, because it's what the commissioner wants," Belgrad told reporters.
"Schaefer says he was conned by NFL process," by Vito Stellino, *The Sun*, Baltimore, Dec. 2, 1993.

CHAPTER TEN, "CLEVELAND AND THE 'JAKE'"

p. 199: ...the LeFevre deal collapsed when bickering among the investors spilled over into court.
Jack Torry, *Endless Summers: The Fall and Rise of the Cleveland Indians* (South Bend, Ind.: Diamond Communications Inc., updated 1996), p. 170. Hereinafter referred to as *Endless Summers.*

p. 200: By insisting that each limited partner turn control of his stock over to him, ...
David Jacobs died in 1992.

p. 201: This $330 million worth of construction changed the face of the city.
Endless Summers, note 1, at 182.

p. 203: A club seat rented for $1,215, not including the required season ticket.
Paul Much and Alan Friedman, *Inside the Ownership of Professional Sports Teams: the complete directory of the ownership and financial structure of pro sports* (Chicago, Ill.: Team Marketing Report 1995), p. 15. Hereinafter referred to as *Inside the Ownership.*

p. 203: The Indians raised their ticket prices 39 percent for the inaugural season.
1994 Major League Baseball Fan Cost Index (Chicago, Ill.: Team Marketing Report). This is an annual compilation of the cost of tickets, selected food, and merchandise at baseball stadiums.

p. 203: ...the Indians were well on their way to becoming one of the richest teams in baseball.
Inside the Ownership, note 4, p. 15. In its 1996 annual review of sports team finances, *Financial World* magazine estimated the Indians' worth to be $125 million.

p. 204: "...the urban backdrop of Camden Yards, and the nooks and crannies of Fenway Park."
"What Others Had to Say," staff and wire reports, the Cleveland *Plain Dealer*, April 5, 1994. Like Camden Yards, the "Jake" became an attraction unto itself. Thousands of fans now pay $5 apiece to tour the park on days when the team isn't playing.

p. 204: Otherwise, the team kept all of the money collected on parking, advertising, concessions, tickets, and luxury suites.
Inside the Ownership, note 4, p. 15.

p. 206: ...but had to pay Modell $50,000 in order to do so or else allow Modell to operate the novelty concessions and negotiate a division of revenues.
The Indians' original lease was among the court documents filed in Cleveland's 1995 breach-of-contract lawsuit against the Browns.

p. 207: "It's the city and baseball team that need a dome," he told reporters.
"Dome loses by 2-1 vote," by Gary Clark, the Cleveland *Plain Dealer*, May 9, 1984.

p. 207: ...warning city leaders that the Indians needed a new home or else.
Endless Summers, note 1, p. 227.

p. 207: "That's the only domed stadium I've seen. I'm still collecting information on it."
"Indians' new owners look to possibility of new domed stadium," by The Associated Press, *The Los Angeles Times*, Dec. 14, 1986.

p. 208: "...realize the value a National Football League franchise is to some communities who don't have one," Modell said at the start of the 1988 football season.
"Modell, city stall on stadium deal," by Patrick Holbrook, *The Columbus Dispatch*, Columbus, Ohio, Sept. 14, 1988.

p. 209: Jacobs said he wouldn't contribute to the financing of the project, an estimated $150 million cost.
"Renovation best value, Modell says," by Ed Meyer, *The Akron Beacon Journal*, Akron, Ohio, Aug. 11, 1989.

p. 209: "If I were the owner of the Cleveland Indians, that's what I would pursue," Modell said.
"Modell unveils plan to renovate stadium," by Terry Pluto, *The Akron Beacon Journal*, Akron, Ohio, Aug. 17, 1989.

p. 210: "I'm suggesting that money should be put to use in Cleveland Stadium."
"Doing the Stadium Shuffle," by Bill Livingston, the Cleveland *Plain Dealer*, Aug. 11, 1989.

p. 210: But, in private conversations with White, Modell was just as adamant as he had been in public.
Nov. 19, 1995, deposition of Mayor Michael White taken in Cleveland by attorneys for the Browns.

p. 210: Mayor White, ... told Gateway's executive director, Tom Chema, that he would support the project only if it provided an economic boost to the city, not just to the sports teams.
Endless Summers, note 1, at 221.

p. 210: ...the team played to better than 90 percent capacity in the 20,000-seat arena.
Inside the Ownership, note 4, at 50.

p. 211: ... it agreed to pay 27.5 percent of the skybox revenue and 48 percent of the club-seat receipts, as well as a per-ticket fee similar to what the Indians paid.
Ibid.

p. 211: "... we may be finding ourselves confronting a subject that we want to avoid," Vincent warned darkly in 1990, on the eve of the stadium-funding vote.
Endless Summers, note 1, at 227.

p. 212: "A deal's a deal," he said. "We'll live with it."
"White, Modell huddle on franchise's future," the Cleveland *Plain Dealer*, Jan. 11, 1994.

p. 213: The smart player opts for a deal that pays the most up front.
For example, a $10 million, five-year contract would be paid half upfront and the rest spread over the term, rather than in five, $2-million increments.

p. 213: ...his actual payroll that year was $62 million, more than $1 million a player, and nearly 50 percent above the league average.
Data provided to reporters in 1996 by the National Football League Players Association.

p. 213: "It's stadium economics," Chicago Bears vice president Ted Phillips complained in 1995.
"Down ... And Out," by Peter King, *Sports Illustrated*, New York, N.Y., Nov. 13, 1995.

p. 214: ...In 1991, baseball owners' shared income from broadcast fees and sales of licensed goods totaled only 26 percent of total revenues.
Report of the Major League Baseball Economic Study Committee, December 1992.

p. 214: Some of the more affluent clubs spent more on payroll than other, less well-off teams were taking in.
Ibid.

p. 214: This meant there were no small-market NFL teams, ... clamoring for an overhaul of the sport's economics and a dramatic ... change in the relationship with players
"The Changing Structure of Professional Sports: Economic Trends, Opportunities and Future Strategies," report by Paul Much and Gregory Smith, Houlihan Lokey Howard & Zukin, Chicago, Illinois, Sept. 17, 1992.

p. 214: Some teams with lavish stadium deals prospered, and those without them faltered, creating a baseball-like world of "haves and have nots."
The leading proponent of this theory is Paul Much, senior managing director of Houlihan Lokey Howard & Zukin and an acknowledged expert in this field. See *ibid.*

p. 215: ...when Gund Arena and Jacobs Field opened and their 225 skyboxes were immediately sold out.
From material prepared by the Browns for their defense in the 1995 Cleveland lawsuit.

p. 215: "... The carbonated condition of the concrete, which allows reinforcing steel to corrode, is comparable to a creeping cancer," they concluded.
"Limited Structural Corrosion Conditions Survey for Cleveland Stadium," by Webster Engineering Associates Inc., Cleveland, Ohio, Nov. 22, 1993.

p. 216: "I know what that does to the set of discussions that I've got to have with Art Modell."
"Several cities trying to lure away the Browns, White says," by Steve Luttner, the Cleveland *Plain Dealer*, Dec. 31, 1993.

CHAPTER 11, "A STADIUM HANGOVER"

p. 218: ...calling it "a sports palace for the Republican privileged."
"Council Slaps at Voinovich, delays budget," by Stephanie Saul, the Cleveland
Plain Dealer, April 5, 1984.

p. 219: ...the team would eventually agree to contribute to stadium costs.
Mayor Michael White deposition, Cleveland, Ohio, Nov. 19, 1995.

p. 220: White told Modell that he had appointed an attorney, ... to lead the talks,
and that the city was "ready to go."
Ibid.

p.220: "If they can't give us fair treatment, ... then that's something we have to
take into consideration."
"What Art Modell Wants to keep the Browns here," the Cleveland *Plain Dealer*,
Feb. 13, 1994.

p. 226: One popular message read: "Jump, Art."
"Modell has always taken risks and doesn't plan to stop now," by Thomas George,
The New York Times, July 21, 1991.

p. 226: "... I'd rather have the hostility than apathy," Modell said after the
season was over.
Ibid.

p. 226: "...I will get out of football and Cleveland."
"Bitter End," Ch. 4, note 13.

p. 227: ... they were one of only 10 teams that in 1994 had failed to ever make the
Super Bowl.
The San Diego Chargers played in Super Bowl XXIX on Jan. 29, 1995.

p. 227: "Right there, we'd have anybody who urinates voting for us in the next
poll," Modell quipped.
"Browns Don't Rate in Value Ranking," by Bud Shaw, the Cleveland *Plain Dealer*,
Sept. 24, 1994.

p. 228: Browns officials began to worry that the mayor was merely buying time
while figuring out what to do.
Art Modell deposition, taken in Cleveland Nov. 18, 1995 by attorneys for the city
as part of its breach-of-contract lawsuit against the Browns.

p. 228: ...he had counted on Cuyahoga County to pay for much of the work, as it
had with Gateway.
"City Presumed County Role in Stadium Remake," by Stephen Koff and Timothy
Heider, the Cleveland *Plain Dealer*, Nov. 22, 1995.

p. 228: "...we didn't have $130 million we could just get out of the bank and fix
the stadium," White recalled later.
White deposition, note 2.

p. 228: ...the Cavs could stick Gateway with a $10 million penalty, payable to the team, if the arena was not ready in time for the 1994 season.
"How Gateway went awry," by Joel Rutchick, Timothy Heider and Stephen Koff, the Cleveland *Plain Dealer*, July 9, 1995.

p. 229: And its elected treasurer, Francis E. Gaul, was convicted of dereliction of duty and sentenced to 90 days in jail.
"Gaul sentenced to 90 days in jail," by James Ewinger, the Cleveland *Plain Dealer*, Jan. 20, 1996. Gaul's conviction was overturned, and he was acquitted on appeal in 1997.

p. 229: "Maybe the mayor has a rabbit he can pull out of his hat."
"Stadium facelift put at $130 million," by Benjamin Marrison, the Cleveland *Plain Dealer*, Aug. 19, 1994.

p. 229: "I don't think the taxpayers in Cleveland want to subsidize the Browns like that," he added.
Ibid.

p. 229: "We're not there yet."
"White pushes $285 million lakefront plan," by Stephen Phillips, the Cleveland *Plain Dealer*, Sept. 28, 1994.

p. 229: "The theme song for this ought to be the *William Tell Overture* because the mayor is certainly the Lone Ranger."
"Lakefront projects sneak up on council," by Evelyn Theis, Stephen Koff and Stephen Phillips, the Cleveland *Plain Dealer*, Sept. 29, 1994.

p. 229: He invited the region's top business leaders to a meeting to hear Modell make his case directly.
White deposition, note 2.

p. 230: ...he never threatened to leave town or suggested that he was experiencing any financial duress.
Ibid.

p. 230: He called Municipal Stadium "an old, decrepit stadium that other teams don't want to play in" and said its owner — the city — does "bear a responsibility."
"Browns could leave Cleveland. If the stadium isn't refurbished by 1999, team will move, Modell said," by Arnie Rosenberg, *The Akron Beacon Journal*, Akron, Ohio, Dec. 10, 1994.

p. 230: "I don't want to wake up with a Baltimore hangover," he said.
"Mayor says stadium is a priority; plea to taxpayers: Browns could move," by Bonnie DeSimone, the Cleveland *Plain Dealer*, Dec. 10, 1994.

p. 231: "...The Governor believes there has to be local public and private financial support before the state should be asked to participate."
"Ohio Governor not committing to Stadium," by Tribune Staff, wire services, *The Tampa Tribune*, Tampa, Fla. Dec. 19, 1994.

p. 231: Then the Browns and the state would have to split the cost
"There's no money for stadium, Hagan says," by Steve Luttner, the Cleveland *Plain Dealer*, Dec. 15, 1994.

CHAPTER 12, "MODELL DROPS THE BOMB"

p. 236: The report raised the specter of Gateway-like overruns and strongly prompted public officials to come to agreement with the Browns "in the very near future."
"Cleveland Stadium Task Force Report," May, 1995. David Hoag, task force chairman.

p. 237: "It's simple. We don't have the money," Hagan said.
"Funding would come from a range of sources," by Stephen Phillips, the Cleveland *Plain Dealer*, May 4, 1995.

p. 238: "...opposition which surfaced even before the task force recommendations were finalized."
"$154 million renovation proposed by task force," by Timothy Heider, the Cleveland *Plain Dealer*, May 4, 1995.

p. 238: The mayor had no immediate public reaction to the report, but the next day convened a press conference and dropped a bomb.
"Parking tax would go on ballot, White says," by Robert J. Vickers and Stephen Koff, the Cleveland *Plain Dealer*, May 5, 1995.

p. 238:...he thought that it would be politically safer to start with a higher cost estimate and have the project come in below-cost, rather than the other way around, as had happened at Gateway.
White deposition, Ch. 12, note 2.

p. 239: "My belief was we had to try to reach some point of consensus so that we would be able to get this issue resolved," he recalled later.
Ibid.

p. 239: He said he didn't want to bargain for a lease until the mechanism was in place to pay for the stadium work.
Ibid.

p. 239: "We've been getting guarantees since 1989 that something's going to be done," David Hopcraft, a governmental affairs consultant for Modell, told reporters.
"Stadium renovations, not yet OK'd, already lag," by Stephen Koff and Timothy Heider, the Cleveland *Plain Dealer*, May 14, 1995

p. 240: ...extension of the sin tax would require state legislative approval, something White said he hoped to have by Sept. 1.
"Mayor offers 4th Stadium plan," by Stephen Koff and Evelyn Theiss, the Cleveland *Plain Dealer*, June 2, 1995.

p. 240: "We believe we've come to a point where action is necessary and we must move rapidly."
Ibid.

p. 240: "...Nor are we willing to endure a campaign associated with either an initiative or recall referendum on the November ballot."
June 5, 1995 letter from Art Modell to Mayor White.

p. 241: "... I'm getting ready to jump. What are you doing to me?" he joked.
White deposition, note 5.

p. 241: ...White would continue working behind the scenes; he himself preferred that such maneuvering be done quietly.
Ibid.

p. 241: "... what I didn't tell him was that I was deathly afraid that if we didn't put a package in front of him before the end of the season, we would be out of the ball game."
Ibid.

p. 241: They needed to have something by the end of the season, he explained to them, "or it was all over for us."
Ibid.

p. 242: "...assure that there is a viable home for the Browns in Cleveland wane."
June 6, 1995, letter from White to Modell.

p. 242: ...the City of Cleveland, ... is doing everything within its power to provide the Browns with a competitive economic package ..."
June 21, 1995, letter from White to Tagliabue.

p. 243: ...the owner of the Browns hasn't given us any indication that this isn't an exercise in futility," Hagan said at a commissioners meeting.
"Modell won't guarantee the Browns will stay put; commissioners schedule," by Timothy Heider, the Cleveland *Plain Dealer*, Aug. 30, 1995.

p. 243: "Don't do it in the name of the Browns," he implored.
"Maybe Art is singing a swan song for us," by Mary Anne Sharky, the Cleveland *Plain Dealer*, Aug. 30, 1995.

p. 244: "We all wish Mother Teresa owned the Browns. It'd be an easier sell."
"Commissioners to let voters decide on stadium tax plan," by Timothy Heider, the Cleveland *Plain Dealer*, Sept. 2, 1995.

p. 245: ...and running back Leroy Hoard ($1.5 million).
"Lombardi Defends Contracts," by Tony Grossi, the Cleveland *Plain Dealer*, Nov. 17, 1995.

p. 246: The 91-person administrative staff was considerably larger than the league average.
"Browns woes run deep," by Diane Solov and Ted Wendling, the Cleveland *Plain Dealer*, Jan. 7, 1996.

p. 246: ...Modell claimed that the team suffered a $21 million "cash loss," though he wouldn't specify what the team's actual profit or loss was.
A "cash loss" occurs when cash outlays exceed revenues during a given period. The shortfall is made up by borrowing. It is different from an actual loss, which is incurred when all expenses — including loan payments — exceed revenues. Some of the extra employees, however, could be explained by the fact that the Browns were operating a stadium as well as fielding a team.

p. 247: ...said Roger Noll, a Stanford University economist who reviewed the league's financial statements and testified on behalf of the players' union in the 1992 court case.
"Browns woes run deep," by Diane Solov and Ted Wendling, the Cleveland *Plain Dealer*, Jan. 7, 1996.

p. 248: "Art just kept getting more and more discouraged and finally said, 'We need to start talking to Baltimore.'"
"A Combination of Circumstances," an interview with Alfred Lerner, the Cleveland *Plain Dealer*, Dec. 16, 1995.

p. 248: "And I think it's an issue where we would also be helping ourselves."
"Football; NFL owners debate TV deal," by Thomas George, *The New York Times*, March 17, 1992.

p. 250: "...he wanted, he was being labeled as not being forthcoming, and he felt kind of trapped between those two lines."
"A Combination of Circumstances," note 25.

p. 250: "...Art was yesterday's hero, and Dick Jacobs was today's hero."
"Bitter End," Ch. 4, note 13.

CHAPTER 13, "DARTH VADER"

p. 257: "...the NFL trails other sports leagues in the number of new facilities that have been built or are under construction in recent years."
Jerry Richardson's Stadium Committee Report, meeting of Sept. 7, 1995.

p. 257: He read with interest Art Modell's expressed frustration with the progress of his talks.
Deposition of John Moag Jr. taken Jan. 10, 1996, in Baltimore by attorneys for Cleveland as part of the city's breach-of-contract lawsuit against the Browns. Moag and the State of Maryland were later added as defendants.

p. 258: "...Isn't that the guy who's talking about suing the league?"
Ibid.

p. 258: Among his options, he said, was moving to Baltimore.
"Bengals left with fewer choices," by Geoff Hobson, *The Cincinnati Enquirer,*
May 31, 1995.

p. 259: ...and would probably take just about anything the community offered him to stay.
Moag deposition, *supra,* note 2.

p. 259: "I think you have a very good shot at landing an NFL franchise in your city," he said.
Ibid.

p. 261: There was very little discussion.
Ibid.

p. 262: He could delineate the list of reasons but didn't want to bore his guests, he said.
Ibid.

p. 262: ...he would need either a lease with a franchise or a legally binding resolution from the NFL promising a team, he said.
Ibid.

p. 262: "...we would be very interested in talking to you, and I hope that you will convey that to Mr. Modell," Moag said.
Ibid.

p. 262: But Lerner did urge Baltimore to pursue the resolution with the league.
Ibid.

p. 265: "'...That's it, I got one place to go, it isn't worth it here, here I go,'" Lerner recalled later.
"A Combination of Circumstances," Ch. 13, note 25.

CHAPTER 14, "THE DEAL"

p. 271: "...Memorandum of Agreement among Maryland Stadium Authority and Cleveland Browns Inc. and BSC, LLC."
"BSC, LLC" is an abbreviation for Baltimore Stadium Corp., Limited Liability
Corp., a team-affiliated stadium operating company controlled by Art Modell.
In structure and purpose, it appears similar to the Cleveland Stadium Corp.

p. 272: Once in the new stadium, the team would pay no rent, but reimburse the state for all operational costs, estimated to run about $4 million a year
It's not entirely accurate to call this reimbursement-in-lieu-of-rent scheme a "rent-free" deal. It was devised to skirt federal regulations on tax-exempt bonds. If the
state were to take in "rent" above a certain level, the bonds would lose their tax-exempt status, and the state would pay millions of dollars more in taxes.

p. 273: (…The city of Baltimore also had to kick in $1 million a year.)
These payments, which began with the opening of Oriole Park, were a good-faith gesture necessary to win state funding for the twin stadium complex. The payments were offset by the city's 20 percent take of ticket taxes and a $200,000 payment from the Stadium Authority in lieu of property taxes.

p. 273: Lerner and the younger Modell then broke out victory cigars.
"Dagger of the Deal," by Jim Duffy, Geoff Brown, Shari Sweeney and Jay Miller, a joint project of *Baltimore Magazine* and *Cleveland Magazine*, January 1996.

p. 274: "'…Art and I think you guys should be out of town before then.'"
"The Modell Women," by Petey O'Donnell, *Style Magazine*, Baltimore, July/August 1996.

p. 275: "What does it say of an organization to kick a city in the teeth that has been so supportive?" White asked reporters.
"Leaders work to derail deal," by Timothy Heider, the Cleveland *Plain Dealer*, Nov. 5, 1995.

p. 275: "We're not even going to come close to that," said Frederick Nance, White's chief counsel and the man who would eventually lead the city's various lawsuits against the Browns.
"Cleveland may find Browns' offer hard to beat," by Stephen Koff, the Cleveland *Plain Dealer*, Nov. 5, 1995.

p. 276: The team had a worldwide network of 310 Browns Backers fan clubs registered in 39 states, 9 countries, and 5 continents — stretching from Ohio to Japan to Australia.
Written testimony of Cleveland Mayor Michael White to the Senate Judiciary Committee's Subcommittee on Antitrust, Business Rights and Competition, Nov. 29, 1995.

p. 276: "Ohio is the cradle of football."
"Browns loss stings Voinovich; Governor angered by way Modell handled situation," by Alan Johnson, *The Columbus Dispatch*, Columbus, Ohio, Nov. 7, 1995.

p. 276: "…they had to go and take a team from an existing city."
"Ex-Browns great Groza can hardly talk about the move," by Marla Ridenour, *The Columbus Dispatch*, Columbus, OH, Nov. 9, 1995.

p. 276: "It's a cash deal, no heart involved."
"Revenge lacks sweetness, brings whiff of hypocrisy," by Michael Olesker, *The Sun*, Baltimore, Nov. 7, 1995.

p. 277: "…I believe he would be a great hero in Baltimore, by this simple gesture of good will."
Letter from William Donald Schaefer to Alfred Lerner, Nov. 9, 1995, provided to author by Mr. Schaefer.

p. 277: "...the citizens of Baltimore, who know the pain and embarrassment of losing a team," Schaefer wrote.
Letter from William Donald Schaefer to Paul Tagliabue, Nov. 16, 1995, provided to author by Mr. Schaefer.

p. 277: "... Well, George, you continue to be a great governor and are still my candidate for Vice President."
Letter from William Donald Schaefer to George Voinovich, Nov. 16, 1995, provided to author by Mr. Schaefer.

p. 277: "Modell can remove the scarlet letter, or add to his former city's misery."
"What's in a name? Shame, if it's stolen," by Ken Rosenthal, *The Sun*, Baltimore, Nov. 7, 1995.

p. 278: "Congratulations if you made it through yesterday's announcement ceremony without becoming nauseated."
"The gloating was nothing to cheer about," by John Eisenberg, *The Sun*, Baltimore, Nov. 7, 1995.

p. 278: "...because of his ineptitude as an owner, money is about the only thing that still matters in his wretched cesspool of a life."
"Modell's actions show him to be spineless thief," by Bob Hunter, *The Columbus Dispatch*, Columbus, Ohio, Nov. 7, 1995.

p. 280: An airplane flew overhead, towing a banner that read "MODELL YOU CAN'T HIDE HERE!! WOOF. WOOF."
"Can't Hide Here! Fans chant," by Christine Stapleton, *The Palm Beach Post*, Palm Beach, Fla., Nov. 27, 1995.

p. 280: "Unfortunately, some communities are willing to spend tax dollars to do that, like Baltimore."
"City-hopping NFL teams infuriate GOP governors," by Benjamin Marrison, the Cleveland *Plain Dealer*, Nov. 21, 1995.

p. 281: "It seems to me we've reached the point of absurdity if it means the Cleveland Browns and the Los Angeles Rams are the teams that are moving."
"NFL unlikely to stand in way of Modell on Browns' move," by Tony Grossi, the Cleveland *Plain Dealer*, Nov. 5, 1995.

p. 282: "You wouldn't wear a dog mask to your brother's funeral, would you?" he asked rhetorically.
"Down ... and Out," Ch. 11, note 25.

p. 283: "The shots are coming from all over."
"Browns can't sneak win," by Mary Kay Cabot, the Cleveland *Plain Dealer*, Nov. 20, 1995.

p. 283: Police, anxious to avoid aggravating an already hostile crowd, chose not to interfere.
"Browns, city check damage to stadium; 2,000-3,000 seats damaged or destroyed at season finale," by John F. Hagan, the Cleveland *Plain Dealer*, Dec. 19, 1995.

p. 285: "We have a message for the NFL. You ain't seen nothin' yet," White declared.
"Save Our Browns kicks off two-week campaign," by Michael K. McIntyre, the Cleveland *Plain Dealer*, Jan. 3, 1996.

CHAPTER 15, "THE RAVENS KICK OFF"

p. 294: "I was born a raven but was raised by humans," explained 23-year-old Steve Lehner.
"Zany Ravens Fans Flock to Baltimore's NFL Return," by David Ginsburg, *The Associated Press*, Sept. 1, 1996.

p. 296: In 1996, an *average* NFL player was earning about $750,000, *three times* the top annual salary he earned in uniform.
"Catching up with Johnny U," by Kevin Cowherd, *The Sun*, Baltimore, March 23, 1996.

p. 297: A courier service that he and some other investors operated in Baltimore flourished for a few years but failed in 1984 when an accountant allegedly absconded with $250,000.
"The Decline and Fall of a Champion" by Bill Glauber and Michael Ollove, *The Sun*, Baltimore, March 17, 1991.

p. 297: ...Unitas allowed his name to appear in advertisements for a football gambling sheet called "All Pro Football Report."
Ibid.

p. 297: ...he filed for personal bankruptcy, listing assets of $1.4 million and liabilities of $3.2 million.
Ibid.

p. 297: One read: "In from Cleveland, Luv those Raiders. Art you filthy Stinkin Traitor."
"Art Modell won and Cleveland lost," by Greg Couch, *The Orlando Sentinel*, Orlando, Fla., Sept. 2, 1996.

p. 298: Each table had a white chocolate box filled with candy and adorned with a dark chocolate Ravens football.
"Pat and Art Modell throw a party worth raving about," by Sylvia Badger, *The Sun*, Baltimore, Sept. 8, 1996.

p. 299: "Baltimore did this the way Irsay did it to us. But now that they're here, we have to support them."
"Art Modell won and Cleveland lost," note 7.

p. 299: "...It's not vindication. It's a new day. We never gave up hope."
"Zany Ravens Fans Flock to Baltimore's NFL Return," note 1.

p. 305: The Ravens, with $7 million in commitments to prior players, were used as an example.
"Tagliabue chides misuse of cap by Ravens types," by Vito Stellino. *The Sun*, Baltimore, March 11, 1997.

p. 307: "...You can take the Browns out of here, but you can't take the spirit," remarked one fan, John York.
"Opening Day in Cleveland: No Team? No Problem," by Ken Berger, *The Associated Press*, Sept. 1, 1996.

General note: Even after the Colts left Baltimore in 1984, area fans still consumed live football at fairly high clips. Fueled by the NFL's expansion snub, attendance at Baltimore's Canadian Football League games was among the best in the league. The need to maintain a link with the past was obvious. Until the NFL and the Indianapolis Colts won a court order to stop it, the CFL team called itself the Colts. The courtroom skirmish only enlivened fan support in Baltimore. For a few months, the team was officially the no-name "Baltimore football club." Public-address announcers at the games would leave out the name, referring to "Your Baltimore ———," waiting for the fans to shout "Colts" on cue. In 1995, the no-name team became the Stallions.

The Colts/Stallions made it to the Grey Cup, the CFL's Super Bowl, in both of its Baltimore seasons, losing the first year to the British Columbia Lions, 26-23, then beating the Calgary Stampeders, 37-20. Modell's announcement eclipsed the Stallions' day in the sun, however, and the team moved to Canada, where it became the Montreal Alouettes. In 1996, the Alouettes failed and folded.

The CFL experience wasn't the first that Baltimore had with a pro-football league after the Colts left.

The city enjoyed much success with the United States Football League, which was organized in 1982 as a rival to the NFL. The USFL played its games in the spring and lasted three seasons: 1983, 1984, and 1985. Its franchises traded cities and owners at a breathtaking pace. The Stars, a charter member of the league, played their first season in Philadelphia, where the team, despite a championship appearance, drew an average game attendance of only 19,692.

But their luck changed the next season when they moved to Baltimore. Unable to secure a lease at Memorial Stadium, the Stars practiced in Philadelphia and played at the University of Maryland's stadium in College Park. They went on to win both the 1984 and 1985 championships, beating the Arizona Wranglers, 23-3, and the Oakland Invaders, 28-14.

The team anticipated a move to Baltimore proper in 1986. Some local boosters were hoping that the USFL's antitrust suit against the NFL would result in a forced merger of the leagues. But it didn't work out. The USFL won its lawsuit, but the jury awarded only $1 in damages, and the USFL folded.

AFTERWORD

p. 310: An average NFL game drew 62,682 fans, 2,278 fewer than in 1995.
Figures provided by the National Football League.

p. 310: Television ratings also dropped by nearly 7 percent.
"Final NFL regular season network ratings: are there diminishing returns?,"
The Sports Business Daily, Arlington, Va., Jan. 8, 1997.

p. 310: In what supposedly was a down year, consumers spent $3 billion on NFL
hats, jerseys, CD-ROM computer games, and other team-related merchandise.
Figures provided by *Team Licensing Business* magazine.

p. 310: On average, more than 12 million viewers tuned into an NFL regular
game telecast; and 130 million watched the Super Bowl.
Figures provided by Nielsen Media Research.

p. 310: Budweiser gladly paid up to $400,000 a minute to broadcast its ads on a
football Sunday, knowing for certain that 1 out of every 10 American males ages
21 to 34 would be watching
Figures provided by Anheuser-Busch, Inc.

p. 311: More and more, as stadium costs climb, stadium construction money is
coming from taxpayers.
"Playing the Stadium Game," by Dan McGraw, *U.S. News and World Report*,
June 6, 1996.

p. 312: ...Maryland estimated that a Baltimore football team would bring $86
million a year and the equivalent of 1,170 full-time jobs to the local economy.
"Projected Economic Impact of the Proposed Baltimore Pro Football Team on the
State of Maryland," Md. Dept. of Economic and Employment Development, 1991.

p. 313: During the 1994-95 baseball strike, bowling alleys and movie theaters
nationwide reported a business upturn.
Joseph Schoenberg, director of Special Projects for the Bowling Proprietors'
Association of America, said of the baseball strike: "In areas where there were
Major League Baseball teams, there were real, definite blips."

p. 313: ...Robert A. Baade, chairman of the economics department at Lake Forest
College in Lake Forest, Ill., in a 1996 study.
"Professional Sports as Catalysts for Metropolitan Economic Development,"
by Robert A. Baade, *Journal of Urban Affairs*, vol. 18, no. 1, 1996, pp. 1-17.

p. 314: "A sports strategy ... will not be an economic stimulus for a community
or region."
"Sport and downtown development strategy," by Mark S. Rosentraub, David
Swindell, Michael Przybylski, and Daniel R. Mullins, *Journal of Urban Affairs*, vol.
16, no. 3, 1994, pp. 221-39. Rosentraub has also written the authoritative *Major
League Losers: The Real Cost of Sports and Who's Paying for It* (New York: Basic Books,
1997).

p. 315: ... the service said the state's "sunny day" fund, used to help attract and retain conventional businesses, creates jobs at an average cost of $6,250.
"Tax-exempt Bonds and the Economics of Professional Sports Stadiums," by Dennis Zimmerman, CRS Report for Congress, The Congressional Research Services, Washington, D.C., May 29, 1996.

p. 315: "And we know without question that owners, players, and NFL season-ticket holders are more affluent than the public at large."
"Field of Fantasies," by Robert A. Baade and Alan Sanderson, The Heartland Institute, Intellectual Ammunition, March/April 1996. (This is a feature on the Internet.)

p. 315: ...flourished with the diminished competition.
"L.A. sports industry found healthy," by Nancy Rivera Brooks. Los Angeles Times, June 11, 1997.

p. 317: ...led Mr. Irsay to accept an offer from Indianapolis to play in a new dome in that city," Moag said.
Written testimony of John Moag, Jr., before the Senate Judiciary Committee's subcommittee on Antitrust, Business Rights, and Competition, Nov. 29, 1995.

p. 318: ... having a tax exemption on stadium bonds saves state and local stadium authorities from 17 percent to 34 percent of their stadium-building costs.
"Tax-exempt Bonds and the Economics of Professional Sports Stadiums," *supra*, note 11.

p. 318: ... a Nov. 29, 1995 hearing before the Senate Judiciary Committee's subcommittee on Antitrust, Business Rights, and Competition.
The excerpts in the text are taken from prepared testimony filed with the Senate Judiciary Committee's subcommittee on Antitrust, Business Rights, and Competition for the Nov. 29, 1995 hearing. The Heartland Institute's Heartland Policy Study was obtained from the Internet.

p. 320: Putting on football games, the charter says, is "incidental to its purpose."
From the corporate charter of the Green Bay Packers, Inc., provided by the team.

p. 321: "...nor any charitable organization or entity not presently a member of the League shall be eligible for membership."
National Football League Constitution and Bylaws, sec. 3.2(a).

TIMELINE: HOW THE BROWNS GOT TO BALTIMORE

1974

January: Art Modell signs a 25-year stadium lease and pledges not to move the Browns for the duration of the agreement.

1983

May: Modell offers to return control of the stadium to the city, but Mayor George V. Voinovich declines the offer, and Stadium Corp., which has managed the stadium since 1974, retains control.

1984

January: Modell, hoping for a new facility, endorses Cuyahoga County commissioners' proposal for a domed stadium.

March 28: The Baltimore Colts move to Indianapolis, leaving their city in the middle of the night.

May: A Cuyahoga County-wide property tax referendum to pay for domed stadium fails at the polls.

November 5: The US Supreme Court upholds the appellate decision allowing the Raiders to move to Los Angeles.

December 5: A group of Baltimore businessmen, including H&S Bakery chief John Paterakis, almost purchase and move the New Orleans Saints to Baltimore.

1985

January: Cleveland considers putting an inflatable dome over Municipal Stadium, but Modell opposes the idea.

1986

March 17: The City of Baltimore vs. Indianapolis Colts lawsuit is settled, with the team paying its former host $400,000 and promising to support Baltimore in expansion.

April 7: Maryland General Assembly establishes the Maryland Stadium Authority(MSA).

September 6: Herbert J. Belgrad is named MSA chairman.

1987

January 21: Baltimore Mayor William Donald Schaefer is sworn in as Governor of Maryland.

April 29: Maryland General Assembly approves finances for a baseball and football stadium at the Camden Yards complex of Baltimore.

1988

January 15: The St. Louis Cardinals, after considering Baltimore, move to Arizona.

May: Cleveland Mayor George Voinovich asks the City Council to approve a new lease that would raise the Browns' rent and force the team to pay up to $10 million if they left the city. The proposal dies.

1989

February: Modell rejects participation in Gateway and decides to stay at the stadium, saying Gateway would be fine for the Indians but not the Browns.

August: Modell unveils his plan for an $80 million renovation during a news conference, standing on second base at the stadium. Voinovich and other politicians don't show up, and Modell never forgets the snub.

1990

January 26: The NFL announces that it's exploring expansion.

May: Cleveland voters approve a sin tax for the twin-stadium Gateway complex for baseball and basketball.

1991

May 22: The NFL announces that it will add two teams by 1994.

September 16: The MSA files an application for an NFL expansion team. Among the investors listed as potential owners or heads of investment groups are novelist Tom Clancy, retail executive Leonard "Boogie" Weinglass, financier Malcolm Glazer, developer Nathan Landow, and Colorado oilman J. Thomas Stoen.

1992

March 17: Baltimore is named one of the five NFL expansion finalists.

April 6: Oriole Park at Camden Yards opens.

September: The NFL delays expansion plans.

1993

August 30: Baltimoreans lease 100 sky boxes and 7,500 club seats as part of the NFL expansion test.

September 25: Modell asks for a meeting with Cleveland Mayor Michael R. White by the year's end to discuss a stadium renovation or the possibility of a new stadium. Modell comments, "We've got five years left on our lease. Beyond that, I don't know."

October 1: Alfred Lerner, minority owner of the Browns, sells MNC Financial Inc. to NationsBank.

October 26: The NFL awards an expansion team to Charlotte, North Carolina, and delays announcing the second city. After the vote, representatives of the Cincinnati Bengals approach Baltimore officials to talk about a relocation to Maryland.

November 15: Maryland recruits Lerner as a possible franchise owner.

November 30: The NFL awards the second expansion franchise to Jacksonville, Fla., after the Redskins announce they are moving to Laurel, Md., a town 15 miles south of Baltimore. Modell was on the committee that recommended Jacksonville and Charlotte after comparing them with Baltimore, St. Louis, and Memphis. After the vote, representatives of the Los Angeles Raiders contact Baltimore officials to explore a move to Maryland.

December 7: The Washington Redskins announce their intent to move to Laurel.

1994

January 21: A Baltimore group's bid for the New England Patriots fails when the team is sold to Boston investors.

February 12: Modell says he is planning to keep the Browns in Cleveland but wants a better facility. He says a renovation would be acceptable.

April 4: Jacobs Field opens for the Cleveland Indians, leaving Modell's Stadium Corporation without a spring and summer tenant.

September 29: Cleveland's Mayor White says stadium renovation is necessary to keep the Browns in Cleveland, and promises to work towards a "consensus plan" among civic and political leaders.

October 12: The Washington Redskins' move to Laurel is blocked by a county zoning officer in Maryland.

October: Cuyahoga County, Ohio announces steep losses in investment fund. Gateway complex revenues fall short.

December 12: Mayor White appoints a task force of business and civic leaders to tackle stadium funding and to decide if a new facility is necessary.

1995

January 16: Glazer outbids Baltimorean Peter Angelos and buys the Tampa Bay Buccaneers for Tampa Bay.

January 17: The Los Angeles Rams reject a Baltimore bid and announce that they are moving to St. Louis for the richest-ever stadium deal. The deal is widely criticized as a municipal giveaway.

January 26: Mayor White's task force recommends a renovated stadium and continues to study financing options.

February 9: John Moag is named chairman of the MSA under new governor, Parris N. Glendening.

May 3: Mayor White's task force recommends a 15 percent parking tax in order to finance a Cleveland Stadium renovation. The following day, White says 15 percent is too high, and creates a new study group for stadium funding.

June 1: Mayor White announces that the parking tax will be 10 percent; Cuyahoga County commissioners discuss extending the sin tax to contribute to renovations.

June 5: Browns break off talks with Cleveland. Modell says "it will allow the political and economic environment to stabilize. I want to give this community every chance it wants and all the time necessary to see what it can assemble for the good of the franchise and the town at large. We're not inviting any contact [from other cities], we're not making any contact..." White refuses to halt the process.

June 8: Cincinnati Bengals president Mike Brown visits John Moag in Baltimore.

June 12: Voinovich, now Ohio's governor, says that unless White and the Cleveland City Council stop arguing over how to pay for the renovation, Cleveland will risk losing the Browns and will be stuck with an empty 'hulk' that will need to be torn down.

June 23: The L.A. Raiders owner Al Davis signs a letter of intent to move his team back to Oakland, California for a renovated stadium and a $31.9 million relocation fee. By doing so, he rejected an offer from Maryland.

June 29: The Cleveland City Council passes an 8 percent parking tax and an additional 2 percent admissions tax to help fund stadium renovations.

July 6: The Ohio legislature wrangles over whether to allow the Cuyahoga County commissioners to extend the sin tax without a public vote.

July 12: County commissioners say they will not consider a sin tax extension until $28 million in outstanding construction bills for Jacobs Field and Gund Area are paid, thereby putting the stadium renovation plan in jeopardy.

July 28: Alfred Lerner secretly talks to John Moag at BWI Airport about the Browns moving to Baltimore. Talks continue over the telephone.

September 18: Moag meets with Modell in New York.

October 27: Modell signs the agreement to move his team to Baltimore.

November 6: The Cleveland Browns announce their move to Baltimore.

Sept. 1, 1996: The Baltimore Ravens play their first game.

Fall, 1999: Cleveland Browns scheduled to resume play in Cleveland, as per agreement with the NFL.

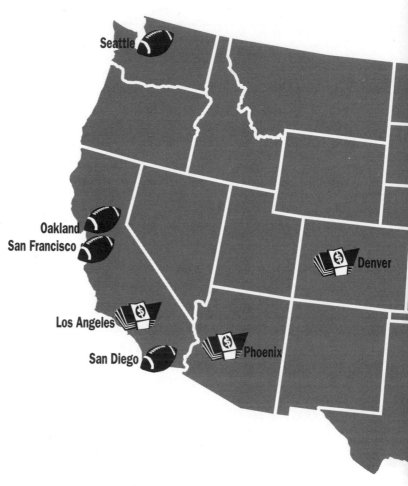

 **HAVE FANS, NO DOLLARS
FOR STADIUM**

Arizona Cardinals
Chicago Bears
Cleveland Browns
Denver Broncos
Green Bay Packers
Indianapolis Colts
Los Angeles (future franchise)
Minnesota Vikings
New England Patriots
Pittsburgh Steelers
Philadelphia Eagles

**THE NEW NFL:
NEW OR RENOVATED
STADIUMS**

Atlanta Falcons
Baltimore Ravens
Buffalo Bills
Carolina Panthers
Cincinnati Bengals
Detroit Lions
Jacksonville Jaguars
Nashville (Houston) Oilers

New Orleans
Oakland Raiders
St. Louis Rams
San Diego Chargers
San Francisco 49ers
Seattle Seahawks
Tampa Bay Buccaneers
Washington Redskins

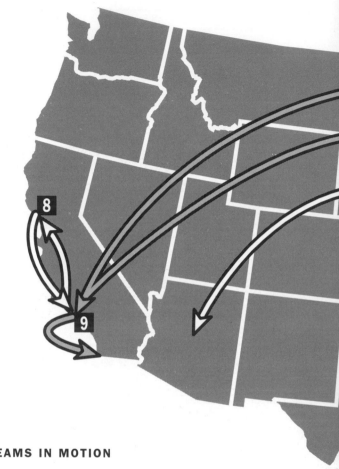

FOOTBALL TEAMS IN MOTION

1. Miami Seahawks — Baltimore Colts, '47-'49
Baltimore Colts, '55-'83 — Indianapolis Colts, '84- present

2. Boston Redskins, '33-'36 — Washington Redskins, '37- present

3. Chicago Cardinals, '45-'59 — St. Louis Cardinals, '60-'87
St. Louis Cardinals, '60-'87 — Arizona Cardinals, '88- present

4. Cleveland Browns, '46-'95 — Baltimore Ravens, '95- present

5. Cleveland Rams, '44-'45 — Los Angeles Rams, '46
Los Angeles Rams, '46 — St. Louis Rams '94- present

6. Portsmouth Spartans, '30-'43 — Detroit Lions, '34- present

7. Dallas Texans, '60-'62 — Kansas City Chiefs, '63- present

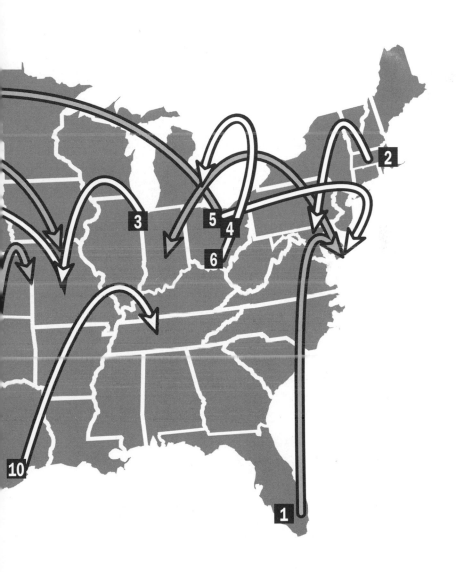

8. Oakland Raiders, '60-81 — Los Angeles Raiders, '82-'94
Los Angeles Raiders, '82-'94 — Oakland Raiders, '95- present

9. Los Angeles Chargers, '60 — San Diego Chargers, '61- present

10. Houston Oilers'60-'96 — Nashville Oilers, '97- present

ABOUT THE AUTHOR

JON MORGAN, one of the nation's few journalists to cover the business of sports, writes for the Baltimore *Sun*. His work in Baltimore has included investigative stories on the exaggerated value of franchises to cities, trends in sports labor relations, and the effect that "stadium economics" have on the relationships between cities, fans, and sports teams.

A Chicago native, Morgan holds a BS in Journalism from the University of Illinois, and was a Fellow at the University of Maryland's Knight Center for Specialized Journalism, where he studied Finance and the Business of Sports.

For his writing and investigative journalism, Morgan has won a number of honors, including the Frank C. Porter Award for Labor and Business Reporting and top rankings from the Associated Press Sports Editors and the Maryland-DC-Virginia Press Association.

He lives in Baltimore, Maryland, with his wife and three children.